AUTHORITARIAN ARGENTINA

AUTHORITARIAN ARGENTINA

The Nationalist Movement, Its History and Its Impact

DAVID ROCK

UNIVERSITY OF CALIFORNIA PRESS

BERKELEY LOS ANGELES LONDON

University of California Press
Berkeley and Los Angeles, California

University of California Press, Ltd.
London, England

First Paperback Printing 1995

Library of Congress Cataloging-in-Publication Data

Rock, David, 1945–
    Authoritarian Argentina : the Nationalist movement, its history
and its impact / David Rock.
        p.   cm.
    Includes bibliographical references and index.
    ISBN 0-520-20352-6
    1. Nationalism—Argentina—History—20th century.   2. Argentina—
Politics and government—1910–1943.   3. Argentina—Politics and
government—1943–1955.   4. Argentina—Politics and
government—1955–1983.
    F2848.R56   1992
    982.06—dc20   92-108

Printed in the United States of America
9 8 7 6 5 4 3 2

The paper used in this publication meets the minimum requirements of
American National Standard for Information Sciences—Permanence of
Paper for Printed Library Materials, ANSI Z39.48–1984. ⊗

To Rosalind

For there are many unruly and vain talk-ers and deceivers whose mouths must be stopped, who subvert whole houses, teaching things they ought not, for filthy lucre's sake.

Saint Paul

Contents

Acknowledgments

This book began as a set of interests and inquiries soon after the fall of the Argentine military regime of 1976–1983, at a time when the authoritarian factions in Argentina were regrouping to resist the newly restored democratic government of Raúl Alfonsín. The focus on ideology, the power of language, and the authoritarian subculture of Argentina springs chiefly from innumerable evening conversations with my wife, Rosalind Rock, in which she suggested how the concerns of literary criticism, in particular its stress on the content of language, might be applied to a study in Latin American history. I acknowledge my wife's part in this book not only for her constant moral support but also for the central conceptual contribution she has made to it.

I have addressed audiences in the United States, in Argentina, and on one occasion, in Uruguay on several aspects of this work. My thanks go to Georgette Dorn, Sandra McGee Deutsch, Hilda Sabato, Jorge Lanzaro, Leandro Gutiérrez, Steven Topik, Leslie Bethell, David Bushnell, Richard J. Walter, and others for opportunities to discuss or write about this book. I also thank Carlos H. Waisman for help in identifying important literature and Perry Anderson for some lively criticism. Tulio Halperín Donghi and Ezequiel Gallo, Jr., two of Argentina's most distinguished historians, have encouraged me to believe that it has been worth the effort to complete this study. I warmly acknowledge the support of colleagues, students, and staff at the Department of History, University of California, Santa Barbara, in particular, Héctor

Lindo-Fuentes and Fernando Lopez Alves, a member of the Department of Political Science with whom I have worked closely during the past few years. Fernando Rocchi, a graduate student from Argentina currently working with me in Santa Barbara, read the manuscript and spotted a few errors I am very glad to have corrected. However, I do not blame him or anyone else for any mishaps that remain. The translations in this book are my own unless otherwise indicated.

A fellowship from the John Simon Guggenheim Foundation provided invaluable funds and time that enabled me to finish the manuscript. Other important material assistance came from the Social Science Research Council of New York and from the Academic Senate and the Interdisciplinary Humanities Center of the University of California, Santa Barbara. I particularly acknowledge the skill and efficiency of Eileen McWilliam, my editor at the University of California Press.

Preface

In Argentina during the late 1970s, thousands of people were kidnapped, secretly imprisoned, tortured, and then never again seen alive. The nation's highest military leadership instituted these measures and justified them by the need "to save western Christian civilization."[1] When the military's terrorist state, as it became widely known, finally collapsed in 1983, Argentines reflected grimly on "the greatest and most savage tragedy of our history."[2] The repression was a "technology of hell . . . applied by sadistic yet regimented practitioners."[3] During these years,

the word "subversive" . . . came to be used with a vast and vague range of meaning. In the semantic delirium where labels such as Marxist-Leninist, traitor to the Fatherland, materialists and atheists, enemies of western Christian values abounded, anyone was at risk.[4]

This book explores the political ideas and the chief ideological threads that created the "semantic delirium" of 1976–1983. Rather than focusing exclusively on the military or the so-called dirty war of the 1970s, this study is a history of the antidemocratic political movement known as "Nationalism" (*nacionalismo*). It examines the part the Nationalists have played in Argentina's modern history, the conditions that governed the ebb and flow of their influence, and some of the reasons their strange fundamentalist movement pledged to violence and dictatorship remains entrenched today in Argentine politics. I address the following broad

xiii

questions: How did the Nationalist movement originate? What were its main ideas? Who adopted these ideas and why, and how were they communicated? Under what conditions did the Nationalists become particularly powerful or influential? Why has the Nationalist movement managed to survive into the last decade of the twentieth century?

As I attempt to show, the influence of the Nationalists went far beyond the military alone and the events of the late 1970s. It extended throughout Argentine society: the arts and literature, the schools and universities, the church, the programs of the political parties, and the population at large. In examining the Nationalists, we confront not only jackbooted generals, paramilitary street thugs, or pathological torturers but also outwardly respectable clerics, poets, historians, and journalists. Over many decades, these people often shaped the national agenda in Argentina in multiple ways. To ignore their influence would be to pass by or to misrepresent some major currents and issues in the country's modern history. To some extent, Ernst Nolte's comments on European fascism might be applied to the Nationalists, who "claimed more victims than any . . . in history, and for this reason demand the utmost effort at understanding."[5]

The Nationalists created the influential school of history known as revisionism, which attempted to create blueprints for the future through a mythic reinterpretation of the past. The Nationalists kept archaic clerical and scholastic ideas alive in Argentina's educational institutions. Nationalist conceptions of the state and society helped to impel numerous political groups to see themselves as organic movements as opposed to pluralist parties. Nationalist slogans became a means to rally the masses in the streets. The Nationalists encouraged the military to perceive itself as "the last aristocracy" and the guardian of a "sacred territory and the western Christian way of life," which answered not to the people or the law but to "God and history."[6] In the late 1980s, Nationalist ideas found yet another expression in the dissident, antidemocratic military faction known as the *carapintadas* (painted faces).

Most surprising of all, the Nationalists had a major influence on the Argentine revolutionary Left: its myths and icons, its ideological outlook, and its propaganda techniques. The New Left of the 1970s inherited the cult of authoritarian leadership from the Nationalists and copied their attempt to create a radical counterculture that used historical invention, xenophobia, and conspiracy theories. The Left's brand of anti-imperialism that denounced the antinational machinations of international monopoly capitalism had some of its roots in the onslaughts of the Nationalists against what they termed Jewish or Masonic conspiracies inspired from abroad.

As a "living museum of the past," to use an expression coined by E. J. Hobsbawm, the Nationalist movement represented an important bridge between the nation's modern and historical forms. The movement had a connection with nineteenth-century federalism, and because of this link, its roots may be traced back to the colonial era and ultimately to medieval Spain. Even so, the Nationalist movement represented only one side of Argentina's past: the "second tradition," "the dark underside of Argentine history," or to use the term made famous by Domingo F. Sarmiento, "barbarism."[7] In these guises, Nationalism became the twentieth-century expression of the deep-rooted historical forces in Argentina that continually challenged and resisted the mainstream liberal conceptions of the state and society.

Unlike the nineteenth-century Federalists, however, the Nationalist movement never grew beyond a small fraction of the population, and it was almost invariably divided into numerous rival groups. The Nationalists often penetrated or influenced the political parties but were never themselves a party. Although the Nationalists often formed militia-style organizations, they were more important as a dissident intelligentsia, whose main influence stemmed from their doctrines and from their links with power groups led by the military. As a fringe group of the intelligentsia rather than as politicians, the Nationalists represented, as one of them put it, "not Action but Truth."[8]

The term "Nationalist" is used here because since the early 1930s, the movement's members themselves have most commonly adopted this title. But in many respects, the term is a misnomer. Although the movement possessed an indigenous base, it derived most of its ideas from the nations of south-western Europe led by France, Spain, and Italy. Thus, despite their claims to a unique authenticity, the Nationalists were typical of Latin American political movements in general, which commonly developed as an unending blend of native and imported ideological currents.

The Nationalist movement, of course, represented the extreme Right in Argentine politics. Yet the term "Right" might be misleading in the sense that the Nationalists always considered themselves outside the formal political system rather than at some point along a spectrum within it. Here the Nationalists became closely reminiscent of José Antonio Primo de Rivera's description of the Falange Española in 1933: "not a party, but a movement . . . I might almost say [it is] an anti-party [because it] belongs . . . neither to the Right nor to the Left."[9] "Conservative" and "ultraconservative" were other labels frequently applied to the Nationalists. By no means all conservatives, however, were Nationalists, and the term "conservative" in Argentina referred more commonly to those right-wingers who belonged to the liberal, and therefore anti-Nationalist, political mainstream.

Whether or not the Nationalist movement may be labeled "Fascist" has been a subject of unending debate. This designation, invariably rejected by the Nationalists themselves, appears constantly in the propaganda of their detractors. According to Ronald Dworkin, to mention only one example, in the 1970s "a substantial proportion of the military were fascists. They thought of themselves, not as the servants of constitutional government, but as the true ruling class of the nation, guardians of its values and way of life."[10] If we accept Nolte's famous notion of the different "faces" of fascism, there seems little reason to avoid using the term to characterize the Nationalists. Equally, it is hard to deny that at least some of the leading Nationalists—most of all, Leopoldo Lugones after 1919—were Fascists at one time or another.[11]

Even so, most of the literature on the movement has tended to avoid the term "Fascist" and preferred other designations: "Catholic integralism," "oligarchic Nationalism," or "philo-

Fascists." As Cristián Buchrucker, for example, has recently written, "philo-Fascists represented an important sector of the Argentine Nationalist movement . . . until 1945, and in many cases long after that date."[12] A reluctance to apply the term "Fascist" unconditionally, which this study shares and continually attempts to document, is meant to underscore some important differences between the Nationalists and at least the classical Fascists of interwar Italy and Germany. Moreover, establishing these differences provides the key to understanding the most crucial weakness of the Nationalists—their incapacity to galvanize the masses.

Hugh Trevor-Roper draws the important distinction between "traditional clerical conservatism" and "dynamic fascism," which were as different as "the divinely consecrated absolutism of the Stuart kings and the naked unconsecrated absolutism of Hobbes."[13] Eugen Weber similarly distinguishes movements based on "conservative pessimism" and "revolutionary fascism."[14] Unlike the Italian and German Fascists, the Nationalists remained closely connected to the church. Indeed, several of the most prominent Nationalists—Julio Meinvielle, Leonardo Castellani, Gustavo Franceschi (a more debatable case)—were priests. In its classical form, fascism represented a kind of renegade and perverted socialism committed to mass mobilization and a revolutionary transformation of society. The Nationalists, by contrast, were pure reactionaries who always looked to the past for the society and government of the future. This distinction became particularly marked in the respective conceptions of the state offered by Fascists and Nationalists. While the Fascists glorified the state and sought to impose total centralization, the Nationalists placed a strong emphasis on the "liberties" of society's subordinate components.[15]

Again unlike the Fascists, the Nationalists usually opposed the idea of basing their movement on popular support and mobilization. Whenever the Nationalists sought the allegiance of the masses, they demanded unconditional support with a minimum of reciprocal concession and social change. While fascism—by virtue of its connection with socialism—grew out of the ideological trunk that emerged from the

French Revolution, the roots of the Nationalist movement lay in the European counterrevolution that sought to retreat to the era before 1789. In Weber's terms, fascism marked the "logical conclusion of the democratic principle of mass sovereignty," whereas the Nationalist movement remained totally divorced from this principle.[16] The Fascists were pragmatic "relativists," but the Nationalists at least claimed to uphold the absolute, perennial truths of natural law. Nationalism was rural and partly patrician in origin, but according to the standard literature, fascism had a mostly urban lower-middle-class base. Thus, in Nolte's words, "it is generally well-known that all fascist movements . . . were middle class movements."[17] Following Trevor-Roper, the "lower middle class provided the social force of dynamic fascism."[18]

The Nationalists failed to meet Nolte's so-called Fascist minimum because of their opposition to totalitarian rule and their failure to unite party and military.[19] An Italian Fascist observer in the 1930s dismissed the Nationalists as merely "patriotic," "insufficiently social revolutionary," and too circumscribed by nostalgia and retrospectiveness.[20] In Argentina, the Fascist revolution had its greatest impact on the Peronists as opposed to the Nationalists, and when Peronism began to develop along lines reminiscent of fascism, most Nationalists rapidly turned against it. In sum, the Nationalists were Mussolini's half-cousins, not his progeny.

Among the philosophical foundations of the Nationalist movement was the archaic Aristotelian dictum of "man as a social animal." The other chief ideological anchors of the movement lay in the world of kings, estates, guilds, and "natural inequalities" that preceded the French Revolution. In this guise, the Nationalist movement of Argentina was hardly unique. Its parallels in Latin America included the *sinarquistas* of Mexico and the *integralistas* of Brazil, and in Europe, the possible comparisons ranged from the Rexists of Belgium to Codreanu's Iron Guard in Romania.[21] The closest European analogues, however, were Portuguese *integralismo* under Antônio de Oliveira Salazar and the Spanish nationalist movement under Francisco Franco. Like the members of these two movements in the Iberian peninsula, the Nationalists became extreme authoritarians without ever quite being totalitarians. The Nationalists differed in one fundamental respect from most of their analogues in Latin America and Europe: they did not die out around 1945 or (as in Spain and Portugal) in the early 1970s, but they have lived on into the 1990s. The longevity of the Nationalists and their ability to keep alive until the eve of the twenty-first century a bundle of political ideas that appeared antediluvian even in the era of the French Revolution—these are among the main reasons that the Nationalist movement is so strikingly unusual and fascinating.

Typical of the Nationalists was the view that the Western world was dominated by two intellectual traditions, one they repudiated and one they upheld. The former tradition was "French rationalism," which "exalted reason and will at the expense of faith" and "ended in the masonic liberal democracy from which sprang Marx, Engels and Freud." The latter tradition was "Catholic communitarianism," invented by the Spanish scholastics led by Francisco Suárez, which offered a vision of "heroes and saints," of peoples who were "naturally social," and of the "social pact" between the governors and the governed.[22]

As formulations like these suggested, the Nationalist movement created its own peculiar jargon that was full of archaic terminology and abstruse incantations. The Nationalists, for example, called their movement an "authentically Argentine struggle for Catholic truth and hispanic tradition," which was the enemy of "liberal philosophy, formal democracy and ideological colonization."[23] The Nationalists considered their movement an embodiment of the "spiritual" over the "material," whose mission was to prevent "the breakdown of the country's spiritual unity." "We are heirs to a millenary civilization," the Nationalists typically proclaimed, "grounded on Christian teachings, Greek philosophy and Roman order."[24] On numerous occasions, the movement's adherents proclaimed a "crusade," whose object was "moral purification" and the "defense of the national soul." To the Nationalists, all politics, by which they meant electoral or democratic politics, was "low-born"; its practitioners were "hypocrites," "dema-

gogues," or "hacks" (*politiqueros*); political parties were no
more than "sects."

In this odd lexicon, the Western world became "western
Christian civilization" and communism an "exotic ideology"
that threatened the country's "classical roots [*cultura greco-
latina*] nourished by religion."[25] Communism symbolized
"the ulcer of extremism," "a disease corroding the country's
entrails," an invisible creeping "poison" or a "cancer." As the
"enemies of the nation," the Communists were aiming at the
conquest of "man's psyche." Communists invariably acted in
secret through "an underground and silent infiltration of the
state, clever propaganda through the media . . . [and a] grad-
ual substitution of one set of institutions for another."[26] The
Communists and their sympathizers could not even be considered human beings. One of the generals who led the
repression in the 1970s felt that "it was not people who [be-
came his victims] but subversives, terrorists or pacifists [*sic*],
who were trying to change the prevailing institutions and to
impose a political system contrary to humanity and Christianity." Those like the Nationalists themselves who resisted the
Communists were "antibodies," or "the natural reaction to a
sick body."[27]

The Nationalists upheld authoritarian rule and the concept
of the organic society; they opposed liberalism, democracy,
and communism. Yet as its interminable factional squabbles
revealed, the movement never existed in a pure form. Tactics,
opportunity, interest, or changing domestic or international
conditions constantly induced shifts in emphasis and changes
in direction. The Nationalists surfaced as major contenders
for power only at times of threatened political breakdown,
usually amid real or imaginary challenges from the revolutionary Left.

The movement's earliest incarnations occurred in the 1880s
during the conflicts over state education. A second phase
came between 1910 and 1920 during conflicts over immigration and labor unions. Later the Nationalists played a leading
part in all the major political upheavals of the twentieth century: in the late 1920s, as popular democracy tottered toward
collapse; in the early 1940s, on the demise of the liberal oligar-

chy; during the struggles against Juan Perón which ended in the revolution of 1955; in the military coups of 1966 and 1976; and finally during the late 1980s, when the military carapintadas fought against the newly restored democracy.

Whenever the Nationalists appeared in government, they usually did so in an unstable coalition with mainstream "liberal" conservatives. These partnerships often formed as the liberals sought to exploit the willingness of the Nationalists to use violence to achieve specific and immediate goals. When the need for force abated, tensions usually appeared between the two wings of the coalition, and the Nationalists became isolated and were eventually excluded from power. The Nationalists succeeded in winning these struggles with the liberals on one occasion alone in 1943, but even then, the Nationalist regime under Generals Pedro Ramírez and Edelmiro Farrell survived for only a brief period before Juan Perón and his movement supplanted it. The Nationalists were heavily represented in the military regimes of 1966–1971 and 1976–1983 but again never completely dominated either of them. While the strength and longevity of the Nationalist movement stemmed largely from its connections with the military and the church, its perennial weaknesses were a lack of any popular base, internal divisions, and a lack of standing among the so-called *fuerzas vivas* (living forces)—the economic interest groups led by the great landowners, merchants, industrialists, and bankers.

If the Nationalist movement may be seen as part of a cultural tradition shaped primarily by the church and the residues of federalism, it should also be understood as the ideological and political response of certain groups to the conflicts that dominated Argentina's modern history. In the early twentieth century, these conflicts arose principally as a result of immigration and rapid social change. Later, the conflicts emerged in conjunction with the careers of two great popular leaders, Hipólito Yrigoyen and Perón. In the late twentieth century, the Nationalist movement became a manifestation of the prolonged stagnation and deadlock that supervened during the late 1940s and continued during subsequent decades.

This book differs from earlier studies in range, structure,

and approach. Previous authors, for example, have mainly focused on the interwar period alone, omitting the movement's
nineteenth-century background and its links with the military
governments of the 1960s and 1970s. The approach taken here
contains a stronger emphasis than others on the European
antecedents of Nationalist ideas and on the diffusion of Nationalist ideas into society at large. This work attempts to trace
the relations between the Nationalists and the Radicals in the
better-known period between the wars in more detail, as it
offers a closer look at the intellectual trajectories of leading
Nationalist figures like Carlos Ibarguren, Manuel Gálvez, and
Leopoldo Lugones. Finally, this work attempts to avoid treating the Nationalist movement as a set of ideas devoid of any
historical context. It is not a study in the history of ideas but
rather addresses the way ideas became the expression of
group interests, and it therefore subscribes to a view once
advanced by Lugones: "ideas do not govern but necessities."
Nationalist ideas continually reappeared in twentieth-century Argentina because they were "needed" by certain social
groups—segments of the provincial landed classes, some
middle-class Catholics, and factions within the church and
the military. Among the recurrent themes here are the impact
of immigration and social change, the relationship between
Nationalism and mass mobilization, and the links between
the Nationalists, the military, and the church. Other major
themes are the ways the Nationalists have continually
adopted and reshaped ideas from abroad, using them to influence the national agenda that emerged during the course
of the twentieth century.

The basic structure and content of the book are as follows.
Chapter 1 traces the origins of Nationalist ideas in the European counterrevolution and in the writings of some of its
major figures, particularly Joseph de Maistre, Marcelino Menéndez Pelayo, and Charles Maurras. Chapter 2 explores the
indigenous origins of the Nationalist movement, its connections with federalism and the nineteenth-century church, and
the early literary expressions of the movement among writers
led by Gálvez and Lugones. Chapter 3 examines the political
manifestations of the Nationalist movement from around 1910

until the late 1920s, with particular emphasis on the periodical *La Nueva República*. Chapter 4 is an extensive review of the movement during the 1930s, and chapter 5 is an examination of its role in the 1943 revolution and its immediate aftermath. Finally, chapters 6 and 7 trace developments after 1945, first under Perón and afterward under the military juntas of 1966–1973 and 1976–1983. Chapter 6 attempts to show how, unlike so many similar movements elsewhere, the Nationalist movement survived the downfall of the Axis powers in 1945, and chapter 7 discusses the movement's influence in the 1960s and 1970s and briefly summarizes conditions between 1980 and 1990, an unconcluded period that will eventually deserve separate treatment.

Chapter One

The Incubus of Doctrine

The Nationalist movement represented a curious relic of a broader counterrevolutionary tradition whose roots and origins lay in Europe. The tradition rested on Catholic natural law and on an aspiration to reconstruct the patrimonial states and societies that prevailed before the nineteenth century, the odious "age of progress." The counterrevolutionaries upheld absolute rule and forms of social organization based on hierarchies, corporations, and particularisms. They opposed the natural righteousness of man proclaimed by Jean Jacques Rousseau, the theories of popular sovereignty that began with John Locke, and the classical economics based on the concepts of laissez-faire, specialization, and comparative advantage originating with Adam Smith.

Like the European counterrevolutionaries, the Argentine Nationalists embodied "a futurism of the past" that aimed to reconstruct a conservative authoritarian government and to restore the temporal power of the church, particularly over education, that the anticlerical liberals had taken away. Again like the counterrevolutionaries, the Nationalists were often less easily identifiable by what they actually proposed than by the "vigor of their negations."[1] These negations were directed chiefly against the modern world, which the Nationalists reduced to a string of reified abstractions: liberalism and individualism, democracy and capitalism, socialism, communism, and "cosmopolitanism," Judaism and Masonry.

1

The Discourse of Counterrevolution

The Nationalists drew eclectically from many different sources, their notions often "bundled together or left in a liquid state, so that anyone could extract a twig or take a sip and believe that he had discovered the truth."[2] Typical of such ideological promiscuity and blurred referents was a statement in 1933 by the young Nationalist Julio Irazusta, who proposed the following principles to achieve the country's "salvation" during the Great Depression:

Traditional political doctrine, . . . restore order, . . . renew the eternal tradition of humanity, innovate conserving and conserve innovating, reestablish the primacy of the political over the economic, restore destroyed or subverted spiritual hierarchies.[3]

Irazusta's vocabulary of "salvation" and "subverted spiritual hierarchies" echoed the nineteenth-century Catholic ultramontane movement. His expression "traditional political doctrine" evoked Edmund Burke or Joseph de Maistre. The self-contradictory phrase "renewing the eternal essence" was a borrowing from the nineteenth-century European Right, which originated in German idealism. "Innovate conserving and conserve innovating" contained a pragmatic note reminiscent of Franklin D. Roosevelt's inaugural speech in 1933, while "the primacy of the political over the economic" imitated Charles Maurras's precept *politique d'abord* (politics first).

The cosmopolitanism the Nationalists perennially decried thus obtruded constantly in their own ideological formulations to a point that the movement often appeared little more than a plagiarism of its European forerunners. The Nationalist movement enshrined Catholic dogmas whose origins lay in ancient Greece, while reflecting precepts of Roman law like the concessionary theory of sovereignty: the only groups able to function as such in society were those formally and explicitly recognized by the ruler.[4] Following the legal code known as the *Siete Partidas* of medieval Spain, the Nationalists assumed that each person was not "atomistic" or individualistic but belonged within a broader fabric that was "social and organic."[5] The opposition of the Nationalists to what they called centralized despotism and their quest for a church free of subjection to the state recalled Spanish Carlism. Like its French counterpart in the late nineteenth century, the Nationalist movement could at times be accurately characterized as "a synthesis of antirationalism, antipositivism, racism, and nationalism."[6] Like Portuguese integralismo, Nationalism began as "traditionalism," an aesthetic cult of the past, before it evolved into a political movement.[7] The rabid version of Nationalism that appeared in Argentina in the mid-1970s often bore striking resemblances to the movement led by Franco during the Spanish civil war.

Many of the institutional vehicles the Nationalists created and led had European precursors. The Liga Patriótica Argentina of 1919, for example, echoed the French Ligue des Patriotes of 1882. The campaigns of the Nationalists against political parties and parliamentary "corruption," or in favor of "class solidarity," had innumerable European parallels such as the Italian Idea Nazionale of 1911.[8] There were other strong similarities between the ways the Nationalists deployed history and myth for political purposes and the manner these were used by the Legion of the Archangel St. Michael in interwar Romania.[9]

The Nationalist movement in Argentina had several close parallels in Latin America, although none of these other movements commanded quite the same influence or achieved a similar longevity. Like the Mexican sinarquistas in the 1930s and the early 1940s, for example, the Nationalists strongly supported Franco's movement in Spain. Both Nationalism and *sinarquismo* were suspected of Axis sympathies during the war, and both combined the rhetoric of scholasticism with Maurras's notion of *le pays réel* (the real country).[10] A sinarquista text of 1941 replicated one of the core doctrines of the Nationalists, as it aspired for "the old regime, the one before the French Revolution. At that time there was spiritual, social and political unity."[11] Like the Brazilian Integralists of the late 1930s led by Plínio Salgado, the Nationalists depicted their movement as a "dike against the destructive avalanche of the values of nationality" and as the opponent of both communism and capitalism. Integralists and Nationalists shared a concept of revolution that signified not the conventional figurative sense of the word as the beginning of something new but its literal meaning as a "constant regression to the origin, a return to the point of departure." An Integralist, expressing sentiments entirely in keeping with the Nationalists, declared that in the modern age, each human being was becoming "an automaton. . . . Capitalism wants to deprive man of his last spiritual residues. . . . The instinct of the machine is enslaving everything."[12]

Throughout its history, the Nationalist movement maintained a web of contacts abroad. The fastest messages to penetrate from Europe came from Rome, disseminated by priests who worked part-time as journalists and political activists. A flourishing trade in books with Spain kept the Nationalist intelligentsia abreast of current Spanish fashions. French influences, by contrast, often arrived more slowly and sometimes indirectly by way of Spanish or Latin American writers. In the early twentieth century, for example, Argentines grew familiar with the ideas of French writer Hipolite Taine through the works of Spaniards like Angel Ganivet and with those of Ernest Renan through the Uruguayan author José Enrique Rodó.

Spanish, French, Italian, and Portuguese influences always predominated above all others. In the 1920s and 1930s, the only English-language authors the Nationalists discussed with any frequency were Hilaire Belloc, G. K. Chesterton, and Sinclair Lewis. Lewis's *Babbit*, for example, provided an abundance of ammunition for the anti-American campaigns in Argentina during this period, although Babbit himself often sounded like the Nationalists. Thus, Babbit saw New York as the Nationalists viewed Buenos Aires, as "cursed with unnumbered foreigners," and he lumped together "foreign ideas and communism." He regarded European countries as "old dumps" and attacked the "long haired gentry who call themselves liberals and radicals."[13] Fifty years later, in the mid-1980s, the catalog of a Nationalist bookstore in Buenos Aires listed a total of thirty-four "classics" of the European Right. Fourteen of the authors of these books bore Hispanic names, eight were French, and three were Eastern European, but only two bore Anglophone names and only three German names.[14]

Before 1914, conservative Catholics, Latin American anti-positivists, and the writings of the Spanish "Generation of 1898" represented the strongest influences on the intellectuals later identified with the Nationalist movement. French influences led by Maurras, whose writings one Argentine commentator dubbed the "romantic manifestations of anti-romanticism," became prominent in the 1920s.[15] By the 1930s and 1940s, the leading Nationalists, who often possessed advanced classical educations, were drawing ecumenically from a wide range of different sources—from ancient authorities like Plato and Thucydides and from contemporary writers like the Russian mystic Nikolai Aleksandrovich Berdiaev, whose tract *The New Middle Ages* commanded great popularity.[16] After 1945, Argentina remained one of the few countries in the world where the notorious *Protocols of the Elders of Zion* remained on display in book shops. In the mid-1980s, Nationalist publishers continued to stock new editions of such canons of the genre as Louis Veuillot's *L'illusion liberale.* Other books bore quaint or ominous titles, for example, *Vatican II and the Liberal Error, Masonry, Communism and the Atomic Bomb at the Service of International Judaism,* and *Was Marx a Satanist?*

The Nationalist movement thus remained a slave of fashion, continually embracing and discarding its foreign mentors. Such mentorship took several different forms. The Nationalist periodicals often reproduced extensive fragments from foreign works they admired, using them as sources of authority and propaganda. Sometimes, however, the influence of European writers became more difficult to document, since it consisted of unattributed practical applications of ideas or concepts originating abroad that reappeared in heavily mutilated forms. The works of the European philosophers or the classical authors admired by the Nationalists were often ingested slowly over long periods in university classes or other organized study groups. As a young man, Federico Ibarguren, for example, recorded his first contact with the writings of the medieval scholastics in classes offered by the lay religious association Acción Católica (Catholic Action). He and many of his classmates, he admitted, were "lazy adolescents [and] ill-prepared." But these classes eventually induced Ibarguren's "second religious conversion" and a life-long commitment to counterrevolutionary Catholic philosophy.[17]

The roots of the Nationalist movement lay in the counter-revolution, but beyond that, its ideological linkages stretched back over two thousand years through medieval scholasticism to the Greeks. Inherent to the Nationalist outlook, for example, was the view of the early Christian philosophers led by Saint Augustine who depicted the universe and its constituents as a hierarchy under God, in which the "higher" properly ruled the "lower." Thus, society, or the earthly city, as Augustine called it, should be "an ordered concord of its members in rule and obedience," and those members belonged to the two commonwealths of church and state.[18] The vindication of what the Nationalists called "national tradition" recalled the still older Aristotelian idea that "a thing contains what is necessary to fulfilling its purpose." Therefore "each People, like each person, has through history a charge, a mission," and "history has the end of promoting civilization."[19] These were the basic connections that in Argentina inspired Jordán B. Genta to define his inflammatory teachings as a "humanist pedagogy, with a classical content."[20] As another member of the movement put it, the Nationalists rejected

all the modern errors: materialism, positivism, pantheism, and that false, gross philosophical movement that began with Descartes and culminated in Kant. We sustain Aristotle and St. Thomas Aquinas: great and glorious thinkers . . . rooted in ancient Greece.[21]

The Nationalists viewed absolute rule and a society composed of corporate institutions as natural to humanity, part of the order established by God. The legitimacy of absolute rule stemmed from the proposition of the scholastics led by Aquinas that men in a community "form a single mystical body . . . a necessary whole, which therefore needs one single head."[22] Thus, "the head of state concentrates in himself complete sovereignty, and does so by God's grant, Lord of all power."[23]

However, an obligation to serve the *bonum commune* (common good) and to avoid the arbitrary and tyrannical abuse of power limited the ruler's authority. If the ruler misused power, he or she could be legitimately overthrown. In practice, although each society could possess only one sovereign "head," power became diffuse and decentralized, and society was constituted as "cells," "nuclei," and "vertebrae."

The principal cell of the nation has to be the municipality and the family; the nucleus is the province; and the vertebrae which give shape to the whole system is the state.[24]

At least in principle, the Nationalists therefore adhered to the archaic style of absolutism that posed a government of "compromise, conciliation, and accommodation" and a system of decentralized power based on implied consent: once more, the ruler had no superior but ought never to become a despot.[25] The Nationalists subscribed to Aristotle's dictum that "man is a social animal," so that without the subsocietal institutions to bind them together, men and women became "beasts." Social inequalities were "natural," since society comprised the same rank order of intelligences and abilities as it did cells and nuclei. The concept of freedom was understood by the Nationalists in the terms defined by natural law as being derived from God rather than from some mythical Rousseauistic state of nature or as the juridical concession of a temporal power. The Nationalists often pointed to the medieval guilds as prototypes of the corporate institutions on which they aspired to reconstruct society. Finally, people themselves could not legislate, only fulfill the divine law: "The decisions [of men] do not go beyond a purely regulatory power of the divine laws which create the constitutions of the peoples."[26]

The Nationalists viewed the French Revolution as a "rebellion against God" that had destroyed the "natural order" of society under the anciens régimes and "corrupted the blood of the Christian world . . . with the poison of liberalism."[27] The revolution "killed, massacred and mutilated twenty million people, destroyed the natural hierarchies . . . and infected the world with absurd doctrines."[28] In abolishing the guilds, the French Revolution extinguished, in Burke's phrase, the "historic, peculiar institutions" and the "intermediate authorities" that formed a necessary link between the individual and the state.[29]

In the liberal era following the French Revolution, the Nationalists contended, morality ceased to be an absolute fixed by natural law and instead became a purely relative notion determined by the reasoning of each person, who thereby became "the center of all." Liberalism inflated a person's vain and "unbridled feeling of selfhood," which the Nationalists condemned as "the Judaeo-Protestant God of the inward conscience."[30] Erroneously following Rousseau and "believing man good," the liberals "had cast aside all his constraints in favor of laissez-faire" but in doing so induced "moral anarchy."[31] The liberal principle of "freedom before the law" again assumed the false notion of human beings as individuals. The "individual" of the liberal scheme was the "unsocial" and alienated human being, who was therefore scarcely human at all. For all these reasons, liberalism led to the "unmanning of man." Thus, liberalism

has destroyed social solidarity and exalted the isolated individual, the modern specimen of the rootless man; the inhabitant of the great world cities, egotistical, atheistic, destructive. . . . With the liberal revolution the naked citizen appears, the perpetual climber, grasping, dominated by his appetite, unruly.[32]

De Maistre, Menéndez Pelayo, and Others

Leonardo Castellani, a priest and one of the leading Nationalist writers between the 1930s and the 1960s, listed several nineteenth-century French and Spanish writers as the chief sources of the movement's basic ideological stances: Joseph de Maistre and the Count Gustave de Bonald and Juan Donoso Cortés, Jaime Balmes, and Marcelino Menéndez Pelayo.[33] There were countless references to these writers in all the major Nationalist books and periodicals, from *La Nueva*

República in the late 1920s to the monthly publication *Cabildo* issued during the military dictatorship of the late 1970s.[34]

From his home in Savoy, de Maistre had led the conservative onslaught against the French Revolution. "*Nous ne voulons pas la contre-révolution, mais le contraire de la révolution*"; de Maistre wanted not only to destroy the revolution but also to construct a new society that was its exact antithesis. He rejected all written constitutions: "The rights of peoples are never written," or if they are written, they amount to no more than "declaratory enunciations of prior [unwritten] rights."[35] He argued that the rights of a people proceeded from concessions by a sovereign in accordance with natural law, and he attacked all representative bodies as perennial sources of subversion. The French *parlements*, for example, were "Protestant in the sixteenth century, '*frondeur*' [i.e., anti-absolutist supporters of the Fronde] and Jansenist [i.e., antiorthodox Catholic] in the seventeenth, Enlightenment-contaminated [*philosophe*] and republican in the eighteenth."[36] Furthermore, "among all monarchs, the harshest, the most despotic and intolerable is the people-monarch" embodied in the movements led by Jacobinism.[37]

Rousseau's social contract was de Maistre's other principal target. "It is a capital error," he contended, "to represent the state as the consequence of a choice based on the consent of men, upon a deliberation, and upon a primitive contract."[38] Rousseau had "constructed his whole philosophical edifice on the anti-Christian proposition that Man is good."[39] Instead, according to de Maistre, human nature was depraved and required an absolute monarchy, supported by the church, to subdue and contain it. De Maistre's writings displayed other strong influences of natural law: forms of government should reflect the "nature" of peoples; governments achieved peace when rulers observed the "fundamental law"; the basic nuclei of each nation were the family and the corporations.[40]

Bonald's writings developed many of the same themes. The strong xenophobic streak in the Argentine Nationalist movement, for example, became reminiscent of Bonald's warning that the great danger of representative government lay in the opportunity it "offered for foreigners to intervene in [national] affairs with their gold."[41]

The men of the [revolutionary] party do not belong to their own country. . . . The Revolution is their homeland. . . . [Moreover the Revolution shows] a profound hatred for Catholicism, whose destruction is the single aim of its policy.[42]

Bonald attacked the doctrine of popular sovereignty with arguments similar to de Maistre's. Political power, he claimed, was independent of men, since it "resides in natural law. . . . It is divine, because God is the author of all the natural laws of the states."[43] As another apologist of the ancien régime, Bonald viewed absolutism as sanctioned by natural law and therefore completely legitimate. He drew the distinction between absolute power, which he regarded as legitimate, and the arbitrary and therefore lawless power he saw as having arisen during the French Revolution. "Absolute power," he said, "is power independent of the subject, but arbitrary power independent of the law. And when you erect the people as the power, you necessarily confer upon it an arbitrary power, that is, power independent of the law."[44] Finally, Bonald stood out among the early European counter-revolutionary writers as one of the first to lament the rise of an industrial society and the impersonal production and consumption relations it fostered.[45]

Gustavo Franceschi, a Catholic dignitary in Argentina connected with the Nationalists, declared that "Spanish philosophy, from Seneca to Balmes, will be a perennial source of wisdom, an art of living, a limitless land of vital experience, of practical discipline, of intimate creations."[46] Among the Spanish philosophers the Nationalists most widely admired, Donoso Cortés was remembered as an eloquent opponent of liberalism during the 1848 revolutions and as a proponent of military dictatorship to protect public order.[47] "When legality can save society," Donoso contended, "uphold legality; when it cannot, embrace dictatorship."[48] He was an early prophet of the impending ideological war between Catholicism and socialism, and he viewed the latter as "Jewish-inspired."[49] Socialism was the most obvious enemy, but Russia, he pointed out, represented the great lurking danger to the Western world.[50] Balmes, a nineteenth-century Spanish priest, became influential in Argentina during the 1920s and 1930s as another critic of the French Revolution who sought to resurrect the old guilds the revolution had abolished. From this position, Balmes became one of the main precursors of modern corporatism.[51]

Among these five seminal ideologues of the counterrevolution, however, Menéndez Pelayo, "the lay saint of the Falange" as Raymond Carr has called him, left his mark most deeply in Argentina. In the nineteenth century, Menéndez Pelayo led the quest to restore what he called Spain's "true Catholic self" and its "providential mission."[52] "Only through [religion]," he declared, "did the Spanish people develop its own way of life and an awareness of its collective strength, only through religion did Spain gain legitimate, well-rooted institutions."[53]

In his quest for the "real Spain," Menéndez Pelayo disparaged the eighteenth century, the age of the Enlightenment, and exalted the medieval era and the Golden Age of the sixteenth century. "In the Middle Ages, we never ceased to consider ourselves one People."[54] Spain's past greatness would revive, he urged, when it rekindled the Senecan discipline and the militant crusading spirit that had prevailed under Ferdinand and Isabella, *los reyes católicos*. Spain had reached its acme in the sixteenth century when it was "most intolerant," when it expelled the Jews and launched the Counter-Reformation. At this point, religion inspired "Spain the evangelist over half the earth, Spain the hammer of the heretics, Spain the light of the Council of Trent, Spain the cradle of Saint Ignacio [Loyola]."[55]

Menéndez Pelayo lauded the Spanish Inquisition: "Never was there more or better writing in Spain than in the two centuries of the Inquisition."[56] The eighteenth-century Enlightenment, however, "the most perverse and ungodly age in history, dismantled stone by stone the beautiful edifice of old Spain. . . . Spain then forgot its religion, its language, its science, its arts, and everything that had made it wise, powerful, and feared in the world."[57] At that time, Spain fell victim to the pernicious influence of the philosophes, Jansenists, Masons, and Jews. Menéndez Pelayo abhorred the tolerance, skepticism, relativism, and materialism he believed had arisen during the Enlightenment and denounced them as incompatible with Spain's intrinsically "spiritual character."[58] His "myth of Castile" exalted the "most Catholic purity" of both Spain and Spanish America and depicted the Spanish conquest of the Americas as a vast evangelical enterprise accomplished by armies of priests and soldiers: the "union of the cross and the sword."[59]

In Argentina, the Nationalists betrayed many traces of the rhetoric and the conceptual schemes of Menéndez Pelayo. Thus, the Catholic church, the Nationalists often claimed, "represents the historic essence of our nationality."[60] Under the spell of Menéndez Pelayo's "myth of Castile," the Nationalists extolled the "ancient apostolic and warrior spirit of the Middle Ages and the Catholic kings" that had accomplished the conquest of the Americas. When the Nationalists urged the reunification of Latin America, they usually meant unity on the essentially metaphysical foundation envisaged by Menéndez Pelayo: "a unity of the peoples on the basis of the Catholic, Apostolic, Roman faith."[61] "We belong to the Christian west," proclaimed Genta in Argentina, "because Spain sowed this territory with the spirit of the two Romes, the human spirit of Caesar and the divine spirit of St. Peter."[62]

In the same mode, the Habsburg kings of the sixteenth and seventeenth centuries became "the source of honor and authority as the incarnation of the state, the first servant of the res publica, the first slave to duty, and the minister of God." The eighteenth-century Bourbon dynasty, by contrast, was "inspired in French despotism" and therefore "centralist and all-absorbing."[63] The Bourbons made religion subject to the state," and they were the source of "the foreign and liberal" malignancies that had arisen since the late eighteenth century.[64] Under the Bourbons, the "reasoning" that characterized the hated Enlightenment superseded "spiritual vocation and an acceptance of the metaphysical." A world based on "Reason" replaced that founded on Aristocracy, and "Single Truth [i.e., Christian revelation interpreted by an infallible

Pope] became a matter for each man's judgment."[65] According to Federico Ibarguren, the Bourbons transformed Spanish America, "this ancient land of missionaries and soldiers, into an underdeveloped colony, into an immense factory with no soul."[66]

At first, the Nationalists appropriated the ideas of Menéndez Pelayo and his Spanish followers almost verbatim, but by the late 1930s, the Argentine historical revisionists were beginning to modify this vision of Spanish history into the autochthonous cult of Juan Manuel de Rosas. In the version of Argentine history created by the revisionists, Rosas occupied the same role as the Catholic monarchs and the Habsburgs in Menéndez Pelayo's Spain, and the Rosas regime became the archetype for the indigenous, Catholic, and paternalist autocracy the Nationalists wished to establish. For the revisionists, Rosas's "liberal" successors, as the instigators of spiritual decline and the conduits of a destructive materialism, occupied the same position as the Bourbons for Menéndez Pelayo. The Argentine liberal oligarchy, Nationalists declared, "ruled the country after [the fall of Rosas] under the [Bourbon] system of enlightened despotism."[67]

In all these cases, history became the mistress of politics and propaganda, as the revisionists sought to chart the directions of the future from the starting point of a mythic past. Like Menéndez Pelayo, the Nationalists established cults of the symbolic events and the historical figures who supposedly embodied the values they aspired to restore. No effort was to be spared to propagate these ideas among the general population. Thus, education, Federico Ibarguren believed, should always be based on a national "historical apologia."[68] "The revision of our history," said José M. Rosa, "is a thankless but deeply patriotic task. . . . From this task will emerge the Argentina of tomorrow."[69]

Other Authorities:
Renan, Taine, and Maurras

The Nationalist movement bore strong traces of two nineteenth-century French conservative writers, Ernest Renan and Hipolite Taine, and it was deeply influenced by a third French writer, Charles Maurras. Renan's popularity stemmed from his opposition to the "profoundly materialist" society he claimed followed the adoption of universal suffrage. Renan yearned for the return of the old France before 1789 with its "patriotism, enthusiasm for beauty, love of glory." "Justice and government," he lamented, "have been taken over by the mass, and the mass is crude, gross, dominated by a sense of superficial self-interest." Democracy stood at odds with "God's design," while liberal utilitarianism was "blind to beauty."[70]

The environmental determinism created by Taine saw each "civilization" or nationality as the product of a "directing principle" (*faculté maitresse*) that sprang from a synthesis of race, milieu, and "moment," or historical situation.[71] Like Renan's, Taine's influence in Argentina spread slowly and indirectly through works such as Angel Ganivet's *Idearium Español* written in 1898. Ganivet converted Taine's faculté maitresse into what he called the *espíritu territorial* (territorial spirit), national character that sprang from the synthesis between environment and history. Thus, for Ganivet, Spanish history from the Roman conquest onward was "a permanent struggle for independence," first against the barbarians and then against the Moors.[72] Taine's view that "at root history is a problem of psychology" reappeared in Ganivet's version as "every society possesses a personality."[73] Finally, like Taine, for Ganivet, "all peoples possess a real or imaginary hero who embodies their own [ideal] qualities." Among the examples Ganivet submitted were Don Quixote and Robinson Crusoe.[74] In Argentina, this idea also influenced the cult of Rosas.

In mid-nineteenth-century Europe, the ideas that emerged from the counterrevolution were for a long time at odds with these more secular threads associated with Renan and Taine, since Catholics considered the latter tainted by the Enlightenment and German idealism. De Maistre and his successors had objected to Kant, the leading Idealist, as strongly as to Rousseau, since it was Kant, they claimed, who had invented the pernicious "God of the inward conscience." In making morality and belief into an issue of personal choice, Kant's ideas mortally threatened Catholic metaphysics based on natural law and the Fall of Man.[75] Kant's German successors, led by Johann Fichte and Johann von Herder, developed his notion of the self-directing individual into the concept of the self-determining *Volk*, which became the philosophical foundation of modern nationalism, the claim that nations had the right to self-determination.[76] From around the middle of the nineteenth century, the Catholics faced other challenges from positivism and Darwinism, the former proclaiming itself a new religion to replace Christianity and the latter preaching what Catholics perceived as the pagan cult of the winners.

The Nationalist movement in Argentina bore the imprint of the deep clashes in the nineteenth century between the primitive counterrevolutionaries and these later ideological currents—national self-determination, positivism, and Darwinism—and of the ways such clashes were eventually resolved. In the nineteenth century, the French clerical historian, Fustel de Coulanges, attempted to resolve the conflict between the clericals and the Nationalists by presenting the church as the chief agent of national identity. He sought to demonstrate the "spiritual," and therefore clerical, foundations of France, arguing that the church had served as the leading institutional nucleus of the evolving national community. For the same reasons, the Catholic clergy represented a vital force in France's origins and development.[77] The scheme created by Coulanges also provided a way of reconciling clerical doctrine with positivist and even Darwinist thought since the history of each nation could now be viewed as a process of ascent and selection, as positivists and Darwinists insisted it should, except that henceforth, religion and the church held center stage in the whole process.

These attempts to update the clerical counterrevolution took numerous forms. "Christianity," wrote Menéndez Pelayo, for example, "constructed the unity [of Spain]. The church educated us in our hearts by its martyrs and confessors, its fathers, the admirable system of its councils. Through this we became a nation, a great nation."[78] Italian social theorist Wilfredo Pareto divided society into what he called the

exceptionally gifted minority and the "mediocre" majority.
Thus, society formed a pyramid, as it did in the eyes of the
counterrevolutionaries, although the "natural elite" now
claimed this distinction not by virtue of birth but in accordance with the laws of natural selection.[79] Writing around
1880–1914, Maurice Barrès offered yet another way to link
the doctrines of counterrevolution with those of nationalism.
Barrès shared the nostalgia of the counterrevolutionaries like
de Maistre for the local and provincial "liberties" that prevailed in France before the revolution. However, on top of
this idea, Barrès placed Taine's idea of national identity
rooted in the "directing principle": the triad of race, ancestry,
and "spirit." He then proposed to restore France as a "living
unity" based on the old "liberties" and a perception of
common roots and a common biological inheritance but
at the same time depicted French history as a teleological
quest for its inner "character," "genius," and *disposition
primitive."*[80]

In Argentina, Barrès's influence paralleled that of Menéndez Pelayo's. Using historical myth in much the same way,
but omitting Menéndez Pelayo's strong, typically Spanish
clerical emphasis, Barrès contended that France had stood at
its peak in the seventeenth century under Louis XIV. But it
then declined as Voltaire and Montesquieu infected it with
the "Jewish and German spirit" of the Reformation.[81] Barrès
thus integrated the provincial particularism that characterized
the counterrevolutionaries with the new brand of nationalism
that emerged from Darwinism and positivism.[82]

The works of Gustave Le Bon, a French contemporary of
Barrès, were republished decade after decade in Spanish and
Argentine editions, and he, too, became another strong influence on the Nationalists. Le Bon stood out as one of the early
theorists of irrationalism, stressing instinct and intuition as
opposed to reason as motivating forces in human behavior.

In all our acts the part played by the unconscious is immense and
that played by reason so small. Reason is too new in humanity, and
too imperfect to reveal to us the laws of the unconscious, and still
less to replace them.[83]

Le Bon saw popular democracy as mass irrationalism in action and combined his mistrust of reason with Taine's notion of "the mental constitution of a people" formed by its history.

The life of a people, its institutions, its beliefs and its arts [represent] the visible thread of its invisible soul. [Each people is] an organism created by the past. . . . Infinitely more numerous than the living, the dead are infinitely more powerful than they.[84]

The Nationalists displayed the influence of many other European writers, among them Georges Sorel, who proposed using myth for political purposes to create "an epic state of mind" among the general population.[85] The popularity of Berdiaev in Argentina stemmed principally from his idea that socialism and democracy wrongly neglected the "ontological communities. [They reduced] the world to atoms . . . as if there were no history and no religion." Socialism, he wrote, imposed a compulsory brotherhood and was an outcome of "Jewish chiliasm," since it embraced the same false notion of the redemption of humanity or the "millenarian deception," as he called it, as Judaism. Berdiaev led another onslaught against Kant, whose "God within Man" provoked the "revolt against God" that characterized the modern age.[86]

But among all the leading figures of the European Right, Maurras always commanded greatest attention and popularity in Argentina.[87] "Maurras's influence," declared Marcelo Sánchez Sorondo, a prominent Argentine Nationalist, "was such that he inspired the first nationalist movements outside France, including ours."[88] To Juan E. Carulla, another leading Nationalist, Maurras seemed "one of the greatest political philosophers of all time."[89] Following Maurras's death in late 1952, Irazusta acknowledged him as "our greatest teacher of politics of his time." Alberto Falcionelli, another Nationalist writer prominent in the early 1950s, felt that Maurras's key contribution was to stress that the state should encourage "the multitude of small, spontaneous associations and autonomous groups that existed before the state itself and would probably survive after its demise." Maurras, he said, "was our Thomas Aquinas."[90] Finally, writing as recently as the mid-1970s, Enrique Zuleta Alvarez depicted Maurras as "the most notable political thinker to have arisen in France during the past two centuries, and one of the great figures in western letters and thought."[91]

The leader of Action Française and the founder of Integral Nationalism, Maurras devoted his long career, which spanned from the Dreyfus Affair in the 1890s to the fall of the Pétain regime in 1944, to a campaign to restore the French monarchy. In the present age when monarchy no longer ruled, Maurras asserted, the rule of justice was replaced by the rule of gold, which was now "the judge of all thinking." The rule of gold was "indifferent, the most absolute, the least responsible" of all possible forms of government.[92] As gold held sway, society passed

from the authority of the princes to that of the merchants. Gold is without doubt a representation of force. . . . Tenacious and volatile, it is also impersonal. Its rule is indifferent, regardless of friend or enemy, of citizen or foreigner.[93]

Resurrecting the ancien régime, Maurras claimed, would replace the "laws of gold" of a society corrupted by materialism with the "laws of blood" that would reunite France and restore its past grandeur. Like Menéndez Pelayo, Maurras aspired to an absolutist regime acknowledging local autonomies and customary rights, and like Barrès, he idealized the folk cults of old provincial France. Here among the provinces, he asserted, behind all its institutional superficialities and legal superstructures, lay le pays réel.

Maurras joined the cult of seventeenth-century France led by Barrès and others, and like them, he viewed the French Revolution as the greatest catastrophe of modern history. "Saving civilization," as Maurras put it, meant destroying "Rousseau's optimistic metaphysics," "Kantian idealism," and the "God of the inward conscience" espoused by Protestants and Jews, concepts he viewed as the "microbes of romanticism and Revolution."[94] Liberalism, too, he declared, was the "first beast to kill." Maurras saw popular democracy as the "monstrous Judaeo-Masonic regime" or the "Dictatorship of the Mob." He echoed the counterrevolutionaries as he lamented the destruction of the guilds or "natural corpora-

tions" by the French Revolution and denounced the order
that replaced them as one that "leaves men naked before capital and the state" and "exalts the egotism of bad passions."
Individualism, he contended, isolated "the individual from
his peers," dragged "him systematically out of society, [and]
separated man from the basic requirements of existence."[95]

In most respects, Maurras lacked true intellectual originality, and his remarkable influence stemmed chiefly from his
striking rhetoric. His republican followers in Argentina ignored or rejected his plea for monarchy but took from him the
biting epigrams he used to attack the liberal-democratic state.
"Society," Maurras proclaimed, as he repudiated Rousseau's
contract theory of the state, "arises not from an act of wills,
but from a fact of nature." Democracy falsely assumes that
men are "small, similar cubes, equal in height, in dimension,
and in weight."[96] Maurras dubbed the Protestants "Catholics
who have abandoned the idolatry of the Trinity for Jewish
monotheism."[97] He hailed the Catholic church as "the last
obstacle to the imperialism of gold, the last bastion of free
thought."[98]

Maurras too became a rabid xenophobe, who was constantly attacking France's foreign residents. *"Les métèques,"*
he called them, in a term derived from ancient Greece. He
sought to utilize anti-Semitism as an instrument to mobilize
the masses. "Everything," he once remarked, "seemed impossible or extremely difficult without the providence of anti-
Semitism."[99] At one point, Maurras taunted a Jewish member
of the French government as "a symbol of the foreign," threatening "to kill him like a dog" if he continued to attack Action
Française.[100] He attacked the "four confederate states: Jews,
Protestants, Freemasons and *Métèques*." Maurras's doctrine
of politique d'abord, politics first, transformed the conventional definition of politics as the art of the possible into an
objectified pure science whose truths could be discovered
and put to practical use. But as he effected this change, he
divested the practice of politics of any moral restraints or ethical boundaries and therefore legitimized the use of violence
or terrorism for political ends. Those who mastered the science of politics, he claimed, were justified on the authority of

such mastery in seizing power and ruling as an "enlightened" elite.

Yet Maurras's influence on the Argentine Nationalists stopped short of being total and all-encompassing, not because of his support for monarchy but because he was an unbeliever who regarded the church merely as an arm of the state. This position left Maurras suspect among Catholics, who also looked askance at his idea of politics first because it endowed men with powers they believed belonged to God. When the Vatican condemned Action Française and its doctrines in 1927, the clerical and Nationalist groups in Buenos Aires immediately followed suit.

To say that politics comes first [as in politique d'abord] is to assert that the body politic is constructed prior to the existence of Christian morality. . . . For Action Française the nation before all: *Salus populus suprema lex est.*[101]

Subsequently, the so-called Maurrasians in Argentina explicitly disavowed this label, describing it as "flattering but unacceptable. . . . Action Française is directed by an unbeliever . . . and its doctrines on the relationship between politics and morality [are] unsatisfactory."[102]

The Ideological Synthesis in Argentina

The controversy over Maurras in the late 1920s offered an important clue to the basic ideological affiliations of the Nationalist movement. Despite its confusion, heterogeneity, and mutability, the movement's ultimate loyalties lay with conservative clericalism and the European counterrevolution and only second with the European New Right that emerged immediately before 1914. Nevertheless, the Nationalists borrowed continually from Maurras and Action Française. Using Maurras's language, they denounced liberalism as "not equitable but tyrannical." Liberalism "does not enhance human personality, but cheapens and degrades it."[103] Liberalism contradicted "national tradition" and was therefore "bastard," the result of a "foreign Masonic weed," "a malignant heresy."[104] A person educated by liberals would become the odious "international type," a mere "machine for production and consumption." Liberalism produced "social depersonalization" and the "dehumanization of culture."[105] Liberal universities were the sources of "subversive ideas, which have infected the whole [national] organism."[106]

Democracy met with similar condemnation and rejection. Universal suffrage and the secret ballot conferred an "unconditional and irresponsible liberty" and falsely assumed "everyone's capacity to govern with no other restriction than having reached the age of eighteen."[107] Democracy's false egalitarian dogmas induced a "flattening of hierarchies at the behest of the multitude."[108] Among the other reprehensible manifestations of democracy stood feminism, whose origins, the Nationalists contended, lay in "the United States, which has encouraged [feminism] in order to spread pacificism" and to weaken resistance to American imperialism.[109]

Drawing from the European tradition, the Nationalists led other onslaughts against capitalism and "materialism." Capitalism led to "moral perversion" and the enthronement of avarice and envy.[110] To envy someone, said the Nationalists, meant wanting to be that other person, and as this was impossible, envy implied a death wish. They quoted the Spanish proverb: *Querer ser otro es ya querer no ser* (To wish to be someone else is to wish not to be).[111] Because capital itself was impersonal and mobile, capitalism also represented "anonymous and vagabond wealth." In this "vagabond" guise, capitalism became the instrument of foreign penetration. Faced by the inroads of world capitalism, one Argentine writer saw his country as having become "a foreign degeneration of liberalism."[112] Nationalists dismissed the nineteenth century, the age of capitalist "progress," in the terms made famous by Léon Daudet, one of Maurras's collaborators, as "the stupid century."[113]

Nationalists viewed Socialist and Marxist ideas as offshoots of liberalism, products of the profane myth that human beings were capable of achieving perfection. Thus, leftism of every hue represented "the summit of the rationalist deviation"; the Left was a consequence of the "pagan Renaissance," "the false Protestant Reformation."[114] The deviation had reached its final abysmal expressions in Rousseau and Marx.

Luther became the precursor of Thomas Münzer, the ideologue of [sixteenth-century] Anabaptist communism, and of René Descartes, the father of all the forms of modern Idealism, including the mechanicism [sic] of Rousseau and the historical materialism of Marx.[115]

Liberalism and socialism were alike, too, in the sense that "the principle of the equality of all born from liberalism is the same principle as the leveling of all" embodied in socialism.[116] "Communist theory and practice," proclaimed Genta, "are no more than modern liberalism carried to its final conclusion as the negation of western Christian order."[117] If liberalism undermined society through its notion of person-as-individual, the leftist movements, as doctrines of class and international brotherhood, split the nation's natural organic unity. The Nationalists often echoed a remark attributed to Lenin in 1914: "Marxism cannot be reconciled with nationalism, be it even the most just, purest, most refined, civilized breed."[118] Allegiance to communism and socialism were incompatible with citizenship. In 1934, a Nationalist observer saw only misfit immigrants, reminiscent of Maurras's métèques, rather than true Argentines at a Communist party rally in Buenos Aires. The demonstrators were "sinister looking mulattoes, Galician [gallego] taxi drivers, Basque milkmen, and fanatical women."[119] The Nationalists followed their European mentors into the "stinking marshes," to use Weber's characterization, of xenophobia, anti-Semitism, and anti-Freemasonry. Foreigners contaminated the "national essence" and polluted national tradition: "Let us clean out of the country all the whining dross who are the failures from abroad," urged Lugones.[120] For decades, the Nationalists led campaigns against immigration, to halt the inflow, for example, of the "thousands of Czechs, Poles, Armenians, Bulgarians and Russians who have invaded our shores."[121] Xenophobia at times lapsed into overt racism. The country should impose an absolute ban on non-European immigrants: "Asians [amarillos], Muslims, Syrians," as Federico Ibarguren described them.[122]

For the Nationalists, Jews were "the deadly enemies of the nation and of the Catholic faith of the people."[123] Jewish "materialism" stood in irreconcilable opposition to the "spiritual character" of the Latin peoples. Jews, the Nationalists argued, were the occult sources of the spirit of "skepticism," "tolerance," and "relativism" that appeared during the Renaissance and then took over most of the Western world. Jews had prompted the liberal or Socialist quests for the new world order they eventually intended to dominate. In offering the opportunity of earthly paradise and salvation, socialism and communism represented a new version of the Judaic myth of the coming of the Messiah.[124] As the Great Depression deepened in 1931, one Argentine anti-Semite explained its causes as follows:

The present state of the world, with its profound illness, its universal disorientation, its enormous unemployment . . . has a hidden cause, which manipulates, intensifies and coordinates the other more visible causes with incredible and tenacious intelligence: this is the Jewish war against the Christian world.[125]

In Argentina, as in Europe during this period, Jews were commonly depicted as "creeping along in darkness with a dagger in one hand and dynamite in the other."[126] Jews were scheming to inoculate "Christian governments" with "liberalism" to kill them, to destroy the landed classes by taxation, to form great industrial monopolies, and to seize world supremacy by controlling gold supplies.[127]

The "world league" of Freemasonry became another instrument of the Jews. The Freemasons aimed

at the destruction of the Christian faith and its replacement by ancient paganism; since Freemasonry too does not acknowledge any Fatherland it has become the natural ally of the Jews against church and state.[128]

Freemasonry was "mixed up in nearly every antireligious and political disorder that has divided and bloodied [the country]."[129] In the terms that Genta viewed the world, "Jewry, Masonry, and communism are the three ideological manifestations of the negation of the Divine Redeemer."[130]

Finally, Jews, Masons, or simply foreigners posed other threats because of the economic power they wielded in Argentina. Between the wars, and to some extent after 1945, the Nationalists led campaigns against the Jewish or formerly Jewish families in Buenos Aires which owned the grain-exporting houses and against the consortium headed by Otto Bemberg which dominated the Argentine beer industry. Jewish-owned businesses, Nationalists often claimed, formed part of an international conspiracy to subjugate the country to the imperialists. In 1933, Nationalists invoked this idea as they launched an abusive campaign against Sir Arthur Samuel, a British government minister of Jewish family who had tactlessly suggested that Argentina join the British empire.[131] In this period, it was common to link economic nationalism, directed mostly against the British, with antagonisms against the Jews. In 1935, a Nationalist journalist complained about the criticisms of the German Nazis that appeared in the *Buenos Aires Herald*, a local English-language newspaper. "Either the *Herald* receives money from the Jews to attack Germany," he declared, "or the *Herald* is a Jewish newspaper, edited by Jews and written by Englishmen."[132] By 1940, the British and the Jews, "the Siamese twins" as they were now being called, had openly banded together in a military campaign for world domination.[133] Throughout, propaganda against the British bore the heavy taint of the techniques of anti-Semitism. "We have before us," wrote Raúl Scalabrini Ortiz, in a reference to the British in Argentina,

an enemy whose techniques of world domination have the following features: astuteness, cunning, indirect maneuvers, ill-faith, constant lies, the subtle manipulation of its local agents. And let us not forget that this enemy has been here for the past hundred years. Let us not forget that we are victims of an educational system [created by this enemy] designed to deprive us of an awareness of reality.[134]

Simultaneously, the Nationalists scorned the United States and the "Jewish-Yank plutocracy in Wall Street."[135] "The Yank film," another Nationalist believed, was "a weapon of social corruption controlled by the nation-less Jews, which poisons the souls of our boys."[136]

In sum, behind the multiple and intertwined ideological threads at play in the Nationalist movement stood some identifiable primary elements. The roots of the movement lay in scholasticism and the early-nineteenth-century counterrevolution. On top of these roots stood a range of more contemporary influences led by Taine, Menéndez Pelayo, and Maurras. In synthesis, the Nationalists were opposed to the modern world and to the ideas, systems, or social groups they regarded as its embodiments.

Chapter Two

The Threads of Tradition

The Nationalists claimed to embody a national essence originating in classical antiquity and the birth of Western Civilization. These connections were often more imaginary than real, since the Nationalist movement was above all an invention and a consequence of the twentieth century and of the conflicts and pressures that reflected the rise of a mass society. More than a simple emanation from the past, the movement embodied the rediscovery and redefinition of the past in a way that placed its heroes on center stage and represented its own principles, often quite falsely, as part of some timeless autochthonous tradition. Like similar movements elsewhere, the Nationalists suffered a "pervasive false consciousness."

[Their] myths invented reality; [they claimed] to defend folk culture while in fact [they were] forging a high culture; [they claimed] to protect an old folk society, while in fact helping to build up an anonymous mass society.[1]

In this respect, the Nationalist movement again resembled many of its European counterparts. But in Argentina, unlike Europe, history was brief, and the threads connecting the past with the present were relatively thin. Manuel Gálvez, one of the leading Nationalist writers, recognized this difference and the issues it raised as he pointed to the most striking contrasts between Argentina and Spain.

The ancient soul of Spain will never be forgotten because it lives on in the medieval churches, in the paintings of El Greco, in the picaresque novels. But the soul of Argentina has to be traced through the few traditions we have . . . and among those few villages where contemporary civilization has not yet penetrated.[2]

In Argentina, there was no baroque church to exalt or memories of the medieval guilds to invoke as the institutional foundation for the Nationalist "new order." "In Italy or Belgium," pointed out Franceschi,

where the streets and houses of the ancient corporations still survive, [corporatism] is possibly applicable. There a professional corporate tradition survives. But here where there are men from all over the world with so many contrasting customs and backgrounds . . . the very base of the corporation is absent. . . . In Europe the corporation is a resurrection, while here it is an invention.[3]

Although Spanish settlement in this region of South America stretched back to the mid-sixteenth century, for centuries the country subsisted as little more than a thin string of tiny, isolated communities in the midst of a primitive pastoral economy. After 1860, Argentina suffered the impact of the liberal revolution on a scale virtually unmatched throughout the world. Subsequently, in a country with an economy expanding at breakneck speed and an almost entirely new population of European immigrants, very little survived to evoke the long centuries of Spanish rule or even the tumultuous early years of independence. Yet, as Gálvez noted, the liberal revolution never entirely eliminated the past, whose remnants remained visible in the country's more underdeveloped regions and in institutions led by the church. "Religious intolerance still exists," commented a visitor from the United States in 1886, "especially in those sectors . . . little affected by foreign influences."[4]

Although the Nationalists themselves continually magnified and distorted them, there were at least some links binding their movement to the preliberal past. In its formative stages before World War I, the Nationalist movement displayed strong provincial connections, an entrenched parochial mentality, and a bias against the city of Buenos Aires. These features evoked federalism, the movement that emerged during the wars of independence after 1810 to resist the political dominance of Buenos Aires and a central govern-

ment dominated by mercantile interests. By the 1870s, following their defeat by the liberals under Bartolomé Mitre and
Domingo F. Sarmiento, the Federalists became virtually extinct as a political force. Yet their influence lingered into the
twentieth century as a collection of folk memories expressed
in verse, music, or local festivals. In the early twentieth century, some still remembered the old Federalist war cry, "Religion or Death!" Particularly in rural areas and in the old cities
of the interior led by Córdoba and Salta, the mistrust or resent-
ment toward Buenos Aires and the foreign influences it was
said to represent still remained. Buried within these survivals
were resonances of still earlier eras, among them, for example,
the tradition of local self-government under the cabildos established during the earliest years of Spanish settlement.

The Seeds of Clericalism

The church became one of the principal bridges linking the
antiliberal sentiments among the Federalists in the nineteenth century with those among the Nationalists in the twentieth century. The church itself, however, barely survived the
almost general breakdown of Argentine society between 1810
and 1860. During this time, the country lost its Spanish bishops, who on the outbreak of the wars of independence fled
home to their native land. When the new Creole rulers of the
Río de la Plata usurped the *patronato*—the Spanish Crown's
jurisdiction over ecclesiastical appointments—Rome severed
all contact.[5] Mastei Ferretti, who later became Pope Pius IX,
visited the country in 1824, and it seemed to him what remained of the local clergy had been taken over and completely corrupted by the incumbent regime of Bernardino Rivadavia. Members of the Argentine clergy, he declared, were
"the miserable instruments of Rivadavia," who taught "the
most perverse doctrines."[6] A British visitor in 1826 found that
"in general, the churches are deserted, and inside them only
one or two decrepit old women are to be seen."[7] Even under
Rosas a decade or two later, who converted the church into
an arm of his dictatorship, the institution remained "torn in
pieces, left in anarchy, and oppressed." The clergy, whose

chief functions were as propagandists for Rosas, remained a "sad skeleton."[8]

In this period, bishoprics remained unfilled for decades, seminaries closed, priests were few and in many parts nonexistent. Diocesan sees remained vacant in Buenos Aires from 1812 to 1834, in Córdoba from 1810 to 1831, and in Salta from 1812 to 1860.[9] In 1836, Rosas allowed a small number of Jesuits into the country, but they remained for only five years before being expelled for refusing to submit to his authority.[10] As late as 1864, the diocese of Buenos Aires contained only thirty-five secular priests.[11] During the late eighteenth century, members of the clergy totaled almost 10 percent of the population but in the 1850s, less than 2 percent.[12] Relations with Rome remained in abeyance for more than four decades, and the church's only contact with Europe lay through a papal delegate lodged in Rio de Janeiro and through a handful of European priests who braved a few years in the country before returning to their native lands.

As a result, the indigenous forms of clericalism were few and scattered. But they existed nevertheless. During the Federalist period, priests denounced the liberals, or *unitarios* as they were then known, in the language the European counter-revolutionaries used against the French Revolution.[13] Clerical attitudes were particularly entrenched in the city of Córdoba and in the northwestern towns led by Salta. As Sarmiento wrote during the 1840s,

The spirit of Cordova is monastic and scholastic; the conversation of its society always turns on processions, the saints' days . . . [and] taking the veil. . . . The city is a cloister surrounded by ravines, the promenade is a cloister with iron gates; every square of houses is a cloister of ruins or friars; the colleges are cloisters; the jurisprudence taught there, the theology, all the medieval law is a metal cloister within which the intellect is walled up and fortified against every departure from text and commentary.[14]

The church began to expand once more following a mission to the pope in 1857 led by Juan Bautista Alberdi which paved the way for diplomatic relations between Rome and the Argentine government.[15] During Mitre's presidency between

1862 and 1868, the diocese of Buenos Aires gained its own archbishop, finally freeing itself from the jurisdiction of the old colonial authorities in La Plata, Bolivia. Newly established seminaries were now training priests for the fast-developing cities of the pampas frontier; by 1868, the seminary in Buenos Aires, for example, had forty-eight students. Following the fall of the Bourbon queen, Isabel, in 1868, several hundred Spanish priests moved to Argentina.[16] By 1880, there were eighty-four priests in the diocese of Buenos Aires.[17]

An active and forceful clerical movement now surfaced in Argentina. This movement possessed an indigenous base, but it crystallized as an import from Rome, echoing the conflicts of the Italian Risorgimento and the split between liberals and ultramontanes in Europe after the 1848 revolutions. When the new Italian state created by Cavour tightened its grip around Rome in the 1860s, a torrent of papal bulls and encyclicals launched Pius IX's counterattack against the false doctrines of "progress." In the *Syllabus of Errors* of 1864, "the solemn synthesis and condemnation of the most common and dangerous errors," the pope refused to accept "progress, liberalism, and modern civilization" as "absolutes." He denied that elections or plebiscites could by themselves confer political legitimacy on a government, and he attacked the "materialist concepts of authority" embodied in socialism and communism.[18] "Reason," insisted the ultramontane supporters of the pope, did not necessarily lead to "truth"; the will of the majority could not replace Catholic "certainty"; nation-states could not displace Christian truth by the fallacious claim of their own omnipotence.[19]

In Argentina, priests now began to attack the "laicism" being practiced by the local liberals.[20] Between 1865 and 1867, the church repeatedly condemned the governor of Santa Fe, Nicasio Oroño, who suppressed a convent, instituted civil marriage, and sought to eliminate the church's control over cemeteries.[21] In 1870, several Argentine bishops attended the Vatican Council in Rome where they witnessed the Declaration of Papal Infallibility and then returned home brimming with Rome's rhetoric against the liberals.

In this spirit, the self-defined "noble and holy purpose" of

El Católico, a newly established periodical in Buenos Aires supported by the bishop, was "to leave that monstrous and most evil liberalism without a single unbroken bone, wherever it should raise its ugly snout."[22] Liberalism, *El Católico* thundered, was a "universal evil," whose nefarious consequences were most recently visible in the "execrable" Paris Commune of 1871.

Liberalism insinuates itself into every part of the world. . . . It represents a falsification of liberty; it is the source and essence of Revolution . . . [and it is] the suppression of God.[23]

El Católico continued with a diatribe against "materialism."

Everywhere we see the cult of purely material interest, an insatiable thirst for gold, pleasure, enjoyments, rewards, power, and honors, . . . a resurrection and glorification of paganism and idolatry.[24]

By the mid-1870s, there were violent outbreaks of anticlericalism in Argentina, and in 1875, a mob of foreign workers destroyed a Jesuit seminary in Buenos Aires, the Colegio El Salvador.[25] Conflict continued during the 1880s. At this point, taking its cue from Bismarck's measures in Germany and others of a similar kind in France, the Argentine government under President Julio A. Roca introduced a slate of anticlerical reforms in Congress. They included the institution of lay education and civil matrimony and the abolition of church cemeteries, parish registers, and religious oaths.[26] Legislation establishing lay education passed Congress in 1883, and a civil matrimony law passed in 1887. Each of these measures provoked a strong reaction among the Catholics. In 1883–84, the Catholics in Córdoba organized an association of upper-class women, the Sociedad de Damas Católicas (Society of Catholic Ladies), which conducted unruly campaigns against the government. In retaliation, the minister of education, Eduardo Wilde, dismissed several church functionaries in Córdoba and elsewhere. Wilde eventually managed to impose lay education, but to do so, he was forced to expel the papal nuncio and once again to sever relations with Rome.[27] In this way, as a Protestant visitor saw it, "intolerance [was] now roused to renewed activity by the law ejecting the priests from the schools."[28]

Catholic opposition to the lay reforms of the 1880s marked the emergence of many of the ideas that were later adopted by the Nationalists. In July 1883, Pedro Goyena, a Catholic deputy in congress, denounced lay education in terms that were to recur on numerous occasions in the future. "A school without religion," he declared, "a school from which the notion of God has been proscribed, and in which God's name is not even mentioned, that school is damned."[29] Catholics also began to oppose the government's programs of subsidized immigration on the grounds that "cosmopolitanism," as they dubbed the supposedly contaminating influences brought by the immigrants, was corrupting "even our language, which is being adulterated by . . . foreign idiocies and exposing us to the seductive influences of materialism and sensuality."[30]

José Manuel Estrada, the leading figure among the Catholics during this period, relentlessly attacked liberalism as the cause of "upheaval and catastrophes and as no more than illusions and lies."[31] "What else but liberalism," he asked,

dragged along by its egalitarian delirium, its quest to destroy the organic societies and to convert them into disarticulated masses, has wrecked the homes of the poor, shattered the guilds [*gremios*], wiped out families, small fortunes, and small properties? What else but liberalism has annihilated the permanent bonds of social cooperation [*patronazgo*]? . . . Liberalism has cast the working classes under the tyranny of wage labor, leaving them subject to the daily contract, incapable of defending themselves against the rich [and] incited to barbarous explosions of anarchy by the Communist, Socialist, or nihilist sects—sects that are no more than variants and derivatives of liberalism, the originating cause of conflict and conflagration.[32]

In the 1880s, the Catholics proclaimed their support for what they called the "free Republic." But "while the rift prevails between religion and liberty, [our nation] shall be liberal . . . but never free," declared a speaker at a congress of Catholics in Buenos Aires in 1884.[33] We are "true democrats and republicans," said another Catholic, but never liberals.[34] The doctrine of state supremacy that the lay legislation embodied, Catholics argued, originated with the "impious" Bourbons, but "a republican and free society should erase the state despotism of the absolutist kings of Spain."[35]

As these terms suggested, in the Catholic view, "freedom" had prevailed before the Enlightenment and the rise of liberalism but had since been lost. Similarly, "liberty" did not originate in liberalism but in natural law. "There are only two ways to understand the principle of sovereignty," Estrada declared:

Either you profess the revolutionary version: sovereignty reposes in the capricious will of the masses. Or you profess the alternative: that sovereignty belongs to the Supreme Legislator of the Universe, and the source and essence of all power is divine. . . . All power comes from God.[36]

Both liberty and sovereignty therefore stemmed from God rather than the popular will, and the protection of liberty by the state meant ensuring each person's pursuit of "moral duty" and a Christian life. Equally, liberty meant upholding the traditional powers of the church in such spheres as education. The Argentine state, Estrada held, had completely failed to protect liberty in the ways Catholics understood it. The liberal reforms deprived the church of its power to determine morality, and secular power inflated to this degree instituted the godless and tyrannical "caesaro-papist" state endowed with temporal and spiritual sovereignty that Catholics had condemned since 1789. Natural law obliged rulers to serve the "common good," but the Argentine liberal state was oligarchic and its congress unrepresentative: this mere "part" of the people represented by the regime could reflect neither the will of the people nor the "common good."[37] In Argentina, there was "no bond of sympathy between the people and the liberal oligarchy."[38] The leaders of the oligarchy "whose god is their stomach . . . forget that peoples and individuals live not only on bread but on truth and justice."[39]

In 1888, Estrada stridently denounced the plan to institute civil marriage as a plot orchestrated by revolutionaries, Masons, and Jews.

The revolutionary parties and the Masons . . . who control the government, and the Jews who control the money, those conspirators against law, justice, and the true conscience of nations: they are the sources of the laws of civil marriage in the world.[40]

The tyranny of the liberal state was such, Estrada concluded, as to justify its overthrow by revolution. "Revolutions are those great invocations [*apelaciones*] of natural law that the people may legitimately employ . . . against tyrants who rule contrary to justice."[41] Employing this doctrine, in July 1890, the Catholics joined the revolutionary coalition that took up arms against the liberal regime of Miguel Juárez Celman.

In the 1870s and 1880s, Catholics articulated some of the basic ideas that reappeared among the Nationalists. Salient among them was the demand for the control of education by the church; the contention that liberalism had destroyed the "organic societies"; the claim that liberal institutions were unrepresentative and oppressive; the view that "materialism" and "cosmopolitanism" were the consequences of liberalism and that all leftist movements were the warped offsprings of liberalism; and finally, the conviction based on natural law that it was legitimate to overthrow "tyranny" by revolution.

Subsequently, in the 1890s, the church developed another basic tenet of the Nationalist movement, the doctrine of "class harmony." This idea took shape as the church became drawn into the social and political conflicts that arose from mass immigration and the expansion of the eastern cities. Facing the growth of a new immigrant working class and of militant anarchist and Socialist movements attempting to co-opt its support, clericals and liberals buried their earlier differences and drew together to resist a common enemy.[42]

The papal encyclical of 1891, *Rerum Novarum*, helped to shape these realignments. It attempted to offer Catholic alternatives to liberal capitalism and the socialist concept of class conflict. The encyclical thus attacked capitalists as "a small number of very rich people [who] have been able to lay upon the masses of the poor a yoke little better than slavery."[43] It then condemned Socialists as "crafty agitators [who] pervert men's judgments and . . . stir up the people to sedition."[44] By denying private property, Socialists "confiscate wages," because property is merely wages "in another form."[45] Property, moreover, conformed to the law of nature that endowed human beings with the "reason" to accumulate resources for the future. Inequality among people was also "natural," but

the great mistake is to believe that class is naturally hostile to class; that rich and poor are intended by nature to live at war with one another. So irrational and false is this view that the exact opposite is the case.[46]

The social classes, the encyclical declared, should therefore maintain "bonds of friendship."

Rerum Novarum looked favorably on governments willing to protect an "equilibrium" between the classes, to prevent the accumulation of excessive wealth, and to strive for "distributive justice, . . . public well-being and private prosperity."[47] The encyclical asserted people's rights to form associations, defining these rights as inherent to the "natural sociability" of human beings. Governments should encourage and protect such associations but were bound to take action against those

imbued with bad principles, [who] are anxious for revolutionary changes. . . . The state should intervene [against] these disturbers, to save the workmen from their seditious acts, and to protect lawful owners from spoliation.[48]

Rerum Novarum thus wove an ambiguous synthesis of reactionary and apparently progressive prescriptions. Its basic message was to urge resistance against "class struggle," by repression if necessary, and to fight for "class harmony" by a program of paternalist reform, indoctrination, and institution building. In Argentina, the encyclical prompted Catholic leaders like Estrada to found "Catholic Women's Centers" to keep working-class women safe from Socialists and anarchists and to sponsor workers' housing projects to fight high urban rents.[49] Both these initiatives survived many years after Estrada's death in 1894, as groups of "Social Catholics," as they became known, continued his work.[50]

The most important of the new Catholic organizations inspired by *Rerum Novarum* were the workers' circles (*círculos obreros*), which were modeled on similar institutions in Europe and introduced in Argentina in 1892 by Fernando Grote, a German priest.[51] By 1912, there were seventy-four of these associations in different parts of the country. The workers' circles typified late-nineteenth-century Catholic thinking on social issues. They acknowledged men's and women's "natural right" to association but were designed primarily to isolate workers from leftist influences. The circles denounced "class struggle" as "antisocial and damaging to worker's interests" and as encouraging "union leaders to become the bosses of the working masses."[52] They pledged to "resist . . . the activities of all those who threaten the welfare of the Nation, Religion, Family, and Property."[53] They petitioned congress for legislation to make Sundays an obligatory day of rest, for the regulation of female and child labor, for compulsory arbitration of labor disputes, and for workers' housing programs.

Several other Catholic institutions of a similar kind appeared during this period. The Liga Social Argentina (Argentine Social League) founded in 1908 pledged "to sustain the Christian organization of society, to combat every error and subversive tendency."[54] The Christian Democratic League founded in 1902 declared itself

equally apart from both liberal individualism and socialist collectivism, two different forms of the same tyranny, [and supported] a reconstruction of society on the basis of the corporations [*gremios*] and professions adapted to the requirements of progress and modern civilization; the kind of organization in which the individual will lose none of his liberty but will receive full protection against the strong. . . . [The league therefore] upholds the individual in the corporation, the corporation in the state, and the sum [of these various parts] forming the nation.[55]

These associations illustrated the prominent part the old guilds destroyed by the French Revolution played in Catholic thinking. Like the guilds, at least as the Catholic imagination portrayed them, these bodies were intended to "unite" workers and employers in a single entity and to act as mediating instruments between the individual and society at large. In the view of Catholics, the national community itself should be constituted as an organic assembly of such associations, or "gremios." The Catholic concepts of "class harmony" and "distributive justice" bore their original Greek connotations of balance, measure, or proportion. In sum, Catholics rejected the laissez-faire and Socialist states and aspired for an organic and paternalist system modeled on the European anciens régimes to implement social reform and institute "justice."

The Traditionalists

Positivism, or *cientificismo*, reached the height of its influence in Argentina between 1880 and 1910. At its most basic level, the positivist movement defined itself "as the critical examination of what is given, the so-called absolute truths," and its followers aimed to discover "whatever is objective, real, natural, and whatever means progress in the sphere of society and politics. . . . The 'positive' is conceived as a function of social progress, progress also bereft of any need of the metaphysical."[56] The main targets of the positivists were natural law and the teachings of the church. Florentino Ameghino, for example, one of the leading *científicos* in Argentina, devoted his career to refuting the Christian version of the origins of humanity and to research in palaeontology to prove its material, evolutionary, and Godless beginnings. By 1900, the positivist movement was entrenched not only in the sciences but in art, philosophy, sociology, and politics, indeed "in every domain of the spirit."[57] "We had absolute faith in science, . . . in indefinite progress to be achieved by advances in technique that would bring contentment to the peoples," declared one of the movement's young adherents.[58]

The first secular, as opposed to clerical, manifestations of the Nationalist movement began as a critique of positivism and as a reaction against the concepts of "progress," "materialism," and "cosmopolitanism" it represented. The opponents of positivism followed the church in denouncing the movement as a pagan onslaught against Christianity. In an effort to extol the "native" against the "foreign," which they identified with positivism, they also attempted to create a cult of preliberal and preimmigrant Argentina.

This "traditionalist" movement emerged soon after the war

of 1898 between Spain and the United States. Spain's swift
and shattering defeat in 1898 focused attention throughout
Latin America on the vast industrial and military power of
the United States and provoked fears that the Latin American
republics could be its next victims. Numerous Latin American
writers denounced the "materialism" they saw embodied in
the United States, as they also discovered a newly awakened
sympathy and fraternity with the "spiritualism" they saw represented by Spain.

At the turn of the century, Uruguayan José Enrique Rodó
became the best-known Latin American writer to capture and
develop these ideas. Rodó's *Ariel*, published in 1900, drew
extensively on the nineteenth-century European conservative tradition, in particular, on Renan's essay, "Caliban, suite
de la conquête." Many of Renan's ideas and stances reappeared in *Ariel*. "Democracy," declared Rodó, for example,
lay at odds with "God's design"; the modern world was subject to an unrelenting contest between "utilitarian democracy" and "spiritual values."

Serious concern for the ideal is completely opposed to the spirit of
democracy. . . . Whoever speaks the word democracy . . . [means]
the progressive development of individualism and the decline of
culture.[59]

Rodó contrasted his notion of the "spiritual," represented by
Ariel, with the "utilitarian conception," embodied in Caliban,
that striving to achieve equality established "the mediocre as
the norm."[60] He saw the United States as "the incarnation of
the word utilitarian," since in that nation there was no "sense
of the ideal. Force substitutes reason, quantity substitutes
quality, [and] democracy consists of the equality of all in common vulgarity."[61]

In 1901, a small group of law students at the University of
Buenos Aires led by Gálvez, then an aspiring novelist, created
a new literary periodical, *Ideas*. The *Ideas* group, as Gálvez
later recalled, constituted itself in a deliberate gesture of opposition to the overwhelming majority of law students who
were "materialists [and] made one god of Spencer and another of Comte." "We," by contrast, declared Gálvez, "were

nearly all upholders of the spiritual, [dedicated to] a heroic struggle against the prevailing ambience of discredited materialism."[62] The "scientific materialism" that positivism embodied, the *Ideas* group contended, "offers no afterlife," and therefore could not explain the mysteries of being. Humanity had to be something more than an "evolved animal."[63] The group attacked José Ingenieros, a leading positivist of the day, for "his militant materialism, his cult of scientific method [cientificismo], his negation of God. . . . He has intellectually perverted thousands of young people."[64]

Gálvez defined the mission of the *Ideas* group as the same as "that in Spain assumed by the generation of thinkers that emerged after the disaster [of 1898]: Ganivet, Macías Picavea, Costa, Unamuno."[65] Rodó's influence on the *Ideas* group became manifest in Gálvez's claim that "we possess the secret of energy."

But ours will never be a barbarous, automatic energy like that which boils away unceasingly in the United States. Ours is a harmonious energy, a force tempered by Latin spirit.[66]

"I have racial sensitivities," said Belisario J. Montero in a 1904 article in *Ideas*,

: am Latin and regard the civilized barbarian in the North with an inherited sense of mistrust. Today [the United States] has become a colossal society and now wants to impose its industry, its commerce, and its imperialism [throughout Latin America]. Each citizen of the union is a kind of stockholder . . . [upholding] an ideal of material perfection above moral perfection and equating civilization with the triumph of industry and commerce. We, by contrast, descendants of the Latins and educated by the Greeks, regard that person as most civilized who is most morally perfect. . . . I am proud to say I am bored with railroads and chimneys.[67]

Gálvez conceived "the heroic struggle" of the *Ideas* group as a defense of "intellectual and spiritual values" in the face of what he called an *ambiente extranjerizante y despreciador de lo argentino*.[68] This so-called foreign atmosphere that "depreciated things Argentine" referred to the European immigrants, of whom a proportionately larger number now dwelled in Argentina than in the United States.[69] By this time, immigration was inducing a sense of panic among native Argentines and an atmosphere of profound, irreversible change that threatened to engulf the native population, its customs, institutions, and language.[70] A contributor to *Ideas* in 1903, for example, lamented that "the Argentine people [*raza*], especially the old inhabitants of Buenos Aires," were disappearing, "on account of the flood of immigrants. And our people are our nationality, and our nationality is our country."[71]

Tensions between natives and immigrants in Argentina already had a long history. In the 1870s, for example, José Hernández's famous poem, *The Gaucho Martin Fierro*, asked, "I'd like to know why the government / Enlists that gringo crew / And what they think they're good for here."[72] By the 1880s, not only Catholics like Estrada but some of the liberals were beginning to question the benefits and consequences of immigration. In 1881, Sarmiento himself, who had been among the architects of the policies that encouraged and subsidized European immigration, complained at the division he now perceived between a political nation of natives and an economic nation of immigrants. The latter, he alleged, were unduly concerned with self-enrichment and used their own schools that taught in their own languages to resist assimilation. He wrote,

Growing and expanding, we shall build, if we have not already built, a Tower of Babel in America, its workmen speaking all tongues, not blending together in the task of construction, but each persisting in his own. . . . One does not construct a homeland without patriotism as its cement, nor does one build . . . a city without citizens.[73]

In the 1887 novel *En la Sangre*, Enrique Cambaceres used a garbled version of Social Darwinism to denounce Italians as a people carrying an inherited stigma.[74] Likewise, José M. Ramos Mejía, another of the leading científicos, denounced immigrants as biologically and culturally inferior to the native stock of Argentina: "Any [Argentine person] is more intelligent than the immigrant just arrived on our shores."[75] Julián Martel's novel *La Bolsa*, written during the political and economic crisis of 1890–91, became the first major anti-Semitic tract to appear in Argentina, although the book was little more than a plagiarism of Edouard Drumont's then notorious piece, *La France Juive*.[76]

The nativism adopted by the traditionalist writers at the turn of the century abandoned the strain of Social Darwinism favored by liberals and científicos, recognizing that it belonged to the positivist viewpoint they were attempting to dislodge. Their own concerns were not with quasi-biological and incipiently racist categories like "blood" or "craniates" but with cultural concepts, "values," and "traditions"—the approach that derived from the Catholics and from writers like Rodó. Rodó, for example, condemned immigration for producing what he called a "zoocracy," which typified the false positivist claim that a melting pot of nationalities would produce "progress."[77] In 1906, Emilio Becher, a member of the *Ideas* group, urged his countrymen

to defend what is national against destructive outside invasion and to strengthen our society on the cement of solid tradition. For a time the cosmopolitan ideal [advanced by positivists] appeared to us a humanitarian philosophy and persuaded some incautious persons [to accept] its promise of an attainable utopia. [Cosmopolitanism preached] that an anarchy of peoples represented the image of future society and that the language of the future was to be the language of Babel.

Despite the great flood of immigrants, Becher continued, "our civilization has not changed at its core," and he urged his countrymen to reaffirm "the indestructible soul of [their] Hispanic ancestry."[78]

Echoing the nineteenth-century Federalists, the traditionalists portrayed the relationship between the city of Buenos Aires and the provinces in the light of the contrasts they drew between "materialism" or "Spencerian notions of progress," on one side, and the "spiritual" or "tradition," on the other. Using this framework, they depicted Buenos Aires as the embodiment of materialism but the provinces as the embodiment of spiritualism. As Gálvez noted, several leading members of the *Ideas* group were of upper-class provincial background and possessed strong ancestral roots in preimmigrant Creole Argentina. Gálvez himself, for example, origi-

nated in Entre Ríos and Becher in Rosario.[79] Gálvez, in particular, drew great pride from his connections with the "ancient
city" of Santa Fe, founded in 1573, and the descent he claimed
from an aristocracy "rooted among the conquerors and the
first Spanish colonizers."[80] He lamented Santa Fe's demise
as the small frontier village it had remained for centuries until
the coming of the immigrants and "progress."[81]

Gálvez contrasted the way of life of the old rustic provincial
communities with the corruption and decadence he perceived in the capital. He derided the tango, now becoming
famous as the great cultural symbol of Buenos Aires, as a
"product of cosmopolitanism, hybrid and ugly music, . . . a
grotesque dance, . . . the embodiment of our national mess."[82]
In *Nacha Regules*, which told the story of a prostitute and
her eventual redemption, Gálvez denounced the white slave
traffic, of which Buenos Aires was then the epicenter.[83]

The traffickers inveigle girls into their control in Austria or Russia.
Sometimes they even marry them and bring them into Buenos Aires
as their wives but keep them virgins to get a better price from their
sale. Then the women are auctioned away to other traffickers. . . .
These fellows make millions. . . . They rape and torture the women.
It's as if Buenos Aires were a great market of human flesh.[84]

Making much the same point in a less lurid way, Ricardo
Oliver, another contributor to *Ideas*, regretted that Buenos
Aires never revealed

any fondness for spiritual matters, the mark of higher civiliza-
tions. . . . Perhaps from time to time the din of its workshops and
the shouts of its politicking plebs have been stilled, and some other
sound may be heard apart from the pounding of metals. . . . But such
an event would last for only a brief moment, as in an instant all
energies returned to the pursuit of fortune and pleasure.[85]

For the most part, the traditionalist writers developed such
an outlook rather than being born with it, since several of
them started out with left-wing connections. "In less than four
years," Gálvez recalled, "I was a Tolstoyan, a Socialist, an
anarchist, a Nietzschean, a neo-mystic, and finally a Catholic
in succession."[86] A visit to Spain in 1906, a religious reawak-
ening in 1907, and then a long journey through the far interior

as an inspector of schools in 1910 slowly induced in Gálvez the sensation of having become a "true Argentine" but at the same time "a Spaniard and a Christian."[87] As a "patriot," he was now aware of the "bitter sadness of the vanquished races [in the interior]." He said, "In the old cities and primitive villages, I have smelled the incense of colonial tradition."[88]

As he underwent this spiritual transition, Gálvez began to peer into the past in search of a vision for the future. In *El diario de Gabriel Quiroga*, a book published in 1910, he wrote,

The present hour demands of us, the Argentines, all our efforts to achieve the rebirth of the spiritual life that in our past we lived intensely. . . . We have abandoned the ideas that once formed the noblest ornament of the Argentine people, and we now think of nothing more than increasing our wealth and speeding the progress of the country. Only a few years ago our people were poor . . . and we lived amidst continuous wars and revolutions. But at that time there was a national spirit, and patriotism inspired our soldiers and writers. . . . Then we were truly Argentines.[89]

Gálvez reflected ironically on the effects of European influences in the country. At the instigation of liberals led by Alberdi, a man of "European spirit, who lacked the spirit of his own land," he declared,

we began to bring in multitudes of rustic peoples from the Italian countryside. . . . Then we started to imitate English and French customs. Jews and Russian anarchists came. . . . The old Creole squares became English parks; the barbarous and poor Spanish language has been smoothed out and enriched with many Italian, French, English, and German words. . . . We have forgotten our own traditions and those ridiculous old-fashioned customs. . . . Today anyone can read Voltaire, Marx, Kropotkin, or Bakunin for a mere thirty cents. As everyone can see, we're now completely civilized.[90]

El diario de Gabriel Quiroga stood out as one of the first published writings that attempted to denigrate liberal-positivism using the technique of historical reinterpretation. In the Argentina of 1910, Gálvez discerned numerous survivals of the conflicts a century before between the liberal Unitarists and the conservative Federalists. He then depicted federalism as the embodiment of the country's "traditional" and therefore real identity. Thus the "spirit" of the two factions remained "latent," he declared. The Unitarists were liberal, pro-European but anti-Spanish "doctors," whereas

the Federalist represents the opposite type. . . . He scarcely ever flaunts the title of doctor: he is a rancher, a general, a commander of the rural militia. He has no specific ideas about what the country is or should be but has an intense sense of the country. . . . He is part of the land. . . . He has the vitality of the gaucho. . . . He is straightforward and democratic. . . . [But] the Unitarist . . . is a parasite opposed to tradition we need to get rid of. . . . He is an atom of foreignism, of manic Europeanism. . . . He contradicts our American character and bars the resurgence of our national tradition.[91]

Gálvez then defined the concepts he was now advancing as "Nationalism."

In the past few years a vague and complex sentiment has arisen . . . that has been called Nationalism. . . . This means, above all, the highest regard for our people and our country, . . . the protection of our past, loving our history, our landscapes, our customs, our writers, and our art. . . . Nationalism resists . . . every idea, every institution, and every habit that can in any way contribute to suppressing one atom of our Argentine character.[92]

In a style closely reminiscent of Menéndez Pelayo, Gálvez argued that the two other main components of Nationalism were the church and the Federalist caudillos. "Religion, like language," he proclaimed, "is one of the essential foundations of our nationality."[93] The caudillos, he continued, were the "obscure architects of our nationality [who embodied] national consciousness and the eternal spirit of the future nation."[94]

La restauración nacionalista by Ricardo Rojas, published in 1909, represented another attack on "destructive individualism" and "cosmopolitanism," particularly as these values were enshrined in the system of public education. According to him, immigration had destroyed the country's "moral unity" and produced an unstable society because so much of its population remained "rootless." To rebuild a sense of community, the authorities should use the schools "to renew our history, cultivate our own legends, revive an awareness of tradition," because "from a sense of its past, a people develops a more powerful commitment to its future. . . . It is now time to impose a nationalist character on our education through the study of history and the humanities."[95]

Rojas reiterated the criticisms that appeared in Gálvez's writings: "cosmopolitanism, . . . the dissolution of the old moral nucleus, . . . a growing forgetfulness of tradition, the corruption of language, . . . the unscrupulous pursuit of wealth." As another writer of provincial origin from Santiago del Estero, Rojas attacked the "corrupting ideas and sentiments" in Buenos Aires.[96] He unearthed the primitive brand of economic nationalism common among the Federalists. "The capital," he declared, "rich and populous as it is, [has] an excessive influence over the rest of the country to the extent that the fourteen provinces subsist upon its ebb and flow [*viven de su ritmo*]."

The apparent greatness of Buenos Aires springs from individual self-serving efforts and from international interests. . . . Behind the appearance of spectacular progress, we remain spiritually the same as in colonial days, . . . waiting for the next ship, which in days past used to come from Cadiz but now comes daily with the news from France or England. . . . Today [in 1910], as we celebrate the first centenary of our political independence, we still feel ourselves a colony of the old metropoli.[97]

The coming generation, Rojas continued,

will have to decide between those who want progress at the price of civilization, those willing to hand themselves over to the foreigner without a fight, and those who want progress along with the content of our own civilization which can only develop upon the substance of our own tradition.[98]

Once more Rojas conflated "national character" with federalism and the caudillos. That age of "barbarism," he wrote, "so reviled by our historians,"

was the most authentic source of our character. . . . There were greater affinities between Rosas and the pampas, or between "Facundo" [Quiroga] and his mountains than there ever were between

Rivadavia or [Manuel] Garcia [the Unitarists] and the country they sought to govern.[99]

In a later work, *Eurindia*, Rojas deprecated the derivative, imitative character of the arts and literature in Argentina and urged a quest for "spiritual autonomy" through the forging of an independent national culture. He listed the artistic movements that had recently appeared in Argentina.

Each of these schools has done some partial good, but almost all of them amount to foreign importations. . . . We now need aesthetic doctrines based on national history, something born here . . . to affirm that as a nation Argentina has reached maturity, that the country has learned to explain itself in its own terms. . . . Political colonialism has ended, but we still have our intellectual metropoli. We need to assume a spiritual autonomy.[100]

Carlos Ibarguren, a leading figure in both literary and political circles during this period, illustrated more of the basic features of the early Nationalist movement. Ibarguren belonged to a leading family in Salta and, like Gálvez, claimed descent from "among the first conquerors, . . . the *encomenderos* of that region."[101] Like Gálvez's nostalgia for old Santa Fe, Ibarguren's childhood memories of Salta recalled a now lost world that stretched far back into the past.

My early childhood was an echo of times gone by. [I remember] the ancient Carmelite monastery, . . . the church with its centuries' old facade, the little shrine that contained a discolored and weather-beaten image of the Virgin, the ornate door of the convent with its great rusty locks, the quiet streets traversed from time to time by silent pedestrians, by grave-looking clerics, and by lowly women shrouded in dark shawls.[102]

The church Ibarguren evoked was not the new institution created by the liberal revolution but the much older one that survived in Salta from the colonial and Federalist eras. Similarly, the society he venerated was preliberal and patriarchal. In his youth, Ibarguren's writings lamented the rise of the capitalist bourgeoisie at the expense of the old feudal nobility.[103] More than fifty years later, in his memoirs, he recalled the story recounted to him as a child, when in 1867 the *mon-*

tonera rebel, Felipe Varela, had invaded and pillaged the city of Salta.[104] Ibarguren had no sympathy for such brigands because, as he put it, Varela had threatened society's leading citizens, or *personas distinguidas*.[105]

The qualities Ibarguren admired most in people were those of an aristocracy. Commenting on some of the public figures he had known during his career, he praised Roque Saenz Peña, president of Argentina between 1910 and 1914, for his "deep filial sentiments, his lofty spirit, the noble firmness of his character."[106] In Indalecio Gómez, who served as Saenz Peña's minister of the interior, Ibarguren saw "talent, an exquisite breeding, finely tuned eloquence." Gómez was "a superior spirit . . . [and] the nobility of his physique lay in concord with the natural harmony of his movements."[107] In his kinsman and fellow *salteño*, General José F. Uriburu, who was president from 1930 to 1932, Ibarguren discerned a "patriot and a gentleman." He praised Uriburu's "disinterestedness, his sense of honor" and for having lived "religiously dedicated to the army."[108]

These writings contained several common threads. "Tradition" became closely identified with federalism and explicitly opposed to unitarism and the liberals. The traditionalists sought to promote "spirituality" and condemned "cosmopolitanism," an equally capacious and indistinct term whose meanings ranged from immigrants, urban life, and culture in Buenos Aires to fashionable philosophical movements like positivism and Social Darwinism. The traditionalists commonly expressed concerns over the debasement of their native language as a result of linguistic intrusions from abroad. They idealized the provincial communities of Creole Argentina, the church, and the old Hispanic families.

There were echoes of the culture of antiquity in some of their writings. "Cosmopolitanism," Rojas alleged, for example, bred "an indifference to public affairs," a complaint that recalled the Greek idea that all members of the polis should participate in its activities and that indifference would lead to its demise.[109] At the same time, these writings contained numerous resonances of more recent foreign mentors. Gálvez remembered Becher, for example, as "an Argentine Renan

[who] thought and wrote like the French, above all Renan and [Anatole] France, in whose works and spirit he was saturated."[110] Gálvez's own writings brimmed with references to Renan and Barrès. He defined the church, for example, in exactly the terms used by Barrès or Fustel de Coulanges as the embodiment of the country's "moral physiognomy."[111] Gálvez's pantheistic depictions of provincial landscapes closely resembled Barrès's portrayals of Lorraine.

Strong Spanish influences also appeared in this literature. "Fascinated by Spain," Gálvez declared, "the most profound and disturbing country I know, I experienced the deepest emotions in my life, and I took from Castille many precepts."[112] In liberal Argentina, he contended, Spain was unjustly "forgotten and ridiculed." The old Spanish cities, quite unlike those in Argentina, were "illustrious and full of essence."[113] Gálvez learned from the Spanish Generation of 1898 "to teach incessantly love of country, for our landscapes, for our writers, for our great men."[114] Expressions and phrasing commonly employed by the traditionalists in Argentina were taken from Spanish writers. In Gálvez's writings, the nation possessed "a historic personality," "a psychological structure," "a real constitution," or represented an "irreducible nucleus." The task of the writer was to "spiritualize the national conscience," to mobilize the "national soul," to foster "collective idealism," and to weed out the nation's "intrahistory."[115] Gálvez's whole approach, which rested on the assumption that in the interior of Argentina lay the "truth," evoked the phrase that Ganivet had taken from Saint Augustine: *Noli foras ire; in interiore Hispaniae habitat veritas.*[116] Similarly, Rojas's concern to defend the linguistic purity of the Spanish spoken in Argentina betrayed the influence of Miguel Unamuno. Language, he wrote, represented "that great psychological archive that conserves the common values of peoples."[117] The work of Francisco Giner de los Ríos, head of the famed Instituto de la Enseñanza Libre in Madrid, heavily influenced Rojas's proposals for the reform of education in Argentina.[118]

Leopoldo Lugones stood out as the most creative and controversial of the early Nationalist writers. Like Gálvez, Rojas, and Ibarguren, Lugones was of provincial origin and felt himself "a lifelong foreigner in Buenos Aires." He was "a son of Córdoba. From Córdoba he received his first impulses toward intellectual activities, and to Córdoba he always returned."[119] Lugones came from a "poor but distinguished family" that was steeped in religion. In her village home in Córdoba, his mother had lived "like the truest believer, submissive to the priest to the point of blindness, as attentive to her duties as a Christian as the soldier to his orders."[120] Lugones's ancestral roots stretched far back into the past. "Among his ancestors was a colonel in the army of independence. . . . His imposing grandmother would solemnly recall that she had been born in Year Two of the Homeland [i.e., 1812]."[121] Lugones's poetry commemorated still earlier ancestors among the first Spanish *encomenderos*.

> A don Juan de Lugones el encomendero
> Que, hijo y nieto de ambos, fue quien sacó primero
> A mención las probanzas, datas y cualidades
> De tan buenos servicios a las dos majestades
> Con que del rey obtuvo, más por carga que en pago
> Doble encomienda de indios en Salta y en Santiago.[122]

Another of Lugones's verses captured his sense of an enduring connection between himself and the provincial village, Santa María del Río Seco, where he was born and raised. Lugones considered himself "no more than an echo" of his birthplace.

> En la villa Santa María del Río Seco
> Al pie del Cerro del Romero, nací
> Y esto es todo cuanto diré de mí
> Porque no soy más que un eco
> Del canto natal que traigo aquí.[123]

Lugones's writings betrayed still more strong foreign influences. The French modernist writers led by Baudelaire and Verlaine propelled him into a quest for the "mystery of subjective life," into the arena of the intuitive and the subconscious, and into the cult of aesthetics.[124] The ancient Greeks inspired Lugones's major prose writings. In *Prometeo*, published in 1910, he depicted Argentina as "a new land suitable for growing any seed," but the seed, he contended, should be the ideals and systems of the Greeks that would "spiritualize" the country. The Greeks, he claimed, lacked the sense of "unease" [*inquietud*], "that terrible modern illness" he regarded as the distinctive trait of the modern society corrupted by materialism.

[The Greeks] resolved the four great problems of existence: the social through institutions that satisfied everyone because they were creations of the community; the individual by establishing the principle of obedience; the spiritual through the knowledge of a future life; the moral through a rational concept of the good. . . . Today we have no idea why we live; all human solidarity has disintegrated into anarchy: [we occupy] a world of separate people.[125]

Also in *Prometeo*, he wrote,

If our present civilization does not wish to die in the shame of mercantilism that Plato and Aristotle believed the labor of slaves, or in a servile philosophy that purports to show the links between men and beasts [i.e., the theory of evolution], it will have to reach a similar synthesis [as the Greeks].[126]

Yet for Lugones, unlike Gálvez or Ibarguren, and in spite of his own mother's influence, spirituality had no connection with Christianity. He scorned the Christian faith as the origin of individualism and therefore materialist greed: "I am the personal enemy of God," he proclaimed ostentatiously.[127] Instead of having any Christian connection, spirituality meant a Hellenic pagan polytheism erected on "three gigantic entities": the Pampa, the Río de la Plata, and the Andes.[128] From this different perspective, however, Lugones's targets remained the same as those of the other traditionalists. He attacked the liberal-positivist idea that "morality was a physical science"; he condemned the liberal individualist assumption that, as he put it, "egotism [underlay] all civilized societies"; he derided liberal democracy as "rule by irresponsible mobs."[129] "From Aristotle to Renan," he declared, "history shows that the best governments are the enlightened oligarchies."[130]

In "El payador," published in 1916, Lugones explored what he saw as the legacies of Greco-Roman civilization in Argentina's national culture. Among them were the old gaucho songs as they were performed by wandering troubadours, or *payadores*. The payadores, he claimed, "were the most significant personages in the creation of our people." In inventing a "new language, . . . another [local] form of Castilian," they "established the foundation of the nation." In their music, Lugones discerned the same technical features and forms of instrumentation as the music of classical antiquity. Moreover, music constituted "the initial word," or first step, in the development of civilization.[131]

The gauchos became another of Lugones's themes in this essay. He depicted these wandering cowboys as prototypes of the Argentine people at large, embodying their traits of physical bravery and introspective pessimism, their disinterest in material wealth: all that was "properly national," he declared, derived from the gaucho.[132] Much of "El payador" was devoted to a critical appreciation of Hernández's *El gaucho Martín Fierro*. Lugones lauded the poem as an epic, the concrete proof of the existence of an Argentine people, since the epic form illustrated the unique style in which each "people struggles for justice and liberty." *Martín Fierro* explored the "formation of a people and the secret of its destiny"; it represented a "certificate" of a people's "vitality" and its "heroic life." Years later in his *Nuevos estudios helénicos*, Lugones reiterated some of the central themes of "El payador": "We on account of our Latin blood . . . belong to the peoples of Beauty, and we therefore descend in a straight line from the Greeks, the progenitors of Beauty."[133]

The traditionalists emerged from the provinces to combat what they perceived as the destructive consequences of the liberal revolution: the all-engulfing tides of immigrants, the proliferation of foreign languages, the hybrid and false doctrines of "progress," in short,

the ugly materialism that today shames and insults us. . . . This materialism is a recent phenomenon that has appeared with the fever for wealth and has come from Europe. The immigrant who has made his fortune has brought with him a new concept of life. His sole intention is to enrich himself, and in doing so he has contaminated the Argentines.[134]

"We have confused national greatness with money. . . . We have placed our honor in commerce," proclaimed Lugones.[135] In this society of foreigners wrought by the liberals, he perceived mere "anarchy bereft of any human or even patriotic solidarity."[136]

The traditionalists aspired for a world of accepted hierarchy and pastoral changelessness, free of the oppressive influence of Buenos Aires. They saw their forefathers as "soldiers, poets, artists" in a now extinct heroic age, which they contrasted with the current generation of "shopkeepers, peddlers, and usurers." The traditionalists felt a close intimacy with the land where they were born. Carulla, for example, who belonged to a later generation of Nationalists, described his native village in Entre Ríos as a place in which "the wilderness reached to within a few steps" of his family home. His origins, he explained, had strongly influenced his ideas "because the earth [*lo telúrico*] strongly conditions our soul and our spirit [*nuestro ser espiritual-anímico*]."[137]

The traditionalists possessed other common features. Except for the aristocratic Ibarguren, they came from declining gentry families that had fallen on hard times. The families of Gálvez, Rojas, and Lugones all prospered in the 1880s under Roca but then lost heavily in the financial crash of 1890 under his successor, Juárez Celman.[138] In the early 1890s, both sides of Lugones's family, for example, forfeited *estancias* they had possessed for generations, and for many years Lugones himself was obliged to eke out a living in Buenos Aires as a postal employee.[139] Common to all the leading members of the group was a sense of exclusion and alienation from the golden age of liberalism after 1890 which had left them behind.[140]

Whereas women often played a prominent role in the clerical movement of the 1880s, the traditionalists were almost without exception men. Gálvez later recalled that among the *Ideas* group, "women were completely absent. There was not a single woman writer at that time. Women were absent even from our conversations."[141] The claim contained some exaggeration, since during this period, in particular, Gálvez was strongly influenced by his wife, Delfina Bunge de Gálvez. The sister of another prominent writer, Carlos Octavio Bunge,

Bunge de Gálvez possessed strong connections with the Order of Franciscans, which apparently stimulated her closeness to what she called the "poetry of little things," which included the small towns of the Argentine interior from which Gálvez himself drew his inspiration.[142]

Except for Rojas's *La restauración nacionalista*, whose appeal stemmed from its link with the fiercely debated issue of education, these early Nationalist manifestos had little apparent impact. Gálvez, for example, sold only five hundred copies of the first edition of *El diario de Gabriel Quiroga*. The traditionalists never completely succeeded in emancipating themselves from the type of personalities they deplored or from the outlook and convictions they were attempting to subvert. The *Ideas* group willingly welcomed to its ranks persons of immigrant stock like Alberto Gerchunoff, who was Jewish. Another member of the group was Guillermo Leguizamón, who later became a railroad magnate and was eventually knighted for his services to the British railroad interests.[143]

In much of the writing of the traditionalists lay the eclectic mixing of philosophical or literary traditions of the type that led Rodó, for example, to aspire for a "spiritualized society" through a process of "natural selection."[144] Gálvez's novels often used techniques borrowed from Émile Zola and introduced Zolaesque characters whose flaws stemmed, Darwin-style, from heredity and natural selection. Gálvez dedicated *El diario de Gabriel Quiroga* to Argentina's great liberals, Mitre and Sarmiento, "these august and unforgettable names," and among the great liberal patriarchs, he confined his criticisms to Alberdi alone. In *Nacha Regules*, he appeared to contradict the sympathies he professed for the Federalist tradition, as he attacked the men "of good name" belonging to the Argentine elite who traveled through Europe

insulting civilized people by their arrogance. In Paris they mix with prostitutes and cause scandals in taverns and cabarets with their South American manners. Mixtures of the civilized and the barbarian . . . they are the descendants of gauchos. Unscrupulous beings [they are], lacking any morals and discipline, obeying no law but their caprices and their pleasures.[145]

Other liberal remnants survived in Lugones, who wanted "human dignity" for workers but could suggest for its achievement only the old liberal plan of handing out free land to newly arrived immigrants.[146] Throughout these years, Ibarguren, who still professed himself a positivist, remained a leading figure in the liberal oligarchy.

The writings of the traditionalists were filled with borrowed techniques, phrasing, and analytical approaches, but as yet, the connections they made with the European counterrevolution were shallow and incomplete. Gálvez's memoirs captured the atmosphere that prevailed in Argentina before 1914 and the limits and ambiguities of the protest he sought to lead at that time. "The only thing wrong with that age," he wrote years later, "which was perhaps the result of the prevailing well-being, was materialism."[147]

Throughout this period, the Catholic movement remained similarly small and weak. To José E. Níklison, a national labor department official writing during World War I, all the Catholic groups evinced "passivity and a truly lamentable inertia." By 1913, the workers' circles possessed barely 20,000 members throughout the country, the Argentine Social League only a few hundred, and the Christian Democratic League had collapsed in 1908.[148] The league's feeble corporatist organizations, as Franceschi, one of its founders, later admitted, merely copied the ideas of "the French sociologist La Tour de Pin" and proved completely unsuited to the dynamic, mobile societies of urban Argentina.[149] The Nationalist movement was thus beginning to stir but so far had failed to find its full voice. "Before the war," declared Lugones, capturing the outlook of the Nationalists in general at this point, "it was [still] possible . . . to believe in liberty, democracy, and equality."[150]

Chapter Three

Rule by the Capable

World War I launched the Nationalist movement as a political force, refashioning a diffuse nativist cult into a crusade for counterrevolution. The war, exclaimed Lugones, finally exposed as a "great illusion" the boasts of the liberals to have created universal and perpetual peace. The war achieved "a renaissance of patriotism." Only after 1914,

> we began to understand that for the nation, power was more important than law and sovereignty more significant than liberty. Life was no longer a legal or moral system but consisted of force, while the nation redefined itself as an expression of victory, as a dominion.[1]

The Nationalist movement developed an incipient political identity around 1910 as a result of the tensions that stemmed from immigration. The war then strengthened and diversified the movement, establishing the first links between the Nationalists and the military through the Liga Patriótica Argentina founded in early 1919 and launching the Nationalists on the quest for a "new order" of society. Afterward, during the late 1920s, the Nationalists played a major part in the struggle against Hipólito Yrigoyen, president of Argentina in 1916–1922 and 1928–1930, which in 1930 brought the destruction of constitutional democracy.

The Nationalist movement came alive when the established "liberal" order appeared to be under threat of destruction or disintegration: these conditions appeared immediately after the war and then in a more profound and protracted way toward the end of the 1920s. In less critical periods, however,

Nationalist ideas and positions were continually usurped by other political movements. For a time, Yrigoyen himself, for example, successfully incorporated many Nationalist themes in his own diverse movement. The Liga Patriótica Argentina betrayed the same tendency to combine ideas typical of the liberals with those of the Nationalists. By the end of the 1920s, the Nationalists achieved greater self-definition as the opponents of popular democracy and the proponents of "counter-revolution." Even so, they still remained unclear or divided on many specific issues: on economic nationalism, on social reform, and on the kinds of structural changes they wanted in the political system. The most striking division lay between Lugones, who emerged as the supporter of a centralized military autocracy, and the clerical wing of the movement, whose members aspired for a patrimonial state preserving local self-government and provincial autonomy.

The Nativist Reaction

By 1910, most of the writers who formed part of the traditionalist movement were supporting the social reforms sponsored by the Catholic groups. Gálvez, for example, now viewed such reform as an instrument to construct a national community and to "spiritualize" a society corrupted by materialism. He played a leading part, alongside economist Alejandro E. Bunge, conservative congressman Juan E. Cafferata, and Monseñor Miguel de Andrea, a leading cleric who was now the "spiritual director" of the workers' circles, in the effort to construct institutions promoting "class harmony."[2]

Meanwhile, Rojas continued to campaign for a system of "patriotic education."[3] As a minister in the Sáenz Peña administration of 1910–1914, Ibarguren proposed, although unsuccessfully, social reforms he later claimed represented a foundation for a social security system.[4] In 1915, Ibarguren drew up the program of the Progressive Democratic party, at that time the largest of the conservative political factions. Here Ibarguren reiterated his support for social reform, while adding several other measures "to give us economic independence from the foreigner."[5] In another vague foretaste of the future, Gálvez criticized the liberal ruling classes in Argentina for accepting "French and British [liberal] ideas too uncritically," thereby identifying themselves with the "cosmopolitan spirit" he deplored.[6]

But in this early period before 1914, it was Lugones who betrayed the strongest hints of the political attitudes that characterized the Nationalists. For many years, Lugones had portrayed himself as a supporter of the Socialist ideal of "perfect equality as an expression of perfect justice."[7] In *Prometeo*, he lamented that "the poverty of a single Argentine is a disgrace in a country that boasts of the ease of its riches."[8] Yet it was said of him that even in his youth he dreamed of "redemptory enterprises under the dual banner of religion and homeland."[9] Some time before 1914, his friend Rubén Darío, the Nicaraguan poet, became convinced that behind Lugones's show of "red perspectives" lurked a real identity that was heavily reactionary, or "completely white."[10] "From the time I was very young," recalled Lugones's son, "I noticed in him a strong disdain for the plebs. . . . He abhorred the mob."[11] In "El payador," Lugones denounced all politics in Argentina as a "national scourge." "Everything in this country that means backwardness and wretchedness stems from politics," he wrote.[12] Despite his professed sympathies for the oppressed, during a visit to Europe in 1911, Lugones expressed strong disapproval of the attempts by the French and British governments to reach negotiated agreements with strikers. "*No se pacta con el desorden*," he proclaimed.[13]

In 1911, both Lugones and Rojas publicly criticized the Saenz Peña government's proposals for a male suffrage law and the secret ballot. Lugones did so as an opponent of "mob rule" and Rojas because the reform failed to impose a literacy test on voters.[14] Ibarguren, by contrast, called for a corporatist-style suffrage law that would represent not individuals but "concrete" entities: farmers, merchants, the professional classes, workers. A congress of the fuerzas vivas, or "living forces," he claimed, using the language typical of corporatism, would sustain "social equilibrium."[15]

These ideas appeared sporadically and in isolation and in the absence of any organized political movement to push them forward. At this point, social conflict spawned by rapid change provoked expressions of concern and disquiet and a strong sense of nostalgia for the past but failed to yield the political space for the Nationalist movement to take shape. The political dominance of the liberals seemed total. Government and congress alike opposed the social reforms proposed by Catholics on the dogmatic grounds that they would impede the allocation of resources through the market or lead to steep increases in public spending. The conviction was entrenched, similar to the Horatio Alger myth in the United States, that Argentina remained a classless society of open opportunity in which fortunes were at hand for anyone willing to work for them. "In our country," declared *La Prensa*,

classes do not exist. . . . Natural inequalities may appear, as in any other society, but these are based solely on the capacity of each person, on the success of some and the failure of others, upon the good and evil fortune that befalls every human being. . . . The workers of yesterday are the employers of today.[16]

Although liberal Argentina paid little heed to the pleas for reform that stemmed from *Rerum Novarum*, it shared the encyclical's uncompromising defense of property rights, its determination to use force to defend them, and its facile willingness to attribute all social unrest to "crafty agitators." In 1899, the writer and politician Miguel Cané began to attack "immigrant agitators." His campaign concluded three years later in the Ley de Residencia (Residence Law), which authorized the government to deport "undesirable" foreigners within three days and without trial.[17] In the same year, 1902, the army established its own police branch, the Orden Social, whose purpose was to keep the anarchists under close surveillance. During the next ten years, it became routine procedure for the police to break all strikes and demonstrations by force and to arrest and often mistreat and then deport the "agitators."[18]

Despite this constant show of force by successive governments, frictions between natives and immigrants continued. In this period appeared a relatively small but significant hint of what could happen if the government's resolve to use coercion ever weakened. When a Russian Jewish anarchist assassinated Ramón Falcón, the chief of police in Buenos Aires, in November 1909, a strong current of anti-Semitism swept Buenos Aires. Rojas, for example, singled out for special criticism the Jewish schools teaching in Yiddish or Hebrew as examples of the immigrant institutions that resisted incorporation and assimilation.[19] Gálvez too muttered occasional complaints against Jews. As Jews entered the urban professions, he declared, they were narrowing opportunities for the natives.[20]

In late 1909, Falcón's assassination triggered the formation of an organization of self-styled "patriotic" students known as the Juventud Autonomista. Six months later, in May 1910, when the anarchist labor unions threatened a strike to disrupt the celebration of the national centenary, members of the Juventud attacked immigrant workers in the streets. Shouting out the verses of the national anthem, they ransacked and destroyed the premises of the city's anarchist and Socialist newspapers. The following night, in a belated act of revenge for the assassination, the gang set on the small Jewish community in Buenos Aires, assaulting its members and looting some of their homes.[21] A month later, congress passed additional legislation directed against "agitators" known as the Law of Social Defense. On this occasion, members of congress denounced "the criminal hordes" who have

neither a country nor a religion and who are plotting in the shadows the most deadly methods to kill old men, defenseless women, and innocent children indiscriminately and in cold blood. . . . These monsters are outside any kind of law.

Unless the agitators were checked, the country ran the risk of "chronic war and daily lynchings."[22]

In *El diario de Gabriel Quiroga*, which appeared in the latter half of 1910, Gálvez sarcastically applauded the anarchists who, in provoking a violent reaction against themselves, had "saved the country and deserved the nation's sincere gratitude." The Juventud Autonomista, he added, demonstrate "our national energy" and

teach us that immigration has not completely destroyed our native spirit, that we still maintain something of the Indian in us. . . . These acts of violence have upset the materialism of the present a little, produced some nationalist sentiment, and revived dormant enthusiasms.[23]

It is notable that even before 1914, Gálvez was proposing that violence possessed a subliminal power to cleanse, mobilize, and unify and that the targets of violence—anarchists, Jews, leftists, or foreigners en masse—could be utilized as the instruments to "save the nation."

In Gálvez's work, too, lurked the even more threatening idea that "saving the nation" required foreign war. "Salvation lies in war with Brazil," he announced. "War will bring the people together, unite them in a common ideal, and awaken the spirit of nationality."[24] But in 1910, Gálvez could not imagine Argentina winning a war against Brazil. Still remembering Spain in 1898, he expected the sense of nationhood he craved would be forged not by military victory but by defeat. Gálvez ended his meditations with another sardonic word of gratitude to the anarchists. By making themselves the target of the "patriots," the anarchists provided a means to avoid "a war and a catastrophe that until now seemed an absolute therapeutic necessity."[25] It was wiser to let off steam against a few helpless foreign workers than to risk national destruction in a war with Brazil.

In 1912, in an effort to defuse years of growing political threats from the immigrants and from the numerous native groups that remained disenfranchised, the ruling conservative oligarchy under Saenz Peña introduced the secret ballot and a system of compulsory voting for native men aged eighteen and above. In 1916, the Radical party and its leader Yrigoyen captured the presidency in national elections. These events split the traditionalists, illustrating the absence of any common ground among them on political issues. While Lugones continued to vituperate against "mob rule" and Ibarguren remained a leading member of the conservative alliance opposed to the Radicals, Gálvez and eventually Rojas emerged as strong sympathizers of the new regime.

The Radical party, or *yrigoyenismo* as it later became known, strongly supported popular democracy and therefore seemed to fit squarely in the liberal tradition. But interwoven with Yrigoyen's pledges to elections free of the fraud and corruption of the past lay numerous traces of the preliberal and Catholic strains typical of the traditionalists. Echoing the Catholic tradition, Yrigoyen, for example, defined the Radicals not as a party but as a movement, which implied that they represented society in its entirety and were committed to the common good rather than merely sectional or partisan interests. Similarly, Yrigoyen conceived the state in terms more akin to *Rerum Novarum* than to classical liberalism. The state should arbitrate between competing interests: its task was reconciliation, social unity, and "distributive justice."

Yrigoyen's political ideas bore other traces of "Krausism," a set of ideas originating in early-nineteenth-century Germany which were adopted by Spanish liberals around 1850 and later spread to Argentina and other parts of Latin America.[26] In essence, Krausism was Catholicism without the church, a body of ideas that became so popular among Spanish and some Latin American liberals because it enabled them to reject the conservative church as feudal or reactionary but to uphold a more secular version of many of its tenets and to enlist support among a population steeped in Catholic values.

The Krausists shared with Catholics the idea that freedom consisted of will governed by moral purpose; like the Catholics, too, they viewed society as an interlocking organic hierarchy composed of "all the parts that constitute the living organism"; equally, Krausists and Catholics alike judged the value of the state and other institutions not by the liberal standard of "utility" but by their capacity to promote the "common good." Krausists agreed with Catholics that moral concerns should underlie every facet of human action and behavior and that a superordinate moral framework little different from Catholic natural law limited the autonomy of each person.[27]

Yrigoyen received some schooling in Krausism far back in his youth in the 1870s, and his political ideas contained a hybrid blend of liberal-democratic, mainstream Catholic, and Krausist ideas. Like the democrats, for example, he argued that clean elections were necessary to "fulfill" the constitution of 1853. "Public opinion," he wrote, "demands nothing more than honest elections . . . as the indispensable condition for the exercise of [political] rights."[28] But then, in a way reminiscent of the Krausists, Yrigoyen related "public morality" to "national character." The "moral" individuals and public figures of the Radical party, he argued, would produce the "moral" state. Thus, "a people," he wrote, "ought to develop and maintain its national character by public morality; only by virtue of such morality does a people gain respect."[29] Finally, Yrigoyen conflated his emphasis on free elections with the Catholic idea of the common good. He condemned the "competing pressures" that characterized liberal societies, and like the Catholic natural law writers, he anthropomorphized the nation, investing it with traits of a human being: "drowning," "breathing," or "vital." When honest elections were instituted, Yrigoyen wrote,

we shall see the differences between a Nation drowned in competing pressures [i.e., the unacceptable liberal nation] and a Nation breathing in the fullness of its being [i.e., the "organic" nation to be instituted by the Radicals], spreading its immense vitality for the common good.[30]

Yrigoyen's language was replete with Christian imagery: "purification," "martyrdom," "believers," "apostolate." In his terminology, the Radical movement became "the Cause," and its conservative opponents were dubbed "the Regime" or "the Argentine Bastille." "I have consecrated my life," Yrigoyen declared, "my repose, my well-being, my possessions, while refusing every temptation [to abandon my opposition to the oligarchy] a thousand times, in return for the cruelest proscriptions and sacrifices."[31] Referring to the Radical party, he proclaimed that

the majesty of its mission is sublime. . . . Its labors will endure; powerful are its forces. It is constantly strengthened and revitalized by the purest currents of opinion. It is a school for the coming generations.[32]

Such conflation of several objectively disconnected ideological strands played a major part in Yrigoyen's success in assembling an extremely diverse constituency before the 1916 election. In the province of Córdoba in 1916, for example, the Radical coalition ranged from "ultramontane Catholic elements to the most vehement anticlerical liberals."[33] Yrigoyen cultivated the church by donating his salary to a clerical charity and by strongly opposing attempts in congress to legalize divorce. Echoing *Rerum Novarum*, he pledged his government to "a moderate form of state intervention to alleviate the rigors of laissez-faire."[34] Under Yrigoyen, many of the proposed Catholic social reforms reappeared in congress as government measures, although opposition from conservatives still stymied them.[35]

At the same time, the Radicals seized on many of the themes popular among the traditionalists. October 12, the anniversary of Columbus's discovery of the Americas, became Día de la Raza, a national celebration of the country's historic link with Spain. In the provinces, the Radicals identified themselves with the native folk traditions popular among the traditionalist writers. As they marshaled their forces for local elections, the Radicals deliberately evoked the old Federalists as they rode into the villages on horseback "clothed in colored ponchos, white headbands, and armed with long cane lances with filed-down points."[36] By criticizing "ungrateful foreigners," the Radicals sought to present themselves as the representatives of the interests and attitudes of native Argentina. During the war, Yrigoyen catered to local nationalist sentiment by refusing to join the Allies and repeatedly pledging neutrality. He criticized the nations that he thought embodied "materialism," telling a British diplomat, for example, that

he had no confidence in the United States and regarded [Woodrow] Wilson as an Imperialist who aspired to exert authority throughout the Americas. Of England he has a holy horror. . . . He regarded England as a power sunk in materialism and which, having grabbed half the world and being sated, could now put on a hypocritical mask of generosity.[37]

Yrigoyen thus claimed that his movement embodied the "nation" and "patriotism" in much the same terms as the traditionalists understood these abstractions. His gestures persuaded Gálvez to hail the Radicals as "the solid and exalted expression of national sentiment."[38] Yet the gestures were unable to prevent Yrigoyen from almost being consumed in the violent outburst of xenophobia that exploded in Argentina a few weeks after the armistice in Europe in November 1918.

When they took power in 1916, the Radicals announced they would no longer repress strikes and labor unions. Henceforth, the government would remain "equidistant from both sides . . . the freedom to strike will not be violated at the point of the bayonet or the blow of the saber."[39] In other departures from established practice, Yrigoyen granted personal audiences to labor leaders and encouraged government officials to arbitrate labor disputes. These steps, the government claimed, marked the beginnings of "distributive justice."[40]

But the policy quickly lay in ruins, as steep inflation caused by the war induced mushrooming labor unrest. Strikes on the British-owned railroads in 1917 and early 1918 quickly provoked British accusations that the government was allowing German saboteurs to disrupt vital food supplies to Britain. The British then found allies among the local business community and conservatives in congress who began, as the strikes mounted in number and intensity, blaming them on "foreign" or "revolutionary agitators." The campaign then focused against the government. Yrigoyen's so-called equidistance, declared conservatives, imperiled public order and gave free rein to violence, "agitators," and "Bolshevik" conspiracies. The current wave of unrest was thus the consequence of

the weakness with which the authorities have proceeded, . . . above all their responses to the strikes. . . . The strikers have committed crimes of all kinds against persons and property. . . . But instead of imposing its authority, the government has remained impassive. . . . Anarchists and Bolsheviks have been allowed unrestricted access into the country, given complete liberty to preach violence . . . to organize meetings . . . and to fly the Red Flag, the symbol of destruction.[41]

This kind of outlook had prevailed in Argentina for decades. What was new in 1919 was the growing obsession at the end of the war with the surreptitious hordes of Bolsheviks, with the Red Flag, and with the idea, which sprang from Russia's fate in 1917, that in democracy lay the seeds of revolutionary anarchy. In the eyes of his opponents, Yrigoyen was rapidly becoming a Kerensky. In late 1918, a conservative congressman described a demonstration of striking workers he had recently witnessed in the streets of Buenos Aires.

When the mob passed the Argentine flag . . . there were howls of "Down with the Argentine flag!" . . . [which was] an insult to our country. . . . Throughout the length and breadth of this country are vast numbers of professional agitators . . . who are offering the mob the maximum program [Bolshevism]. . . . The maximum program recommends any form of violence to attain its ends. . . . Today we are entirely defenseless. . . . Let us rise up and put an end to the evil which is undermining the cement of Argentine society.[42]

In early January 1919, a storm of violence erupted. The *Semana Trágica* (Week of Tragedy) began with a strike of metalworkers in Buenos Aires which ballooned into a general strike and a mass protest march. The strikers burned streetcars and automobiles, ransacked and destroyed a church, and later, under cover of darkness, laid siege to several police stations. The strike was quickly put down by troops, but then the events of May 1910 began to repeat themselves, although on a much greater scale, as gangs of "patriots" ran amok through the streets attacking foreigners, particularly Jews, as "Bolshevik agents."[43]

The Semana Trágica brought to a head the tensions brewing for more than a generation between natives and immigrants. The outburst demonstrated the weak roots of popular democracy and marked the first major political intervention by the army: without waiting for orders from the authorities, troops had marched into the city to repress the general strike and then for several days held Yrigoyen at their mercy. In triggering a deep-rooted and long-lasting fear of communism or Communist penetration, the Semana Trágica became one of the chief springboards of the Nationalist movement. Looking back more than thirty years later, Carlos Ibarguren still believed that "Russian agents, the revolutionary agents of the Soviet," had provoked the general strike.[44]

This violent episode led to the formation in early 1919 of an organized paramilitary movement, the Liga Patriótica Argentina, which during the early postwar years enjoyed strong support among the upper and middle classes, the military, the church, and the leading business associations. The members of the league combined the now ingrained fear of "agitators" with some of the attitudes of the traditionalists and with a new cult of the military.

Before the war, the army was seen as important to the interests of native Argentines in two principal ways. First, the army represented "the only organized force that society can turn to to oppose the multitudes united in revolutionary solidarity."[45] Second, the growth of a professional army based on conscription, many believed, would assist the efforts of the schools to create a strong sense of national identity in a population largely descended from immigrants. World War I, however, portrayed the army in a new light—as vital to national survival. Thus, although Argentina had been neutral throughout the war, the war achieved a profound metamorphosis in the status and self-perception of the army. The manifestos of the Liga Patriótica Argentina reflected this transition, as they sought

to inspire the people with love for the army and navy, that to serve in their ranks is a duty and an honor. . . . They are the ultimate guardians of our homes, of order, liberty, dignity, and the fortunes of the nation.[46]

The rabid chauvinism of the league, the violent class hatreds it enshrined, and the armed brigades it established suggested comparisons with the paramilitary organizations, led by Italian fascism, that appeared in Europe soon after 1918. But unlike the Fascists, the league upheld strong links with conservatives and the church, associations that became particularly manifest in its heavy emphasis on "respect," "order," and "harmony." The league's followers identified themselves with the "cross that has civilized the world," committed themselves to the "moral reform of the individual," and repeatedly condemned "the utilitarian principle" that plunged society into "moral chaos . . . into anarchy, into an illness symptomized by events like this general strike." The only way to correct such ills was to return to "Christian morality." Labor unrest, declared one national senator sympathetic to the league, was "the outcome of society's lapse from Christianity." "The social question is not only economic," he declared.

Man does not live by bread alone. . . . It is principally and fundamentally a moral question, for which there are no economic remedies without the introduction of the moral factor to restrain intemperance, to halt the excessive pretensions of the capitalists and the unbridled demands of labor; without the moral factor it will always be difficult to keep ambition within the limit of what is just. . . . The remedy lies in the moral reform of the individual.[47]

Thus "moral reform" that sought to undercut alien "corrupting influences" and to stifle the "agitators" emerged as the main response among supporters of the Argentine Patriotic League to the Semana Trágica. The league itself launched new attempts to impose "patriotic education" of the type proposed by Rojas. Upper-class women recruited by the league led other efforts to establish new Catholic workers' associations. They produced a few league-controlled unions known as "workers' brigades" and some "workshop schools." These institutions pumped out "Argentine values": piety, obedience, punctuality, deference.[48]

The league illustrated that the upper classes, the so-called *gente bien*, were now starting to assimilate the arguments advanced by the traditionalists over the past two decades. The slogan *¡Salvemos el orden y la tradición nacional!* (Let us safeguard order and national tradition!) exemplified the idea proposed by Catholic writers like Gálvez that "order" and "tradition" were synonymous and inseparable. Manuel Carlés, who became president of the league, encouraged efforts to increase attendance at church, arguing that the church alone could correct the sins of envy and covetousness plaguing the alienated inhabitants of large cities like Buenos Aires. "A soul without faith," Carlés declared, "easily becomes the victim of anxiety, . . . the great illness of the large cities which afflicts those who covet luxury."[49] In September 1919, the bishops of Argentina, who were closely linked with the league, sponsored the "Great National Collection," which quickly raised an enormous fund, mostly from contributions by big business. Its proceeds were be used to wean the working class away from leftist labor unions by philanthropy and indoctrination.

Despite its strong military links, the Liga Patriótica Argentina was thus typical of the clerical associations of the past thirty years which sought to resolve the "social question" by a combination of repression and "moral reform." Equally, the league avoided any commitment to the deeper changes in government and society proposed by the Fascists or other radical right-wing movements in Europe. Finally, there were some strong liberal influences in the league, whose members, for example, continually scorned their enemies as *montoneros* or *mazorqueros*, derogatory labels entrenched in the local liberal tradition which anathematized all memories of the Federalists and Rosas.[50] When Carlés condemned "class struggle," he usually avoided the clerical term "class harmony," which was temporarily in disrepute because of its association with Yrigoyen. Instead, he drew on the liberal thesis that class conflict belonged in "old Europe" alone and was inappropriate or "artificial" in the American "Eden" that Argentina embodied.

The fury . . . and the madness that injustice has provoked in the exhausted lands of Europe have invaded our Eden, the country of light, . . . of abundance, seeking revenge here for the wrongs committed abroad. . . . We can understand [class warfare in Europe]; but here, where everything yields such abundance, [and] . . . everything lies within reach of the intelligent, here such protest appears false and artificial.[51]

The Impact of War

World War I produced a state of intellectual ferment in Argentina which extended across the political spectrum. Ibarguren, for example, now looked at society in a totally different way. Whereas earlier he had possessed "complete faith in science

... and indefinite progress," he now completely abandoned these ideas, calling them the causes of "the terrible world war [and the product of] industrialism with its imperialist struggles."[52] In a series of public lectures in Buenos Aires in mid-1919, Ibarguren discussed some of the French and German writers whose works had appeared immediately before the war. These writers, some of whom had since died in battle, shared a vision of a "new order," which they defined as a society reorganized along collectivist lines, purged of liberal influences. Ibarguren depicted the war itself as the start of the new order, since it had provoked, he claimed, a "revolution of values" on a scale unknown since the rise of Christianity.

We are witnessing the collapse of a civilization and the conclusion of an historical epoch. ... The century of omnipotent science, the century of the bourgeoisie emerging under the flag of democracy, the century of the financiers and the biologists is sinking in the midst of the greatest catastrophe that has ever afflicted mankind.[53]

The new order, Ibarguren believed, would produce a society infused with "force, virile action, glory, heroism, and sacrifice."[54] He predicted that the "formidable spiritual exaltation that has swept through all the peoples that have been at war" would continue in its aftermath and bring about "a new age of spirituality," sweeping aside the world in which, as Ibarguren saw it,

people act out of instinct rather than through controlled feelings, and society is a terrible conflict of discordant interests ... where money rules. ... Money has been an obsession, which in fostering the gambling instinct leads to constant theft, intrigue, and conspiracies. ... Society lacks a soul; its dominant forces are violence bred by envy and a mass of unbridled appetites.[55]

To Gálvez, Spain, "where life had stopped three centuries before," continued to embody the "spiritual" values he wished to create in Argentina. Yet Gálvez's language, too, now became notably sharper and more forceful, and he now depicted himself, and those sharing his views, as "Nationalist evangelists."

It is the writers, especially the young writers, who must fulfill this task of evangelization. ... A harsh struggle is ours. We must fight through our books, through the press, and from the lectern, every-where against the Calibanesque interests created by materialism. We must teach patriotism manically. . . . We must disentomb the idealism and originality of our past.[56]

Another brand of nationalism emerged after the war in the writings of Bunge, the economist who was among the Catholic supporters of social reform and at that time a close friend of Lugones.[57] During the past decade, the Argentine economy had undergone extreme cycles of decline and expansion, cycles that convinced Bunge of the need for a major effort to reduce the country's dependence on foreign markets. He described the existing economy as "primitive," "monotonous," and "disturbing." He criticized the control of foreigners over trade, warning that if foreign markets ever collapsed, the country would fall with them. Bunge pointed out that Britain, currently Argentina's largest overseas market, was now moving toward a policy of imperial preference, making it unlikely that the prewar system of trade could ever be restored. He warned against trends in Europe toward "super-nationalism" and autarky, while pointing out that Argentina would never be able to use the United States as a substitute market because it would quickly resort to protectionism to defend its own farm economy.

The solution to these problems, Bunge argued, lay in a program of economic diversification: the substitution of imports, the planned colonization of the land, the growth of construction and manufacturing, increased investment, especially in new technical skills, and an expansion of the state in the economy. In "economic independence," he argued, was the opportunity to create a genuine national culture and to establish a real base for social and political consensus. The "Argentina of tomorrow," Bunge concluded, would no longer be the old country of the rancher and the importer but the new country of the farmer and the manufacturer.[58]

Even more striking still were the new directions Lugones was now taking. In 1914, Lugones became a strong supporter of the Allies and the enemy of "Prussian militarism," although he continued to oppose democracy and now dismissed social-

ism as a "German invention, . . . Prussian discipline by definition."[59] By the end of the war, he had changed his mind
again: he was now an archreactionary pledged to the "Prussian" values he had earlier condemned. As his son later described the transition, "the European war, the Russian Revolution, and the January days [of 1919]" engendered in
Lugones a "new mental formation." At the center of his latest
position was the concept of force.[60] "The war," Lugones himself proclaimed, "has shown the power of force. It was the
Bolsheviks who did it. . . . Lenin said that pacificism and liberty are bourgeois prejudices. . . . The present historical moment is for all peoples the unfolding of a contest of force."[61]

After the Semana Trágica, Lugones condemned all strikes
as "acts of rebellion" and harbingers of Bolshevism.

We have sought to fulfill the mandate of our fathers and to make this
country . . . a great concordance. Those from abroad have brought us
to discord. . . . We have recently witnessed two strikes, . . . acts of
rebellion, supported by . . . foreigners, and [favoring] Russian
Bolshevism.[62]

He now depicted the "foreign influences" he despised as an
invisible, creeping poison that attacked the "spirit" or the
"conscience." The measures he proposed against such malignancies carried allusions of war and were expressed in metaphors of cleansing, purging, and purifying. Thus, Lugones
portrayed the Semana Trágica as a war fought by the nation
against a foreign enemy. There could be "no civil war against
foreigners," he insisted, "because all wars with foreigners are
national wars" requiring full-scale military mobilization. The
citizens of Argentina exercised absolute dominion over the
foreigners resident in the country: "We govern and we command. . . . We are the masters of this country." In exercising
the right of command, citizens had an obligation to root out
the foreigners Lugones now referred to as "poisoners of
minds." "We must clean up this country, . . . making life here
impossible for the pernicious elements, either the petty criminal or the poisoner of consciences [*el salteador de conciencia*]."[63] Lugones, too, was now closely watching European
trends. "Italy under the heroic Fascist reaction led by the

admirable Mussolini has just taught us how to restore a real national sentiment," he declared soon after the March on Rome in 1922.[64]

By 1923, what Lugones called "national" was ceasing to denote the abstract prewar concepts like "spirit," "language," or "communities" and now carried a much stronger connotation of *people*, particularly poor people of native descent in the rural areas, whom Lugones depicted as the human remnants of a glorious historical past. Similarly, what he called "Nationalism" now possessed a growing association with reform and redistribution—striving to achieve the physical and moral betterment of the native population. Thus, while striking down the foreigners by military force, he would elevate and redeem both morally and materially the "real" Argentines. Lugones blamed prevailing conditions on the Argentine upper classes, whose eyes looked constantly abroad and whose backs were turned on their own people. "Many rich people," he complained, "have made donations to feed the hungry in Russia when our own working countryfolk are dying of hunger, want, and disease without any of this moving the rich in the least."[65]

Like Ibarguren, Lugones began to dream of the revolutionary "new order," of which he saw the army as the architect. His "Hour of the Sword" speech in Peru in 1924 dismissed liberalism as the "dead" nineteenth-century constitutional system and popular democracy as incorrigibly "demagogic." Lugones hailed the army as the agent of national independence, the origin of nationhood, the single source of "all we have achieved until today." The army, he affirmed, represented the only surviving institution that preceded the birth of the liberal order in Argentina, and the hierarchical structure of the army represented the nucleus of the new political order he aspired to establish.

The army is the last aristocracy, the last hierarchical organism that has escaped destruction at the hands of demagogy. At this historic moment only military virtue represents a superior form of existence.[66]

The army should refashion society in its own image, imposing "the necessary order and an adherence to rank which democracy has undermined," because democracy's "natural consequence [was] either demagogy or socialism." The speech ended in a plea for dictatorship and in a panegyric to the "predestined leader, the man who commands on account of his innate superiority, lawfully or not, because law, an expression of power, becomes conjoined with his will." Lugones now saw "life itself as a state of force," and life meant "four words: arms, combat, command, instruction."[67]

The "Hour of the Sword" speech marked the conclusion of Lugones's long pilgrimage from the anarchism of his earlier years to the extreme authoritarianism of his last fifteen years. Of the little that remained to connect these two extremes was Lugones's persistent paganism. In 1924, he still refused to acknowledge the church as the second great institution in Argentina whose origins stretched back beyond the liberal era, even farther back in fact than the army's. He had no desire, he declared, to organize "life on charity and compassion but only on force."[68] This position, however, continually kept him in a category apart from the other Nationalist intellectuals, some of whom were beginning to despise and even fear him. "I have spent an hour with Lugones," complained Gálvez, "and came out with the sensation of having been with a viper."[69]

Lugones continued to develop these ideas throughout the 1920s. He denounced representative democracy as a "regime of bribery"; he demanded a "government of the best," which could no longer be the "enlightened oligarchy [because] I consider soldiers better than politicians."[70] Resolving social conflict, he declared in March 1926, did not lie in making "concessions but in force. Lenin in Russia and Mussolini in Italy have suppressed class conflict by imposing authority."[71] In May 1927, Lugones reiterated his demand for army rule. "Created by means of compulsory military service, [the army] constitutes a more genuine form of representation than any other," he declared. He observed that the people of ancient Rome "delegated its sovereignty to the commander of its army," and Rome became "the greatest political and social success ever known in the world. . . . We too need a government based on organization and command."[72] He campaigned for large increases in military spending because "more than unarmed, we are defenseless. Our peace depends on the will of outsiders." The expansion of the military would strengthen "discipline in general" and banish "social immorality."[73] Lugones wanted citizens and soldiers to be "synonymous" as in ancient Greece; patriotism had to be a "religion." According to him, "the Nation stands above Reason and Conscience," that is, above the individual and above the church.[74]

Meanwhile, Lugones's xenophobic outbursts grew stronger and wilder.

Foreigners fill our jails; foreigners are the vast majority of the criminals on the loose, . . . the beggars, those who abandon and exploit children, the drug dealers and traffickers in pornography, the alcoholics.[75]

The purpose of education, he declared in another stab at liberals, was to prepare "men for the Argentine Republic, not abstract entities for humanity."[76] The ruralist strain of the early Nationalist movement then resurfaced as Lugones complained at the "excessive privileges of urban labor, most of it foreign." Social reform for the urban population would depopulate the rural areas, feed the growth of government jobs and bureaucratic sinecures, and increase the numbers of women in prostitution.[77]

Yet in the midst of these wild outbursts were some unusual elements. Despite his attempts to glorify the army, Lugones sometimes acknowledged what he called the "democratic" origins of the Argentine state.

For us democracy as a system and the republic as a political organization are inseparable from our concept of nationality and independence. The name of our country is the Argentine Republic, and its appearance before the world implied an enthronement of the principle of "noble equality."[78]

However, Lugones had his own peculiar sense of what democracy meant. At times, it signified "rule by the capable" or a type of aristocracy; at others, it meant, in the language typical of corporatism, "a system of normal equilibrium between the individual and the nation."[79] In the 1920s at least, Lugones's antagonism toward the clerical movement led him to reject anti-Semitism, which he called "barbarous" and blamed on the church.[80] Last, the cult of the military state induced him to repudiate federalism. In 1810, he observed, "Independence transformed the viceroyalty into the Argentine Nation. The provinces came afterward as a product of civil war. Federalism therefore represented a transaction with anarchy."[81]

The Assault on Popular Democracy

By the mid-1920s, Lugones's voice became the loudest in a growing chorus of protest now focusing increasingly on "demagogy," a term applied pejoratively to the system of popular democracy implanted in 1912. This issue emerged during 1919–1922, the last three years of Yrigoyen's government when the president turned to a political spoils system to extend his popular support. At this point, Yrigoyen strengthened his position in the provinces and congress through Federal Intervention, the legal instrument that allowed the central government to dissolve provincial governments and to rule the provinces through an appointed delegate (intervenor) until elections were held and a new local administration was formed. Yrigoyen used both these techniques with great success. By the end of his term in 1922, he had constructed a large and enthusiastic popular following, and his party controlled most of the provinces. In 1922, Marcelo T. de Alvear, Yrigoyen's personally nominated successor, won the presidential elections with a large majority. In this election, Ibarguren headed the now demoralized conservative coalition that attempted to challenge Alvear for the presidency.

Unable to regain power through the ballot box, from henceforth the conservatives attacked Yrigoyen, who was now attempting to remain the power behind the throne, as incorrigibly corrupt and arbitrary. They were particularly incensed at the way lowborn Radicals, many of them sons of immigrants, swept them out of their positions in congress and the provinces and trampled on their entrenched self-image as a natural ruling class. Under the old oligarchy, Ibarguren, for example, had been destined for the highest offices and in all likelihood for the presidency itself; he and others now turned openly against the system that denied them their due.

The atmosphere briefly improved in 1922–23 when Alvear renounced Yrigoyen's tactics and adopted a set of orthodox conservative policies. But as he switched policies, Alvear quickly lost his popular support. When the Radical party split in 1924 between the minority supporting the president and the vast majority defecting to Yrigoyen, it became clear the *yrigoyenistas* intended to launch a new bid for the presidency in 1928 that no one could stop. At this prospect, the return of the "inept" whose habitats were "cockfights and bars," popular democracy itself came under assault.[82] Yrigoyen's supporters, said one critic, were "owners of gambling dens and brothels, . . . Arabs, Turks, Russians, and other trash thrown out of their own countries."[83] To another critic, they were "a horde of Bedouins headed by a neurotic self-styled saint."[84] Carlés, the leader of the Argentine Patriotic League, called the yrigoyenistas "abnormal, rootless, ignorant, and disreputable."[85] To Benjamín Villafañe, yet another inveterately hostile observer, Yrigoyen's threatened resurgence spelled "the death of justice, dignity, duty, and patriotism in this country. . . . Today this country has become a paradise for cowards and criminals."[86] By mid-1927, many of Yrigoyen's opponents discerned a "grave crisis in our parliamentary system" that they blamed on

the destruction wrought by yrigoyenismo in every branch of government and public affairs. . . . If the Parliament cannot improve itself in time, it will be overthrown by antidemocratic forces that perceive the coup d'etat the only way to cure the whole system.[87]

In December 1927, a few months before Yrigoyen swept back into power in a landslide election victory, a new periodical, *La Nueva República*, appeared in Buenos Aires which brought to the fore a new generation of Nationalist writers. The group of four at the head of *La Nueva República* had in common a provincial background, membership in well-established but not quite upper-class families, and elite Catholic educations. At least three of the four had spent several years in Europe, where they established contact with ultra-conservative ideas and movements.

Carulla, at thirty-nine the oldest of this quartet, was a physician from Paraná in the province of Entre Ríos, which was also the birthplace of Manuel Gálvez. Carulla was educated at the National College of Concepción del Uruguay, and again like Gálvez, he sympathized in his youth with anarchists and Socialists.[88] Between 1914 and 1916, Carulla fought as a volunteer in the French army and in the late 1920s remained an expert on both French and German politics, with a familiarity, for example, with the Nazi movement some time before it took control of Germany in 1933. Carulla's diatribes against Yrigoyen in *La Nueva República* often strongly suggested that he supported the Nazis and wanted a Nazi-style political system. However, Carulla himself claimed he was a lifelong supporter of France and Britain and that his opposition to Yrigoyen stemmed from his refusal to join the Allies during World War I.[89]

Carulla was an anti-Semite and a particularly vindictive and strident opponent of the enfranchisement of women. The origins of his anti-Semitism lay in Entre Ríos, which in his youth at the end of the nineteenth century, contained a number of Jewish agricultural colonies mostly composed of refugees from central and eastern Europe. The Jews of Entre Ríos, Carulla later wrote, were "dirty and broken in health. Their faces bore the pain of their long odyssey. Many of them even now seemed to feel the agony of the whips and sabers of their European oppressors. There was nothing at all that was attractive about them." In Entre Ríos, Carulla claimed, the Jews had brought epidemics of typhus.[90] Such early prejudices hardened into bigotry during the violent episodes of the Semana Trágica; like Ibarguren, Carulla was never to be moved from the conviction that the general strike was a revolutionary plot led by Jews.[91]

Ernesto Palacio, the second of the four leading contributors to *La Nueva República*, was another former anarchist who became a convert to the Nationalist cause when he rejoined the church and became a practicing Catholic. Better known in the 1930s and 1940s than at this point in the late 1920s, Palacio later gained some stature as a Nationalist historian. The other two leading figures in the group were Rodolfo and Julio Irazusta, brothers who, like Carulla, came from Entre Ríos, where the Irazusta family possessed cattle ranches. The family had a long connection with the Radicals that went back to the party's creation in 1891. However, the Irazusta brothers themselves abandoned the Radicals after Yrigoyen "intervened" in Entre Ríos, displacing the local Radical government and imposing the rule of his own nominee from Buenos Aires.[92]

In *La Nueva República*, Rodolfo Irazusta became known as the hard-line opponent of "liberalism." "The very word would infuriate him," remembered Carulla. "It was like a red rag to a bull." As the author of an article entitled "The Constitution Is Not Democratic," which appeared in most issues of the periodical, Irazusta established himself as the group's leading political commentator. Julio Irazusta, born in 1899 and the youngest member of the group, possessed a different temperament from his brother. Carulla remembered him as "studious, erudite, disciplined and hardworking."[93] During several years in Europe in the early 1920s as a student at both Oxford University and the Sorbonne, Julio studied intensively the writings of Burke and Bonald.[94] However, his main interest was history, and he later became one of the most prolific and influential of the "historical revisionists." Among the more occasional contributors to *La Nueva República*, along with Gálvez and Lugones, were César Pico and Tomás de Casares, the two leading clerical theorists of this period.

For several years before 1927, Carulla attempted to create a periodical like *La Nueva República*. In 1925, he led the small group that established its short-lived precursor, *La Voz Nacionalista*, which campaigned for military officers to be allowed to lecture in the universities on a regular basis. *La Voz Nacionalista* attracted several important subscribers, among them General José F. Uriburu, the inspector-general of the army, and José Figueroa Alcorta, a former conservative president who now served as head of the Supreme Court. But *La Voz Nacionalista* proved premature; in 1925, Nationalist ideas commanded almost no support, and the publication folded in less than nine months. Carulla recalled a meeting he arranged in 1925 to raise funds for his venture.

When I arrived [at the meeting] I was surprised and disappointed to find a mixed group of people, most of them very old. Among them was a marquess, a lady in her sixties, . . . two Italian counts, a captain in the Italian army who had been horribly mutilated in the war, and a gentleman who said he was a specialist in "corporatism." Only three of us were Argentines.[95]

But only two years later, with Yrigoyen once more an impending threat, conditions were changing rapidly, and Carulla's second venture into political journalism proved far more successful.

"Let us organize the Counter-Revolution. We have on our backs more than half a century of intellectual disorientation."[96] With this ringing proclamation, in December 1927, *La Nueva República* launched its three-year campaign against the yrigoyenistas and for "a government of order to allow the country to regain its moral energy, free of the need to flatter the masses."[97] The group rejected what it called "the dictatorship of the mob as a necessity imposed by the so-called laws of history and economics."[98] It pledged "to combat errors [that sprang] from liberalism with its Protestant and imbecile origins" and campaigned with great intensity against all democrats, Socialists, foreigners, and Jews.[99]

La Nueva República attacked such apparently innocuous organizations as the Young Men's Christian Association and the Salvation Army as "sects of Anglo-Saxon origin." The former, it declared, was "directed and supported by the United States," while the latter was an "English enterprise for exploiting poverty."[100] In December 1928, *La Nueva República* greeted Herbert Hoover, then president-elect of the United States, as the "heir to the empire we see preparing itself for dominion over the world."[101] Meanwhile, the periodical denounced British "hypocrisy." In India, for example, "the British had granted freedom of the press and an elected parliament, while they were killing the Indians by starvation."[102] In Latin America, *La Nueva República* led another propaganda onslaught against the "sanguinary tyrants of Chapultepec" led by Plutarco Elías Calles who had emerged victorious from the Mexican Revolution.[103]

In Argentina, *La Nueva República* wanted voting rights to be withdrawn from all foreigners and illiterates and a constitutional reform to specify that the "Rights of the Nation" preceded those of the individual.[104] The group demanded the abolition of lay education and universities free of "Communist propaganda," in which students would no longer have a voice in university government, the concession they had gained as a result of the university reform of 1918 under Yrigoyen. "Women were not made for public life," thundered Carulla. If women were let into the political clubs, they would become the scene of "great orgiastic dances." When allowed out of the home, women would fall into "anarchy and moral disorder [and become] suffragettes or, worse still, sans culottes." Feminism was a "spur to revolution and destruction."[105]

La Nueva República combined such absurd and comic features with attempts at serious philosophical and literary commentary. Its writers quoted Plato, Thucydides, and Aristotle, the leading nineteenth-century counterrevolutionaries led by de Maistre, Bonald, and Donoso Cortés, and contemporary figures such as Maurras, Berdiaev, Maeztu, and Chesterton. Among the local writers the leaders of *La Nueva República* admired stood the young poet Jorge Luis Borges, who won their praise for his depictions of the country life and the gaucho.[106] The group lauded Simón Bolívar because he had proposed that the Latin American states should be ruled by "kings with the name of presidents."[107] The intellectual nemeses of *La Nueva República* were Hobbes, the source of "individualism," and Rousseau, who made "man into God."

The leaders of *La Nueva República* carefully cultivated military leaders led by Uriburu who were known to be at odds with Yrigoyen but deliberately distanced themselves from the mainstream conservatives who were trying to combat Yrigoyen through elections and in congress.[108] These conservatives, they declared, were the "liberals" and "positivists" who had sponsored the electoral law of 1912, which had opened the gate to Yrigoyen.[109] Overall, the group stood much closer to the position represented by Gálvez than that by Lugones, in that it echoed the clerical line that demeaned "materialism" but stopped short of endorsing a monolithic and centralized military autocracy.[110] Julio Irazusta, in particular, illustrated this position. He was a "spiritualist and an antipositivist." Saint Thomas Aquinas represented "the axis of his political thought," and he often attacked Lugones on the issue of the church.[111]

La Nueva República's links with the Federalist tradition, another of its points of disagreement with Lugones, became visible in its attacks on the yrigoyenistas for subverting the "municipal authorities." Yrigoyen used Federal Intervention in a way that made the country into an "enormous Asiatic empire. Only those countries that have a system of local government can enjoy the benefits of liberty." The provinces should be allowed to subsist alongside the central government "in a different but parallel orbit," *La Nueva República* argued.[112] The federal system of government could not be reconciled with democracy because the latter required the surrender of all subordinate rights to the absolute sovereign residing in the "people." The historians of *La Nueva República* led by Palacio and Julio Irazusta attempted to demonstrate the historical connections between the systems of local government that prevailed under the Federalists and those of the Habsburg monarchy.[113]

These particular concerns signaled the similarities between *La Nueva República* and Action Française. Carulla and Rodolfo Irazusta had met Maurras in Paris, the former during World War I and the latter in 1923.[114] *La Nueva República* followed Maurras in opposing political centralization in both its autocratic as well as its democratic forms and in denouncing the French Revolution and the "sophistries of romanticism" it had produced.[115] Later in life, Irazusta acknowledged that his political ideas, particularly his objections to democracy, were based on Maurras.[116] Yet on several occasions in the late 1920s, the members of the group disclaimed any connection with Maurras because in 1927 his movement had been proscribed by Rome.[117]

Carulla's memoirs, published in 1945, provided deeper insight into the relationship between *La Nueva República* and Maurras. In 1910, Maurras struck a political alliance with Georges Sorel, and Carulla, as an admirer of Sorel at that time, was therefore drawn into examining Maurras and his strange "dynastic doctrines."[118] When he enlisted in the French army in 1914, Carulla visited the headquarters of Action Française in Paris and later encountered some of its members among the soldiers in the trenches.[119] His contact with Action Française then gradually freed Carulla from his earlier Socialist or "utopian" leanings, particularly as he watched the "indecorous and servile" European Socialist parties lining up behind the militarists in 1914. Henceforth, Carulla decided to support what he called "the ethical state" proposed by Maurras, but he then quickly realized that it could only be achieved through the church, or, as he put it, through "fulfilling the truths of the Evangelist." As a result, although Maurras still seemed to Carulla "one of the great philosophers of all times," he himself ceased to be a Maurrasian and became a Catholic.[120] In this position, he remained committed to a government of "order," "hierarchy," and "tradition," which would "remedy the evils of democracy, or demagogy, and the exaggeration of democracy, or communism."[121]

In essence, *La Nueva República* was therefore another clerical association, a successor of Estrada's movement in the 1880s which became an important expression of the Catholic revival in Argentina in the late 1920s and early 1930s.[122] Thus, *La Nueva República* upheld the authority of natural law that viewed the "law of God" as superior to all "arbitrary human law." As Casares argued from the natural law perspective, democracy represented a false doctrine because it converted the people into God.[123] The legitimacy of a government, claimed Palacio, depended not on its origin, as the followers of Locke and Rousseau claimed, but on the extent to which it obeyed the fundamental law and served the common good. The people had the right to be well governed as opposed to the right to rule. The democracies that claimed the power to enact whatever laws they pleased, Palacio continued, showed a disdain for "ancestral values," and "the rupture with the

past" they caused became a "negation of eternity" and therefore a denial of God. The Kantian idea that proposed the moral
autonomy of the individual produced "rebels and heretics"
and a society plagued by anarchy and alienation.

Such were the basic assumptions that underlay the war of
propaganda led by *La Nueva República* against Yrigoyen's
"popular tyranny." The group cited Plato's opinion that bad
government would invariably result "in all those parts where
poor men, hungry for goods," like the yrigoyenistas, sought
power.[124] Yrigoyen could no longer disguise his true identity
behind his "vague clericalism," declared Julio Irazusta; he
represented "the [mob] revolution in all its crudity."[125] Only
a "slick demagogue" like Yrigoyen would "flirt with the
Church and the Revolution at the same time." Yrigoyen was
creating "a nation of bureaucrats" and using the public administration as a "formidable electoral syndicate." He had
failed to protect the country against communism, and he was
a tool of the Jews, who controlled Argentina's grain exports.[126]
The past decade and a half of so-called democracy had totally
corrupted public morals. "How much more will women be
allowed to undress themselves?" asked *La Nueva República*,
insisting this was what democracy was encouraging them to
do. "The history of clothing is the history of civilization
itself." Democracy marked the rule of "the incapable, the
dishonest"; it brought "corruption, waste, the annihilation
of culture, incompetence, parasitism, overblown cities and
agitators."[127]

In May 1928, Carulla published a satirical piece in *La
Nueva República* entitled "The Ultimate Consequences: The
Year 1932." By that time, after four more years of Yrigoyen, he
surmised, the land would have been taken over by rebellious
peasants crying "Land and Liberty." By 1932, trade would be
completely dominated by Jews and the country flooded with
Jewish immigrants. By that time, too, Yrigoyen would have
complete control of the press, including the upper-class conservative newspaper *La Prensa*, whose owner, Ezequiel Paz,
would continue to attack the regime from his refuge in Biar-
ritz. By 1932, Yrigoyen would have added 800,000 persons to
the government payroll and possess his own army, having

abolished the old one. Some private property would still survive in 1932 but only as long as its owners paid exorbitant taxes. By 1932, a pizza in Buenos Aires would cost fifty pesos, about one-third of the current workingman's wage. Finally, by 1932, Carulla ruminated, Chile would have taken over Patagonia, and the United States would control the national customs because Yrigoyen had defaulted on the foreign debt. The article ended as if this were a "History Written in the Year 1940 by Order of the American Governor of Argentina."[128]

This satirical fantasy captured several aspects of the outlook of the Nationalists in the late 1920s. Carulla freely indulged his anti-Semitism; he seemed obsessed with foreign invasions and takeovers; he feared a rural revolt of the type that had swept Mexico less than twenty years before; Yrigoyen was planning to abolish the regular army and to establish his own militia. Carulla's remarks on *La Prensa* and Paz, and his fears of inflation and high taxes, betrayed his social position within the professional middle classes and his sense of separation and distance from the great liberal elite that Paz represented.

According to Carulla, *La Nueva República* enjoyed a substantial readership among "cultured groups in Buenos Aires and the interior, the university youth, the army, and Catholics."[129] Nevertheless, during the late 1920s, the Nationalists remained a small, marginal group of misfit, nihilistic intellectuals. In his novel *Hombres de Soledad*, Gálvez drew a caricature of the young Nationalist types he had met. In the eyes of the Nationalists, he wrote, the whole country was "a rotten mess." "Here there is no character," his imaginary Nationalist exclaimed,

no energy, no youth, no patriotism, no discipline, no passion. This is a people enslaved by skepticism, by the sensual tango, by the pleasures of the flesh, by the races, by booze. . . . My aim is purely moral. I want to change myself and change everyone else. I want danger, combat, violence! . . . Our revolution will establish a dictatorship. It will do away with elections, adulation and mediocrity. We'll clean up this mess and impose a despotism of decency, intelligence and austerity. . . . We'll shoot the bribers, the pimps, the robbers, and those with anti-social ideas.[130]

Although united by this passionate iconoclasm, the Nationalists were often deeply divided on most other issues. In June 1928, Julio Irazusta, now sounding like a true cattleman, objected to Gálvez's support for social reform. There should be no eight-hour-day legislation he argued, for example, in a country "where there are so few workers."[131] But other Nationalists often took the opposite view. Despite its more common stress on local government and traditional forms of authority, *La Nueva República* at times endorsed Italian fascism, which contrasted with "the chaos of democracy where each class is trying to take power." In Italy, Mussolini had achieved "class harmony," which implied higher living standards, cheap housing, and progressive social reforms like the eight-hour day.[132]

In defining itself as "Nationalist," *La Nueva República* meant little more than placing a vaguely defined national interest first and denying that a democracy could ever do this. During the prosperous late 1920s, economic nationalism of the kind put forward after the war by Bunge still remained almost dormant. In its first issue in December 1927, *La Nueva República* complained that the "mother industries . . . pay an enormous tribute to foreign capital." But a few months later, Julio Irazusta condemned proposals by the yrigoyenistas to force the British railroad companies to lower their freight rates as "confused and ingenuous economic nationalism."[133] *La Nueva República* opposed the great campaign led by Yrigoyen which began in 1927 to nationalize the oil industry. Despite his apparent Nazi sympathies around 1930, Carulla later professed himself a lifelong anglophile. His memoirs recalled the English and Scottish gentlemen farmers he had known in Entre Ríos in his youth, many of whom in 1899 cheerfully enlisted in the British army for service against the Boers in South Africa, although few returned alive.[134]

Yet by September 1930, on the eve of the "surgical operation," as the Nationalists called the military uprising that finally swept Yrigoyen from power, there were hints of new directions. Rodolfo Irazusta was now complaining that Britain had helped Argentina to gain its independence from Spain during the early nineteenth century but only to replace one "monopoly" by another that was "less visible but much more prejudicial." British dominance, he continued, had induced an "excessive development of commerce," and to correct this damaging legacy, Argentina should embark on the development of manufacturing industry.[135]

World War I, the Bolshevik Revolution, and the rise of yrigoyenismo were thus the chief motive forces in the formation of the Nationalist movement. Before 1914, the movement existed in almost entirely prepolitical forms but after 1918, rapidly developed as a radical critique of liberal democracy. During this period, the ideological armory of the Nationalists strengthened and toughened. From the flashes of ill-temper and violence directed at anarchist "agitators" which continued into the early 1920s, the Nationalists by 1930 were beginning to conceptualize their vision of a new society constructed on liberation from liberalism.

Chapter Four

The Nationalist Crusade

In the 1930s, the Nationalists lacked the milieu, the opportunities, and the great popular constituencies that enabled the European dictators in Italy, Germany, and Spain to construct and consolidate their briefly titanic power. Although Argentina suffered considerable political and economic disruption from World War I and the Great Depression, it escaped the profound moral collapse these cataclysms provoked in Europe which gave rise to the Fascists and the Nazis. Nor was Argentina like Spain, where Franco's victory in the civil war of 1936–1939 came as the great climax to political conflicts that stretched back for more than a century. In Argentina, the Nationalists were too constrained by their narrow social base and their close identification with the church and the military to capture much support among the urban middle class. Except for a brief intermission in 1930–31, liberals clung to power, and the main issue before the country remained that of choosing between the liberal oligarchy, championed by conservatives, and the return of liberal democracy, supported by the Radicals.

Nevertheless, the 1930s marked a crucial period in the development of the Nationalist movement. In this period, the Nationalists infiltrated the military to such an extent that it became impossible to expel them. The Nationalists developed their philosophical critique of liberalism and adopted a bellicose anti-imperialism that struck at the relationship between the oligarchy and Great Britain, Argentina's chief trading and investment partner. The school of "historical revisionists" appeared and attempted to replace the standard liberal version of the country's past with an alternative created by Nationalists. Finally, in this period, Nationalism became coupled with the concept of "social justice," which aspired to enlist the proletariat under the Nationalist banner.

In the 1930s, none of these ideas, issues, or approaches were entirely new, and they all developed on a base established during earlier periods. But in the harsh atmosphere of the 1930s, the Nationalists became increasingly militant and aggressive. What before were only attitudes or points of view now hardened into dogmatic certainties that were hurled at the general population. Palacio, for example, judged the Nationalists of the 1920s "pure aesthetes" who believed in "the supremacy of intelligence and spirit" and were "anesthetized by material prosperity." But when "the hard times" came in the 1930s, he wrote, the Nationalists "no longer smiled. . . . They lifted their fists and prepared for combat."[1]

The Right to Good Government

By the late 1920s, General Uriburu had served in the army for almost forty years. As a junior officer in July 1890, he took part in the rebellion supported by Estrada and the Catholics against President Juárez Celman. Later, Uriburu spent several years training in Germany, which during World War I led to suspicions that he supported the Axis. But at least during the early war years, Uriburu behaved like a good democrat. He became a deputy in congress representing the Progressive Democratic party, whose leader, Lisandro de la Torre, campaigned unsuccessfully for the presidency in the 1916 elections. During his stint in congress, Uriburu emerged as one of the early champions of industrial development and self-sufficiency in oil, which he argued were essential to national defense.[2] Among conservatives, Uriburu enjoyed great respect as a "born military man" who embodied the army's devotion to rigid discipline.

Firm of character, . . . pure in intentions, clean, loyal, he showed that rare combination of personal valor, which is so common among [the Argentines], with civic awareness, which is so scarce.[3]

Uriburu was known as the hard-line opponent of strikers and "agitators" who made no secret of his antagonisms toward Yrigoyen and the Radicals. On at least one occasion soon after the war, Uriburu issued a strong warning to Yrigoyen to abandon his links with the labor unions.[4] At this point, like Lugones, Ibarguren, and others, Uriburu began to abandon democracy as a lost cause and turned toward the Nationalists. In 1925, he became one of the few subscribers to *La Voz Nacionalista* and in late 1927 to *La Nueva República*. In 1927, Carulla presented Uriburu with a copy of the Italian Fascist labor charter, the *Carta del Lavoro*, and urged him to stage a coup d'etat to prevent Yrigoyen's return to the presidency. The general listened but at that point could do nothing.[5] Twelve months later, in December 1928, two months after Yrigoyen's return to the presidency, Uriburu accepted an invitation by *La Nueva República* to be guest of honor at the group's first annual banquet. Carulla recalled that at this time, the government had such overwhelming support that he was unable to fill the banquet hall with the supporters of *La Nueva República*. In an effort to impress Uriburu, he gathered a crowd of Latin American tourists from the streets and gave them a free dinner.[6]

But only a year later everything had changed, as Yrigoyen's popularity began to wilt in the face of the mounting political pressures that emerged from the depression. For several months in late 1929 and early 1930, *La Nueva República* ceased publication as Carulla and the others took part in the organization of a paramilitary force, the Liga Republicana, whose members fought for control of the streets against a rival Radical group dubbed the Klan Radical. By late 1929, the league claimed three thousand members, and it was now bent on bringing down the government.[7] Its manifestos denounced the 1928 election as a fraud and insisted that despite his election victory, Yrigoyen had no right "to act against the nation. . . . Majorities are only worthy of respect when they elect well. There is a right prior to the rights of the citizens, which is the Republic's right to be well governed."[8] When *La Nueva República* resumed publication toward mid-1930, it dismissed democracy as "a dictatorship of incompetence."[9] Throughout the world in 1930, it claimed, "the failure of the [democratic] system is almost absolute."[10] Democracy, whose weaknesses stemmed from its exclusively "liberal and British" origins, divorced "each people from its own traditions. . . . The time was ripe to think of replacing it."[11]

After months of political crisis, on September 6, 1930, Uriburu led battalions of army cadets from the garrison at Campo de Mayo outside Buenos Aires to overthrow the government. The uprising met with virtually no resistance.

Nobody raised a hand to defend the legal government. The workers were disinterested, apathetic, no strike was called, no demonstration was held, no plant or shop closed. [No one] minded exchanging the legal but insolvent, vitiated government of a senile, dreamy, insincere reformer for a general's government which could be expected to be favored by the banks, pay salaries on time and reward its followers handsomely.[12]

As he assumed office as provisional president, Uriburu at first claimed that the revolution was a democratic movement, "responding to the clamor of the people."[13] The people remained "the only sovereign," and the country would continue "to follow its honorable tradition of democracy."[14] Several times, Uriburu declared that "democracy" itself was not at fault so much as the way the system had functioned under Yrigoyen. During the early weeks of the provisional government, there were indications that Uriburu intended to hold early elections and expected his old comrade de la Torre to succeed him.

Even so, there were indications that Uriburu was planning to do more than simply replace Yrigoyen. The president claimed that under the corrupt yrigoyenista party committees, "democracy" had declined into "demagogy" and "tyranny." The fallen regime had acted not "for the common good but to satisfy personal appetites."[15] The only way to overcome these failures was to achieve "true representation," while "good government" meant rule by the "best qualified." These objectives could be met, Uriburu suggested, by a new system of representation in congress: "When the representatives of the people cease being merely the agents of committees, and workers, ranchers, farmers, and manufacturers occupy the seats of congress, democracy will become more than a fine label."[16]

In Córdoba, where he had been sent as interim governor, or *interventor*, Carlos Ibarguren echoed the sentiments of the provincial president. Reform was necessary, he insisted, to ensure the election of

genuine representatives of true social interests . . . to avoid a return to demagogy and the rule of the committees. [Such a system] will prevent the professionals of electioneering from monopolizing the government, placing themselves between the state and business and labor.[17]

In pursuit of "a true revolution to modify and transform many of our institutions," Ibarguren assembled joint boards of workers and producers to supervise the distribution of food supplies.[18]

Many conservatives, including de la Torre, as well as Radicals and leftists, condemned such ideas as Fascist. Uriburu rejected this charge and decried fascism as a "foreign doctrine." He would rule, as he put it, in accordance with "the language and the ideas of the French Revolution," phrasing that was again meant as a pledge to restore democracy.[19] But there was now great confusion and uncertainty among the Nationalists on this issue. Even Carulla, who thought "Fascist corporatism headed by the Grand Council . . . the best system," concluded that "for us the problem requires another system, something simpler."[20]

The ambiguities persisted for several months as the depression deepened and Uriburu's initially strong support began to decline. Eventually, in April 1931, the regime staged a trial election in the province of Buenos Aires using the old electoral system: so long as the right candidate won the election, it would be unnecessary to adopt the divisive route of electoral reform. But contrary to expectations, the Radicals swept to victory in the election. At this point, Uriburu concluded that democracy could not be reformed and had to be replaced.

Following the April election, which he instantly annulled, the Nationalist content of his discourse became more heavily pronounced. Speaking at a meeting of farmers in Rosario in July 1931, he urged his audience into

cooperative action to join together rural workers in great and disciplined forces, . . . something that [liberal] individualism could never achieve. . . . We cannot accept that a country of farmers and ranchers be represented in the chamber of deputies by fifty-nine lawyers, thirty-six physicians, nine ranchers, and two workmen.[21]

Uriburu now repeatedly disparaged "urbanism" and "electoral professionalism." "Genuine representatives of real social interests" would replace the political parties. The new organizations would be state regulated, and their task was to select "the best" for the task of government. "True democracy," he now proposed, was "government of the most practiced by the best."[22]

Uriburu's followers then launched a campaign to reform Article 37 of the constitution, which defined the composition and functions of the chamber of deputies. The specifics of the plan never became public, but the attacks made by its sponsors on the secret ballot instituted in 1912, along with their numerous references to "guilds" (gremios) and "corporations," left little doubt as to their general intent. But still no one would admit that the proposal marked the first step toward fascism. The most Uriburu himself would say on this subject was that "if we had to decide between Italian fascism and Russian communism or the leftist political parties, let no one doubt what our choice would be."[23]

Despite the denials, in mid-1931, with Uriburu's support, Carulla played a leading part in creating another paramilitary organization, the Legión Cívica Argentina, whose members wore Fascist-style uniforms and used the Fascist salute. In 1931, enlistment in the Legión Cívica topped 10,000, including several hundred women.[24] Yet the organization failed to achieve a lasting impact because no one knew quite how to use it. Carulla himself thought the organization's only purpose was to defend the government against the resurgent yrigoyenistas.[25] Neither he nor Uriburu made any attempt to use the Legión Cívica in the way the true Fascists might have done as a mass movement controlled by the state. "It never passed through [Uriburu's] mind," Carulla declared, to replace our democratic laws with others of an absolutist type. How far he stood from the totalitarian position! His natural gentility, compassion, and Christian humility kept him apart from the lies and racist infatuation of the Nazi-Fascist leader and politician.[26]

Uriburu thus represented an example of a Nationalist who seemed incapable of becoming a Fascist and whose outlook was traditional and Catholic. He defined the corporatist institutions he wanted to create in limited conservative terms as "the modernized forms of a system whose long historical contributions justified its revival."[27] In the document entitled "The Doctrine of the September Revolution" that Uriburu issued on leaving the presidency in early 1932, there was no sign of fascism at all. As its justification for the coup d'etat, the doctrine repeated the arguments based on natural law that Estrada had employed against Juárez Celman more than forty years before.

The supreme authority's reason for being . . . is . . . the fulfillment of the collective welfare. . . . Any government that fails to serve that end, either through the abuse of its authority or by abandoning its responsibilities, is a tyrannical government. . . . The tyrannical government is a seditious government because in sacrificing the common good, it compromises the unity and tranquillity of society, which exists to ensure the welfare of its members. . . . And every seditious government ceases, by definition, to be a government, so that a revolution that overthrows it is quite legitimate so long as its objective is to restore the collective welfare.[28]

Structure and Personalities

After the miscalculated election of April 1931, Uriburu and his followers lost the secretive power struggle they were waging against the rival liberal factions. The latter comprised the great majority of the landed and mercantile classes and the preponderant force in the army. These groups opposed the corporatist reforms offered by Uriburu, preferring to maintain at least outwardly democratic forms on condition that the Radicals were kept from power. In late 1931, Uriburu imprisoned the leading Radicals, including Yrigoyen and Alvear, and staged rigged elections. Finally, in February 1932, Uriburu was succeeded by General Agustín P. Justo, the leader of the military liberals, whose presidency signaled the end of dictatorship and the return of oligarchy under a democratic facade.

When the Uriburu clique fell from power, the Nationalists launched a new crusade against liberalism and its "ill-educated doctors" and against Justo, the "fat Mason," they claimed had cheated them of power.[29] Throughout this period, dogma prevented the Nationalists from ever trying to develop as a "party," because all parties implied the acceptance of liberalism. Instead the movement developed as a disjointed confederation of factions bearing high-sounding paramilitary or clerical designations. Among the Nationalist groups of the 1930s were first the Liga Republicana and the Legión Cívica, which were followed by the Legión de Mayo, Restauración, the Milicias Cívicas, the Guardia Argentina, and numerous others. These bands drew from much the same clientele, mostly Catholic students or former students from the upper-middle-class Barrio Norte district of Buenos Aires.[30]

The Argentine liberals frowned on these noisy parodies of the storm trooper gangs in Europe. In 1931, for example, *La Prensa* strongly objected to training what it called "schoolchildren" in the use of lethal weapons.[31] But the militias were all very small, altogether totaling only a few thousand members. In 1931, the Legión Cívica claimed 10,000 followers, but ten years later, a mere 1,500 remained. Some of the other groups numbered no more than a few score.

The militias led noisy marches through the streets of Buenos Aires and other cities and periodic gatherings of the faithful on the anniversaries of the September revolution and Uriburu's death, which occurred in April 1932, less than three months after he had left the presidency. Again usually only a few hundred people attended these meetings, although in April 1934, two thousand gathered at the Recoleta cemetery in Buenos Aires in memory of Uriburu.[32]

At this point during the early 1930s, the term "Nationalist" finally established itself in common usage. "Only three years ago," remarked Gustavo Franceschi in October 1932, "it was bad taste to call oneself a Nationalist, but it is no longer so today."[33] Yet the Nationalists were united in name only, above all because they lacked an acknowledged leader. Uriburu had failed in this role, and there was no one else at hand with the power and prestige to follow him. Lugones stood out as a propagandist but was a complete failure as a political organizer. In 1930, Lugones helped pave the way for the coup d'etat through the rhetoric that depicted the army as "the religion of the nation, the civilization of force."[34] He then wielded some influence under Uriburu as the author of a "Confidential Memorandum" to the president that called for intensified repression and censorship. The government should shut down *La Vanguardia*, the leading Socialist party newspaper, Lugones demanded sanctimoniously in this document, for continually ridiculing "our women for having joined the Legión Cívica as the 'legionary ladies' [*las damas legionarias*]."[35]

Later Lugones demanded a government by an alliance of the army and the "men of culture" like himself.[36] But by now in the mid-1930s, the Justo government had managed to shunt Lugones off to the sidelines. As he passed sixty years of age, the poet was becoming a spent force, scoffed at by his many enemies, hated by the clerical groups, and smirked at even by Nationalists in the army because, as one officer complained, "he talked too much."[37] It was rumored that Lugones had finally returned to the embrace of the church, but in February 1938, after several years of virtual silence, he committed suicide.[38] His death occurred only days before the inaugural of Roberto M. Ortiz as the second liberal president to succeed Justo and expressed a sense of total failure and disillusionment at a time when the destructive ideas he represented seemed even farther from realization.

Ironically, while Lugones entered this period of decline toward the mid-1930s, the Fascist cause he often appeared to represent was reaching its zenith, at least in Europe. Lugones resembled the Fascists most closely in his cult of violence and the centralized state. But there were many doubts expressed, even among his contemporaries, as to the true extent of his identification with fascism. In Gálvez's view, for example,

Lugones was never a Fascist because he remained so bitterly opposed to popular politics: to the end he remained committed to a form of aristocracy, "government by the best," as he had called it.[39]

Arturo Jauretche, a prominent Nationalist intellectual associated with the Radicals, later dismissed the leading Nationalists of this period as "the declassé of the ruling class, the poor cousins of the oligarchy." The movement's great weakness lay, he thought, in its refusal to engage with the "masses," which left the Nationalists in the ambiguous position of tacitly upholding the liberal oligarchy and only pretending to threaten it. The Nationalists, he wrote, "separate the idea of the nation from that of the people and propose authoritarian forms that perpetuate the enlightened despotism of the oligarchy."[40] Seen like this, Nationalism became reduced to a form of tactical expediency as opposed to the revolutionary alternative it proclaimed itself. Felix Weil called the Nationalists "semi-feudal overlords." In his view, they were were no more than posturing reactionaries concerned with the protection of their own social position.[41]

While such judgments underestimated the Nationalists, they accurately pointed to their most striking weaknesses and to some of the reasons they were unable to establish a larger popular following. The movement now possessed a foothold in the cities, but its roots remained in the provinces. Some of the leading Nationalist figures, like the Irazustas, were conservative ranchers; others, like Ibarguren, were "oligarchs." Personal interests often induced the Nationalists to compromise with the system they ostensibly deplored. Nationalist lawyers, for example, often accepted briefs from the foreign companies their writings condemned.[42] Some Nationalists appeared to support the movement merely for tactical or opportunistic reasons before eventually returning to the liberal fold. Writing during World War II, Juan Carulla, for example, later looked back on his career during the 1920s and 1930s with what seemed a genuine sense of remorse and repentance. He had failed to "achieve any of [his] objectives. [He] had written nothing of any merit. [He] remain[ed] confused and perplexed."[43]

In the 1930s, the Nationalist factions squabbled constantly, attempted to cannibalize each others' followers, and continually accused one another of entering into secret deals with the government. "In that turbulent camp," observed *La Vanguardia*,

of the hundreds of legionnaires, brigades, and assault troops, there is neither unity nor decency. Such and such a "Nationalist" group declares war on the one next to it. The boss of this or that Fascist band bears a deadly hatred toward the boss of the other. The great Fascist family presents the spectacle of dogs fighting over a bone.[44]

Indeed, the divisions were acute. The fundamentalist clerical groups often opposed any form of political activity because, they said, real change could only be "spiritual" in nature. The extreme xenophobes opposed corporatist institutions as a threat to sovereignty, arguing that under corporatism, foreigners or foreign business interests would obtain too much political influence.[45] The young hooligans in the militias who thirsted for violence complained at the intellectuals who were "too fond of theory and floated about like women."[46] Nationalists in the military often opposed the use of violence by civilians, claiming that violence was their prerogative alone.

In fact, in a period of strong government and powerful policing, violence in its deadlier forms remained comparatively rare. Whenever the Nationalists used force, they faced storms of abuse from the left-wing press led by *La Vanguardia* against the "bands of Fascists, reactionaries, . . . [and] the agents of the fraudulent oligarchy."[47] Even so, during the six years of Justo's presidency, the Nationalists made several attempts to challenge the government. There was a week of high drama in March 1935, for instance, when Justo decreed a Federal Intervention against the province of Buenos Aires whose governor, Federico Martínez de Hoz, had appointed several Nationalists to high positions in his administration. On news of the decree, several hundred armed members of the Legión Cívica marched from Buenos Aires to La Plata, the provincial capital, where they announced their determination to resist the intervention. But the resistance quickly collapsed when the government threatened to send the army into the city.[48]

These failures to shake the political system led the more intelligent Nationalists to conclude that their chief weapon should be propaganda and to concentrate on increasing their support in the universities and, above all, the military. As this effort began, the movement lost its character of the 1920s as "juvenile, theoretical, free-spirited, and romantic," as Carulla put it. It now became "strong and corrosive, . . . particularly for having infiltrated the army."[49]

Throughout the 1930s, the Nationalists flattered the army as "the living image of the force of the nation."[50] They applauded "the military spirit" as the "highest form of the idea and sentiment of the nation."[51] In characteristic style, a Nationalist pamphlet circulating among army officers in 1935 depicted the soldier as a saint. Liberalism, this document claimed, "emasculates" the soldier, and it urged the army to watch "the internal front" and be prepared for "rapid, decisive action."[52] The Nationalists campaigned for the military to be brought into the schools and given control over larger segments of the economy. Occasional references in the army itself to its "civilizing mission" suggested that growing numbers of officers were listening to Nationalist propaganda.[53] As later events were to show, the Nationalist movement established a permanent bridgehead in the military during this period, but as yet the link remained mostly invisible. Justo and his successor, Roberto M. Ortiz, in particular made determined efforts to keep Nationalist influences in check, and at this point, most of the military officers who sympathized with the Nationalists found it more prudent to keep their opinions to themselves as they quietly climbed the promotion ladders.

Under Justo, two senior military men in particular openly declared themselves Nationalists. The first of them, retired General Emilio Kinkelín, succeeded Carulla at the head of the now-dwindling forces of the Legión Cívica. Kinkelín spent most of his time touring the country on a quixotic search for "agitators." In April 1935, for example, he announced from the province of Tucumán that he had discovered a Jewish plot to take control of the area's sugar mills.[54] But a few years later,

Kinkelín's career as a Nationalist ended when he declared his support for rigged elections, a step that indicated his return to the camp of the liberals. From around the mid-1930s, Colonel Juan Bautista Molina took Kinkelín's place as the leading military Nationalist. Molina organized numerous minor conspiracies to overthrow the government, but Justo always managed to outmaneuver him.[55]

In the 1930s, the Nationalists became entrenched in the weekly clerical periodical *Criterio*, whose editor Franceschi had been active for many years in the Catholic organizations led by the workers' circles. *La Nueva República* ceased publication toward the end of Uriburu's government, but two successors emerged, *Crisol* (Crucible) and *Bandera Argentina* (Argentine Flag) established by Carulla.

As Nationalists of the second generation began to appear, parts of the movement now began to develop into a clanlike network of families. Some of the leading Nationalists had enormous families. Typical of them was the Nationalist novelist, Gustavo Martínez Zuviría, a man with twelve children, including three sons who later became senior officers in the army, and forty grandchildren.[56] Two of the sons of Carlos Ibarguren, Federico and Carlos, Jr., became increasingly prominent in the movement, as did Marcelo Sánchez Sorondo, the son of Matías Sánchez Sorondo. The elder Sánchez Sorondo served as Uriburu's minister of the interior but fell from power after sponsoring the ill-fated election of April 1931. Marcelo Sánchez Sorondo made his name as the correspondent of *La Nación* in Spain during the civil war. Like some of their predecessors, several of the more prominent newcomers of the 1930s, like the two journalists Ramón Doll and Justo Pallarés Acebal, were lapsed leftists who converted to the Nationalist cause at the climax of the struggle against Yrigoyen. As Nationalists, both men gained notoriety for the particularly rabid brand of anti-Semitism they promulgated.

Thanks once more to the struggle against Yrigoyen, the Nationalists were now attracting persons of immigrant and metropolitan background like writer Roberto Laferrère, who was of French descent. On his mother's side, however, Laferrère resembled the older Nationalists since he numbered among his ancestors Encarnación Ezcurra, the wife of Juan Manuel de Rosas. Laferrère often recounted the tale of another of his local ancestors at the time of the second British invasion of Buenos Aires in 1807. On news of the landing of the British, this man had hurried to join the militia "to wait for the Bretons [*sic*]," as he called the intruders.[57]

Clericalists, Jews, and Fascists

Weak, divided, and largely ineffective as a political force, the Nationalist movement nevertheless grew more intense in delivering its message, at the heart of which lay the assumption of a world of universal truths as they were determined by the Catholic, Apostolic, and Roman faith. Any idea to the contrary was dismissed by the Nationalists as relativism or rationalism. According to this outlook, the laws of humanity remained beyond the scope of reason, either in the form of the scientific investigation promoted by the positivists or in the form of the deliberative assemblies proposed by liberals. The Nationalists saw the roots of the false deities of relativism and rationalism in Judaism and traced its development through the Renaissance, the Reformation, the Enlightenment, and the French Revolution. Liberalism stood out as the end product of this nefarious tradition, and the Saxon, Protestant, and commercial societies led by Britain and the United States represented its embodiments.[58]

To counter liberalism, the Nationalists urged "a return to tradition, to the past, to sentiments authentically Argentine, . . . [to] the reintegration of the nation with its essential values."[59] Prominent among these essential values stood the church, and "to Her the Nation should be linked as the body to the soul."[60] The church, most Nationalists argued, should be independent of the state since it possessed "prior rights" to those of the secular authority. In the 1930s, the Nationalists renewed the struggle against lay education, or "Masonic laicism" as they now called it, and demanded the return of clerical control over the schools.[61] In their efforts to defend the rights of the provinces, the Nationalists approvingly quoted Saint Thomas Aquinas's designation of provinces as "natural republics," agreeing with his view that "just as there is a common good for the nation as a whole, there is a similar common good in each province."[62] The Nationalists continued the cult of the "guilds" and corporations as "the natural organization of the forces of production, the authentic expression of national life, . . . the link between the individual and the state."[63] The creation and development of new corporate bodies would enable a "regime of unity, that is to say, a government of one person, who will lead the multitudes to the attainment of the common good."[64]

The continuing clerical flavor of many of these pronouncements reflected the growing influence of the church throughout Argentine society during the late 1920s and early 1930s. During this period, the number of church parishes in Buenos Aires increased from 39 in 1929 to 105 in 1939. Membership in Acción Católica increased from 20,000 in 1933 to 80,000 in 1940 and to 100,000 in 1943.[65] Catholic influences reached a high point in 1934 when the Vatican staged the International Eucharist Congress in Buenos Aires, an event that had an enormous impact on the Nationalists. "The miraculous spring of the congress broke upon the enormous city," one Nationalist writer declared extravagantly as he remembered the ceremonies.

Not even in the days of the Apostles, not in the Catacombs, not even in the Crusades did the eyes behold and the ears receive such expressions of collective faith. Radiant days, clear nights, friendship among persons unknown to one another. Sweetness on bitter lips. . . . Buenos Aires found itself in a state of grace.[66]

The young Federico Ibarguren attributed what he called his "second religious conversion" to the congress. Hitherto, Ibarguren had seen himself as a "Maurrasian" and had spent much of his time taunting the police in Nationalist demonstrations. But he now abandoned this "irrational belligerence" to devote himself more fully to Catholic philosophy.[67] In 1934, one of Ibarguren's friends, Rodolfo Martínez Espinosa, a young bank clerk, circulated his treatise, *Politeia*, which set out his own ideas for a new constitution. *Politeia* was a piece of straight scholasticism coated with a thin secular veneer taken mostly from Maurras. Scattered throughout the document were notions like the "real being" or "nature" of the nation, "popular will" as a manifestation of the "divine will," and the aspiration to restore the *civitas argentina* that liberalism had destroyed.[68]

Under these influences the Nationalists now created a vision of the political system in which monarchist elements became particularly pronounced. "The chief of state ought to concentrate all government completely in his own person," the Nationalists believed. "His power comes from God alone, Lord of all power. The people are not, and never can be, sovereign."[69] The ruler's duty was to respect the "fundamental law" and "to ensure liberty within order for the purposes of welfare and progress." The ruler should pursue these objectives through "Authority, Discipline, Hierarchy."[70]

In the 1930s, the Nationalists continued to denounce the "Red plots," whose aim was to destroy "God, the Nation, and the Family."[71] They urged a "national dictatorship" to quash "this internal enemy."[72] In liberal democracy, they endlessly intoned, lay the seeds of Communist revolution, because democracy "allows all sorts of seditious propaganda. A powerful Communist organization has arisen among us. . . . Democracy hands us over unarmed to these forces of extreme socialism and anarchy."[73]

The cult of rural life still formed a strong element of the movement. For Lugones, there was "no better citizen than he who works the land."[74] "The man of the country," declared *Crisol,*

is superior to the man of the city. The former is a producer, . . . the latter is worthless. . . . He is an accessory, a mere cog in the wheel. In the land within lies our liberation. We should look there because something that is really ours remains.[75]

The city of Buenos Aires, by contrast, remained synonymous with "bureaucracy, prostitution, and corruption."[76] Immigrants were "parasites and undesirables" who brought the "poison of foreign ideologies" and the "conception of the universe as a great productive machine."[77] In the 1930s, the Nationalists issued numerous demands for tighter immigration controls to reduce "the parasitical hordes of the metropolis."[78] The foreign population of the cities possessed "a quite absurd privilege, while the real workers in the country, whose interests are the nation's interests, are being abandoned to their fate."[79] Although the foreign segment was now beginning to shrink as a ratio of the total population of Argentina, during the depression, fears of " mass protest movements, . . . a rising of the foreigners of the worst types," remained intense.[80]

By this time, there were also concerns about the growth of the mestizo and indigenous populations. Lugones, for example, demanded a ban on all nonwhite immigration.[81] By the end of the 1930s, Bunge's writings betrayed hints of the principles of eugenics—normally anathema to Catholics—as he urged "the wealthier classes" to increase the size of their families. In an article entitled "Splendor and Decadence of the White Race," Bunge urged that "the whole vigor of the race, the patriotism of superior men, and the Christian spirit ought to be invoked, especially among the wealthier classes, to promote the blessings of children and large families."[82]

The "Nationalist Revolution" would abolish the liberal constitution of 1853, "which is not national but foreign. The new law ought to be an expression of the people and not of the Yank treatise-writers."[83] In April 1935, Colonel Molina urged the dissolution of the three powers of government, the abolition of the political parties, the establishment of military dictatorship, press censorship, and campaigns to uproot "immorality": prostitution, rent gouging and speculation, "provocative" dress worn by women, and the *lunfardo*, the "low-speak" dialect widely used among workers in Buenos Aires. Having completed these tasks, Molina's dictator, who he intended of course would be himself, would establish the "guilds" (gremios) and use a "consultative board [to] unite" workers and employers.[84]

"Immorality" stood out as one of the leading concerns of the Nationalists. They dismissed an American film version of Emile Zola's *Nana*, for example, as a "Jewish-Yank production [and] one of the worst of Zola's works."[85] Another despised import from the United States during the 1930s was the "marathon" dance in which women would hire themselves out for hours at a time as dancing partners. Franceschi thought this practice "the ruin of a culture."[86] He condemned the lunfardo dialect for its "bastard and unknown origins."[87] He scorned the tango that had originated, he claimed somewhat improbably, in the Japanese community in Cuba. Its verses were "bad, sick and immoral" and "its subjects the age-old repertoire of romanticism, turned into slum language."

"He cries because an evil woman left him." (Why get mixed up with an evil woman in the first place?) [This rubbish] plagiarizes Armando in "The Lady of the Camelias." But just remember that between the original model and its version [in the tango] there is the great distance that separates a noble line like "*La donna è mobile*" from "*Te fuiste, ja, ja!*" . . . The words of a tango remind me of mayonnaise I once ate in a country hotel made from cactus.[88]

In the 1930s, anti-Semitism did not reach the same violent extremes as in January 1919. Indeed, Gálvez now blandly denied that anti-Semitism existed at all, calling it the "invention of an unscrupulous press." In Argentina, he claimed, there were no ghettoes, or any form of discrimination whatever. The Jewish people were the "most intelligent in the world," he generously conceded, while the Argentine elite itself had blood bonds with Sephardic Jewish immigrants that derived from colonial times. Restricting Jewish immigration, an idea Gálvez nevertheless supported, was meant only to allow the country to maintain "its Latin spirit."[89]

There were other Nationalists, however, who saw Jews as "the deadly enemies of the Nation and of the Catholic faith of the people." Jews were cast in this role because of their alleged prominence in banking and foreign trade.[90] Simultaneously, however, Jews remained the agents of Bolshevism. "Will the Jews be content with their achievements in Russia?" asked one anti-Semite. "Never!" he replied.[91] In 1931, *Criterio* featured lurid anti-Semitic tracts under titles like "The Jewish Plan against the World" and issued a facsimile of the *Protocols of the Elders of Zion*.[92]

The most notorious figure among the Argentine anti-Semites was the Jesuit-educated, former Santa Fe cattleman, Gustavo Martínez Zuviría, who between 1931 and 1955 served as director of the National Library in Buenos Aires. Under the pseudonym Hugo Wast, Martínez Zuviría churned out large numbers of pulp novels to a mass public. Among them was his *Oro* (Gold), published in May 1935. The novel portrayed a clique of powerful Jews grouped together in the *Kahal*, "a mysterious tribunal like a society of Carbonari," who were conspiring to monopolize the world's gold. The plan was to corrupt the goyim (Gentiles), "making them love luxury that they can only pay for by using our loans."[93]

The Jews are the bankers of the world, in possession of three-quarters of the gold that exists. . . . At the signal of the Great Kahal in New York, which is the omnipotent, occult authority that directs this colossal mechanism, part of the gold is withdrawn from circulation. Panic breaks out and a crisis the economists call a crisis of overproduction. Overproduction! Every government falls into the trap; they restrict production, ban sowing grain, destroy the harvests. Meanwhile half a dozen persons monopolize the wealth of the world at the lowest prices. . . . At this moment the best properties of this great city, the richest ranches of the Republic are falling, for nothing, into the hands of Jewish mortgage creditors.[94]

In *Oro*, the infamous *Protocols* reappeared.[95] The Catholic church, it continued, represented the Great Kahal's sworn enemy. According to the book's Jewish caricatures, its influence can be weakened "by spreading liberal ideas."[96] Jewish control of the press exercised from New York, "the Jewish Vatican," meant that when leftists

kill Christians in Mexico, Spain, and Russia . . . our press never reports it. . . . But if there are attacks on the Jews in Germany or Poland, the world will be in uproar: intolerance, pogroms, anti-Semitism. No one mourns the martyrdom of a million Christians in Russia, but there is an enormous row when a Jew loses his chair in Berlin University, or in Buenos Aires when a Jew is thrown out of the country.[97]

For two thousand years, it was claimed, the Jews had been executing their serpentine plan for world domination.

Nine hundred years before Christ the conquest of the world by our race began [when] the serpent departed from Jerusalem. Five centuries later it reached Greece. . . . By 1940 we shall control

Tokyo, by 1950 Buenos Aires, and sixteen years later the Serpent's head will meet the tail in the plains of Moab.[98]

Most anti-Semitism in Argentina was the less dangerous cultural breed typical of some Catholic nations which attacked Jews for the alleged threat they posed to the Christian religion and to national identity. But the anti-Semitism of *Oro* stood very close to Nazi-style biological racism. "Judaism," Martínez Zuviría wrote, "is as indelible as the color of one's skin. This is not a religion but a race."[99] In 1935, there was a storm of protest against *Oro* led by the Socialist party. "The thesis of this Fascist-Clerical author," thundered *La Vanguardia* with the most biting sarcasm it could muster,

is that the Jews are the only ones guilty of the collective misery and the general state of the world. This idea is about as intelligent as another one of Hugo Wast's that Saint Theresa had blessed—we can't remember by what miraculous intervention or other—the revolution of September 1930.[100]

The Nationalists were racists to the extent that, like Lugones and Bunge, they proudly represented Argentina as a "white" nation and were determined to keep it as such. Racial slurs were common in politics: one of the insults hurled at the yrigoyenistas, for example, was that they were "redskins" or "little blacks." However, the extreme racism of *Oro* was exceptional, and in Argentina, attitudes on race usually leaned toward being patronizing rather than aggressive. In 1931, for example, Franceschi commented on the death of a young black Brazilian poet. He noted the "acute note of melancholy in his verses . . . which expresses the endless bitterness of his race in its long painful journey from the heart of Africa, always tortured and cast down."[101]

Not surprisingly, as *Oro* showed, the Nationalists were constantly watching the European Fascists. In 1934, Gálvez published a tract entitled *"Este pueblo necesita."* What "This People Needs," according to Gálvez, was, in part, old virtues like "idealism," "moral reform," and the dethronement of "politics." But by this point, other "needs" had appeared which no longer bore the imprint of nineteenth-century Spain alone but that of contemporary Italy and Germany: "a heroic sense of life," the "cult of youth."[102] "Today no one believes in the survival of democracy," Gálvez wrote.

Sooner or later the social war will begin. At that time to avoid the communist horror, with its crimes, its satanic destructive power, its destruction of man, its militant atheism, the iron hand of Fascism will become necessary: violent, dispensing justice and salvation.[103]

After the 1930 revolution, Gálvez stood virtually alone among the leading Nationalist figures in continuing to support the Radicals. But he now tried to justify his position on the grounds of the similarities he detected between the Radicals and the Fascists.

True Radicalism is not too far away from Fascism. It is nationalist, it believes it must work for the people, and it supports rapid, even violent procedures. . . . Like Italian Fascism it aspires to work for the people, respecting religion, family and social traditions.[104]

In the sloganeering, frequently incoherent writings of Enrique Osés, another extreme anti-Semite who at this time was editor of *Crisol*, Nationalism sometimes meant in standard form "the basis for a return to tradition, to the past, to a sentiment authentically Argentine, to the characteristic Creole virtues."[105] But Osés also portrayed the movement in militant Fascist-like guise as "iron, indestructible unity," which required a state "able to dominate the economic and financial infrastructure." Under a Nationalist dictatorship, Osés declared, the state would become "directing" rather than "directed" and regiment the individual with unlimited authoritarian power.[106] Similarly, he sometimes combined the scholastic justifications for autocracy with elements of the Italian Fascist idea that the *Duce* inherited the powers of the Roman imperator.[107]

The Nationalists admired Fascist Italy for having "inspired an enormous national pride," which contrasted with the "indifference and weakness of character of many of our citizens."[108] By 1934, Carlos Ibarguren sounded virtually indistinguishable from the Fascists as he proclaimed "the hour of the organized masses."[109] Sánchez Sorondo admired Mussolini, "who made brilliant speeches."[110] He drew a distinction between the "aesthetics" of Nationalism, which he called "religious" and "monarchist," and its "politics," which was "Fascist, bitterly Fascist."[111] On occasion, the Nationalists used Mussolini's expression, "the politics of things," which meant a commitment to the ceaseless action and vitality the Fascists claimed to represent. Thus, one of the justifications for dictatorship was that it would "impel action; it will silence ideological dissent; it will do constructive works."[112] In his "Letter to Jacques Maritain," published in 1937, Pico, a leading clerical intellectual, argued that Catholics should be willing to ally with the Fascists to save the world from communism.[113] The same year, the priest Meinvielle judged fascism less "totalitarian" than liberal democracy, because democracy suppressed the "spiritual power" and made society the victim of an all-devouring bourgeoisie.[114]

The streak of destructive nihilism in the attitudes of the Nationalists further evoked the Fascists. In 1935, Federico Ibarguren perceived close similarities between the attempt by the Legión Cívica to halt the overthrow of Martínez de Hoz in the province of Buenos Aires and the turmoil following the wars of independence a century earlier. Then as now, he believed, the only solution to "anarchy" was dictatorship.

Today we live . . . the prologue to another anarchy [like that in the 1820s]. . . . Therefore when society has passed into definitive crisis, another Rosas will have to take power and impose order, but this time with machine guns, planes, and bombs. And then the liberals will tremble![115]

Nevertheless, even at this point in the halcyon era of European fascism, the clerical and elitist connections of the Nationalists continually limited the extent to which they could assimilate and emulate fascism or evolve along truly totalitarian lines. In founding *Bandera Argentina* in 1931, Carulla adopted Mussolini's slogan "Rome or Moscow." Yet Italian Fascist visitors to Argentina found *Bandera Argentina* merely "patriotic" and insufficiently "social-revolutionary." They were at a loss to understand why *Bandera Argentina* never openly attacked President Justo and why the Nationalist movement at large had failed to achieve unity.[116]

Nationalists commonly dismissed fascism on the grounds that it "bureaucratized and used" religion. In 1930, Meinvielle found fault with Lugones for "invoking Machiavelli's Reason of State and Italian Fascism as if the state were an end in itself." Lugones's stance, he said, amounted to a "simple Caesarism which sacrifices all personal initiative to the will of the God-State."[117] In 1933, Julio Irazusta felt that "Fascism or German Nazism are not models to imitate but . . . proof that human effort can solve the most complex situations."[118] A campaign against Catholic groups led by Mussolini in 1931 prompted complaints in Argentina against the "insolent and presumptuous Fascist spirit that does not allow even a shadow of a citizen's liberty."[119] In Argentina, as Uriburu had argued, fascism remained "an imported ideology without firm bases in the vernacular."[120] In other criticisms, fascism was "pagan" and made an "idolatrous cult of the Nation, a fanatical exaltation of the State."[121] "This pagan nationalism will carry us back two hundred years before Christ."[122] In sum, as another observer expressed the difference, "fascism has emerged from the socialist-laicist experience of the nineteenth century," as opposed to Nationalism, which was based on the "old Hispanic cult of personality."[123] Citing the encyclical *Ubi arcano Dei* issued at the time of the March on Rome, Franceschi deplored the "fanaticism that deifies the Nation, that materialist nationalism which represents instinct, covetousness, passion."[124]

In keeping with their traditional allegiances and reactionary impulses, the Nationalists made no attempt to exploit the political potentialities of women. Franceschi thought women unworthy of any consideration beyond the need to "protect them." Women viewed life, he said, "from an exclusively sexual standpoint."[125] In the early 1930s, a few "ladies" joined the Legión Cívica but then seem to have drifted back into their traditional spheres in organized charity led by the Sociedad de Beneficencia. Women writers were virtually unknown in the Nationalist press, except very occasionally when articles written by women in Spain were reprinted in Buenos Aires. The Nationalists, who opposed all voting, were still likely to explode at any suggestion that women be given the vote, although one group in 1935, noting that women in Spain were voting for conservatives, was prepared to accept voting by married women with children.[126] In 1936, *Crisol* described the growing numbers of women entering the labor force as an "invasion" and "an inversion of Christian society, . . . the demoralization of men." Women should return home, "as in Germany and Italy."[127]

Writing after 1945, Mario Amadeo, a junior member of the movement in the 1930s, attempted to summarize the relationship between Nationalism and fascism. The declining respect for liberty and the stress on authority in the 1930s, he wrote, reflected the general "crisis of the institutions encharged with preserving liberty." These conditions made it impossible to prevent much of the youth of the 1930s from supporting those who urged "the strengthening of a weakened authority." Mussolini, Amadeo continued, "who incarnated the restoration of order shattered by the postwar anarchy . . . pushed the youth toward new ideas." Even so, Nationalism was never "a slavish imitation, a gross plagiarism."[128]

Nationalists observed the rise of Hitler and the Nazis sometimes with envy and admiration but just as commonly with fear and even repugnance. In September 1930, Carulla suggested that six million votes for the Nazis in the Reichstag elections represented "hope . . . in the midst of chaos."[129] But in 1936, Alberto Ezcurra Medrano described the Nazi movement in more typical Nationalist terms as "the exaggerated nationalism condemned by the church" and as the outcome of "four hundred years of apostasy" since the Reformation, *El Error*, as he called it.[130] In 1932, Franceschi thought Hitler "no better than the Communists" because he was attempting to restore the "religion of Valhalla."[131] He compared nazism with the Ku Klux Klan in the American South, calling it "anti-Christian and anti-human."[132] Carulla later claimed that during the late 1930s he was frequently offered bribes to steer *Bandera Argentina* toward a pro-Nazi line, a temptation he constantly refused.[133] When in 1938, Carulla ended his career among the Nationalists, he did so following a physical attack by the Austrian Nazis against the Catholic primate of Austria.

He characterized his last article, entitled *¡Basta!* (Enough!), as

an expression of my repugnance for such a monstrous attack. In this text, having explained my reasons for supporting Hitler's early measures, I openly expressed my utter distaste for his aggressive and inhuman policies and the pagan tendencies of his followers.[134]

"The new Germany," concluded Richard Meynen, a Nazi diplomat in Buenos Aires, writing to his superiors in 1939, "is viewed as hostile to culture . . . because of its supposed threat to the Catholic church."[135] Although Nazi-style anti-Semitism had a great impact on writers like Martínez Zuviría and Osés, affiliation in openly Nazi organizations in Argentina remained almost entirely confined to those who were either German-born or of German descent.[136] In June 1939, Congressman R. Damonte Taborda made sensational charges that Nazi front organizations were active in Argentina. Nevertheless, he distinguished between the Nazi groups and the Nationalists, or "national reactionary interests," as he called them. It was not "the spirit of the gaucho tyrant Rosas, popularly elected and inspired by nationalism," which supported the Nazis.[137]

Attitudes among the Nationalists of Argentina toward the Nationalists of Spain led by Franco contrasted strongly with their attitudes toward the Fascists and the Nazis. Empathy with Spain had been one of the major ingredients of the earlier traditionalist writers led by Gálvez. During the early 1930s, the Nationalists became highly receptive to *"hispanidad,"* an idea invented by Spanish conservatives and disseminated in Argentina by visitors led by Ramiro de Maeztu which proclaimed the indelible "spiritual" linkages between Spain and its former American colonies. In the 1920s, the Nationalists strongly supported the Primo de Rivera regime. After Primo's fall in 1929 and the abdication of Alfonso XIII in 1931, they observed the deepening crisis in Spain with growing apprehension and alarm. In 1931, Gálvez denounced a spate of church burning as the "Mexicanization" of Spain, "but I wouldn't be surprised that something worse will follow: the Bolshevization of Spain."[138] Federico Ibarguren found José Antonio Primo de Rivera so attractive because he was "totally

Christian, . . . free of the racist fantasies of Hitler and Rosen-
berg."[139] Franceschi denied that Franco was a Fascist because he ostensibly supported the devolution of political
power to the Spanish municipalities, the redistribution of
property, and only a short-term dictatorship.[140]

In July 1936, the Nationalists rose en masse to support
Franco's rebellion. "Our concept of life," wrote Gálvez, "of
family, of morality, and the dignity of women is in danger.
Our Catholic religion is in danger. Even our language is in
danger, which will become daily more bastardized by foreign
voices and habits."[141] Franco symbolized the "heroic mission
of authentic Christianity," and the Spanish civil war offered
an option between "the highest religious and cultural values
of the West and Marxist barbarism."[142] Franco, enthused
Franceschi, was "filled with a desire for social justice. [He
was constructing] a new state as a bridge between Spanish
traditions and modern conditions."[143] The intervention of
Italy and Germany in the civil war, declared Carlos Ibarguren, was a justified response to the actions of "the supporters
of the Red Spanish regime": the Soviet Union, Britain, and
France.[144] This second alliance proved the Nationalist thesis
that liberalism and communism were father and son. Spain
became the terrifying lesson of what would happen in Argentina if the hated Radicals ever regained power, since behind
the democrats invariably lurked the Reds.[145] Laferrère believed that it was now even more imperative to establish a
dictatorship to avoid the fate of Spain.[146] In sum, Nationalist
Spain became the great model for Nationalist Argentina.

The fields of Spain have become a testimony to God in the blood of
His martyrs and heroes. In community of faith, and inspired by this
example, we shall embark on our own struggle.[147]

Social Justice and Anti-Imperialism

In the 1930s, the Nationalists developed a rejuvenated form
of "social justice" and a strong commitment to economic nationalism. Their interest in the former derived partly from

Mussolini's *Carta del Lavoro* and partly from discussions of social reform in Spain during the early 1930s which were led by José María Gil Robles, whose speeches were often reproduced in the Nationalist press.[148]

The primary inspiration for social justice, however, sprang from the papal encyclical *Quadragesimo Anno* of 1931. Entitled "In the Fortieth Year" to mark the fortieth anniversary of *Rerum Novarum*, the new encyclical took as its starting point the church's opposition to the market economy proposed by liberals. "The right ordering of economic life," it declared, "cannot be left to a free competition of forces." *Quadragesimo Anno* reiterated the proposals of *Rerum Novarum* for Catholic labor unions but abandoned its rigid defense of the rights of property. The duty of the state was to ensure an equal distribution of wealth.[149] The state should therefore adjust "ownership to meet the needs of the public good," although in discharging this responsibility, the state would act "not as an enemy but as a friend of private owners: for thus it effectively prevents private property . . . from creating intolerable burdens, and so rushing to its own destruction."[150]

"By these principles of social justice," the encyclical continued, "one class is forbidden to exclude the other from a share in the profits."[151] Capital and labor represented a partnership, and each possessed a legitimate claim to the value added by the manufacturing process.[152] Wages, too, the encyclical urged, should always be high enough to keep women out of the labor force.[153] *Quadragesimo Anno* lamented once more the demise of the guilds, or "independent associations," and blamed the "political crises" of the modern era on their absence. The state, it contended, was now "encumbered by all the burdens once borne by the disbanded associations."[154]

But on this last issue, a crucial new element had appeared. Earlier, Rome had assumed that the corporatist associations would be established by freely contracting parties. *Quadragesimo Anno*, however, introduced the concept of "subsidiarity," the idea that the state itself should create and support the associations. Thus, "social policy" should aim to reestablish the "functional groups." Second, the state received authority to establish "legal monopolies" in certain areas of the economy, although such monopolies should never reflect "particular political aims" or lead to "economic dictatorship."[155]

In the terms envisaged by *Quadragesimo Anno*, "social justice" now meant much more than simply a state willing to mediate in the interests of "distributive justice," the way Yrigoyen, for example, had conceived it. The new definition implied the presence of a far more powerful interventionist state that would restrict the rights of property owners, favor workers and the poor in the distribution of income and wealth, and establish the institutions to pursue these objectives. Expressed in these terms, there seemed close practical similarities between the Catholic and Socialist conceptions of social justice. However, the former still remained anchored in natural law and upheld its anachronistic devotion to the medieval guilds. There was another sharp difference in the way Catholics and Socialists viewed the state. The concept of subsidiarity suggested the existence of the state prior to the associations, whereas the Socialists tended to view the state as an emanation from the associations. In the Catholic view, the state would dominate civil society; the Socialists posed a reverse relationship, although they conceived of civil society in more limited terms as a set of working-class institutions.[156]

Quadragesimo Anno had an enormous impact on the Nationalists. Applying the typical Nationalist technique of looking constantly to history as the key to the future, Franceschi looked forward to "the approach of the collectively regulated economy that prevailed in the past."[157] *Crisol* argued for a new strong state that would embark on the task of moving people from the cities to the land through a program of land colonization.[158] In 1935, Carlos Ibarguren predicted the emergence of a state-directed economy based on "welfare," "social security," and the control of labor relations.[159]

Thus, side by side with the torrents of abuse they flung at "liberals," "democrats," and "Communists" stood the demands of the Nationalists for social reform and the redemption of the working class. "The lack of equity," declared *La Voz Nacionalista*, "of welfare, of social justice, of morality, of humanity, has made the proletariat into a beast of burden . . .

unable to enjoy life and the benefits of civilization."[160] The
Alianza de la Juventud Nacionalista (Alliance of Nationalist
Youth), founded in 1937, placed "hierarchy and order" at the
head of its proposals, followed by the usual catalog of xenophobic and anti-Semitic slogans. But then came the demand
for "social justice" and a "revolutionary" land reform to destroy "oligarchy." The alliance offered to lead "the proletarian masses, to carry them forward with the rest of society toward the conquest of justice and the grandeur of the
Nation."[161]

In the 1930s, this propaganda quickly left a mark. Toward
the end of the decade, social justice became an increasingly
popular theme in film and theater and was beginning to play
a part in public policy.[162] Its influence became particularly
visible in the province of Buenos Aires in 1936–1940 during
the government of Manuel Fresco. Fresco remained a suspect
figure to many Nationalists because, until recently, he had
been one of the old-style "oligarchs" with shady connections
to the British railroad interests. But by 1936, after a visit to
Italy where he met Mussolini and to Brazil where he made
contact with the Integralists, Fresco was full of rhetoric against
"liberals." As governor of Buenos Aires, he attempted to end
the secret ballot. He used the provincial schools for purposes
of indoctrination and adopted the Integralist slogan, "God,
Country, Home."[163] Fresco spoke constantly of the "social
question" and how he would solve it by "coordinating social
interests." He introduced pilot schemes in land reform and
colonization and attempted to create government-controlled
labor unions and a new system of compulsory arbitration.[164]
Between 1937 and 1943, some of the same techniques reappeared in the province of Santa Fe under Governor Joaquín
Argonz.[165] Fresco and Argonz were widely decried as Fascists, but both could also be seen as the exponents of social
justice along the lines of *Quadragesimo Anno*.

The first great manifesto in the genre of historical revisionism was *Argentina and the British Empire: The Links in the
Chain, 1806–1933* by Rodolfo and Julio Irazusta.[166] The book
appeared soon after the Roca-Runciman trade treaty of 1933,
which afforded numerous concessions to British trade in re-

turn for guaranteed access to the British market for a small elite of Argentine cattle ranchers. Since their own land was located in marginal Entre Ríos, the Irazustas gained nothing from the deal, which they denounced as a sellout of national interests by the liberal oligarchy. The brothers used the treaty to attack the mentality of a ruling class that continually deferred to the British on the grounds that they had made a decisive contribution to Argentina's struggle for independence. Britain's purpose in lending this support, the Irazustas argued, was to capture control of the country as a commercial and investment market and to create a new form of colonial domination to replace that of Spain. As long ago as 1810, the liberals began life as the agents of the British; as the Roca-Runciman treaty illustrated, they were still discharging this role in 1933.

Henceforth, the Nationalists coupled their antagonism to the liberals with a heavy dose of anglophobia. Thus, *Crisol* attacked the Justo government for "handing us over to Great Britain."[167] "It's a foul lie," proclaimed Sánchez Sorondo, "that we owe our historical being to liberalism. To liberalism we owe only the handover of our frontier lands and the tutelage of foreigners."[168] Soon the Nationalists were resurrecting memories of the British invasions of 1806 and 1807, the expansion of British trade after 1810, which they portrayed as having destroyed the local economy, the usurious British loan of 1824 under Rivadavia and the unitarios, and Britain's role in the creation of an independent Uruguay a few years later, which the Nationalists contended had robbed Argentina of part of its rightful territory. In a typical statement, Laferrère claimed that British commercial imperialism had "caused" the civil wars of 1810–1860; Britain had destroyed "the old Hispanic culture, the Catholic religion, traditional customs, the native population."[169] In these campaigns, the Nationalists employed propaganda techniques strongly reminiscent of anti-Semitism, portraying the British, sometimes in alliance with Jews, as a hidden, diabolical force plotting to take over the country.[170]

The Nationalists raised another issue that until now had seemed buried and almost forgotten: Britain's occupation of the Malvinas Islands. The year 1933, which brought the Roca-Runciman treaty, was also the centenary of Britain's takeover of the islands. In early 1934, *Crisol* ran a series of articles under the banner "The Malvinas are Ours!" and then began tying the status of the islands to the disputes over the Roca-Runciman treaty and the British-owned railroads.[171] By 1937, the recovery of the islands stood out as one of the central demands of all the Nationalist groups.[172] Yet by this time, the Malvinas question was only one of several territorial disputes in which the Nationalists were embroiled. In mid-1935, *Crisol* denounced the presence of Chilean "spies" in Patagonia and launched a campaign against Bolivia for occupying territory claimed by Argentina.[173] These campaigns bore the strong imprint of contemporary events in Europe. At the end of 1935, fifteen thousand people attended a Nationalist rally in Buenos Aires to support a number of territorial claims by Argentina. As its organizers explicitly acknowledged, the rally was inspired by Hitler's demands for control over the Saar and the Sudetenland.[174]

Some of the earlier historical writings by Nationalists were written in the form of allegory and analogy. Palacio's *Catiline against the Oligarchy*, published in 1935, for example, became a parable on the revolution of September 1930 and the reasons Nationalists believed it failed. Catiline's career, Palacio wrote, was "instructive for men of our own day, spectators of the universal collapse of the principles on which the legal order is founded."[175] Palacio saw parallels between Catiline and Uriburu as "symbols of the decision to take power by extralegal means" and because the two generals shared a positive view of youth and an opposition to "oligarchy." Both Catiline's and Uriburu's "revolutions" had failed, Palacio argued, because they were betrayed by a patrician class that then upheld its rule by rigged elections.

But history in this form was too esoteric to be of much use as propaganda. Soon the Nationalists were turning to the formula developed by the nineteenth-century European writers led by Taine: the idea that in national history lay a "core" or "essence" that had to be rediscovered and restored and that in history lay the threads that pointed the correct course into the future. As Laferrère declared, "Without an awareness of history there can be no national destiny."[176] Julio Irazusta put the issue more directly. "It is almost inevitable to be involved in politics while writing history," he remarked. "Anyone who lacks a defined position on the politics of a country will find it difficult to understand its history."[177]

The first attempts to develop this approach closely followed Spanish writers like Menéndez Pelayo and were strongly influenced by the notion of hispanidad. Like Menéndez Pelayo, the Nationalists began to extol the Habsburgs and the sixteenth century and to denigrate the Bourbons and the eighteenth century. Thus, the Habsburg king represented the "source of honor and authority as the incarnation of the state, the first servant of the Republic, the first slave to duty, and the minister of God." The Bourbons, by contrast, were "inspired in French despotism. [They were] centralist and all-absorbing" and made religion "the slave of the state"; from the Bourbons came the "foreign and liberal" ideas that had perverted Argentina's development. In the eighteenth century, "reasoning" had superseded "spiritual vocation," "Single Truth became a matter of each man's judgment," and a world based on aristocracy was replaced by one founded on reason.[178]

It followed that national regeneration implied restoring the spirit and the institutions of the Habsburgs before these deviations had taken root. The Nationalists would therefore attempt to rekindle the "ancient apostolic and warrior spirit of the Middle Ages and the Catholic kings" which had conquered and "civilized" the Americas. They would restore "the direction taken by the captains of the conquest, that of the first settlers and colonizers who gave us our identity [raza], our faith and our culture."[179] In the Argentine version of hispanidad, however, the Spanish conquest had created a "separate Hispanic world, with the right to rule this conquered space belonging to those who dwelled in it: this right to rule is what constitutes [our] sovereignty and autonomy."[180]

But even in these modified forms that stressed local sovereignty, there were difficulties with the schemes borrowed from Spain. In the Habsburg period, Argentina had been part of the viceroyalty of Peru and an insignificant corner of the Spanish empire; the creation of the viceroyalty of the River Plate in 1776 under the despised Bourbons marked the country's beginnings as an identifiable territorial entity. Nationhood was then achieved under liberal leadership beginning in 1810. Using the Spanish approach, it became very difficult to argue that the liberals had led the nation astray, since they were its architects.

The Nationalists resolved the matter by making Rosas into a local version of the Habsburgs and his liberal successors led by Mitre, Alberdi, and Sarmiento into substitutes of the Bourbons. The cult of Rosas—henceforth one the great distinguishing features of the Nationalist movement—seemed to erupt out of the blue in mid-1934. In July that year, the press reported the creation of a committee to repatriate the dictator's remains from their burial place in England.[181] Toward the end of the month, *La Vanguardia* issued a warning against the conspiracy to "spread reactionary ideas disguised as historical revisionism."[182] *Crisol* saw the movement as a result of the depression, "that tragedy we are now living through."

The generation born after the turn of the century . . . is seeking the origins of our misfortunes through historical research. . . . Many of the most prestigious figures in our history are disintegrating like pillars of salt in the rain, while the personages of the proscribed are mounting in repute.[183]

In Rosas and his system, the Nationalists discovered the kinds of state and society they wished to restore. Rosas had ruled as a military dictator, but he could be depicted as the Federalist heir of the Habsburgs, since during his era the provinces preserved self-government. Rosas, the revisionists claimed, had supported the powers and privileges of the church while excluding both Protestants and Jews. The revisionists presented the social relations on the great cattle ranches of the Rosas era as an archetype of patriarchy and a native version of the guild system. As the benefactor of the poor, Rosas exemplified the principle of "class harmony" and "social justice," the "collaboration of all elements of society," in a hierarchy composed of "chief, enlightened elite, and mass."[184] Rosas, too, led the great struggle against the unitarists, the nineteenth-century precursors of the modern liberals. He established protectionism to develop the national economy and twice repelled military or naval incursions by France and Britain to impose free trade; he could therefore be depicted as the champion of national sovereignty and the great symbol of resistance to foreign domination. In June 1938, in a large gathering in Buenos Aires attended by Gálvez, the Irazustas, Laferrère, Palacio, and others, the Nationalists inaugurated the Instituto Juan Manuel de Rosas.[185] In the first edition of the institute's *Bulletin,* Palacio mapped out the future directions of the revisionist movement. Rosas, he wrote,

represented the honor, the unity and the independence of our nation. . . . The primary obligation of the Argentine intelligentsia is to glorify . . . the great caudillo who decided our destiny. Such glorification will signal the final awakening of the national conscience. Rosas . . . will make us love our land.[186]

Federico Ibarguren saw the year 1937, when the Rosas Institute was being planned, as marking an important shift in the Nationalist movement. That year, he wrote, the Nationalists "abandoned their conspiracies . . . to dedicate themselves fully to the systematic deepening of their ideas."[187] Historical revisionism stood out among the main results of this transition. The movement implied that by the late 1930s, the clerical emphasis on "Single Truth" was giving way to "Nationalist Truth" and the concern with the "metaphysical" yielding before an extreme relativism: what now mattered was truth "by an Argentine standard." "Revising our history," wrote José M. Rosa, one of the young revisionist historians, "is a deeply patriotic task."

It means to search for the truth and to evaluate that truth by an Argentine standard. From this task will emerge the Argentina of tomorrow, free of foreign tutelage. . . . We shall achieve nothing while our history presents as great men those who did not believe in the country, and whose only intention was to hand over our territorial, spiritual, and economic patrimony [to foreigners].[188]

Growing support for economic development and diversification among the Nationalists became another expression of this transition. Despite Bunge's earlier writings, during the early 1930s, the economic programs of the Nationalists were still little different from those of liberals: what mattered was balancing the budget, cutting taxes, especially on exports, and reviving the flow of foreign investment. As yet, Lugones alone had taken up Bunge's ideas with any enthusiasm. World War I, Lugones argued, demonstrated "the need for self-sufficiency." In 1930, he proposed developing industrial exports, coal and hydroelectric resources, and an iron and steel industry.[189] In the "Confidential Memorandum" of 1931, Lugones repeated many of these ideas and suggested extending tariff protection for national industries led by food-processing, construction, and textiles.[190] Yet there were still numerous traditional remnants among his ideas: he called the state "the worst kind of administrator" and supported new foreign investment; excessive protectionism represented "the negative nationalism of barbarism."[191] In these respects, the "Fascist" Lugones remained an economic liberal.

Bunge quickly recognized that in forcing a contraction of imports, the depression offered an opportunity for industrial development. But his ideas were again slow to catch on. In 1933, Matías Sánchez Sorondo submitted proposals to congress to tighten import controls, subsidize industrial exports, and create an Industrial Bank.[192] In 1934, *Crisol* ran a campaign supporting greater economic self-sufficiency using lengthy citations from the speeches of Sir Oswald Mosley, the leader of the British Fascists. *Crisol* wanted an economy "directed by the state" but unlike Mosley, continued to oppose economic planning for being too close to "state socialism."[193]

In other proposals, the Nationalists supported increasing oil and electricity supplies and efforts to create new foreign markets in Latin America. There were vague ideas for a common market in the southern half of South America through a "powerful and felicitous consortium of five nations in an economic union of the River Plate region."[194] Other groups, by contrast, wanted to expand the internal market. In this era of world economic breakdown, argued Guardia Argentina, all nations had to live "within themselves and of themselves."[195]

The Guardia stressed higher consumption, social security legislation, and an expansion of public works.[196] Bunge strongly endorsed these proposals. Since the country lay "under blockade," he declared, "we ought to conquer our own market."[197] In the 1930s, while the ruralist and antiurban strains among the Nationalists remained strong, the commitment to economic development went furthest among members of the military. A tract written by an army major in 1938, for example, proclaimed that "Argentina ought to be and will become a great power." The key to national greatness lay in industrial development and in the elimination of foreign companies through nationalizations.[198]

Ideological Cross-Fertilizations

The Roca-Runciman trade treaty and other dealings with Britain during the mid-1930s provoked a barrage of economic nationalism in Argentina which went far beyond the ranks of the Nationalists alone. Among its other manifestations was the group known as the FORJA, Fuerza de Orientación Radical de la Juventud Argentina, a think tank of young writers and intellectuals in the Radical party established in 1935.[199] In most respects, the FORJA seemed the antithesis of Nationalism. Far from believing that a Rosas-style dictatorship offered the key to national salvation, the FORJA identified itself with the democratic traditions of Radicalism. The native historical figures FORJA venerated were the caudillos of the independence era led by José Gervasio Artigas who could be depicted not only as anti-imperialists but as popular revolutionaries. "Argentine history," the group declared, "reveals the existence of a permanent struggle of the people for popular sovereignty."[200] If this goal were achieved, FORJA argued, Argentina would automatically divest itself of the imperialists whose domination required the oligarchy as its conduit. FORJA was anti-British and anti-American but also anti-Fascist and viewed the Spanish civil war, for example, as a conflict between rival imperialisms.[201]

By the late 1930s, the FORJA and the Nationalists found themselves competing for leadership over the Nationalist movement at large. As this struggle developed, the two sides began to co-opt each other's slogans, approaches, and ideas. The FORJA's impact on the Nationalists showed in phrases borrowed from the Radicals and Yrigoyen which now crept into their language, such as "apostolate" and "intransigence."[202] Toward the end of the 1930s, the Nationalists began to reevaluate the figure of Hipólito Yrigoyen. He now came to be seen less as the architect of "demagogy" than as the heir of Rosas, who created the type of political movement based on "class harmony" to which the Nationalists themselves aspired.[203]

But as the FORJA influenced the Nationalists, the reverse occurred. Scalabrini Ortiz was one of the young writers associated with the FORJA who made his reputation by his scathing attack on the British railroad interest during the nineteenth century.[204] Except that he was an economic nationalist, little appeared to connect Scalabrini Ortiz with the Nationalists, since he defined himself as a "materialist," took the side of the "masses," and professed a concept of political leadership he called "Leninist."[205] But behind these appearances, many of Scalabrini Ortiz's ideas contained strong Nationalist threads. He described the people of Argentina in terms reminiscent of Taine as "the expression of the land that represents the voice of times past."[206] He aspired for a charismatic political leader who possessed "an indivisible and organic link" with the people.[207] In his attacks on the British, Scalabrini Ortiz used the idea of the "hidden enemy" that evoked anti-Semitism. The British, he declared, were aiming for "world domination"; they were "astute" and "cunning"; they operated by "indirect maneuvers, ill-faith, constant lies, through a subtle manipulation of their local agents." Scalabrini Ortiz depicted the malign hand of imperialism acting principally through the system of education, an idea that echoed the long conflicts over lay education since the 1880s. "We are victims of an educational system," he wrote, "designed to lead us aside from an awareness of reality."[208] In later years, commentators were to dub Scalabrini Ortiz a "philo-Fascist."[209]

At the end of the 1930s, the Nationalist groups remained small and divided, apparently unable to shake the liberals' control over the political system. None of the Nationalists except for Fresco in the province of Buenos Aires and Carlos Ibarguren could be regarded as a leading political figure. Yet as their influence on the FORJA showed, the Nationalists were beginning to reveal their power to mold mentalities and set new priorities. Their slogans, foremost among them, "social justice," were creeping onto the political agenda. Meanwhile, the Nationalists were entrenching themselves in the army, and from here they were about to launch their revolution to demolish the liberal order.

Chapter Five

The Nationalist Revolution

At the end of the 1930s, there were few signs of the deluge about to engulf liberal Argentina. In early 1938, Roberto M. Ortiz replaced Agustín P. Justo as president, and for the next two years, politics appeared to be returning to a situation similar to that thirty years earlier under Saenz Peña. As the economy recovered from the depression, the oligarchy seemed poised for another attempt at political liberalization. Ortiz outlawed the practice of election fraud, a step that in early 1940 allowed the Radicals to regain control of the chamber of deputies. In this scheme, there was no room for the Nationalists, whom Ortiz harried at every opportunity. For two years, the president was locked in conflict with Fresco, the governor of the province of Buenos Aires, and in March 1940 finally ejected him from office through a Federal Intervention.

But in late 1940 and 1941, as Ortiz's failing health forced him to leave office, his program faltered and finally collapsed. Vice President Ramón Castillo, a man from the remote interior province of Catamarca, possessed none of his predecessor's commitment to liberalization and became quickly embroiled in feuds with the Radicals, which shattered the attempts to rebuild a political consensus. At length, in June 1943, the army, led by Nationalists, overthrew Castillo, set up a dictatorship, and plunged into a program of sweeping change.

Throughout this period, Argentine politics was inseparable from the broader context of World War II, the wartime disruption of links with Western Europe and the chronic tangling of

international relations.[1] The war provoked a desperate search
for a new economy to replace the old, opened rifts with the
United States over the issue of neutrality, and finally led to
the birth of a new political movement to fill the vacuum left
by the liberal oligarchy.

However, Juan Perón, rather than a Nationalist, emerged at
the head of this new movement. Although many of the initial
objectives and orientations of Perón's movement betrayed
strong Nationalist influence, some crucial differences quickly
emerged between the Peronists and the Nationalists. Perón
based his regime on popular support rather than dictatorship,
and his aim was not to restore a patriarchy but to forge a new
society based on industrial development and the support of
the labor unions. Thus, Perón failed to become a figure in the
mold of Rosas that the Nationalists aspired to: to their disgust
and increasing disenchantment, he merely "flattered the base
instincts of the masses."[2]

The Ascent of the Nationalists

The declaration of neutrality in 1939 marked an attempt by
liberal Argentina to guard its options. Should Britain survive
the war, Argentina intended to continue its long-established
trade and investment relationship with Britain; if Germany
proved victorious, Argentina hoped to establish a similar connection with the Axis. From Argentina's point of view, the
least desirable outcome of the war was the expansion of the
influence in South America of the United States, the industrial
nation with which its ties were weakest. Argentina's notoriously poor relations with the United States, noted an American observer, were

> not only due to a desire to assert her freedom and independence . . .
> but also to sound economic reasons. Could the United States take
> her surplus exports? . . . Until such time as the United States could
> replace Europe as a principal market, the Argentine would refrain
> from displeasing the actual and potential rulers of the Old World.[3]

In any event, neutrality prevailed until 1945 but failed to
prevent political instability in Argentina, which grew increas-

ingly severe as the war progressed. The crisis struck in mid-1940 as Ortiz vacated the presidency and Castillo replaced him, a transition that reignited party feuds and wrecked the efforts of the more progressive factions in the government to broaden its political base. "No more tragic misfortune could have been inflicted on the Argentine people" than Ortiz's forced withdrawal, wrote Sumner Welles, the United States diplomat. Had Ortiz remained president, he "would have avoided [the revolution of] 1943, achieved democracy, and prevented the diplomatic crisis with the United States."[4]

Yet the origins of the 1943 revolution lay in something more than chance or ill-luck, and Welles failed to recognize the deeper causes of the conflicts that erupted in late 1940. The stable coexistence Ortiz was struggling to reconstruct between the exporting interests, represented by the ruling conservatives, and the urban middle classes, represented by the Radicals, depended heavily on maintaining a steady flow of resources from foreign trade and allowing both sides to benefit from them. But in mid-1940, the fall of Western Europe to Nazi Germany and the Allied blockade of continental Europe that followed provoked a commercial collapse in Argentina on an even greater scale than during the depression a decade before.

In World War II, Argentina faced a far more critical situation than in World War I, when it profiteered from exports of canned and frozen beef to Britain and from large grain exports to France, Italy, and other countries. Between 1939 and 1945, Argentina could continue exporting meat to Britain, but its European markets for grains almost entirely disappeared. As the resources from trade diminished, it became immeasurably more difficult to strengthen the government by co-opting the Radicals, almost regardless of who occupied the presidency. It thus seemed quite likely that even if Ortiz had survived as president, he would have eventually faced much the same fate as Castillo.

In late 1940, several members of the Castillo government led by Federico Pinedo, the minister of finance, sought to escape the threatened breakdown in foreign trade through an approach to the United States, which implied that Argentina would support the Pan-American alliance proposed by Washington if the United States would open its markets to Argentine exports. In his economic recovery plan of late 1940, Pinedo proposed subsidies for farming and manufacturing and using the United States as a substitute market for Argentina's "vast surpluses of unsellable goods."[5] "The great American market offers enormous possibilities," Pinedo claimed. "There is no logical reason our industries should not take advantage of it."[6] However, the plan failed: in congress, the Radicals, as the newly constituted majority in the chamber of deputies, refused to support any of the government's proposals; nor did Pinedo succeed in winning the concessions he wanted from the United States. In early 1941, Pinedo resigned from the cabinet and was followed by several of his supporters, leaving Castillo virtually alone.

The confrontation between a popular opposition led by the Radicals and a shrinking oligarchy under Castillo now dominated Argentine politics. The opposition groups slowly put aside their rivalries and began to evolve into a coalition known as the Democratic Union. Leading this trend was the small Argentine Communist party under Vittorio Codovilla, which was now pursuing the strategy known as "Browderism." Following the German invasion of the Soviet Union in June 1941, Earl Browder, the leader of the United States Communist party, urged Communists throughout the Americas to abandon their earlier struggles against the capitalist "monopolies," to acknowledge their common interests with the "Anglo-Saxon democracies," and to unite with the bourgeois parties in a "peaceful revolution" through social reform.[7] In Argentina, first the Socialists and other smaller parties joined the alliance proposed by the Communists, followed in late 1942 by the Radicals. The party realignments of 1941–42 helped to set the scene for the Nationalist revolution in 1943 by raising growing fears of a Communist "popular front" that would lead to the expansion of Communist control over labor and eventually to a complete Communist takeover.

Increasingly isolated at home and abroad, the Castillo government grew progressively weaker. The Nationalists now returned to their old claim that "liberalism" had failed and was about to degenerate into communism. By 1943, there were some striking similarities between conditions in Argentina and those ten or twenty years before in parts of Europe which led to the rise of fascism. Like the triumph of European fascism, the Nationalist revolution of 1943 in Argentina was

born of fear. . . . Its dynamism sprang from the fear of a revolution, and this time a "proletarian" revolution. As long as "liberal" economics had worked, . . . [society] felt safe. . . . Each stage in the rise of [fascism] can be related to a . . . panic caused either by economic crisis or by its consequences, the threat of socialist revolution.[8]

Under Ortiz, the Nationalists seemed to be drifting into oblivion. Lugones was dead and Fresco about to be overthrown; veterans of the movement, such as Carlos Ibarguren and Gálvez, were no longer politically active; Federico Ibarguren, one of the younger Nationalists, became a schoolteacher.[9] In 1937, Carulla joined Ortiz's election campaign and then resigned as the editor of *Bandera Argentina*. In 1939, Ortiz closed the Consejo de España, the main propaganda organization of the Spanish Nationalists under Franco.[10] The same year, Osés, the editor of *Crisol*, was imprisoned on charges of slandering the authorities.[11] Other leading Nationalists continued their feuds, at times even dueling with one another.[12] At this point, the Nationalists could do little more than carp in frustration from the sidelines. In late 1939, the periodical *La Maroma* (Tightrope) complained,

In Santiago del Estero people have no water. [Elsewhere] there is no bread. In the south the children don't go to school because they have no clothes to wear. But in Buenos Aires a committee made up of two ex-presidents, a vice-president, senators and so on, . . . all of them Argentines, collects funds for the war hospitals in France.[13]

La Maroma led another noisy but vain campaign to restore Argentine sovereignty over the Malvinas Islands. While the islands remained in British hands, it claimed, they could be used as a springboard for an invasion of South America.

The Malvinas should be ours, although they produce nothing. Their value is strategic. . . . We shall always be dominated by the foreign country that controls them. Today that country is Britain, the only country capable of bringing armies to South America and providing them with a powerful base of operations.[14]

The position of the Nationalists immediately strengthened after the German conquest of Western Europe. Although there was no important German strategic interest in this region, Nazi influences for a time became far more obtrusive.[15] Carulla reported meeting senior army officers who were bedazzled by Hitler's exploits and dreamed of emulating them in Latin America.[16] Some officers campaigned for military mobilization on the grounds that Argentina faced a combined attack from Chile and Brazil.[17] In September 1940, Osés founded a new newspaper, *El Pampero*, which became a mouthpiece for Nazi propaganda and war bulletins. As it later transpired, *El Pampero* received secret subsidies from the German embassy. It also advertised the publications of the Rosas Institute, which suggested that the institute suffered no qualms of conscience at its vicarious links with the Nazis.[18] But even at this point in 1940–41, while the Blitzkrieg was sweeping aside everything in its path, there were limits to German influence over the Nationalists. Most of the Nationalists continued to champion "active neutrality," which meant, as one of them put it, "We are not neutral, we are against everyone."[19] The clerical groups continued to criticize the Nazis, and other Nationalists labeled them potential imperialists. In early 1941, Roberto de Laferrère, who two years earlier had openly declared his support for France, equated the local pro-Nazi groups with "some of the men during the May Revolution [of 1810], who supported our independence from Spain but only to make us depend on the English."[20] Laferrère now defined the "true Nationalist" as someone who had no current links with any political party, who had never been a Communist, and who opposed Jewish immigration, foreign capital, and British "tyranny." Yet the Nationalists, he urged, should "resist any kind of link with Nazi groups. . . . Today our worst enemies are the British and the Jews. Tomorrow they could be the Yanks or the Germans."[21] Following the German invasion of the Soviet Union, a small number of Argentine Nationalists joined the Spanish "Blue Brigade," which fought for the Nazis on the eastern front, but the vast majority stayed at home.[22]

In 1941, following the defection of the Pinedo group from the cabinet, Castillo turned to the army and then to some of the Nationalists for support. Among his new cabinet appointees in 1941 was Enrique Ruiz Guiñazú, the new foreign minister, who was an outspoken exponent of neutrality and a passionate supporter of Franco's Spain.[23] The Nationalists now intensified their propaganda, focusing it on the army. "The war is impoverishing, isolating, strangling us," declared Laferrère in May 1941, implying that only the army could stop the rot.[24] The army should organize new sources of weapons to escape its dependence on the United States.

The country has no munitions, and never has had. It is a defenseless country. Here too it depends on foreigners for arms, on the Yank factories. Without these supplies the army would be a laughing stock.[25]

Rather than ridiculing the army, the Nationalists quickly turned to flattering it. "In the armed forces," declared Laferrère in a rather different tone in September 1941, "reposes the independence and honor of the nation."[26] Again in 1941, in a speech to a group of naval officers, Marcelo Sánchez Sorondo called the "military spirit . . . an exaltation of the idea and sentiment of motherland" and the man in uniform "a superior specimen of citizen."[27] In September 1941, a new militant voice appeared among the Nationalist propagandists. Addressing senior army officers at the Círculo Militar, the high-class military club in Buenos Aires, thirty-one-year-old Jordán B. Genta, a former Marxist who was now a rabid and exceptionally belligerent Nationalist, proclaimed that "the warriors represent the most esteemed class of the state, [because] the nation enters into political existence by virtue of war and proves its right to exist in war."[28]

In late 1941 and early 1942, as war erupted in the Pacific, diplomatic tensions with the United States steadily increased when the Castillo government refused to join the Pan-American movement and to break relations with the Axis. As fears of a Brazilian invasion backed by the United States rose, the

Nationalists campaigned for "military preparedness," a message now taken up in the army itself.[29] Bowing to pressure from the military, Castillo established a national directorate of military factories to enable the military to produce weapons, planes, and tanks. Army experts issued a stream of articles under titles like "Industrial Mobilization and Preparation for War," "The Brazilian Steel Plan," and "National Defense and Heavy Industry."[30]

As Argentina's transatlantic links diminished, the Nationalists led another campaign to increase trade in Latin America. Bunge, for example, proposed a customs union of the Latin American nations under Argentine leadership, whose purpose was to establish new markets for exports of manufactured goods. The revisionist historians supported this campaign by reviving the memory of the viceroyalty of the River Plate, which had embraced modern Argentina, Bolivia, Paraguay, and Uruguay in one unit. The viceroyalty, Laferrère wrote in early 1941, reflected the true "nature of things," which a "deranged and suicidal diplomacy bowing to foreign interests" had destroyed. Thus, "a people that was once strong and rich, enjoyed an easy and contented existence, and possessed unlimited prospects in the New World . . . was left dispersed to the four winds."[31] Among these ideas lurked strong currents of imperialism and expansionism.

Throughout 1942 and early 1943, as Castillo's internal position and relations with the United States both continued to deteriorate, the influence of the Nationalists and the clamor of their propaganda grew. "The country's destiny is at stake," proclaimed Laferrère in February 1942, and "it will soon be our task to confront some fundamental problems connected with that destiny."[32] "For the first time," declared *El Ríoplatense* in December 1942, "the Nationalist movement stands in a position of formulating policies of critical significance."[33] Nationalism was "no longer only a doctrine," insisted Sánchez Sorondo in May 1943, "but a fact. It now has body, a physical presence." The movement was advancing from taking over "mentalities" to seizing control of "politics."[34] Ray Josephs, an American journalist in Buenos Aires, noted the rising influence of the Rosas Institute, which now contained "many important Argentine names, and military titles aren't the least of these. . . . They devote much effort to influencing professors, and, through them, hundreds of university students."[35] In Buenos Aires, the Alianza de la Juventud Nacionalista, a youth organization controlled by Colonel Juan Bautista Molina, now led aggressive and increasingly well-attended street demonstrations.[36] Josephs observed the largest of the demonstrations on May Day, 1943.

Down Santa Fe [Avenue] marched 10,000 anti-United States, anti-democratic, pro-Nazi nationalists. They swaggered along shouting "Death to the British pigs." "Death to the Jews." "Neutrality and Castillo."[37]

But the cheers for Castillo had a hollow ring, since only a minority of the Nationalists supported the regime, while the rest condemned it as "electoralist," "corrupt," and "oligarchic." The regime lacked legitimacy because it relied on rigged elections, declared Leonardo Castellani, one of the leading Nationalist priests, which meant the commission of a deadly sin: election fraud abused public authority, which was "sacred."[38] Castillo, warned Rodolfo Irazusta in 1941, "was preparing the way for the dictator, that unknown man, an ambitious soldier, . . . an unscrupulous political adventurer."[39]

On June 4, 1943, the army revolted and finally swept Castillo aside. The coup was planned by a secret Nationalist clique of about twenty senior officers, mostly colonels, known as the Grupo Obra de Unificación (Task of Unification Group), or GOU. The GOU led this revolt as a protest against government corruption, election fraud, and opposition to Robustiano Patrón Costas, a pro-British conservative whom Castillo wished to impose as his successor in the elections scheduled for late 1943. However, the GOU also feared that the forthcoming elections would result in the victory of the popular front led by the Communists. This "popular front" was "the precursor of communism," declared a member of the GOU in one of the group's secret meetings, which represented "a pseudo-democracy, an alliance of fellow-travelers under the thumb of Judaism, . . . an openly revolutionary organization trying to repeat the pattern of Spain where the moderates fell and became communist puppets."[40] From this viewpoint, the chief aim of the GOU was to forestall the elections scheduled for November 1943, which its members feared would carry either Patrón Costas and a clique of pro-British conservatives into power or alternatively the Democratic Union and the Communists. The GOU saw itself as the instrument to awaken the army to these perils; herein lay its task of unification.

Members of the GOU denounced the "international conspiracies" led by Freemasonry they claimed supported the popular front. Freemasonry itself was a

Jewish creation, . . . a fearful secret organization, international in character, . . . a kind of Mafia writ large. . . . Among its works were the French Revolution and the Spanish civil war. . . . It is anti-Catholic and therefore by definition anti-Argentine.[41]

The GOU described the Rotary Club, which was popular among businessmen in Argentina, as "a network of international espionage and propaganda in the service of the United States."[42] Its members defined the Nationalist groups, by contrast, as "the purest forces, those with the most spiritual awareness in the panorama of Argentine politics."[43] Although the GOU was a purely military association, it possessed a heavy clerical accent. Another member of the organization, for example, justified his support for a revolt against Castillo to be followed by a dictatorship on the authority of Saint Augustine, whom he quoted at length to his audience.

When a people is moderate and serious by custom . . . and esteems the interest of all above private interest, the law is just that allows it to elect its own magistrates. But when little by little the people starts to place private interest above the common good, and when corrupted by ambitious men it lapses into selling its votes and handing over government to the depraved, it becomes entirely admissible that the man of goodwill, even a single man with the influence and power, may take away the right to choose the government and submit the people to the authority of one man alone.[44]

The GOU drew up the proclamation announcing the change of government, which portrayed the armed forces as "the guardian of the honor and traditions of the nation." The army was replacing a regime, the proclamation continued, that was "gnawing at the foundations of our nationality," and it warned against the dangers of communism in a country that offered "a plethora of opportunities [to Communists] because of its lack of social legislation."[45] The new government would wage war on "the crude materialism hostile to the sacred interests of the nation," so that one day "Argentines may breathe the air of their land in liberty, enjoy work, bread and an honorable home, . . . venerate our national heroes and pray daily for our nation."[46]

Although the GOU was formed by Nationalists, the military junta itself began as a coalition between the Nationalists and a faction of liberals who represented a much broader constituency in the army. After the coup, four months of secretive infighting between the two factions followed for control of the new regime. The Nationalists won the first battle when they quickly replaced General Arturo Rawson, who rallied the liberal officers into supporting the coup, as president with General Pedro Ramírez, the leader of the GOU. When he took power, Ramírez issued a public communication addressed to Franceschi which immediately betrayed his sympathies, as he pledged his government to "God, the source of all reason and justice." Ramírez promised "to restore the traditional values of Argentine culture, which have been cast aside by a policy of suicidal blindness . . . and dismal negation of national identity."[47] Next the Nationalists issued a volley of anti-Semitic measures against "speculators," "usurers," and "middlemen." A decree of June 18, 1943, echoed the message of the historical revisionists as it condemned the artists and intellectuals in Argentina who possessed too "little interest in historical themes."[48] Meanwhile, the GOU intrigued against the liberal members of the cabinet like Jorge Santamarina, the finance minister, or "one of them" as the GOU described him.[49] In July 1943, the Nationalists defeated a liberal plot to subdue them which used the argument that the Nationalist colonels should obey the mostly liberal generals.[50] Then the Nationalists resisted demands from their opponents to name a date for elections.

Meanwhile, each side struggled to fill the administration with its own followers. On the Nationalist side, this campaign became an opportunity to indulge some of their prejudices against women. "There is great commotion," noted Josephs, "among the numerous women employees in government offices. The new regime is evidently opposed to women in business or public life. . . . All these gals are summarily being cleared out."[51] In September 1943, the Nationalists succeeded in placing their henchmen in many top-level university positions. The clerical theorist Casares, whose "thinking resembles that of Father [Charles E.] Coughlin," remarked Josephs, became the government's delegate (interventor) in the university at Buenos Aires.[52] Genta took over the national university in Rosario, where he immediately launched a project to restore the "metaphysical" in the curriculum and to "aristotelianize" (*aristotelizar*) the university. In Genta's view, the universities had been "taken advantage of by the Marxists to lay the conditions for the total subversion of the principle of authority."[53]

In October 1943, the Nationalists finally emerged as victors over the liberals when an attempt by the latter to enlist the support of the United States backfired. In an effort to increase the popularity of the liberals in the army, the foreign minister, Admiral Secundo Storni, appealed to the State Department to relax an arms embargo against Argentina imposed under Castillo. But American suspicions that the government was "Nazi-Fascist" led to this plea being curtly rejected.[54] After the "Storni letter" debacle, the remaining liberals resigned from the cabinet, and Nationalists replaced them. Among the new appointees was Gustavo Martínez Zuviría, "Hugo Wast," who became minister of justice and education, and General Alberto Gilbert, who as military attaché in Spain had seen

the civil war from Franco's side [and] studied Falangist methods and operations. . . . When he came back to Argentina he brought with him not only Falangist ideas . . . but a conviction that the Partido Unico, one party system, might become necessary for Argentina.[55]

A flood of Nationalist enactments followed the palace revolution of October 1943. The regime stepped up its earlier drive against corruption and profiteering, reduced rents paid by tenant farmers by 20 percent, froze the rents of apartment tenants in Buenos Aires, forced the British-owned Anglo-Argentine Tramway Company to cut its fares, and in early 1944, nationalized another British business, the Primitiva Gas Company. The junta placed the provinces under military governors and imposed tight press censorship.[56] At the end of 1943, it decreed the abolition of the political parties on the grounds that they had failed to represent "authentic public opinion" effectively.[57] Members of the government delivered endless homilies to the population replete with Nationalist slogans: "Honesty! Justice! Duty!" In November 1943, Ramírez lauded the rural population, which was "uncontaminated," he declared, "by the false foreign ideas of the cities."[58]

Although rumors that it was setting up concentration camps in Patagonia proved false, the regime closed down several Jewish associations, dismissed some Jewish teachers, and canceled the citizenship of several naturalized Jews.[59] Led by *Cabildo*, a daily newspaper founded in September 1942, the Nationalist press waged threatening campaigns against prominent Jewish families, accusing them of amassing urban and rural real estate from the victims of credit foreclosures. In April 1944, the government took over the grain export trade and nationalized grain elevators and warehouses. These measures were ostensibly designed to rally the landed interests, but they again had an anti-Semitic slant since they were directed against the mostly Jewish-owned grain export houses known as the "Big Four."

Martínez Zuviría began his tenure as minister with a speech urging a national commitment to

make the country truly Christian. . . . We should increase the birthrate, not immigration; we must ensure a fair share of rewards for labor and put every household under a decent roof; we have to root out doctrines based on class hatreds and atheism.[60]

To the enthusiastic applause of the church, Martínez Zuviría abruptly restored compulsory religious instruction in the schools by decree and then embarked on his own witch hunt for "Communists" in the universities. When students responded with strikes and other acts of resistance, he shut down the universities. Meanwhile, other members of the government launched violent onslaughts against Communists in the labor unions. Mass arrests followed strikes of meat-packing workers in Buenos Aires and La Plata, and the government took over several of the largest labor unions, including the railroad workers, by "intervention." Captured Communists faced some harsh treatment. José Peter, the leader of the meat packers' union, for example, was imprisoned in late 1943 and much of 1944. For the first two weeks, he was held naked in a cell flowing with cold water. For the next six months, his captors left him in rags and refused to address him by name.[61]

Social Justice and Perón

In this way, the Nationalists gave vent to their spleen against "liberalism," "imperialism," "cosmopolitanism," and "communism." "For the first time," noted the Mexico-based Confederation of Latin American Workers (C.T.A.L.), "the men governing a Latin American country openly deny democracy."[62] Yet as it attacked and persecuted its enemies, the junta simultaneously set about constructing "social justice." Within days of the purge of the cabinet liberals in October 1943, Colonel Perón was named head of the national labor department, and those close to the regime immediately pointed to the great significance of this appointment. Perón, declared *Cabildo*, would bring "weight and efficiency to labor problems"; he was aware of "the true needs of the workers' associations" and would support the "unity" of the labor movement, "always trying to avoid and resolve conflict."[63] Perón's task, *Cabildo* continued, was to "make the labor unions into an organic system" (*la organización del sindicalismo*). "I sought out a few labor people today," reported Josephs on the day of Perón's appointment, "and they are really worried."[64] "Long interested in mass psychology and in military strategy," Josephs wrote, "Perón thinks Army techniques can be applied to the organization of the masses."[65] He noted that "the regime now seems to be trying to develop some sort of popular following [and is now] stepping up its propaganda, making special appeals to win labor support, seeking to win over elements within the political parties."[66]

Although he was as yet unknown to the general public, Perón commanded high respect in the army. A career soldier since early adolescence, as early as 1932, he argued for a program of industrialization that was to be led by the military.[67] Between 1938 and 1940, Perón served as a military attaché in Italy where he became familiar with the European dictatorships. As one of the organizers and leaders of the GOU, Perón plotted against Castillo, drafted the revolutionary proclamation that followed the revolt, pushed the nomination of Ramírez as president, and then embroiled himself in the ensuing battles between Nationalists and liberals.

Perón held strong views on the role of armies in modern society that were strongly influenced by late-nineteenth-century German military theorists.[68] He saw the army as the pivot of government and society with a "civilizing mission" of leadership and mobilization. "There are two types of military officers," he wrote in April 1943, "those who believe the army is theirs," by which he meant the selfish liberals, "and those who know that they belong to the army," which meant the public-spirited Nationalists. "In this sphere too lies the difference between materialism and spirituality."[69] During the internal debates in the GOU, Perón did not voice any support for the extreme xenophobes and anti-Semites, but he did betray strong anti-Communist opinions, freely expressing his fears of the popular front and Communist influence in the labor unions. He drew parallels between current conditions in Argentina and those in Spain before the civil war, using the comparison to justify the coup d'etat.[70]

By the rebellion of June 1943, "social justice" had become an issue of almost daily debate in Nationalist circles. The objective of social justice, as the doctrinaire Nationalists saw it, was

to reconstitute the organic groups that compose the nation, the municipality, the family, the guild, the school. [Social justice] will permit the creation of an Argentine philosophy, derived from native-Hispanic traditions to emancipate us forever from foreign modes of thought.[71]

In more practical terms, social justice was now a euphemism for state-controlled unions, a system the Nationalists believed would both keep the Communists at bay and provide them with the instrument to establish their political dominance: as Sánchez Sorondo wrote in May 1943, "The conquest of the state begins with the conquest of the multitude."[72] Immediately after the coup, the Nationalist groups, led by the Alianza de la Juventud Nacionalista, repeated their demands for what they called the "state-protector of the Argentine working class."[73] The recent collapse of Fascist Italy did not discredit the idea, since its supporters in Argentina were now intently observing another model, that of Brazil under Getulio Vargas. "Vargas has given an extraordinary impetus to workers' rights," noted a journalist with Nationalist sympathies in the newspaper *La Razón* in June 1943. "He started with the creation of the ministry of labor. . . . The way they deal with this matter in Brazil . . . invites us to consider it . . . as a basis for study and ideas."[74]

As he assumed control over the Labor Department in October 1943, Perón was thus executing a strategy the Nationalists had been discussing in great detail for several years. Perón too acted with the full support of the military junta, and he quickly offered an explicit statement of his intentions. Two weeks after his appointment, he held an interview with a Chilean journalist. He declared in the interview that "our revolution is essentially a revolution of the spirit."

In Argentina the wealth of the people [ought to remain] in our hands, so that everyone may receive the best return on his labor. I myself am a labor unionist [*sindicalista*], but as such I am an anti-Communist. I also believe that labor should be organized into unions, so that the workers themselves, not the agitators who control them, are the ones to reap the benefits of their labors.

His aim, Perón continued, was to

improve the standard of living of the workers but without tolerating social conflict. . . . I shall not allow free rein to the agents of destruction and unrest, who are often not even Argentines but foreigners. I have working-class issues completely under control, not by force but through agreements. Don't believe we are anticapitalist, we are not. [But] international capital is quite mistaken if it believes it can conquer the national spirit in Argentina, which this government incarnates.[75]

The statement echoed several long-established Nationalist themes and formulations: Perón aspired for "a spiritual revolution"; he saw an alliance of Communists and "international capital" banded together against Argentina; he revived the entrenched idea of the pre-1914 period that "agitators" controlled the labor unions; finally, he argued the need for the collective organization of labor on the principles that sprang from the old debates on the guilds.

This interview in November 1943 marked the first occasion Perón exposed himself to public scrutiny. His performance proved confident and appealing, and it provoked his interviewer into a memorable forecast.

My general impression is that the Argentine government is united, powerful, and strong. . . . Another of my impressions is that Colonel Juan Perón may very soon become the supreme chief in the Argentine Republic, and who knows for how long.[76]

This particular comment caused a ripple of unease in the government which Perón quickly calmed by a public denial that he aspired for anything more than his current position. A few days later in late November 1943, in a decree signed by all eight members of the cabinet, the junta replaced the national labor department by a new secretariat for labor and welfare.[77] The measure unified several hitherto separate state welfare agencies into one body and brought Perón as the head of the secretariat into the cabinet. The secretariat, noted Josephs, "looks as if it's going to be one of the most powerful of the regime's entities and the busy colonel's make or break stepping stone upward."[78]

In a lengthy preamble to the decree establishing the secretariat, Perón again defined his objectives, drawing this time on the clerical ideas of "harmony" and "distributive justice." The new body, he declared, would serve as an "organization that centralizes and controls," to create "greater harmony between the forces of production: to strengthen national unity through a greater measure of social and distributive justice

. . . conceived in the Christian way in the light of the great encyclicals."[79]

Speaking to a group of workers, Perón suggested that the unions should be organized along the same lines as the military.

I am a soldier in the most powerful unionized association of all: the military. I advise you that to achieve the same cohesion and strength we have, always remain united.[80]

If the unions achieved such unity and supported the government, Perón was intimating, they would receive substantial rewards. In December 1943, the secretariat reached an agreement on pay and benefits with the Unión Ferroviaria, the largest of the railroad unions, which offered the union almost everything it had been seeking, until now in vain, during the past fifteen years. The agreement made a great impact, persuading some of the union leaders to bestow on Perón the title "Argentina's Number One Worker."[81] Perón concluded his activities in 1943 with an appeal to employers to grant their workers an extra month's wage as a Christmas bonus. The Nationalist press, led by *Cabildo*, supported the whole campaign with a barrage of propaganda against what it called the "pernicious canker of Manchesterian liberalism."[82]

In late January, Ramírez suddenly fell from the presidency after an embarrassing disclosure by the U.S. State Department that he was secretly negotiating with Nazi Germany to obtain arms. Foreign and domestic pressure now forced Argentina to break diplomatic relations with the Axis, which in turn precipitated several cabinet resignations, including that of Martínez Zuviría. There were other acts of protest by Nationalists, such as that in Tucuman, where the flags on government buildings flew at half-mast.[83] Yet despite the fall of Ramírez, the foundations of the regime remained strong. General Edelmiro Farrell replaced Ramírez, allowing Perón to add Farrell's earlier position as minister of war to the one he already held as head of the labor secretariat. Apart from the break in diplomatic relations, the junta's policies stood unchanged.

In April 1944, the government slapped a five-day ban on *La*

Prensa, its most vocal press critic.[84] In early June, Farrell led the celebrations commemorating the coup d'etat a year earlier. Under the liberal state, he proclaimed, all "sense of rank was lost, all values were subverted. . . . We lived engulfed in the crudest materialism."[85] In a similar rhetorical vein, Colonel Alberto Baldrich, the new minister of education, argued that the revolution had eliminated

a foreign ideology to restore those traditional values which are at one with the missionary objectives of the nation. These values are the common property of the Greco-Latin spirit sublimated in the civilization of Catholic Christianity.[86]

Under Baldrich, public education remained high on the regime's agenda. "Nationalism," declared *Cabildo*, "has two faces. One looks behind and the other forward. . . . Separated from his own tradition a man does not exist." Therefore, "history ought to be at the foundation of teaching to promote a sense of national spirit." School textbooks, it continued, should be "revised," by which it meant rewritten by Nationalists.[87] In April 1944, the regime established an industrial bank to finance manufacturing deemed "of national interest," which meant principally state corporations producing arms.[88] At the end of July, Farrell officiated over a great torchlit gathering in the Avenida Nueve de Julio in Buenos Aires. Before an audience estimated at a quarter of a million, he issued a "declaration of sovereignty."

Today . . . the entire people of the Republic . . . has understood the fundamental truths of Nationalism. . . . [This great gathering] reveals the existence of a powerful national movement pursuing ends that are purely national and that therefore can never be a political party because it does not defend the interests of any part against any other part, but the grandeur of the whole nation.[89]

Still more Nationalist edicts followed. In another echo of the old sensitivities of the Nationalists toward the rural population, a "peasant's statute" (*estatuto del peón*) set minimum wages for rural workers. In October 1944, in an act symbolizing the "union of the cross and the sword" that represented one of the central tenets of hispanidad, Farrell presided over a ceremony "consecrating" the armed forces to "the Virgin."[90]

From the war ministry, Perón launched a massive expansion of the armed forces that in less than two years tripled the number of men under arms. In 1944 and 1945, the army deployed its conscript personnel into new road construction, created new experimental industrial plants, and conducted surveys of the Andean region in a search for industrial raw materials.[91]

From his other position as labor secretary, Perón was now forging a vast popular constituency. In March 1944, large masses of railroad workers demonstrated to support him.[92] On May 25, for the first time ever, the Confederación General del Trabajo (CGT) joined the annual parades led by the military to commemorate the 1810 revolution. In June, Perón gained control over the powerful metalworkers' union, the Unión Obrera Metalúrgica. Perón unceasingly urged unity and social justice. "The new social policy," declared *Cabildo*,

is based on the need . . . to avoid a situation where some men are unduly rich and others unduly poor. The wisdom of the ancients, *in medio veritas*, continues to be valid. . . . Truth stands at the mean, at a due balance being maintained in the sharing of wealth so as to eliminate the absurd polarization between the class of the wealthy and powerful and the class of beggars. . . . [We aspire for] a healthy balance [and for] understanding and conciliation between the classes.[93]

On June 11, 1944, Perón delivered his most widely publicized speech to date in which he advanced his concept of the "nation in arms." War, he declared, was an inevitable consequence of the human condition. To win wars, "one should develop true . . . solidarity [and] create a strong sense of discipline and personal responsibility in the people."[94] Each nation's best deterrent against war was to become militarily strong; military strength, in turn, required the mobilization of all available resources, and effective mobilization meant economic development through industrialization coupled with "social justice." "*Si vis pacem, para bellum*," he proclaimed: if you wish for peace, prepare for war.[95] In July 1944, having ousted his main rival, General Luis Perlinger, from the ministry of the interior, Perón added the vice presidency to his growing list of offices. Perón's supporters acclaimed the "nation in arms" speech, but his opponents in Argentina and the United States cited it as proof the regime was "Nazi." In August 1944, the liberation of Paris was followed by huge pro-Allied demonstrations in Buenos Aires which turned into an outburst against the regime for its "Nazi sympathies."[96]

The Transitions of Perón

Years afterward, Perón's opponents were repeating his alleged remark, "Mussolini was the greatest man of our times, but he made some disastrous mistakes. I shall follow in his steps, while avoiding his pitfalls."[97] In 1946, the American Congress of Industrial Organizations (CIO) called the workers' march of October 17, 1945, "an exact reproduction of the first popular fascist and falangist demonstrations."[98] In Argentina, continued the CIO, "the last scenes of the Nazi-Fascist drama are being unfolded."[99] The "logical end" of Peronism, declared the *New York Herald Tribune* in December 1945, "is tyranny at home sustained by nationalistic war abroad."[100] In Peronism, noted other critics, Mussolini's title *Il Duce* became *El Líder*, and the Fascist youth march *Giovinezza* translated into *Los muchachos peronistas*. Perón's "Decalogue of Workers' Rights," issued in 1947, copied the Fascist *Carta del Lavoro*.[101] Once more like the Fascists, another opponent claimed, Perón sought "psychological uniformity [*masificación*] . . . [by a cult of] instinctive terrors and primitive ignorance."[102]

These judgments—standard views of Peronism among its foreign and domestic adversaries—illustrated the intensity of the conflicts that developed after the revolution of June 1943 as Perón toppled the established political structures. Although there could be little doubt that the European dictatorships strongly colored the emergence of his movement, the label "Fascist" so commonly pinned on Perón during these years was not entirely accurate. Rather than a copy of any single body of ideas, his notions were a hybrid of several influences that the peculiar domestic and international conditions of 1944–45 quickly pushed into some novel and unforeseen directions.

Years later, Perón recalled his decision in 1943 to seek the support of the unions and the proletariat. He perceived at that time, he declared,

the country moving in one direction and the workers in another, and the latter had no part in the former. I discovered the resurgence of the corporations . . . [and] that evolution would lead us, if not towards the corporations . . . because it was not possible to retreat to the Middle Ages . . . then at least towards the formula in which the people played an active part. When I discovered this, I thought that Germany was undergoing a similar process, . . . an organized state for a perfectly organized community. . . . That is how I discovered the whole doctrine. . . . People will say that it was a simple reflection of what was happening in Europe, and I will answer that is so, because that is the way our country has always been. What happens in Europe reaches us ten years later.[103]

On another occasion, Perón traced the origins of his principal political ideas to his sojourn in Europe between 1938 and 1940. "For me," he said, "it all started in January 1938," during a course in Fascist political economy in Turin, an experience that "clarified many things in my mind."[104] Fascist Italy embodied "the first national socialism, . . . a third position between Soviet socialism and American capitalism."[105] In Italy too he perceived the rising influence of communism and that "although the Communist Revolution had not crossed the Urals [*sic*], its influence was being felt over the whole world."[106] Then "I realized that the key to the whole situation at that moment lay in the forgotten department [of labor]. . . . When I said so, they said, 'You're mad. Why do you want to do this?' "[107]

Perón's remarks illustrated the potency of European cultural influences in Argentina. His remarks also captured some of the main ingredients of the movement he led: the corporatist quest for the organic society; the "third position" outside capitalism and communism; the anticommunism that in 1943 and 1944 became the chief declared impulse behind his bid to dominate the labor unions.

In late 1944, Perón's followers published an edition of his

major speeches over the past year entitled *El pueblo quiere saber de qué se trata* (The People Want to Know What It's About) and persuaded Gálvez to write a preface.[108] Here Gálvez hailed Perón as a "providential man," whose programs were "Christian, patriotic, and salvationist [*salvadora*]."[109] Perón's second great virtue, declared Gálvez, was that he "transcended the political racketeers [*politiqueros*]" who invariably dominated the political process under the rule of the parties.

These formulations represented the standard repertoire of the Nationalists, and they reappeared continually in Perón's speeches. In his own words, Perón aspired, for example, to "give labor a sense of dignity, to give capital a human face, to eliminate the materialist conception of life by exalting spiritual values."[110] "Capital and labor," he continued, "form a true human body, all parts of which have to work in harmony to avoid their mutual destruction."[111] Perón objected to the fallen regime of Castillo and his predecessors because it left people "detached" or "distanced" from the state.[112] Under the liberals, an "excess" of individualism produced an "unsociety," in which each person was "the enemy of everyone else."[113] To replace the liberal order, he proposed "an absolute, true, sincere [*leal*] union . . . of all Argentines."[114] Such unity would be achieved through the "organization of the cells that compose society," because without such organization, society lacked the means of "civilized life."[115] "The most dangerous 'mass' is the disorganized mass," he declared, and disorganization was the prelude to "cataclysm."[116]

Perón opposed "base politics, outside ideologies, and false apostles." The first of these phrases, "*la mala política*," meant the same as Gálvez's attack on "racketeering" and evoked the campaigns against the yrigoyenistas in the 1920s. "Outside ideologies" and "false apostles" were expressions borrowed from thirty or forty years earlier during the struggles between the nativists and anarchists, which by 1943–44 had become code words for Communists. In another echo of the old nativism, Perón depicted the Communists as "a cosmopolitan and unassimilated nucleus," who could only be mastered by "social, political, economic solidarity."[117]

Alongside the Nationalist content of Perón's speeches lay the contrasting resonances of revolutionary fascism. Like at least some of the Fascist theorists but entirely unlike the Nationalists, Perón took a favorable view of the legacies of the French Revolution, which he regarded as the origin of "social justice." The role of the "statesman," he declared, was "to fulfill the French Revolution: social justice."[118] In Perón's version, social justice was less the instrument of mere control or a means to return to the past, as the Nationalists stressed, than the agent of revolutionary change that would impel a decisive break with the past. Thus, social justice would construct a future that could "never be rubbed out," a future that was "decided and defined" and therefore permanent and inexpungeable.[119]

Elsewhere in Perón's speeches were echoes of totalitarianism. His visit to Europe a few years before had convinced him, he claimed, of the "evolution of almost all human activities toward a concentration around the state."[120] He proclaimed a "new society" based on the armed forces, the salaried classes, and the workers: they were destined to become consolidated corporate associations bereft of all autonomy and subject to the state.[121] Perón saw himself as the symbol and the agent of unity in the system he was proposing. "I have three titles I display with pride: that of being a soldier, that of being considered the First Worker in Argentina, and that of being a patriot."[122] This statement suggested that Perón regarded himself as the leader of the great power entities in society: the army, the workers, and the propertied classes. And he saw himself as the instrument to achieve harmony between them. In the "nation in arms" speech, Perón introduced another idea closely reminiscent of fascism, as he argued for national integration as a necessity arising from the threat of total war.[123] In early Peronism too lay another Fascist-like orientation toward public acclamation and display. In July 1944, for example, when Perón became vice president, "thousands of workers downed their tools and converged on the historic Plaza de Mayo to show their support."[124]

Mixed elements of both local nationalism and European fascism thus constituted the foundations of Perón's ideological outlook. His affiliations with the Nationalists led him into the hackneyed outbursts against liberals and Communists and into the clerical doctrine of "class harmony." His Fascist side stressed national integration and mass mobilization, developing the country's human potential through social justice and instituting the control of the state over civil society. Perón's conception of the part women would play in his new society typified these combined retrospective and revolutionary impulses. In traditional Nationalist style, he supported action for women to "invigorate the family . . . and to strengthen the nation," because the family was "the very cell" of the nation.[125] However, women workers were "the most heavily exploited" and thus most deserved the benefits of social justice.[126] "If modern society," declared Perón on another occasion, "demands that women function both within and outside the household, adequate recompense for their labor should be a basic requirement of justice."[127]

The military regime of 1943–1946 as a whole contained elements of all the leading right-wing movements of Mediterranean Europe. Baldrich, whose statements often contained a strong hint of Maurras, wanted society and the state to be remodeled on "Portuguese lines" following the teachings of Salazar.[128] Like Vichy France, the Nationalist regime restored religious instruction in the schools. Similarly, the Nationalist slogan ¡*Honestidad. Justicia. Deber!* evoked Pétain's exhortations to *Travail. Famille. Patrie!* Echoes of Spain appeared in the claim by Gálvez that Perón was a "providential" leader, and on occasion, Perón himself drew on the doctrine of hispanidad. Argentina, he declared at one point, was a "product of Spanish colonization and conquest: the cross and the sword. [Now] that same conjunction of extraordinary spiritual forces is about to be reconstituted."[129] There were some general similarities between the powers Perón claimed and Franco's title, "Caudillo by the Grace of God." "The masses are led by intuition," Perón claimed, "and intuition can be granted by God alone."[130] To the C.T.A.L., observing developments in Argentina from Mexico, the affinities with Spain under Franco were the most striking feature of the Argentine dictatorship. This regime, it declared, was an "absurd, clerical, anachronistic government, . . . an attempt to return to the past and to restore the sixteenth-century Spanish state, a violent, intolerant, sectarian, and absolutist regime."[131]

Finally, the military regime in which Perón had now become the leading figure resorted to a style of violence that was to reappear in Argentina at a later date. Detainees became "missing" as the police looted their homes; prisoners fell victim to torture by the *picana eléctrica*, forced cold baths, and sham executions.[132] When Perón's police began arresting demonstrating students in early October 1945, their mothers gathered in protest outside government house in the Plaza de Mayo.[133]

Yet events forced Perón's movement into some rapid changes. By mid-1944, the Nationalist regime was facing intense pressure at home and from the United States to alter direction and hold elections. At first, Perón responded to this campaign defiantly. "True democracy," he insisted, meant "social justice" as opposed to liberal democracy, which embodied "venality, fraud, exploitation, social injustice."[134] In the real democratic state, "individual interest must cede to the welfare of the community."[135] On July 9, 1944, independence day, Perón hailed a procession of workers as "a true democracy on the march."[136]

But immediately afterward his tone underwent subtle changes. At the end of July, he perceived "history" moving away from "individualism" toward "the social man" [*socialización*], but in Argentina, "the best thing would be an evolution within our traditional democracy."[137] A few days later, Perón conceded that "the revolution wishes to return the institutions to the people," a remark implying that he was now willing to stage the elections his opponents demanded.[138]

Thus, despite the still strong corporatist flavor of his public statements, "democracy" had now become Perón's acknowledged goal. During the antiregime demonstrations that followed the liberation of Paris, Perón began searching for allies among the middle and upper classes. "The activities of the secretariat of labor and social welfare," he declared on August 13, "should not be confined to the working class. [I wish] to make contact with the middle class, which I know is long-suffering, hardworking, and virtuous. . . . We also aspire to count on the upper class [*la clase pudiente*]."[139]

Perón's highly publicized speech at the *bolsa de comercio* (stock exchange) in early September 1944 formed part of the same tactic. At this point, he appealed to the propertied classes to support his concessions to labor to prevent a Communist revolution. Argentina resembled pre-civil war Spain, he insisted, except that a civil war in Argentina would be even bloodier than in Spain because "wages were lower." Communism was now spreading in neighboring countries, particularly among "the Indians in the [Bolivian] mines." When the war ended, a Europe dominated by the Soviet Union would confront Argentina, along with an economic depression that would induce "extraordinary unemployment." Under these conditions, the only way to escape the grip of communism was to achieve "real democracy" free of fraud and "social justice."[140]

But when this appeal failed to divide or co-opt the opposition led by the Radicals, Perón was forced back to his core of support among the labor unions.

From that moment forward I recognized I could not count on the Radicals, and I began to work in another direction, to fashion a popular movement through the unions.[141]

As a result, by late 1944, some novel leftist allusions began to appear in the rhetoric of the Peronist movement. Gálvez's preface to *El pueblo quiere*, written in late 1944, illustrated this shift as it juxtaposed the dogmas of Nationalism against echoes of the French and Russian revolutions and the Atlantic Charter of 1941. Thus, according to Gálvez, Perón deserved the title of the "providential man" by virtue of his "revolutionary significance for the proletariat." He would build "a better world" by promoting "equality."[142]

This shift gathered speed in early 1945. By this time, nearly all the remnants of the GOU except Perón himself had left the government, which committed itself to future democratic rule as it signed the Act of Chapultepec in February and then in late March finally declared war on Germany to gain admission to the pending conference in San Francisco to set up the United Nations. At the end of May 1945, the government's statute of political parties, which marked the first concrete move toward elections, acknowledged "democracy" as "a historic mandate" and "the only form of social organization compatible with Argentina's dignity."[143]

In midyear, as he faced a new opponent, the bellicose Spruille Braden who arrived as ambassador from the United States, Perón made another unsuccessful approach to the Radicals.[144] Now desperately seeking to neutralize the opposition, he even resorted to an appeal to the Communists. "The Russians," he said, not the Western allies, "have won the war. . . . The proof of it is that while Britain and the United States occupy only a few small areas, Russia has taken over the whole of Europe."[145] When the effort to attract the Communists failed, Perón predicted the "rebellion of the masses." The Russian Revolution, he declared, would have the same impact on the world in the future as the French Revolution had in the past.

If the French Revolution did away with governments by the aristocracies, the Russian Revolution will do the same with the governments of the bourgeoisies. Government by the popular masses has begun. . . . If we fail to carry out a peaceful revolution, the people will lead a violent revolution. Just remember Spain, Greece, and the other countries that have gone through revolutions.[146]

But as 1945 continued and the decisive political confrontations of September and October approached, Perón again found himself forced back on the support of the unions alone and at this point openly embraced democratic socialism. The victory of the Labour party in Britain in July 1945, he declared, showed "humanity marching toward a new world."[147] Speaking to a group of railroad workers, he perceived "a world experiencing a moment of redefinition, [in which] the working class has come to possess an enormous responsibility in government."[148] Throughout September and early October 1945, Perón urged the workers "to defend their rights for them-

selves if these rights were not to be taken away by their enemies."[149] Further emblematic of the transition was the changing connotation of the term *"descamisado"* in Perón's
rhetoric. Originally the use of the shirt as a political symbol,
as in "shirtless," seemed another example of Perón's Fascist
associations—his own version of the Fascist Blackshirts. But
by late 1945, the descamisado possessed the new connotation
of the sans culotte, having become a metaphor for popular
revolution. "They do not hurt us when they call us 'descamisados,'" Perón declared in December 1945. "We must not
forget that the 'descamisados' of old France showed humanity
a new way forward."[150]

By the election of February 1946, having survived the onslaughts of his enemies the previous September and October,
Perón had reconstructed his following into a reform movement built on working-class consumerism.[151] The State Department's Blue Book issued in February 1946 acknowledged
this transition, as it identified two phases in the development
of Peronism after June 1943. The first phase until late 1944, it
said, "paralleled [the steps taken] earlier by the rising dictators of Italy, Germany, and Spain. They set out to create a
Fascist State." Then came a shift to more democratic forms
during the Chapultepec Conference in February–March 1945.
But this transition, concluded the Blue Book, was mere "defensive camouflage," a response to pressure. At root, all this
implied, Perón had not changed at all.[152]

In a debate with Carlos Ibarguren more than a decade earlier, in 1932, Franceschi commented on the career of the
Roman general Catiline "If Catiline were alive today," he
wrote,

we would call him an excellent sportsman, a robust, agile man, able
to endure hunger, sleeplessness, and pain, who carried out difficult
tasks. . . . But whenever he held a public position, he exploited it to
the limit. His easy language, his generosity, . . . and his outstanding
valor . . . brought him great popularity, as much among his own class
as among those below him. Catiline became the epitome of the
unscrupulous leader who in normal times would never prosper but
who in unstable times could launch the worst kind of revolution.

"If you ask me," Franceschi continued,

how I would apply [Sallust's] *Bellum Catilinarium* to our own day,
I would have to say that I would regret our society ever becoming
like that of the Romans. Evil always begins in the leaders who forget
their duties and let selfishness and vices dominate them. The illness
then infects the people, and it assumes the form of demagogy. This
will then lead to a dictatorship . . . which is the first stage in the
final ruin of the institutions.[153]

By 1946, many of the Nationalists, among them the former
members of the GOU, viewed Perón in much these terms and
bitterly regretted the part they had played in his ascent to
power. When Perón first appeared on the scene, the civilian
Nationalists tried to use him to advance their own power.
Amadeo, who was a former junior member of the *La Nueva
República* group, recalled meeting Perón soon after the June
revolution.

I was attracted by his idea of creating a political movement to advance the ideas of June 4. . . . We were convinced the country
wanted profound change, and we thought it perfectly proper to link
our own aspirations with that unknown movement and its promising
leader.[154]

However, Amadeo's connection with Perón ceased as early
as November 1943. He found Perón "impressive" but "ruthless." He talked, for example, of pitching the men he considered his enemies in the Ramírez junta "through a sixth-floor
window." Against the wishes of the Nationalists, Perón had
decided on "the politics of the masses," and he quickly became impatient with the Nationalists as "theoreticians, intellectuals, lacking any practical value."[155] Amadeo objected to
the "personalist slant" of Perón and his habit of pilfering Nationalist ideas. Peronism, he wrote,

was a great absorbent of ideas. It utilized, popularized, but cheap-
ened . . . the Nationalist agenda. Don't forget that its three slogans,
Political Sovereignty, Economic Independence, and Social Justice,
were stolen from a Nationalist group.[156]

Peronism took

most of its themes from the Nationalists while rejecting their doc-
trinal underpinnings. [Perón himself] displayed the measure of its

incoherencies when he said his movement was so flexible that it could be adapted to the strictest form of liberalism as to the most iron-clad collectivism.[157]

Above all, the Nationalists and Perón parted company on the issue of social justice. In its retrospective and far more abstract Nationalist version, social justice implied tutelage, "hierarchy," and "values," but under Perón, it became a radical commitment to transform the status and material conditions of the "masses." "My policies," Perón declared, "were always directed at wages and living conditions rather than toward moral values."[158] The Nationalists wanted control without concession; Perón was willing to give in order to receive. Equally, nationalism now ceased to be the ill-defined "essence" it had remained under the Nationalists themselves and under Perón was closely identified with the economic advance of the popular classes.[159] Nationalists like the Irazusta brothers became immediately incensed by the way Perón taxed cattlemen like themselves to increase the living standards of the masses.

Throughout, Perón viewed the Nationalists as tools rather than allies and was ready to discard them when it suited his interests. In January 1944, during the disputes that led to the downfall of Ramírez, he supported a decree banning the Nationalist organizations.[160] Approximately one year later, as he faced Braden, Perón purged the Nationalists from the universities to demonstrate his opposition, he declared, to "an intransigent, medieval university," whose sponsors denigrated the "founding fathers of the nation."[161] Among the victims of this purge was Genta, who was hounded out of his position as head of the National Institute of Teachers. In late 1945, as he prepared for the forthcoming election, Perón made a renewed approach to some of the Nationalists to help his campaign as speech writers and propagandists. The Nationalists "drew near once more, convinced that now at last ... they could convert Perón into a mere mouthpiece for their ideas."[162] Yet the Nationalists were disappointed once more, because after the election, Perón "threw their baggage away in a corner."[163]

In sum, the Nationalists could produce some useful rhetoric but in the judgment of Peronists, lacked "an historic awareness of the masses." They thus became "a useless abstraction," representing an underdeveloped form of nationalism that was "literary, reactionary and apocryphal."[164] For their part, the Nationalists soon reacted to this treatment by turning against Perón, attacking his movement as "openly Marxist, class based, and subversive," or a "plagiarism of socialism."[165] In this rift lay the seeds of future political turmoil.

Chapter Six

Perón and After

By 1946, the right-wing dictatorships that earlier ruled much of Europe and Latin America had almost all collapsed and now survived in Spain and Portugal alone. In Rome, the church began to support the new Christian Democratic parties, gradually moved toward the reforms of the Second Vatican Council, and shed its past connections with ultraconservative forces. In Argentina, the Nationalists appeared to have lost their anchors and their targets: the liberal oligarchy had disintegrated, and in the 1946 elections Perón defeated the Democratic Union, including the Communists; immigration ceased to be a political issue; for several years under Perón, the military ceased to act in politics. The Nationalist movement seemed destined for extinction in this distinctly unfavorable environment.

But instead, the movement survived. After his election as president, Perón made no attempt to protect or support the Nationalists, but he did not attempt to eliminate them either. He simply ignored what he regarded as an obsolete sect that would eventually fade away of its own accord. Perón's tolerance and the absence of a concerted purge like those directed at the European Fascists after the war enabled the Nationalists to persist in many of their old bastions. Their roots still lay in the military, the church, the universities, strongholds like the Rosas Institute, and small circles in some of the provinces, particularly Córdoba, which remained the bulwark of reactionary clericalism. From these redoubts, the Nationalists quietly kept their faith alive during the early postwar period.

In the early 1950s, the Nationalist movement underwent a slow renaissance that illustrated the gathering political and economic crisis during the later years of Perón's regime. Having spent the past few years lurking in silence, the Nationalists now reappeared as a political force in the church and the military. In September 1955, General Eduardo Lonardi, who sympathized with many of the general objectives of the Nationalists, led the military rebellion that finally overthrew Perón. For several years afterward, the Nationalists vainly competed to become Perón's successors, first under Lonardi and then at the head of a popular movement under their own control. When this effort failed, the Nationalists retreated into their earlier role as a small but active intelligentsia, whose influence stemmed from their propaganda and from their ability to infiltrate key institutions.

By the mid-1950s, after years of Perón's dictatorship, the Nationalists appeared to have learned the value of personal liberties and democracy; by the early 1960s, however, many of them were again supporting a military dictatorship. In sum, Perón failed to destroy the Nationalist movement; he and his weak successors, along with the deepening atmosphere of violence and breakdown that now prevailed in Argentina, then helped it to bloom once more.

The Confrontation with Perón

During the early years, Perón's regime continued to wear what the U.S. State Department had called its "defensive camouflage" and manifested relatively few traces of its authoritarian origins. Buoyed by a rapidly expanding economy, Perón could reward his supporters and ignore most of his enemies. He now flaunted his credentials as a popular democrat and sought to strengthen his support by "becoming closer to all those who have thought differently from us. . . . All forces can be used in our movement. . . . It is our breadth that will enable us to triumph."[1]

While Perón showered the working class with social justice, Eva Perón campaigned for voting rights for women, a measure she proclaimed would achieve a "new and modern

democracy, in which all would participate on equal terms."[2]
As these words suggested, in 1946–1948, the mainstream rhetoric of Peronism often seemed very similar to that of liberal or social democratic movements in the United States and Western Europe. Perón spoke the same language as the liberal Americans who believed that in the postwar world, "few will consent to a state in which large masses of people are unable to live in comfort and dignity as productive members of society."[3] Perón's impassioned attacks on "oligarchy" and his support for "cooperation" or "unity" recalled American liberals who felt that "we shall fail . . . unless vested interests can be modified, submerged and integrated into a common social purpose."[4] Like social reformers elsewhere, Perón argued that rising standards of living were the key to a permanent partnership between the social classes that would erect an insuperable barrier against communism. Equally, his movement embodied the idea now current throughout the West that unions served as a stabilizer. "Because of labor unions, working men acquire something to trouble over. When his wages rise, his working conditions improve, and he has some kind of claim to his job, he ceases to be revolutionary."[5]

After his election as president, Perón no longer posed as a "providential man." "We do not consider ourselves providential beings," he declared.

I reaffirm our faith in the democratic and republican institutions of our country in face of contrary opinions which predict the failure of these institutions. . . . We firmly believe that only these institutions can ensure the liberty and happiness of peoples; we know perfectly well that their detractors have only two means of replacing them, both of them extreme tendencies, with ideologies based on materialistic principles, which pretend to arise from the deficiencies of the liberal systems [and lead to] regimes of the crudest despotism.[6]

Although the country needed "cooperation," Perón was determined that "we should not stray from the principle that gives the individual supremacy over the state. The state's basic function is to ensure the welfare of the individual in maximum liberty."[7] Not only the Communists but the Fascists, he now argued, "want to sabotage the country's economy. . . . Alongside them we should . . . condemn those who profess totalitarian ideas incompatible with the Argentine constitution [and] the institutions of popular suffrage."[8]

Despite these strong democratic professions, Perón continued to practice many of the ideas the Nationalists had created, supported, or popularized. In 1946, Perón erected an interventionist state in which four institutions became paramount. The state export trade monopoly, the Institute for the Promotion of Trade (Instituto Argentino para la Promoción del Intercambio), or IAPI, broke the grip of the landed classes, the meat-packing plants, and the giant grain firms on exports and channeled earnings from farm exports into urban industry. The newly nationalized Central Bank funneled subsidized credits to manufacturers and extended exchange controls to direct the flow and composition of international trade. Last, the ministry of labor and social welfare directed the swift increases in wages and salaries in 1946–1948 and the growing centralization of labor under the CGT. During his first two years as president, Perón nationalized the telephones and the railroads, repatriated almost all the foreign debt, and embarked on efforts to create a national merchant marine.

These new institutions and policies, many of them of Nationalist origin, attempted to give substance to the slogan that Perón had also usurped from the Nationalists: "National Sovereignty, Economic Independence, and Social Justice." Many of Perón's supporters continued to use the vocabulary typical of the Nationalists. Novelist Leopoldo Marechal, for example, supported Perón because, as he put it, the president would "achieve a match between the state and the interests of man," through

a return to traditional concepts concerning man and his destiny, and in an appeal divorced from the two currents of capitalism and Marxism that are antagonistic to each other, but share the common denominator of materialism.[9]

Occasionally, the Peronists acknowledged the influence of the Nationalists in the development of their movement. "You Catholic Nationalists," admitted Juan José Hernández Arregui, a leading Peronist intellectual, "have contributed . . . to our struggle for national liberation."[10]

In 1946–1948, Perón betrayed other hints of his antidemocratic origins. He purged the supreme court of all but one of its members and forced the resignation of some 1,250 university professors.[11] He swiftly replaced the coalition of trade union "laborites" (*laboristas*) and formerly Radical "reformers" (*renovadores*), which carried him to victory in the elections of February 1946, with a new movement known at first as the "Single Party of the National Revolution" and later as the "Party of Perón" (*Partido Peronista*). Henceforth, Perón maintained complete personal authority over his party and the selection of its candidates for public offices. By early 1947, the government was using its control over the supply of imported paper in an attempt to silence criticism in the opposition press.[12] In February 1947, Perón issued the Declaration of the Rights of the Workers, a document strongly reminiscent of Mussolini's *Carta del Lavoro*.[13]

In late 1948, as the postwar boom collapsed and political unrest began to mount, Perón began to abandon what he called "the generic methods of democracy" and to erect a dictatorship. The shift became visible as the regime placed increasing emphasis on the doctrine of justicialism (*justicialismo*), which Perón depicted as the "third position," the ideological option to liberalism and communism. Among the "Twenty Truths of Justicialism," which rang constantly with the jargon of "justice," "patriotism," "sovereignty," and "equality," were claims that the Peronist movement was both "Christian and humanist." Justicialism represented the "people" against the "circles," a derogatory term of Nationalist and antiliberal origins which the Peronists used to denote the political parties.[14]

By the end of the decade, Perón was again insisting that his own movement and the nation at large were one and the same thing. "No true Argentine," he insisted, "can deny his agreement with the basic principles of our doctrine without reneging on his identity as an Argentine."[15] Following an alleged plot to assassinate Perón and his wife in September 1948, the president's language grew increasingly abusive and violent. He attacked his "immoral," "occult," "class-motivated" (*clasista*) "enemies" and the "infiltrators" in his movement.[16] By

1949, the police were being regularly set loose against the opposition newspapers; opposition politicians were rounded up and imprisoned; rumors of police beatings and torture were widespread.[17]

In 1948–1951, the political influence of Eva Perón reached its apogee. Eva Perón, whose "only religion was Peronism and only tenet was faith in Perón," now sought to recast the regime as a theocracy. During these years, she acted out her self-appointed role as a medium or conduit with Perón in a way that deliberately evoked the place of the Virgin Mary in the teachings of the church.[18] "Following the example of Jesus," she declaimed, "General Perón sought his friends among the poor. . . . We know of no other governor in history who concerned himself so much as General Perón with your words, O Lord, 'Suffer the little children to come unto me.' "[19] Perón was a genius, she constantly insisted, and "the history of the universe is the history of great men."[20] Through her lavishly financed program of "social assistance," Eva Perón organized the vast networks of public charity the regime now relied on to protect its popular support. Adding her voice to Perón's, she urged vigilance against the regime's "hidden enemies."

[We must] keep an alert watch on all sides in our struggle. The danger is not past. The enemies of the people, of Perón, and of the patria do not sleep. . . . Our enemies work in the shadow of treason, and sometimes they hide behind a smile or an outstretched hand.[21]

Eva Perón's appeal to women was now cast in strikingly conservative terms. A woman, she said, was a better source than a man of "spiritual values" and because of her "different sociobiological condition" better able to teach "good behavior."

She is the pillar on which society stands to ensure the best psychological and moral education of the child. . . . [She is] the protectress of the common sense of the species.[22]

Only by "great women can great men be made."[23] The place of the woman was at home, "the sounding board of the country. There where you live alongside your husband and child, where you conceive your children and work."[24]

When we speak of the Argentine household, and of women as the symbols of that household, we speak of the Christian housewife bound to a traditional morality. Every woman should vote in accordance with her sense of religion . . . and with her duties as a mother, a wife, or a daughter.[25]

"To be a Peronist woman," declared Eva Perón in July 1949, meant "faith in Perón, subordination to Perón, and blind obedience to Perón."[26]

In these formulations, there were numerous traces of Nationalist influences. By 1949, Perón too was returning to the ideas he had inherited from the Nationalists five or six years earlier but since discarded. He now lamented the "crisis of materialism of our era." Too many "desires remained unsatisfied," he claimed, because society possessed "too many rights and too few obligations."[27] "Materialism," he declared in an echo of the antipositivist writers almost fifty years earlier, reduced "the perspectives of man, who cannot develop his full personality side by side with the enormous power of the machine." Nearly all Perón's speeches now attacked "uncontrolled liberalism"; "the only solution for the West," he declared, "was to renounce individualism."[28]

In the early 1950s, Perón resurrected his old claim to be a "providential" leader. In *Conducción Política* (Political Leadership), published in 1951, he borrowed from the writings of the pre-World War I German military strategist Alfred von Schlieffen. "Leaders are born, not made," he wrote paraphrasing von Schlieffen, "and he who is born with enough of Samuel's oil needs little more to become a leader."[29] By this time, Perón no longer promised, he commanded and threatened: "society should be a harmony without a single dissonance."[30] Having earlier "organized" the working class, the president declared,

we now wish to organise the other communities. . . . When this is all organised we will have an organised community which will not need to fight, but only to discuss and come to an agreement. . . . [Then] we shall have the most perfect community conceivable.[31]

Perón defined his new system as the "syndical state, the old dream of the human community." Once it was achieved, "all will be represented in congress and government by their own people. The politician will disappear from the Argentine scene."[32] Developing Perón's idea of the "organized community" that would replace "class struggle" with "class collaboration," Peronist propagandists proposed a society based on "syndicates" (*sindicatos*). "Syndicalism," they claimed, was rooted in natural law, since it "was born with human society. It is inherent to the race, belonging to its very nature."[33] The syndicate represented the modern form of the guild, and as a product of "nature," the obligations it imposed on individuals could not be opposed on the grounds of individual rights established by men.[34] Syndicalism would replace democracy, since "syndicalism represents the antithesis of liberal-democratic principles. The word means the need to unite, to express oneself in a social unity . . . as opposed to the idea of one man, one vote."[35] By 1953, the Peronist propagandists were arguing for rule by a single person committed to "paternal" government who embodied the national will and would serve for life.[36] Under this regime, the nation would "transform itself, completely and eternally, into the state."[37]

Beginning in the late 1940s, Perón thus underwent yet another major ideological shift. He reverted to the stance he had taken in 1943–1944 but with the important difference that his chief concerns now lay with containment and control rather than with change and emancipation. In its new extreme authoritarian guise, particularly in the natural law suppositions that underlay the doctrine of the syndicates, Peronism appeared closer to the Nationalist movement than ever before. Yet it was the Nationalists who were now starting to weave the political alliances that would eventually eject Perón from power.

In 1946, the Alianza Libertadora Nacionalista, the largest of the Nationalist groups, contested a few congressional elections but gained only 25,000 votes throughout the country.[38] On the day of Perón's inaugural as president on June 4, 1946, members of the Alliance attacked the headquarters of several liberal and leftist newspapers, including *La Hora*, the newspaper of the Communist party, and a bar in downtown Buenos Aires frequented by Spanish Republican refugees. In the latter incident, the streets rang with the cry of *"¡Viva Franco! ¡Viva Rosas!"*[39] In August 1946, the ratification of the treaty of Chapultepec by congress provoked a week of street violence by the Alliance that led to 600 arrests and a botched attempt to dynamite the dome of the congress building.[40] Similar incidents on a smaller scale followed a year later when congress adopted the vote for women.[41]

Yet these episodes marked the last gasp of the street-brawling tactics the Nationalists had employed over the past few years. By 1946, the movement lapsed into what the priest Meinvielle described as a "confused medley of worries and tendencies of every kind."[42] For some time, the Nationalists appeared completely overwhelmed by the renewed power and vitality of democratic ideas; antidemocratic nationalism had led nowhere; even Catholics, Meinvielle noted, were beginning to adopt "Socialist concepts."[43] In 1945, Carulla published his memoirs, which concluded by reneging on nearly all the ideas and causes he had supported for the past thirty years. Veteran Nationalists, led by Carlos Ibarguren and Gálvez, both of them now approaching their seventies, withdrew completely from politics. Censorship during the last few months of the war took its toll as the Nationalist daily press in Buenos Aires now disappeared, as did some of its leading figures, like Osés, the wartime Nazi collaborator.[44]

A few of the Nationalist intellectuals, Julio Irazusta, Sánchez Sorondo, Federico Ibarguren, and Amadeo among them, managed to slide into university positions in Buenos Aires or La Plata. But fearing for their jobs, they abandoned politics and said or wrote virtually nothing on current affairs for the next ten years. In 1955, Julio Irazusta, for example, declared that he had written nothing on politics over the past decade because of censorship and at one point even abandoned his work as a historian of Argentina for a project in British history.[45] When Perón proposed a new constitution in 1949, Sánchez Sorondo found a rare opportunity to air his views along with other university figures but contributed little to the debate beyond a proposal to abolish the elected senate and to replace it by a "council of autarky" based on corporate representation.[46] Under Perón, the long-influential *Revista de la*

Universidad de Buenos Aires was taken over by Hernán Benítez, another right-wing priest and Eva Perón's confessor, who
used the periodical mostly as a vehicle for propaganda from
Franco's Spain.[47]

As Perón grew increasingly autocratic, the Nationalists
were obliged to express their opinions and sympathies cau-
tiously or indirectly. In August 1951, following the death of
Marshal Pétain, some five thousand persons crowded in and
around the metropolitan cathedral for a commemorative mass
and to hail Pétain as a "martyr to the idea of a united Europe."[48] In late 1952, the death of Maurras, who like Pétain
had spent his last years imprisoned as a Nazi collaborator,
provoked a similar public display.[49] Borrowing one of Gálvez's old techniques, Amadeo commented obliquely on conditions in Argentina by sentimentalizing Spain. At one point
toward the end of Perón's regime, Amadeo was invited to
Spain and in the presence of Franco himself delivered a
speech at Alfajería, "the ancient residence of the Catholic
monarchs." "The ornate room was an imposing spectacle," he
wrote,

in which Ferdinand and Isabella seemed invisibly present. The
purple-robed cardinals stood side by side with the professors of the
academies in their gowns, while the dark suits of the diplomats
contrasted with the brilliant military uniforms. . . . I feel the deepest
admiration for the Spain of tradition and destiny, . . . the Spain that
expresses the highest cultural and religious values of the west
against Marxist barbarism. . . . I am certain that the union of the
American peoples will be accomplished under the banner of the
values of which Spain is the most eminent expression.[50]

In September 1950, Amadeo, Sánchez Sorondo, Julio Irazusta, and another Nationalist priest, Juan Sepich, became
contributors to a new periodical, *Dinámica Social*. The initial
line of *Dinámica Social* was so blurred that its readers complained they were unable to discern whether it was right- or
left-wing, pro-American or pro-Soviet. The periodical's editor, Carlo Scorza, who was a refugee Italian Fascist, deliberately left these issues unclear until he could gauge the opinion of the state censors.[51]

Gradually, the allegiances of *Dinámica Social* became clearer. The periodical pumped out anti-Communist propaganda, vindicated fascism, lauded Franco's Spain and Salazar's Portugal, and denounced liberal economics as "utopian." Amadeo used *Dinámica Social* to praise fascism for its sense of "national destiny," its capacity to transcend class struggle, and its cult of past national glories. He contrasted the prewar Fascist states with what he saw as the weak incumbent democratic governments of Western Europe that could not survive, he claimed, without "American aid and fear of communism."[52] Numerous articles of a similar tenor followed, some written by former Vichyites or refugee Fascists like Scorza who had fled from Europe after the war. The August 1951 issue of *Dinámica Social*, for example, contained several pieces praising Salazar's "new state" in Portugal. "Portugal and Spain," declared one writer, "are the last bulwarks of the European ideals of liberty and civilization."[53]

The overall tone of *Dinámica Social* was abstruse and pseudotheoretical, and its contributors still took great care not to offend the government. Scorza repeatedly praised Perón's doctrine of the "third position" and lauded the "Twenty Truths of Justicialism" as ideas based on "the love that unites men in peace."[54] In late 1951, Scorza joined the chorus of sycophantic approval that followed Perón's proclamation of the "syndical state."[55] *Dinámica Social* thus blew with the wind, avoiding too close an alignment with any particular brand of right-wing politics that might incur the government's disfavor.

Pushed out of day-to-day politics, the Nationalists retreated into "culture": revisionist history, weighty theorizations on corporatism, and disquisitions on national tradition. Typical of the revisionist history of this period was a 1951 piece by Federico Ibarguren which argued that José de San Martín, the liberator of Argentina from Spanish rule in the early nineteenth century, was an opponent of "individualism" and a sponsor of counterrevolutionary ideas.[56] Echoing the old links between twentieth-century nationalism and nineteenth-century federalism, the Tucumán-born writer Bruno C. Jacovella blamed the decay of folk festivals in the interior on the country's unification by Buenos Aires. Increasing contact with the metropolis, he lamented, resulted in the "end of the corporate spirit and the organic community" and the rise "of the extremes of individualism and 'massification.' "[57]

The few explicitly Nationalist texts of this period repeated the standard fare of the previous decade. In a short book published privately in 1947 but probably written several years earlier, Salvador Ferla railed against "subversion and the systematic destruction of values" that threatened society with "an acute crisis."[58] "Nationalism," he declared, rejected all the "modern errors that started with Descartes and reached a climax in Kant." Like the Nationalists of earlier years, Ferla lauded Aristotle and Saint Thomas Aquinas as "great and glorious thinkers who brought to its peak the brilliant philosophy that began in ancient Greece."[59] Democracy he dismissed as the tool of the Jews.[60] Ferla attacked proposals to give women the vote. "Leave the woman at home," he demanded. "Having women in politics is neither good nor necessary."

Where does this women's rights movement come from? From the United States, which supports it to encourage pacifism, to leave the other nations of the world in complete passiveness, and to take away their capacity to react against American pressures. . . . Women are rarely capable of taking a forthright position. It is hard for them to vote for or support a military government. . . . Just think what parliaments are already like [full of shouting, conflict, useless talking] and what they would be like with a score of women in them.[61]

Ferla demanded corporatist representation, an interventionist state, and the type of land reform practiced a decade before in the province of Buenos Aires under Fresco. Ferla acknowledged new trends only to the extent that he called the sindicato an "institution that after the family and the church is the most natural and the most instinctive of all institutions."[62]

In subsequent years, the line remained unchanged. In July 1951, an article by Federico Ibarguren in *Dinámica Social* again recalled the dogmas of the 1930s as it attacked the United States and the Soviet Union for having a common origin in the European Enlightenment.[63] Of better quality but still bristling with Nationalist prejudices was Palacio's *His-*

toria de la Argentina, published in 1954. "Our brief history," Palacio declared in the preface,

does not suffer so much from gaps of information as from errors of interpretation. It is not weakened by ignorance of what happened so much as by deliberate falsification. . . . Although I have tried to maintain a strictly objective position, I cannot deny that on many occasions my blood has been boiling at the injustice, errors, and betrayals [of the liberal historians]. . . . I belong to a slandered people.[64]

Writing in 1956 soon after the fall of Perón, another prominent Nationalist priest, Ludovico García de Loydi, denounced the hidden alliance of liberalism, Freemasonry, and Marxism against the church and against Catholic Nationalism, which he called "the Christian doctrine of our people, . . . the soul of nationhood."[65] The same year, José María de Estrada resurrected Maurras and the clerical counterrevolution as he signaled "the crisis of liberalism" and attacked the "superstition of progress."[66] Estrada labeled Marxism "the summit of the rationalist deviation."[67] Nationalism, by contrast, arose as a reaction against "egalitarian internationalism and the conception of the universe as an enormous production machine."[68] Their links with the church, Estrada claimed, would prevent the Nationalists from succumbing to Nazi-like "excesses," which he defined as the "idolatrous cult of the nation, the fanatical cult of the state."[69] In yet another echo of the past, Estrada denied there was any necessary link between liberty and democracy: liberty was "natural" but democracy man-made.[70]

Throughout this period, the more politically attuned Nationalists were struggling to come to terms with the vast changes wrought by World War II and with Argentina's now much closer relationship with the United States. A striking feature of the early postwar years was a profound revision of attitudes toward the United States. "We must be resolutely against Russia and for the United States," wrote Meinvielle, for example.

Any reservations we may have about the American way of life, American plans for continental unity, and American economic imperialism does not undermine the need to close ranks with the United States against Soviet Russia. . . . This is the only way to ensure the survival of the highest values: the church and the principles of Western civilization.[71]

Some of the historical pieces published during this period showed a similar tendency to bow before the general values associated with the United States. There was now less emphasis on issues concerning authority and more on concepts of freedom and national emancipation. A work by Silvestre Pérez was typical of the Nationalists who romanticized the Habsburg monarchy and Rosas. However, Rosas's great merit, as Pérez now saw it, was not that he was an iron-fisted dictator but that he represented the traditions of federalism and the "great popular masses."[72] Like the contributors to *La Nueva República* in the late 1920s, Pérez laid great emphasis on the colonial representative institutions led by the cabildos.[73] In this example, the blind cult of autocracy typical of the period 1930–1945 disappeared, and a vague conception of liberty replaced it. Later postwar Nationalist writings frequently took up this theme as they defined local government corporate institutions as one of the crucial intermediate "cells" that comprised the nation.

The opponents of the Nationalists swiftly seized on these adaptations, particularly those that favored accommodation with the United States, to denounce them as agents of "imperialism." In correspondence with *Dinámica Social*, Hernández Arregui, a former member of the FORJA, saw prewar Nationalism as a byword for "racism, anti-Semitism, abstract corporatism, . . . [the] ideas that now lie in the great trashcan of ideas which is history." Although they should therefore have disappeared, the Nationalists had survived the impact of World War II, he argued, by becoming "tied up with religious fundamentalism [and] supporting the conservative and opportunist world strategy of the church, which places the United States, the great guarantor of the capitalist status quo, before the national interest." He dismissed the Nationalists as "economic liberals" and quoted an unnamed Nationalist who had recently admitted that he now stood "alongside the

United States, which represents private property, the order desired by God and the ecclesiastical hierarchy against the invasion of Asiatic communism."[74]

In February 1955, another Peronist critic, E. S. Giménez Vega, denounced the Nationalists for their "colonial mentality" (*cipayismo*) and "pro-Americanism." Historical revisionism, he claimed, was based on "historical preconceptions" as opposed to "historical facts." Like the nineteenth-century liberals, who were the chief targets of their propaganda, the Nationalists were "an intellectual minority" and "strangers in their own country."[75]

Such changing attitudes among the Nationalists toward the United States demonstrated the impact of the new international order in Latin America after World War II and the strengthening of "liberal" forces throughout the West. As a result, the Nationalists were left fumbling around for new connections, identities, and external allegiances. The clerical periodical *Criterio*, still under the editorship of Franceschi, continued to publish diatribes against communism, but reversing its position of only a few years, *Criterio* now attacked nationalism. Communism, *Criterio* declared, was "the external enemy" but nationalism "the internal enemy."[76] Catholics should support democracy and "help" Jews.[77]

But underneath this veneer of change, the old allegiances lingered. In 1946, Franceschi published a tract entitled *Totalitarismo* (Totalitarianism), which mostly amounted to an apologia for Catholic corporatism. When practiced by Catholics, Franceschi argued, corporatism meant voluntary association as distinct from the unacceptable Fascist brand of corporatism that was a creation of the state.[78] In June 1946, *Criterio* published a loud defense of Franco's Spain, and in November 1946, when Perón's proposals for public education reached congress, Franceschi issued a vintage-style attack on lay schools. Such schools, he wrote,

cut the links of love and respect in the home between children and parents, corrupt the conscience of public employees and workers by encouraging them to reject authority, drain the people of spiritual awareness, and reduce it to materialist hedonism.[79]

The great issue now facing the Nationalists, however, was
Perón. In late 1945 and early 1946, the Nationalists helped
Perón by playing to the old fear of the popular front and attacking the Democratic Union as the pawn of Washington and
Moscow. Yet all but two Nationalists rejected Perón's last-
minute offer of twelve seats in congress, and the Nationalist
Alliance competed in the elections with its own slate of candidates.[80] At this point, relations with Perón still remained
cloudy and ambivalent. "There were some who hailed Peronism as the incarnation of the nationalist ideal," remarked
a later commentator, "and others who instantly rejected it."[81]

Among the Nationalists who initially supported Perón was
Palacio, who in 1946 became one of the two Nationalists to
accept the offer of a seat in congress. Virgilio Filippo, a priest
whose tract *The Jews*, published in 1939, illustrated the general tenor of his past allegiances, became another self-appointed Peronist propagandist. Filippo's adopted mission was
to "convert" Peronism to Christianity.[82] He sought to portray
Perón as a local version of the European Christian Democrats
whose "doctrines" put into practice the church's slogan,
"Neither individualism, nor collectivism: Christianity in action."[83] By taking control of the unions, Filippo claimed,
Perón was establishing a "non-sectarian labor unionism"; his
emphasis on "unity," "doctrine," and "organization" fulfilled
the aspiration of the Nationalists to "transcend politics."[84]
Like Perón himself, who constantly maneuvered behind a
smokescreen of conflicting historical associations, Filippo attacked "liberalism" while inconsistently hailing the country's
pantheon of liberal heroes led by Manuel Belgrano.[85] Finally,
if more commonly in the tense 1950s than in the freewheeling
late 1940s, some of the Nationalists on Perón's side, such as
Guillermo Patricio Kelly, were gangsters. In April 1953, Kelly
took over the Nationalist Alliance by putting "a gun at the
head" of its former leader.[86] During this period, Kelly organized the regime's goon squads in league with segments of the
police.[87]

Yet Palacio, Filippo, and Kelly represented the minority.
Most Nationalists definitively turned against Perón in 1946 on
the ratification of the treaty of Chapultepec. In Amadeo's

view, "although initially Perón stood at the head of the Nationalist movement," under his leadership Nationalism was "transformed into something new and wrong. The identity its creators had given it over the previous three decades changed into something else. For a time, there was confusion and perplexity" among the Nationalists but then came open opposition.[88] "He made no move to approach me," Amadeo added, "and I made no effort to close the distance that separated us."[89]

The early criticisms of Perón by Nationalists were little different from those made by liberals. In 1946, before retreating into silence, the Irazusta brothers demanded policies to make economic growth a first priority, because without growth, "it will not be possible to achieve social justice, national sovereignty, or liberty."[90] Meanwhile, Meinvielle attacked the expansion of the state under Perón in ways that suggested he supported a liberal, free enterprise economy.

We must return to the traditional notion of the state and the economy. The economy must run itself as far as possible . . . and the government keep to the function of a regulator with only an indirect role in the economy.[91]

"Distribution without accumulation," he warned, "will end in Marxism."[92] Like other Nationalists, Meinvielle dismissed Peronism as "pure improvisation [*empirismo*] and rhetoric . . . that followed the circumstances of the moment."[93] Franceschi condemned Perón's concept of social justice. It was an error, he declared, "to use social justice as a weapon . . . that allows one class to destroy another, or to reduce its application to only one class of citizens." The pope, he continued acidly, supported democracy but condemned demagogy.[94] As Hernández Arregui saw it from the other side, the "pro-Fascist" Nationalists had first supported Perón's revolution under the false impression that it would produce "a hardline, antiworker, antiliberal, and ultramontane regime." But when Perón set up a "popular democracy," the Nationalists became increasingly "divorced from the [Peronist] revolution to the point of complete separation."[95]

Perón's role, the Nationalists repeatedly demanded, was to

contain and defuse the masses, not give them a share in power
or access to the nation's wealth. A policy of "full stomachs for
the wage-earning masses," declared Meinvielle, was nothing
short of an abject collapse into materialism.[96] Perón was unduly "concerned with the popular classes at the expense of
the national wealth," he continued.[97] Meinvielle criticized
Perón's proposals for constitutional reform in 1949 on the
grounds that they treated humanity as a mere agent of production: *Homo faber* as opposed to *Homo sapiens*, as he put it.[98]
The new constitution failed "to address the cultural dimen-
sions of man sufficiently and overemphasized his economic
welfare."[99]

Thus, although Perón continually usurped the ideas, the
rhetoric, and the programs of the Nationalists, he remained
far too "modern" for the Nationalists to stomach. Under
Perón, the archaic system of ascriptive rank and privilege the
Nationalists craved slipped even farther away with the unbridled growth of the "mass society." Perón offered not the neo-
Platonic state ruled by the military, the church, and the intelligentsia which the Nationalists wanted but the enthronement
of himself and the plebs in a system they dubbed "plebisci-
tarian caesarism." Perón, the Nationalists complained, practiced social justice not to achieve genuine "class harmony" or
"social equilibrium" but only to win elections and perpetuate
his personal rule. The Nationalists contended that social reform had gone much too far and that the government ruled
tyrannically by force and demagogy. "Totalitarianism and collectivism are the gangrenes of the Argentina of today," asserted Meinvielle.[100] Perón had "raped and pillaged the Nationalist ideal," claimed Sánchez Sorondo.[101]

Filippo and Palacio, who at first supported Perón, were
soon showing signs of disillusionment. After his election to
the chamber of deputies as a Peronist member in 1948, Filippo
introduced legislation banning Masonry in Argentina but
found himself blocked by party leaders. "Our own party," he
thundered, "is contaminated by Marxism, Masonry, liberalism, socialism and leftism."[102] By 1951, Palacio was supporting the overthrow of Perón by a military coup d'etat.[103]

In September 1951, Rodolfo Irazusta attacked Perón with

the argument common thirty years earlier at the time of the Liga Patriótica Argentina: he was implementing European formulas totally unsuited to conditions in "America."

Instead of the truly national revolution we wanted, we got a social revolution of an international collectivist brand. It applied European ideas suited to the overpopulated nations of the old continent, but not to our American latitudes that are so full of opportunities yet short of people. Instead of a harmony of classes, we have class struggle; instead of a national consciousness, we have a strengthening of the mentalities of class; instead of a stimulus to free enterprise, we have authoritarian regulation; instead of citizen participation, we have iron discipline; instead of prosperity, we have poverty; instead of liberty, we have popular tyranny.[104]

The conviction grew among the Nationalists that in Peronism lay the seeds of Marxism. "I didn't find that Perón was the right man," declared Palacio some years later. "He practiced an underhand demagogy that threatened to bring civil war by intensifying class conflict."[105] When Perón slid into repression in the late 1940s and early 1950s, the Nationalists suddenly discovered the virtues of a free society. "The generation to which I belong," wrote Amadeo only four years after his article in *Dinámica Social* vindicating fascism, "did not count liberty among its major concerns." But Perón forced him into "a profound reevaluation of the issue of freedom" that provoked some "fundamental changes in [his] political ideas." After experiencing the hand of Perón's dictatorship, he now supported constitutional guarantees of individual rights, the rule of law, clean elections, and "civilized habits of political involvement."[106] In future, "the conquest of liberty," Amadeo proclaimed, "must become Argentina's finest acquisition."[107]

Franceschi underwent a similar transition. Throughout the period 1946–1954, *Criterio* made virtually no comment on domestic politics. In eight years, its tone changed only once, in September 1948, when three priests were arrested as suspects in the assassination plot against Perón.[108] Yet silence instantly turned to raucous jubilation on Perón's overthrow in September 1955. "For now at least I shall not write an article brimming with theories of liberty," Franceschi exulted. All he wanted was to "shout the word [liberty] that has been exiled for so long."

At last we can speak by telephone without fear of being overheard, hold a conversation in the street and not have to look out for spies, make a speech without the police listening, write an article without worrying about a lawsuit. . . . The Argentine people has, I hope! learned a hard lesson: how easy it is to lose freedom and how much it costs to recover it.[109]

Perón and the Church

Perón's regime finally collapsed when it turned against the church. In 1946, the church supported Perón by reissuing a 1934 pastoral that forbade Catholics to vote for parties that upheld lay schools, divorce; and the separation of church and state.[110] A year later, Perón repaid his debt to the church by endorsing legislation to ratify Martínez Zuviría's decree three years earlier imposing religious education in the schools. Henceforth, all teaching appointments in the public schools became subject to review by ecclesiastical authorities through a board of religious instruction in the ministry of education. For several years, the church enjoyed a free hand over school curricula, which it exploited to the full. Among the typical messages of Catholic teachers and textbooks to the nation's children during this period were "Protestantism upholds ideas that lead to immorality and crime," and "civil marriage and the lay school are inventions of the devil."[111]

By the end of the 1940s, conditions were changing. Relations with the church began to deteriorate when Perón sought to convert justicialism into a civic religion within the "organized community."[112] Peronists were now called "believers" and the doctrines of justicialism "truths," superior even to those proclaimed by the church. Some of Perón's speeches obliquely criticized the church as a bastion of extravagance and display that conflicted with the regime's professed cult of simplicity. In a "socially just" Argentina, he declared, a "religion of humility" was needed, "the religion of the poor, of those who feel hunger and thirst for justice."[113] "We love

Christ," Perón declared provocatively in 1950, "not because He is God. We love Him because He left something eternal in the world: love between men."[114] In 1950, the regime abolished several long-established religious holidays.[115]

In the schools, Perón no longer wanted ultraclericals but unswerving Peronists who would inculcate blind loyalty to the regime. The teachers, as Franceschi later recalled, were no longer devoted to the teachings of the church but "wrote textbooks that taught the children to identify that woman," as he called Eva Perón, "with the Virgin Mary."[116] As the regime moved in these directions, the church began to brand Perón a tyrant.

Meanwhile, unrest in the military surfaced in 1949 following the ratification of the new constitution that allowed Perón to seek reelection and when a failing economy led to growing scarcities of new military equipment. Unrest intensified in 1951 when Eva Perón made her unsuccessful bid for the vice-presidency.[117] In September 1951, a retired cavalry officer, General Benjamín Menéndez, one of the associates of Colonel Juan Bautista Molina during the 1930s, led a small, premature, and unsuccessful revolt to topple the regime.[118] Perón initially demanded death sentences for the captured leaders of the rebellion but eventually took retribution by imposing harsh prison sentences and carrying out a purge of two hundred senior officers. Civilians like Laferrère, who helped Menéndez draw up his revolutionary proclamation, were also punished by imprisonment.[119]

Perón now staked his survival on ceaseless propaganda and long bouts of repression that soon escalated into mob assaults against his opponents. In April 1953, bombs exploded during one of Perón's mass rallies, and Peronists led by Kelly's organization, the Nationalist Alliance, replied by torching and destroying the premises of the Socialist and Radical parties and of the aristocratic Jockey Club.[120] Perón's few remaining Catholic supporters, like the priest Benítez, made vain attempts to restore his links with the church. "Religion is the strongest of all society's linkages," Benítez warned Perón in 1952. "Without religion, Justicialism will end up just another failed system."[121] But the warning went unheeded.

Soon there was an open rift between Perón and the church. In mid-1952, the church complained that many of the films the government was allowing to be screened in Buenos Aires were immoral and defamatory and tacked this complaint onto others against recent restrictions on religious education in the schools.[122] In another indication of strained relations, in July and August 1952, the church virtually ignored the death of Eva Perón.[123] Still more controversies followed, particularly in 1954 when the church campaigned against the activities of Theodore Hicks, an American faith healer, which the government encouraged in order to tap into the vast crowds attending his meetings for propaganda.[124]

Franceschi's writings in *Criterio* illustrated the way this conflict gradually mushroomed. In late 1953 and early 1954, *Criterio* published several articles on the "worker-priests" in France who were taking jobs in mines and factories to challenge the Communists and Socialists for the control of the labor unions. *Criterio*'s discussion of this issue was explicitly confined to France but implied nevertheless that the same technique could at some point be used in Argentina against the Peronist unions. *Criterio* then pointed to another ongoing debate in France on the activities of the lay organization Catholic Action, which was attempting to enhance popular support for the French church. On both these issues, *Criterio* took the official line supported by Rome that the church should never attempt to become a "substitute for the temporal power" and that priests and lay organizations alike were limited to "the transformation of mentalities, the purification of conscience." Their only contact with the temporal sphere should be to remove "obstacles to the redemption of humanity and the order of God."[125]

In February 1954, however, *Criterio* advertised a succession of public lectures organized by Catholic Action in Buenos Aires entitled the "Argentine Social Week." The lectures were directed at "the middle class" and bore titles like "The Current Situation of the Urban Middle Class," "The Crisis of the Middle Class," and "Will the Middle Class Disappear?"[126] Immediately after the "Social Week," *Criterio* pledged that Catholic Action would now support the union of the middle class with a view to winning its representation before the authorities . . . and promote the formation of professional, cultural, and economic associations for the defense of its interests.[127]

In effect, the church was proposing to sponsor new mass organizations independent of the all-inclusive Peronist movement; hints then followed that the church intended to create a new Christian Democratic party to challenge the Peronists in future elections.[128] In August 1954, Franceschi published a long article to commemorate the seventieth anniversary of the "First Assembly of Argentine Catholics" in 1884 at the height of the conflicts over lay education. In 1884, Franceschi emphasized, the Catholics "united to uphold the predominance of true Christian principles in public life and government," and he then quoted some of the speeches during the 1884 assembly.

When a dominant political party pokes its oar into everything that is sacred and attacks the very foundations of the prevailing religious order, it becomes the duty of Catholics to organize their own parties to defend the principles of faith and the rights of the church.[129]

A month later, in September 1954, church and state collided openly when Catholic Action organized a mass march of high school students in Córdoba in competition with a rally by Peronist students. Perón responded to the challenge by accusing the church of attempting to infiltrate the Peronist trade unions and student organizations. He then imposed an escalating succession of retaliatory measures. The government arrested, imprisoned, or deported a number of priests, outlawed Catholic Action, and further restricted religious teaching in the schools. Congress then instituted divorce, legalized prostitution, and in early 1955 prepared a constitutional amendment to separate church and state. Newly elected members of congress now had the option of taking their oaths in the name of Eva Perón; priests were to apply to the government for permission to preach; the church was banned from organizing religious processions and from voicing its opinions in the press.[130]

In April 1955, after several months of ineffective protest, the bishops finally responded. In a communication they ordered read from every pulpit of the republic, they denounced the proposal to separate church and state. "Every political party," they declared, "that is hostile to religion places the separation of church and state at the forefront of its programs."[131] Perón responded with more anticlerical measures that now seemed to be building up into a general onslaught against the church. "We aspire for the universal truth of authentic Christianity," he declared in a speech in mid-May, and he denounced the bishops as "the last remnants of unjust privilege, the ornaments of hatred and injustice [who] conflict with our aspirations."[132]

In June 1955, the conflict spilled over into violence and bloodshed. In defiance of the government's ban, on June 11, the church organized a mass procession to commemorate the festival of Corpus Christi. Peronists then accused Catholics of burning the national flag during the march. On June 16, a faction of the naval air command revolted and showered the center of Buenos Aires with bombs, killing some five hundred people.[133] The same evening a mob of two hundred Peronists roamed the streets of Buenos Aires burning churches. The burning of the churches, Franceschi cried in anguish, showed a repulsive "hatred and cruelty. . . . The sacred vessels were used as urinals, the statues of the Virgin beheaded, . . . the oldest buildings of the city burned."[134]

Perón held on for another three months. At first he attempted concession, promising to cease being "head of a revolution" and to rule as "the president of all Argentines, friends and adversaries." But as his opponents rejected his overtures, Perón threatened them with extermination. The final act of this yearlong drama came in mid-September 1955 on the outbreak of another military revolt in Córdoba. The so-called liberating revolution (*revolución libertadora*) contained strong clerical and Nationalist elements. The V sign displayed by the rebel airmen meant *Cristo vence*: "Christ conquers."[135] The rebel password in the insurrection was *Dios es justo*: "God is just." In the radio proclamation that followed Perón's defeat by General Eduardo Lonardi, the rebels celebrated a "miraculous" victory. Victory had been won "with the help of Christ and of the Virgin of Rosario to whom the general in charge of operations had dedicated his sword."[136] As Perón fell, the leading Nationalists joined the vast crowds in the streets to express their gratitude "to those who rescued our liberty" from an "infamous and moblike tyranny."[137] Others, like Laferrère, scoffed at Perón's apparent cowardice. *"Cose e parlare de morte e altro morirse"* [*sic*], he remarked, quoting a fractured version of a Italian proverb.[138]

Both the Nationalists and the leading members of the church interpreted recent events as the climax to a long process of national decline that had begun decades before. Materialism, declared Franceschi, lay at the root of the nation's misfortunes. "There is a political problem in this country because of a social problem and a social problem because of a moral problem."[139] The origins of Perón, he claimed in another echo of a long entrenched Nationalist idea, lay in the moral inadequacies of the ruling classes.

The aristocracy has become courtesans, the landowners usurers. Luxury has taken over. To be rich no longer carries responsibilities. Serving the country means taking more, simply grabbing more pleasures.[140]

Sánchez Sorondo took a similar position. "There are no longer any ruling classes or recognized elites," he wrote in 1956. "The Argentine patricians who used to personify the country are gone. There are no leaders, only minorities . . . dissociated from historical tradition."[141]

There were some striking parallels between the struggle against Perón in the early 1950s and the clerical campaigns against the liberal oligarchy during the 1880s. Once more the Catholics sallied forth in battle as the enemies of "tyranny." "Only the totalitarian state," declared García de Loydi, referring to the fallen regime, "monopolizes teaching and makes the schools into instruments of party propaganda."[142] Perón unleashed "the most sadistic persecution of the church in the history of the Argentine Republic."[143] "There were two contradictory Peróns," he claimed,

the colonel, who soaked himself in the Nationalist ideal, and the general, who became the tool of the sordid plans of international liberalism. . . . There was a captivating, attractive Perón . . . and another who was an egotistical Caesar who rubbed out every single human right.[144]

The Nationalists regarded Perón as the "tool of international liberalism" because over the past few years he had reopened the country to foreign investment and a few months before his fall made an agreement with Standard Oil of California to develop the local oil industry. But Perón was simultaneously a tool of international Marxism, since social justice "has become contaminated by Marxist dialectic."[145] The Communists, argued Amadeo, intended to take command of the Peronist movement, since the "Marxist Left only objects to Perón himself, but looks at his movement as a powerful weapon against imperialism."[146] In Sánchez Sorondo's view, Perón fell because he had adopted "the ideas of those who were originally his enemies," the Communists, which led him into the "crazy conflict with the church."[147]

In 1955, the conviction among the Nationalists that Perón had become a Communist fellow-traveler found some characteristically wild expressions. When the battle against the regime was reaching its climax in mid-1955, Perón's opponents fought back against government censorship by flooding the country with anonymous mimeographed cartoons and manifestos. One of the documents in this so-called war of the pamphlets issued in May 1955 bore the title. "Peronism, the Instrument of Soviet Communism in Argentina." It warned the country that "after the decapitation of the unions, the universities, the judiciary, and the church will come the decapitation of the army and the establishment of a people's army as the first step to a dictatorship of the proletariat."[148] The pamphlet claimed that the Soviet Union was "training Communist leaders for undercover penetration"; there were "thousands of Communists [in Argentina] sent by Moscow with false passports, . . . [Communists who were] Jews for the most part."[149] Masons and Jews, it declared, had formed a partnership with Perón to control the white slave traffic to Buenos Aires and the brothels set up by the government, in which "many of the women are Communist spies."[150] By 1955, there was therefore no doubt that in the eyes of the Nationalists, Perón had become the incarnation of evil.

From Lonardi to Illia

In September 1955, the Nationalists once more occupied the most salient command positions in the military rebellion and the liberals the more secondary roles. But again the former proved relatively weak, and they were quickly elbowed aside by the liberals. Franceschi commented that during the early 1940s, the church was commonly accused of "extreme nationalism," a charge he had rejected at the time but now thought "partly justified." The church had long ago abandoned such alignments, he claimed, because the Nationalists had provoked "innumerable disorders" and their ideas were "incompatible with Catholicism." Nevertheless,

even today among some individuals Nationalist tendencies have survived. [They are visible] in antipathies toward democracy, . . . in the aspiration for a leader with absolute power, in a distaste for liberalism, and in the rejection of independent thinking.[151]

For a few weeks in late 1955, these "Nationalist tendencies" promoted chiefly by General Lonardi attempted to use the government to take over the Peronist movement. As he became the president of the new military junta, Lonardi proclaimed the slogan, "Neither victors nor vanquished": he would prosecute the Peronist "criminals" but would otherwise preserve intact the institutions established since 1943.[152] But the plan quickly raised fears of another bout of authoritarian rule under Nationalist extremists. The Lonardi government contained two factions, recalled Juan Carlos Goyeneche, who served as Lonardi's press secretary,

the liberal group that was full of hatred and the desire for revenge . . . and the Nationalist group that wanted to protect Perón's social reforms and eliminate only its mistakes. The Nationalists also wanted to have one or two Peronists in the cabinet to avoid a break with the Peronists that could lead to hatred and injustice.[153]

Within scarcely a month of Perón's downfall, "a head-on struggle between Nationalists and [liberals erupted] in the military and the government."[154] On November 8, the liberals forced the resignation of General León Justo Bengoa, the Nationalist minister of war, whom they accused of failing to purge the Peronists from the military. Then the liberals blocked the appointment of another Nationalist, Luis María del Pablo Pardo, as interior minister.[155] Finally, on November 13, the liberals forced Lonardi himself to resign and appointed General Pedro Aramburu the new provisional president.

For the next two years, the Nationalists turned against Aramburu in the same way they opposed Justo in the early 1930s. Yet on this occasion, the tactics of the Nationalists were very different, since they now emerged as the sponsors of popular rule, elections, and personal freedoms. "No government or ideology can survive," Amadeo conceded, "unless it can capture the people."[156] "It was wrong and tragic," declared Sánchez Sorondo, "to substitute Perón by the same men, parties and policies . . . Perón defeated in elections."[157] Against accusations in *Time* magazine that they were "friendly with dictators and anti-American," the Nationalists retorted that they supported "free elections, democracy, and the rule of law."[158] At this point, as one of their opponents conceded, the Nationalists were using "more measured language, more thought out points of view and more up-to-date opinions." They were at least pretending, he added, "to love liberty and to display a profound respect for the rights of the individual."[159]

Under Aramburu, the Nationalists sought to sponsor a popular movement that would include all "those on this side of the barricade . . . to defeat a minority, traitorous" military junta. In February 1957, Bonifacio Lastra and other Nationalists established a Christian Labor party that included a substantial number of women members.[160] For a brief period, it seemed that the Nationalists were creating a substantial popular constituency. Nationalist rallies frequently attracted large audiences, and a new Nationalist newspaper, *Azul y Blanco*, under the editorship of Sánchez Sorondo, claimed a circulation of 100,000.[161]

The shift to the popular arena marked an attempt to prolong the effort begun by Lonardi to capture control of the Peronist movement. If the attempt succeeded, it would provide the

Nationalists with a ready-made mass base and prevent the Peronist movement from being taken over by leftists. In 1956–1957, the Nationalists curried favor with the Peronists by opposing the restoration of the constitution of 1853 to replace that of 1949. In June 1956, they condemned the execution by the government of the Peronist rebels led by General Juan José Valle and supported the Peronist unions during the repressive onslaught that began immediately after Aramburu became president.

The Nationalists now seemed finally to acknowledge that the era of "mass politics" was irreversible and the backward-looking authoritarianism of the past gone forever. Yet their opponents remained unconvinced by this apparent change of heart. In a study of the Nationalist movement published in 1957, a Socialist politician, Oscar A. Troncoso, exposed its long authoritarian associations and contended that its current democratic leanings were a sham. The Nationalists, Troncoso argued, wanted a new Perón under their own control, who would combine power over the masses with leadership over the army. Amadeo, for example, who had served as Lonardi's foreign minister, Troncoso continued, still referred to democracy as a system that possessed merely "instrumental value," as opposed to being an end in itself. Amadeo's appeals to Nationalists "to assume the concerns, emotions, language, and idiosyncrasies of our people" rang with hypocrisy and opportunism.[162] Quoting José María de Estrada, the latest of the natural law theoreticians, Troncoso demonstrated that the Nationalists continued to separate the notion of liberty from democracy. "Liberty is a value that stands on its own," Estrada had written. Liberty is "linked with natural law. If Nationalists have made the mistake of not granting the idea of liberty the importance it deserves, it is also wrong to view liberty as the consequence of democracy."[163]

Troncoso defined the Nationalists as a "multicolored" movement, whose allegiances changed according to the circumstances of the moment. During successive periods, he wrote, the Nationalists "waved the flaming red of the Federalists, the black shirt of the Fascists, a little later on the brown of the Nazis, and then the blue of the Falange." In 1957, the

Nationalists were embracing the blue and white of the Argentine flag, as in the periodical *Azul y Blanco*, but still covertly supporting a political system like that of Franco's Spain.[164] In the preface to Troncoso's book, Ignacio Martins put the same point of view even more bluntly. The Nationalists, he wrote, were obnoxious "political speculators," who made "facile speeches full of impossible demands"; they were "low," "mediocre," and backed by a "reactionary clergy."[165]

Attacks like these from the press and the political parties rapidly destroyed the hopes the Nationalists cherished of inheriting Perón's great popular constituency. When their popular following declined as rapidly as it had arisen, the Nationalists finally enlisted in the coalition of Radical Intransigents (Unión Cívica Radical Intransigente) led by Arturo Frondizi. They believed Frondizi would be "faithful to the country's traditions, to its sovereignty, and to social justice."[166] Waving the banner of popular nationalism and skillfully negotiating the support of the exiled Perón, Frondizi emerged victorious in the election of February 1958. But when Frondizi assumed the presidency later that year, the hopes of the Nationalists were dashed yet again. Rapidly changing his colors, Frondizi took an anticlerical position on the issue of the schools, jettisoned his nationalist program, and began constructing an alliance with the multinational corporations.

As Troncoso claimed in 1957, the tie between the Nationalists and democracy proved superficial and short-lived. By 1960, the Nationalists were again divided as Amadeo, the leader of one faction, attempted to cling to Frondizi while Sánchez Sorondo, heading another group, bitterly opposed him. Sánchez Sorondo once more endorsed a military government "above parties and factions" and a neo-Maurrasian "organic democracy that recognizes the family, the military, the organizations of labor and production, the municipalities as structural components of the nation."[167] He demanded government by "the best men of the country, . . . [by] the true elite" and "the destruction of the parasitical Marxist cyst in our universities."[168]

In succeeding years, antiquated, marginal, and ineffective as they so often appeared, the Nationalists still remained a force to be reckoned with. In 1963, Arturo Illia, president of another weak constitutional government like Frondizi's, once more felt obliged to seek support from the Nationalists and offered an ambassadorship to Sánchez Sorondo.[169] At this point, the Nationalists continued to control numerous key command positions in the military, the church, and the universities. For several years, for example, Brigadier Hugo Martínez Zuviría, one of the numerous sons of "Hugo Wast," who was described as "a Nationalist who does not hide his admiration for Germany," served as the head of the Escuela Superior de Guerra, the leading military academy.[170] Another prominent military figure with strong Nationalist connections was Colonel Francisco Guevara. The son of a once-rich Mendoza vineyard owner, who was educated by Catholic seminarians, Guevara was said to have sympathized with Germany before World War II, until the "neopaganism" and the "racial persecution" of the Nazis led him to reject them. Guevara had a major role in the revolts of 1955 against Perón and in Lonardi's generous tribute, single-handedly accomplished "90 percent of the revolution; the remaining 10 percent was our job."[171] During the early 1960s, Guevara emerged as one of the leading sponsors of a Nationalist movement of the masses modeled on Nasser's Egypt.

During the 1960s, Nationalist priests like Meinvielle and Castellani continued to publish innumerable books and articles. The Rosas Institute, now directed by Jorge María Ramallo, who held a doctoral degree from the University of Madrid, issued a bimonthly bulletin and offered regular classes in the doctrines of revisionism.[172] Meanwhile, the revisionist historians, led by Julio Irazusta and José María Rosa, piled up more large quantities of new research. The message of the revisionists had undergone little change since the late 1930s. Rosas remained their fixation, because "he organized the most complete regime of collaboration between the different social sectors that the country has ever known."[173]

Under Aramburu, the Nationalists waged bitter campaigns to protect their positions in the schools and universities against a "virulent leftist advance."[174] In 1956, a group of Nationalist law students in the University of Buenos Aires established a "law school union" (*sindicato universitario de derecho*), whose aim was to resist the "Bolshevization" of the university by left-wingers. Ten years later, this association continued to function, continually drawing recruits from each new generation of students.[175] In the late 1960s, law students could still recite the basic dogmas of Nationalism by rote. Since man was a social animal, one of them wrote in 1967, the foundation of "true representation" lay in "integration." In the past, academic history had been "one of the principal means that antinational interests had used for the systematic falsification of our past. . . . To deny the ontological reality of a nation is to deprive it of its true future." The country needed a "ruling class based on superior intellect."[176]

In the 1960s, some of the leading Nationalists used the advent of air travel to reestablish an international network; the Nationalists hosted their ideological kin from Europe and occasionally from the United States in Buenos Aires and made their own pilgrimages abroad. In late 1966, for example, Goyeneche, formerly Lonardi's press secretary, reported on his recent visit to Lisbon to attend an international conference led by the Committee for the Defense of Christian Civilization.[177] Goyeneche's connections with the Nationalists went back to the mid-1930s. During the Spanish civil war, he served as the editor of *Sol y Luna*, one of the main propaganda vehicles in Argentina for Franco and the doctrines of *hispanidad*. During World War II, he fought for the Nazis on the Russian front alongside Spanish volunteers in the "blue brigade." After a brief stint in the Lonardi government in 1955, he played a major part in the attempt under Aramburu to organize a "national front" under Nationalist leadership.

During the early 1960s, Meinvielle was widely suspected of links with the Organisation Armée Secrète (OAS), which led the armed right-wing resistance to French president Charles de Gaulle. At one point, Meinvielle was considered for but eventually denied a position in the Catholic University of Buenos Aires, where some hoped he would counteract the influence of the Catholic reformers inspired by the Second Vatican Council.[178] Genta, once a Mason and a Marxist, now possessed a close connection with senior figures in the Argentine air force.[179] Federico Ibarguren, a vice president of the Rosas Institute, held a teaching position at the University of La Plata.

By the 1960s, the oldest members of the Nationalist movement had been active for more than forty years: they were now old men, and some were dead. Carlos Ibarguren, whose public career ended in the early 1940s, died in 1956; Gálvez, Laferrère, Palacio, and Scalabrini Ortiz during the early 1960s; Rodolfo Irazusta in 1967; and Carulla in 1968 in his eightieth year.

The younger Nationalists often differed from the older in having a lower-middle-class and immigrant background. Typical among these younger figures was Omar Lazuzzi, who was forty-four years old in 1966 and an employee of the provincial government of Córdoba. Lazuzzi joined the Nationalists as a young man during World War II as a supporter of neutrality and the church. He originally supported Perón, too, but abandoned him when he "betrayed" the Nationalist cause during the mid-1940s.[180] Ex-Brigadier Gilberto Oliva, born in Córdoba the same year as Lazuzzi, was an example of the middle-ranking Nationalists in the military. After gaining a law degree during Perón's first government, Oliva joined the Menéndez rebellion in 1951, suffering imprisonment and a dishonorable discharge as a result. He returned to the military after Perón's fall but a few years later, in 1963, was again purged after backing the losing side in internal conflicts in the military.[181] Below such second-rank figures was a highly factionalized contingent of young Nationalists, whose members once more were mainly law students. Some of the youth groups were now resuming the customs and styles of the 1930s, for example, the use of paramilitary uniforms and the Fascist salute.[182]

"No other movement," remarked an observer in a reference to the Nationalists in 1962, "has had such an influence in the realm of ideas . . . and none failed so often in politics."[183] After splitting during Frondizi's government, Sánchez Sorondo and Amadeo feuded endlessly over whether they should support a military dictatorship or attempt to infiltrate whichever government achieved power. Meanwhile, the youth groups chafed against the dominance of those they called the "gray-heads." In the early 1960s, observers sometimes distinguished between the "old" and the "new" Nationalists. The former were pro-Franco, anti-Communist "McCarthyites" pledged to dictatorship, and the latter, like Colonel Guevara, were those who wanted a form of "Nasserism."[184]

From his exile in Madrid, Perón continued to deride the Nationalists for their "hegemonic pretences and their mania for organizing elites."[185] Yet his criticism, which evaluated the movement by the standards of votes or numbers, in some respects missed the point. The power of the Nationalists lay in their ability to raise issues, set goals, and influence the attitudes of even their sworn enemies. "The Nationalist movement has played an important part in the country's political history," concluded Basilio Serrano in 1968.

Its thought and action have influenced nearly all the political groups. It has imposed some strong feelings and ideas on public opinion. Yet I do not think the movement can ever become a united political bloc. . . . In this country ideology appears to be at odds with political success.[186]

Although the Nationalists commanded no overt popular support, there was some validity to their own claim that in one form or another their ideas were "admitted and professed by the vast majority."[187] In 1967, Julio Irazusta observed that although the Nationalists had failed to evolve into a political movement, thanks to their activities, "national consciousness had taken a gigantic step forward." Irazusta compared himself and other prominent historical revisionists with the leaders of the *Risorgimento*, whose efforts had paved the way for the unification of Italy.[188] Denouncing a study of the Nationalist movement by an American historian in 1969 as full of "inexactitudes and verbal violence," a Nationalist reviewer lamented that in her account,

the Nationalist movement appears as little more than a bunch of armed bands, [its] intellectuals debating by what kind of ferocious totalitarianism they planned to replace the decadent liberal state.[189]

Although the academic Nationalists like Irazusta claimed positions of respectability and high public standing, there remained at least in a loose sense ample grounds for the charge of "ferocious totalitarianism." Sánchez Sorondo constantly demanded a dictatorship and the purge of the universities. Genta continued to issue the ultraclerical and militarist diatribes that had been his trademark for the past twenty-five years. The Catholic church, Genta proclaimed in a 1960 piece, for example, represented the only salvation from communism; "Judaism, Masonry, and communism are the three manifestations of the negation of the divine redeemer."[190]

Although overt anti-Semitism among the Nationalists declined after 1945, the early 1960s brought another ugly eruption of hostility toward Jews following the capture and abduction of Adolf Eichmann in Buenos Aires by Israeli agents. With Sánchez Sorondo at their head, the Nationalists denounced this action as an attack on Argentine sovereignty. Subsequently, a Jewish girl was kidnapped, mistreated, and injured, and several synagogues in Buenos Aires were defaced.[191] A few years later, the son of Leopoldo Lugones felt obliged to make a public statement to the effect that gossip among the Nationalists that his wife was Jewish was false.[192]

In 1970, the self-styled Commission for the Defense of Tradition, Family, and Property published an extensive account of the origins and intellectual history of the Nationalist movement. Here once more the usual themes appeared, unchanged over the past forty years. The commission attacked "the ideological deficiencies of the ruling elites" and the "dictatorship of the mob" and upheld the need for "order, rank, authority."[193] The commission pledged adherence to the Catholic doctrine of absolute truth, condemned Freemasonry, praised the Habsburg kings and Maurras, but deprecated the eighteenth-century Bourbons.[194] All leftist movements, the commission claimed, embodied the doctrine of "humanity without a country."[195] The commission denounced Perón as a Socialist, the rival of the Communists rather than their enemy.[196]

By the late 1960s, Walter Beveraggi Allende, who possessed law degrees from Harvard and Boston universities and a long career in the Law Faculty of the University of Buenos Aires, emerged as a prominent Nationalist figure.[197] Beveraggi

Allende began his political career in the 1940s as a left-wing opponent of Perón. His Nationalist affiliations dated from the late 1950s under Frondizi, which convinced him that "the crisis of the regime could never be overcome within the framework of legality."[198] Beveraggi Allende's *El dogma nacionalista*, published in 1969, was dedicated to the nineteenth-century caudillos led by Rosas and to the leading Nationalist authors of the interwar years: the Irazustas, Meinvielle, Lugones, Martínez Zuviría, Scalabrini Ortiz, and Castellani. Like his predecessors, Beveraggi Allende condemned "liberalism" for its cult of "science and indefinite material progress" and "democracy" because it meant "ideological colonization."[199] "True democracy" would be fulfilled through a network of self-governing local communities "truly respectful of the popular will" like the colonial cabildos.

In Beveraggi Allende's eyes, the country faced a multitude of "hidden forces"—capitalism, Marxism, Zionism—and an equal variety of "imperialisms"—British, French, Russian, American, and Jewish.[200] Argentina's only defense against these hostile forces was its "Catholic faith . . . and the formidable cultural force of indigenous tradition."[201] At present, the country was being held for ransom by "international usury," and "twenty million Argentines are working for two or three thousand usurers." *El dogma nacionalista* contained the standard attacks on political parties, Jews, foreigners, and the "privileges" of the city of Buenos Aires. In Beveraggi Allende's view, the wartime holocaust against the Jews had never happened.[202]

Nevertheless, *El dogma nacionalista* contained other expressions of changing times. In 1969, Beveraggi Allende lambasted the International Monetary Fund, psychedelic music, hippies, and erotic literature; he demanded the nationalization of the banks, a three-year crash housing program, and the creation of a national social security system. *El dogma nacionalista* contained several other incongruous features. Beveraggi Allende claimed Mahatma Gandhi as his model for the anti-imperialist struggle in Argentina.[203] He identified Raimundo Ongaro, a radical labor union leader, as a national hero of the stature of Rosas or Lugones. With the single exception that he was a Catholic, Ongaro seemed the absolute antithesis of the Nationalists. Beveraggi Allende's willingness to adopt him illustrated the way the church was now helping to establish linkages between the Nationalist Right and the newly emergent Nationalist Left. Here lay a crucial trend, because in the convergence of these extremes lay one of the main elements in the great conflicts of the 1970s.

Chapter Seven

Authoritarians, Populists, and Revolutionaries

The intense conflicts that followed the fall of Perón in 1955 led to civil war and dictatorship in the 1970s and finally in the 1980s to a renascent but fragile democracy. Throughout this thirty-year period, the Nationalist movement, often to a greater degree than ever before, again strongly influenced all Argentina's major institutions: the military, the church, the political parties and mass movements, and even the ostensibly left-wing groups committed to "armed struggle." The period after 1960 can be divided into three phases. The first marked the emergence of the "doctrine of national security" during the early 1960s and encompassed the military regime led by Juan Carlos Onganía from 1966 to 1970. The second phase, which witnessed the rise of new populist and revolutionary movements, overlapped to some extent with the first phase in the late 1960s but continued until the mid-1970s. The third phase began in 1976 under the military juntas known as the Process of National Reorganization and concluded in late 1983 on their downfall.

The Doctrine of National Security and the "Argentine Revolution"

After 1955, the Argentine military pledged itself to prevent the Peronists from regaining power ever again and to halt the spread of "subversion" from abroad. In pursuit of these objectives, the military adopted the "doctrine of national security," whose main theses were as follows: first, that "subversion" represented a "hidden enemy" and formed part of a "world conspiracy" of Communists against the West; second, that national security and economic development were linked and that the military could not accomplish the former without the latter; and third, that the military had the right to apply certain tests and standards to civilian governments, failing which they could be overthrown.

During the early 1960s, a faction known as the *colorados* ("reds") dominated the military. They were committed to an all-out war on the Peronists and to a military dictatorship that would remain in power for as long as it took to destroy them. The colorados dominated the Frondizi government that took power in 1958 and, after a long string of confrontations, in early 1962 finally overthrew it.

In 1962, however, the attempt to impose a long-term dictatorship failed. A few months after the fall of Frondizi, a rival military faction dubbed the *azules* ("blues") displaced the colorados from dominance. The azules were as strongly opposed to the Peronists as the colorados; the chief differences between the two groups stemmed from the relationship they envisaged between the government and the military. Countering the colorado demand for a military government, the azules argued that direct military rule would taint and discredit the armed forces, as they believed had happened in the period 1955–1958 under Aramburu. They therefore insisted that the government be returned to the civilians and the military withdraw to its proper "professional" responsibilities in national defense and security. The azules, led by General Onganía, seized control of the de facto government from the colorados in September 1962 and then, in armed skirmishes the following April, defeated an attempted comeback by their opponents. Soon after, in July 1963, elections were held, and in October the same year another civilian government took power under the Popular Radical party led by Illia.[1]

While the colorados remained dominant, there was a particularly strong French influence in the Argentine military. Its chief sources lay in the similarities the colorados perceived between their own struggle against the Peronists and the French struggle against the insurgent movement in Algeria. Contact with the French began in 1957 when two senior French officers arrived in Buenos Aires to instruct Argentine officers in the War Academy (Escuela Superior de Guerra).[2] The French specialists, who possessed links with the Organisation Armée Secrète (OAS), argued that the nuclear age had produced a military stalemate between East and West. As a result, the Communists would no longer risk a direct military confrontation with the West. Instead they would attempt to encircle it by slowly capturing control of peripheral nations through "subversion." According to the French experts, subversion did not necessarily mean open revolutionary warfare, rebellion, or acts of terrorism. They viewed the subversives as a "hidden enemy" who would work behind the scenes, surreptitiously taking control of key institutions like the trade unions, the political parties, the mass media, and the universities.[3] Thus, "a new form of war, lateral war, revolutionary war," had begun which would determine the future course of the world.[4]

These French influences became visible in the edict sponsored by the military in March 1960 to combat the Peronists. Known as the Plan CONINTES (*Conmoción Interna del Estado*), or Plan for Civil Insurrection against the State, the measure was directed at "terrorists and their sympathizers" and threatened action not only against those who engaged in "terrorist acts in themselves . . . but against those who have any kind of connection with them: . . . organizers, instigators, promoters, accomplices and anyone helping to conceal terrorists." The Plan CONINTES followed French practice in Algeria by dividing the country into military districts under separate commanders, by granting the commanders wide powers, and by menacing "terrorists" with military tribunals and lengthy terms of imprisonment.[5]

By the early 1960s, the ideas of the French instructors began to surface in the writings of Argentine military strategists. In a work published in 1963, General Osiris G. Villegas proposed the concept of "permanent war."[6] "Peace," he wrote, twisting the famous dictum of von Clausewitz, "is the continuation of war by other means."[7] "The war is developing within our own frontiers," he warned. "Its dangers are as threatening to us as any of the wars fought in the standard fashion."[8] "Subversion is the procedure chosen. The destruction of the nation is the object of this mortal enemy."[9] Subversion operated through the covert penetration "of all the national power structures" including "the labor unions and the universities."[10]

While reflecting the teachings of the French, Villegas was also recycling some long-ingrained Nationalist notions. He described himself, for example, as a supporter of democracy but defined democracy, like the Nationalists, as "a new humanism" opposed to "prevailing materialist ideas."[11] Yet democracy in any form was inherently risky, Villegas believed, because it would allow the Communists greater freedom for "infiltration." "In the course of the revolutionary war," he wrote, "the grasp of the military on political power should be relative to the magnitude of the threat and the effectiveness of the government in combating it."[12] In another comment strongly reminiscent of the Nationalists, Villegas denounced "the new conception of man" supposedly advanced by the Communists which sought "to destroy and supplant the millenary western culture."[13] He drew on the legacy of Lugones as he proclaimed the army's "final responsibility to protect the native spirit against any attempt to destroy it."[14] In 1963, Villegas advised the military to avoid "excessive violence or uncontrolled reactions . . . that will only serve to impede or betray reconciliation and harmony."[15] But aside from this note of moderation—destined to disappear in later formulations—Villegas was advancing the basic principles of the doctrine of national security that henceforth became increasingly embedded in the military command.

Toward the mid-1960s, military thinking took another direction when the azules gained supremacy. In the view of the azules, the armed forces could best fulfill their "professional" mission of national security and defense by becoming the agents of economic and social modernization: in economic progress, they argued, lay the key to national security and the best insurance against subversion. Posing a relationship between security and development was scarcely original, since the idea had been strongly entrenched elsewhere in Latin America, particularly in Brazil, for example, since the early 1950s.[16] In Argentina, the link had hitherto received less attention because it had a ring of Peronism, but it now finally caught on as a reflection of the growing influence of the Alliance for Progress.

By early 1964, links between the azules and the U.S. military had replaced those between the colorados and the French. Although the Argentine military ranked only sixth among the Latin American nations to receive military aid from the United States under the Alliance for Progress, the period 1963–1966 brought a large influx of American military aid, while growing numbers of Argentine officers began training in American military bases abroad.[17] The Alliance for Progress stressed expanding the scope of the military's activities in such areas as road building, irrigation projects, and developing communications. "If during the '50s," commented an observer, "the army began to study the new ideas from France . . . it is in the '60s that it has begun to define new functions for itself."[18] The problem was, however, that these "new functions" had no defined limits, and they indirectly encouraged military leaders to see themselves as responsible for the entire national agenda. Here lay the seeds of a new philosophy of military intervention that in the event quickly destroyed the commitment of the azules to civilian government and to a purely "professional" military.

In August 1964, General Onganía, the leader of the azules, addressed the West Point military academy in the United States. At the commencement of his speech, Onganía restated the position taken by the azules in 1962–63: the military, he declared, should encourage and support government by civilians, which it should obey and respect. But Onganía then completely shifted his ground and issued a long list of hypothetical situations in which the military's "duty to obey" the government became a responsibility to intervene against it. The military, for example, would be released from its obligation to support the civilian government, if Communists [*ideologías exóticas*] were to undermine the government's authority and threaten the basic republican form of government, . . . if there were a violent disruption of the balance or the separation of powers, or the use of government power in a way that destroyed the rights and liberties of the citizens.

The military could step in if "totalitarian organizations" gained control over the political parties or the opposition groups, or "if the government were to allow the growth of a totalitarian movement able to take power; or if internal subversion were such that it disrupted the community and the rights of individuals." Since the military now had the task of ensuring economic development, it could intervene "whenever government policy led to a decline in living standards, and thus fostered an environment favorable to Communist propaganda." Finally, civilian governments, declared Onganía, were under a stringent compulsion to strengthen the democratic system but under the same "inescapable obligation to let the military participate in the broader issues of government."[19]

Under these stiff but vague guidelines, the civilian governments faced an obviously daunting task. Onganía claimed the right to intervene if, in his own judgment as army commander, the slightest semblance of "totalitarianism" were to appear, but it remained a mystery whether he included the Peronists, as well as Communists, under this rubric. The civilian government had to achieve economic growth and consolidate democracy but let the military determine the basic objectives of policy. For Onganía, the government's obligation to uphold "liberty" meant much more than simply protecting basic liberal freedoms. Inherent to his notion of liberty was the successful pursuit of economic progress: without that, liberty did not exist.

The West Point speech had the tone of an academic treatise or a legal brief but was meant as a sharp rebuke to the Illia government. Illia achieved power with the support of barely a fifth of the electorate, and he was soon facing coordinated waves of strikes led by Peronists. As the unrest mounted, it became clear that Onganía believed the government had failed to meet the standards he prescribed. In May 1964, General Julio Alsogaray, one of Onganía's associates, warned that the country was close to a state of full-blown "subversion," which he defined as a stage by stage process beginning with infiltration and climaxing in guerrilla warfare.[20]

Now convinced of the need to take power, Onganía began to lay his plans, marshaling the support of the military and the press and making vague promises of future concessions in an attempt to win the support of the Peronist unions. Finally, in early June 1966, General Pascual Pistarini, who had recently replaced the openly dissident Onganía as army commander, accused Illia to his face of "inefficiency" and of failing to protect "liberty."[21] Only three weeks later came the smoothly executed and feebly resisted coup d'etat that established the government of the *"Revolución Argentina"* (Argentine Revolution).

On taking power, the new regime issued several proclamations that, like so many of their predecessors, rang with the language of the Nationalists. The "Act of the Argentine Revolution" alleged an

appalling conduct of public affairs by the [deposed] government, [its responsibility] for breaking the spiritual unity of the Argentine people, [for the prevailing] apathy and the loss of national sentiment, [for] the absence of order and discipline, [and for] profound social disruption.

Illia's incompetence, the act continued, allowed "covert but aggressive Marxist penetration" and "extremist outbreaks" that exposed the country to a takeover by "collectivist totalitarianism." The mission of the military, declared the act, was "to safeguard the nation's highest interests"; the military was taking control, "as in all decisive stages of our history," to achieve a "profound transformation."[22]

In a similar vein, the "Message of the Revolutionary Junta to the Argentine People" claimed that Illia's government made "electoralism into a system" and encouraged "a collision of antagonistic interests"; government and public services had become the cat's-paws of "electoral games"; the civilian politicians and the political parties had "betrayed the

state" by exposing the country to attack by "powerful enemies" and Marxist infiltration. The coup was thus a

historic imperative. . . . If we wish to preserve our identity as a free
civilized society and the essential values of our way of life . . . we
must unite around the great principles of our Western Christian
tradition.[23]

In all democracies, the message claimed, society invariably
lapsed into a jungle of isolated individuals, who required the
"protection" of an authoritarian government to recover their
"natural" social identity. The "masses" remained perennially
susceptible to "corruption." The new government, the message continued, would regenerate the nation. The role of the
military was to "interpret the [nation's] highest common interests" and to protect and restore "national unity"; its "mission" was to defend Western Christian tradition; it would promote "general welfare," while "raising the country to the
status it deserves."[24]

As this choice of language illustrated, there was a strong
Nationalist presence in the new military government. Onganía himself had close links with the Cursillos de Cristiandad and the Opus Dei, both of them extreme clerical associations of Spanish origin of the type Nationalists had often
patronized in the past.[25] Foreign Minister Nicanor Costa Mén-
dez, Secretary of the Interior Mario Díaz Colodrero, and
Mario Amadeo, who became ambassador to Brazil, were all
members of the Ateneo de la República (Atheneum of the
Republic), a Nationalist club formed in 1962 in readiness for
the day "the military would take power and lead the transformation of every arena of national society."[26] Although the
Ateneo group was considered relatively moderate, the government contained other Nationalists of an extreme bent. Enrique Martínez Paz, Onganía's first minister of the interior,
for example, repeatedly berated "old-style politics." The political parties, he declared, in another Nationalist cliché, had
revealed their "lack of true representativeness, their inau-
thenticity, their egotism."[27]

The Onganía regime also bore the strong imprint of the
azules. According to them, the armed forces had the right to

terminate a government but having done this, they should immediately return to their "professional" activities. As a result, although the regime took power by coup d'etat and nominated a general as president, azul doctrine forbade government by military junta. Instead, Onganía insisted on maintaining the fiction that the military no longer formed part of the government: he would rule alone on the authority of the personal power vested in him by the revolutionary statutes. Illustrating the relationship the azules saw between national security and economic development, the government established the National Council for Economic Development, known as CONADE (Consejo Nacional de Desarrollo), and the National Council for Security, known as CONASE (Consejo Nacional de Seguridad), proclaiming that the two bodies would work closely together and complement each other. In an example of the strong American influences on the azul group, General Villegas, who became the head of CONASE, took as his personal motto a statement by John F. Kennedy that weak societies would perish and only the strong survive.[28]

The leading figures in the regime referred to themselves as "the guiding nucleus of the popular mass."[29] Villegas envisaged revolutionary change being accomplished through what he called a "conscious national project to unify and enthuse the people, by an elite to plan and direct the project, by a leader to interpret it, and by a social dynamic to support and execute it."[30] Yet references to "the people" and the "social dynamic" were more examples of wishful thinking, since despite the expectations he cultivated before the coup, Onganía made only token efforts to win popular support. The government was a dictatorship "impregnated," as a later commentator accurately remarked, "with a hostility to all forms of political mobilization."[31]

On taking power, Onganía closed congress, deposed the provincial governors, and banned and bankrupted the political parties by confiscating their properties and assets. Martínez Paz then embarked on a defamatory campaign against the public universities, denouncing them as "a focus of ideological disruption, a forward trench of the Cold War, an internal front that serves to hide the enemy."[32] In early August 1966, scarcely a month after taking control, the regime "intervened" the universities, which meant eliminating their self-governing authorities and placing them under direct government control. To implement the measure in the University of Buenos Aires, riot police armed with clubs stormed the faculty buildings and inflicted heavy beatings on those inside.

The Nationalists, who were among the chief instigators of this "night of the long sticks," loudly applauded the government's action as an "undoubtedly revolutionary operation [that brought about] the destruction of the Marxist apparatus encysted like a parasite in our universities."[33] The "apparatus," Nationalists claimed, was entrenched in certain disciplines, particularly psychoanalysis. "Marxist psychoanalysis in the universities" was based on

a conception of man that is exclusively materialist and mechanistic. The psychoanalyst wields a pedagogical influence lacking any spiritual or metaphysical content. This conception, which is scientifically and medically false, is dangerous to the social and moral structure. . . . It is essential to wipe out the evil influence of Marxism represented by destructive professors who teach a mechanistic and materialistic form of psychoanalysis.[34]

Even if members of the university faculties were democrats rather than Marxists, it was advisable to purge them too, because according to another time-worn Nationalist dogma, "it is well-known that liberalism engenders communism."[35]

In similar style, in May 1967, Onganía promulgated a vaguely worded "defense law against communism," whose aim was to counteract "ideological infiltration, economic pressure from abroad and subversive action."[36] In yet another illustration of the influence of the Nationalists at this point, Onganía expressed strong support for new forms of political representation through local corporate collectivities, or "basic community organisms." To Martínez Paz, the "basic sectors," as he called them, implied "true democratic representation," and he urged "such groups to grow and increase their influence. . . . Old-fashioned politics has been banished so that together government and people may launch a new form of

politics."[37] According to Díaz Colodrero, the government
wanted to establish new forms of federalism at the local government level to foster "revolutionary social cohesiveness."[38]

The regime depicted these ideas as "revolutionary," but
they were at least one hundred fifty years old. The "community organisms" were merely new representations of the old
Catholic aspiration to revive the guilds, or "intermediate
cells," between the individual and the state. Among the chief
intellectual mentors of the plan was Jacques Marie Mahieu,
an exile from Vichy France now settled in Argentina. Mahieu
was a veteran of the Nazi armies on the eastern front and
before that claimed to have been a member of an École des
Hautes Études Corporatifs in Paris. In postwar Argentina, *Dinámica Social* gave him a new forum for his corporatist theories. In a 1968 interview, Mahieu emphasized the similarities
between Onganía's "basic communities" and the medieval guilds. "Communitarianism," as he called the system,
represented a "midway point" to "rescue man from his soli-
tude before the forces of capitalism and from his subjection
to socialist totalitarianism."[39]

Nationalist supporters of the basic communities hoped they
would replace the political parties, which they deemed "unrepresentative" or "egotistical." The idea, however, brought
few tangible results. During subsequent years, the province
of San Luis organized a "congress of municipalities," and
Santa Fe published a "plan for communal action" designed
to pave the streets and construct new public buildings. Elsewhere, other vague proposals surfaced to represent local communities in both the provincial and national senates as soon
as these bodies were restored, which they never were under
Onganía.[40] Among Díaz Colodrero's schemes for "genuine
participation" was a "representative congress of production,
commerce and consumption."[41] Raúl Puigbó, another Nationalist in the government, hinted at subsidies for initiatives that
sprang from the municipal level.[42] In July 1968, Onganía
loftily proclaimed that the "basic organisms" would eventually lead to a "community of solidarity." A few months later,
he bestowed his patronage on a similar but no better defined
project he called conciliarism (*consejalismo*).[43]

Municipal corporatism had a few short-term results in Córdoba alone under the government of Carlos Caballero, another rabid Nationalist who gained power under Onganía. In parts of Córdoba, local clubs and neighborhood associations, as opposed to individual voters, nominated the members of municipal councils.[44] During these years, Córdoba emerged as the hotbed of popular radicalism but simultaneously lived up to its long reputation as a bastion of clericalism. In early 1971, for example, another Nationalist governor of Córdoba, José Camilo Uriburu, was heard to utter the claim that "governors speak with the word of God."[45]

The Armed Bands

The Grupo Tacuara de la Juventud Nacional (Tacuara Group of National Youth) first appeared in late 1957. *Tacuara* is the term for a gaucho lance and illustrated the group's sympathies with the historical revisionists. The group consisted of remnants of earlier Catholic student organizations, including some branches of Acción Católica. Its original purpose was to achieve the return of religious teaching in the schools, a ban reimposed by Perón shortly before his overthrow and upheld by his successors.[46] In the early 1960s, however, Tacuara became known as a gang of violent right-wing hoodlums whose ideological line stood at some indistinct point between nazism and falangism. Alberto Ezcurra, a descendant of General Uriburu and the leader of Tacuara at this time, unabashedly proclaimed himself a Nazi, although most members of the organization, including Ezcurra himself, also emphasized their links with the church.[47] Indeed, beyond bigotry and a devotion to violence there was no clear line.

Tacuara had an unsavory reputation and some dubious connections. During the early 1960s, it was responsible for the rash of anti-Semitic incidents that followed the abduction of Eichmann. Some claimed that Hussein Triki, the representative of the Arab League in Argentina, had instigated these incidents and denounced him as a former Nazi sympathizer who was now paying Tacuara to attack Jews and synagogues.[48] Tacuara had another, better-documented connection with Meinvielle, who was once described by its members as their "only mentor."[49] There were other rumors that the group had a connection with Genta and through him enjoyed the protection of the Argentine air force.[50] Although Tacuara was outlawed, observers became suspicious as the group arranged periodic public press conferences that the police did nothing to prevent.[51] At one of the conferences, Ezcurra declared that Tacuara would

defend Catholic values against Marxist-Jewish-liberal-Masonic-capitalist imperialism. We are not anti-Semites with racialist aims, but we are enemies of Jewry. In Argentina the Jews are the servants of Israeli imperialism [who violated] our national sovereignty when they arrested Adolf Eichmann. In this struggle we have much in common with Nasser.[52]

Between 1960 and 1963, Tacuara underwent several splits whose main causes, beyond numerous purely personal rivalries, lay in disputes over goals and strategies following the Cuban and Algerian revolutions.[53] In November 1963, for example, a breakaway group led by José "Joe" Baxter appeared. A former student then in his early twenties, Baxter proclaimed "an opening to the Left" and the slogans "War on Imperialism!" "On March toward National Liberation!" His "strongly anti-imperialist" movement, he announced, would be modeled on the Algerian revolution but would align itself with the masses through an attachment with the Peronists. Under cross-examination by journalists, Baxter declared that he still subscribed to the basic tenets of the Nationalist movement, in particular, to historical revisionism, but was withdrawing from Tacuara because he disapproved of its tactics and procedures. The members of Tacuara, he said, did little more than act as "police informers" and as the "shock troops of the oligarchy." He attacked the "McCarthyism" of Tacuara and labeled its anti-Semitism "artificial" and "diversionary." He then spoke patronizingly of the "honest Jews" he knew. "No one can call Fidel Castro an anti-Semite," he declared, "but as a Cuban nationalist he has done away with the exploiters and so most of the Jews had to leave."

In Baxter, juvenile ingenuousness and superficiality were combined with a heavy streak of opportunism. He was abandoning the Right and taking up with the Left, mainly because, as he blandly put it, the Right had been on the losing side in 1945. Baxter announced his break with Tacuara in the Law Faculty of the University of Buenos Aires, a move that suggested he intended the faculty to be his main recruiting ground.[54] Baxter's group remained active for the next year or so. Among its exploits were a botched attempt to assassinate General Villegas, a major bank robbery, and several efforts to enlist support in the shantytowns of Buenos Aires and other cities by raiding food stores and organizing handouts to the poor. Soon Baxter was on the run and eventually fled the country, first to Nasser's Egypt and later to Ghaddafi's Libya.[55]

Baxter's activities were typical of the Tacuara groups, both right- and left-wing, whose exploits included forcing army conscripts to provide them with weapons and sometimes using them to ambush police officers. By March 1963, rumors were afoot that the police planned to retaliate by organizing death squads.[56] Yet at this point, the "armed bands," as they were known, were sporadically disruptive but small. In 1964, Tacuara itself was reckoned to have only sixty active members, of whom a mere fifteen could handle guns. Members of the bands were mostly well-educated young men (women were uncommon until around 1970) with backgrounds in the upper middle classes. Reflecting Meinvielle's influence, the right-wing groups were "profoundly religious, all of them Catholics," and the leftists of an ostensible intellectual bent who constantly "devoured philosophical and political literature."[57] Yet these intellectual pretensions failed to dispel an odor of corruption. Observers noted a "phantasmagorical range of alliances" among the bands which they attributed to their quest for money and patrons. Thus "anti-Peronists wound up becoming Peronists," or like Baxter's group, "representatives of the extreme Nationalist Right later moved over to the far Left."[58]

While some of the armed bands attempted to penetrate Peronist youth groups, others tried to fasten onto labor union leaders by offering their services as bodyguards. In 1965 and 1966, for example, members of the right-wing Movimiento Nueva Argentina (New Argentina Movement), which emerged from a 1962 split in Tacuara, acted as a self-appointed bodyguard for Isabel Perón during her visits to Argentina as Perón's representative.[59] But in the early to mid-1960s, efforts to infiltrate the Peronist movement proved unsuccessful. In 1961, the Peronist leader John William Cooke, who ironically enough was to emerge as the great intellectual mentor of a later generation of the armed bands, scorned "the tiny groups . . . that in Perón's name . . . hunt Jewish students and betray those they call Marxists to the police. Do we need this scum? If one day we win, we shall have to shoot the lot of them."[60]

Similarly unsuccessful were the attempts by the leftist groups to penetrate the small Communist party. Communists invariably rejected the intruders as "bourgeois," "right-wing Nationalists," "Catholics," and latent anti-Semites and condemned their tactics of confrontation and violence. For the Communists, the main task was grass roots work to entice support among the Peronist labor unions.[61]

In March 1964, one of the right-wing offshoots of Tacuara, the Guardia Restauradora Nacionalista (Nationalist Guard of the Restoration), the group at that time rumored to have close links with the air force, issued an incendiary proclamation warning the country of an impending Marxist uprising and urged the military into instant preparations.[62] A brief flurry of violence followed as right-wingers shot and murdered a young leftist.[63] But then the issue cooled for some time, as attentions focused on the growing crisis between Illía and the military. In July 1966, Onganía's minister of the interior, Martínez Paz, provoked a brief furor when it became known he had granted an interview to one of the leaders of Tacuara.[64] In September 1966, the New Argentina Movement gained more publicity when its members launched the "Condor Operation": the group hijacked an airplane, forced it to land on the Malvinas Islands, and from there loudly proclaimed Argentina's sovereignty over the islands. The incident concluded when the hijackers were returned to the mainland and imprisoned by the government.[65] Soon afterward, in December 1966, Tacuara itself was disbanded.[66]

The armed bands were a warning symptom of deepening political crisis but at this juncture commanded relatively little influence. Their importance lay in their role as precursors of the guerrilla groups of the 1970s that adopted and developed many of their techniques. The armed bands set the precedent of attempting to use the Peronist movement as their vehicle to power. The early 1960s illustrated the ease with which extreme right-wing groups shifted allegiance to the far Left. Finally, Tacuara and its offshoots invented new forms of political violence but in doing so, swiftly raised the specter of retaliatory death squads.

The Populist Resurgence

Despite its strong Nationalist connections, the Onganía regime quickly evolved into another political hybrid when the president entrusted control over the economy to a team of liberal technocrats led by Adalbert Krieger Vasena. This permutation of arcane Nationalists with ultramodern liberals led Cooke to describe the regime sarcastically as "a mix of the twelfth century, the nineteenth century and western technocracy."[67] Between early 1967 and mid-1969, Krieger Vasena achieved great success in combining rapid economic growth with a large influx of foreign investment and a steep fall in inflation. In late May 1969, however, the edifice he had built came crashing down following the great popular rising of workers and students in Córdoba known as the *cordobazo*. The cordobazo too proved the beginning of the end for Onganía. Having first dismissed his entire cabinet, Onganía then spent a year flailing around helplessly, until finally in early June 1970, he fell to another coup led by his army commander, General Alejandro Lanusse.

The Nationalists played a complex role in the events that led to the downfall of Onganía. In the early 1960s, the leading Nationalists remained divided, with some, like Meinvielle and Sánchez Sorondo, backing the hard-line colorados and others, including the Ateneo group, turning to the azules.[68]

By early 1967, much the same situation prevailed, and the movement remained "a mosaic of conceptions and attitudes."[69] Although the Ateneo group was supporting Onganía, other Nationalists were moving into the opposition. The primary causes of the latest division were the policies of Krieger Vasena as economy minister which stressed the expansion of foreign investment and extending the country's ties with the multinationals.

In 1967, Sánchez Sorondo and his periodical *Azul y Blanco* led the Nationalist opposition to Onganía and Krieger Vasena. Only a year before, *Azul y Blanco* had acclaimed the coup d'etat, rejoiced at the violent takeover of the universities, and waged verbal warfare against "Communists," led by prominent Jewish publisher Jacobo Timerman, entrenched in the media.[70] But the tone changed abruptly on Krieger Vasena's appointment in early 1967. Sánchez Sorondo now denounced Onganía as another Frondizi who was attempting to force the country under the yoke of "big capital." The Nationalists in the government, Sánchez Sorondo contended, were a "right-wing Catholic facade, a means to disguise the plan to alienate the national wealth to the international monopolies."[71] By late 1967, Sánchez Sorondo was continuing to shift gears as he began to urge the formation of a "popular front" to fight the government. The front would be headed by a dissident general, "any loose Colonel Blimp [*espadón*] who was hanging around," as one of Sánchez Sorondo's critics put it, but would include the banned political parties and the labor unions.[72]

For the moment, Sánchez Sorondo's new populist line remained only a veneer on his customary right-wing militancy. *Azul y Blanco* responded to the student riots of May 1968 in Paris, for example, by publishing an *Ode to Marshal Pétain*, which implied that Pétain alone and the ideals of Vichy, not President Charles de Gaulle, could succeed in maintaining public order in France.[73] Sánchez Sorondo attacked Krieger Vasena with anti-Semitic innuendoes, claiming that his success in attracting the multinationals to Argentina was due to his close relationship with Jewish-American politicians like

Senator Jacob Javits.[74] Meanwhile, Sánchez Sorondo kept up a barrage of demands for the British to quit the Malvinas Islands, an issue that became particularly intense in 1967–68 when the Labour government in Britain appeared ready to open negotiations over the status of the islands.

But simultaneously some strange and surprising new elements were starting to emerge in Sánchez Sorondo's weekly articles. In October 1967, *Azul y Blanco* dwelled, incongruously and uncharacteristically, on the plight of the urban poor in the shantytowns of Buenos Aires to attack Onganía's policies on housing and foreign investment.[75] Totally reversing the position he had taken only a year before, Sánchez Sorondo now declared himself "unworried by hypothetical speculations" among members of the government that the country faced a threat from leftist subversion.[76] He thought it "ridiculous and depressing" that Onganía was willing to become the "champion of professional anti-communism to score points in the eyes of the United States."[77] In yet another untypical move, Sánchez Sorondo sought to ally himself with Raimundo Ongaro, the radical labor leader who was now attempting to create a parallel labor movement to challenge the government.[78] Finally, Sánchez Sorondo embraced new trends in the church that attacked monopoly capitalism.[79]

Sánchez Sorondo and *Azul y Blanco* reflected changes taking place in the Nationalist movement at large, as the opponents of Onganía began to search for allies among Peronists and even the leftists.[80] In mid-1967, Meinvielle, for example, announced his support for *Populorum Progressio*, the newly issued papal encyclical. The church now recognized, he declared, that it had "to begin anew on every level" and must no longer work "from above. It had to create a new order from below." Meinvielle's normally conservative line on economic issues began to echo the newly emergent left-wing "dependency" writers. "The country has achieved its great leaps forward in economic development during the world wars" when "imperialism" had weakened, he wrote. The secret of future prosperity and national grandeur therefore lay in a "policy of independence" under a "directive elite" linked to the popular masses.[81]

By late May 1968—exactly twelve months before the cordobazo—Sánchez Sorondo was prophesying a popular insurrection in Argentina that would match the recent explosion in Paris. "The outbreak is imminent and inevitable," he wrote. "It will come like a gigantic, sudden spasm."[82] Dismissing Onganía's vision of the "community of solidarity" as "gaseous," he attacked the president for failing to create effective channels of popular representation. The government was being torn apart, he claimed, by conflicts between the liberals led by Krieger Vasena and the Nationalists of the Ateneo group. Thus, "a united people unable to make itself heard" faced "governing groups that are absurdly segmented and divided."[83] In the past, he argued, the true Nationalist movement, as distinct from the traitorous Ateneo faction, had served as a way of breaking "political deadlock" (*decompresión política*) and as an instrument of "cultural revolution." Its third, and now imminent, role was to lead the "National Revolution and eject the liberals from their bastions of power."[84]

There was now an open convergence between the Nationalists and segments of the Argentine Left. In September 1968, *Azul y Blanco* displayed advertisements by local publishing houses which listed the works of classic Nationalist authors like Enrique Osés and José María Rosa alongside those of former Communists like Rodolfo Puiggrós.[85] The same month, *Azul y Blanco* contended that the members of a small guerrilla band recently taken prisoner in the province of Tucumán were not leftists, as the government claimed, but government-paid provocateurs.[86] The regime's declared reasons for supporting the creation of a Pan-American military force to combat guerrillas was based on an "unserviceable theory." Rather than manifestations of a "worldwide Communist offensive," as the national security doctrinaires like Villegas were claiming, the guerrilla movements of Latin America were propaganda inventions of the United States designed to "force the South American governments into letting the Pentagon meddle in their military plans and preparations."[87]

In Argentina the "anti-subversion struggle" was being used as "an excuse to repress non-Marxist nationalist forces."[88] The government, Sánchez Sorondo claimed, had hired Guillermo Patricio Kelly, the gunman who had served Perón, and it was the government that was therefore responsible for the rising climate of violence now pervading the country.

Since the government . . . hires gangsters . . . it has no right to protest if citizens react violently to defend themselves. . . . It's a bad sign that gunmen are being set loose under government protection, and even worse that honest men have to do for themselves what in any orderly society is carried out by the agents of law and order.[89]

Sánchez Sorondo still pandered to Ongaro, although in an interview with *Azul y Blanco*, Ongaro declared that he was awaiting a new "Che Guevara ready to campaign along the frontiers of Argentina." Ongaro grandly depicted himself as one of Gramsci's "organic intellectuals," preparing to hurl the proletarian masses into a popular revolution. Using the term that denoted the rural militias that fought for the Federalists during the nineteenth-century civil wars, Ongaro described his own movement as a *"montonera."* The word "guerrilla," he explained, "suggests a minority [but] *montonera* a national majority."[90] By mid-1969, shortly before being banned by the government following the cordobazo, *Azul y Blanco* was supporting the Left-leaning nationalist regime established in Peru the year before. "In Peru," it declared, "the people, the church and the military are united. They represent the constituent powers of the National Revolution."[91]

The Montoneros

These were some of the more striking stages and features in the strange shift to the Left by formerly extreme right-wing groups during the late 1960s. Under Onganía, the military establishment remained constantly alert against the threat of "subversion." In September 1966 and October 1968, Argentine delegates at inter-American military conferences supported the formation of an international force ready for deployment anywhere in Latin America the leftist guerrillas dared raise their heads.[92] In October 1967, immediately after the destruction of the small guerrilla band led by Ernesto Guevara in Bolivia, the army began practicing field maneuvers in preparation "against the Communist internal enemy."[93] But for some time there were no enemies to be found, and these preparations brought few rewards. In October 1968, the rural police captured the weekend guerrillas of uncertain affiliation in Tucumán, whom Sánchez Sorondo denounced as provocateurs. In April 1969, the police arrested a former member of the Tacuara who now claimed leftist connections but turned out to be a mere armed robber.[94] A month or so later, the government blamed the cordobazo on a "subversive plan with a perfectly well-known ideology," by which it meant Cuban communism, but it could never back this claim with any evidence.[95]

Guerrilla warfare finally erupted in early 1970. In late May, a string of minor incidents reached a sudden, devastating climax when the *Montoneros*, an armed band of Peronists, kidnapped and murdered former president Pedro Aramburu. For the next two years, guerrilla actions slowly gathered momentum. In a two-month period in June–July 1971, for example, guerrillas invaded and occupied the town of San Jerónimo in Santa Fe, repeated Joe Baxter's tactic of commandeering and distributing foodstuffs to the poor, and assassinated a former chief of police of Córdoba.[96] Three Peronist groups now were active: the Fuerzas Armadas Peronistas (Peronist Armed Forces), or FAP, the Fuerzas Armadas Revolucionarias (Revolutionary Armed Forces), or FAR, and the Montoneros. Independent of the Peronist groups was the Ejército Revolucionario del Pueblo (People's Revolutionary Army), or ERP, which emerged as the armed wing of the small Trotskyite party, the Partido Revolucionario de los Trabajadores (Revolutionary Workers' Party), known as the PRT.

Of all these groups, the ERP alone was Marxist. The Peronists, particularly the Montoneros, were mostly Catholics who claimed to be Socialists but remained inveterately opposed to what they called "godless and antinational communism."[97] The source of this outlook lay in the background, education, and early connections of the guerrilla leaders. Fernando Luis Abal Medina, for example, the co-founder of the Montoneros, who was killed in a skirmish with the police soon after the Aramburu episode, had joined Tacuara at the age of fourteen, seeing it as the local equivalent of the EOKA, the Greek guerrilla organization then fighting British rule in Cyprus. An admirer of George Grivas, the right-wing leader of EOKA, Abal Medina was also "a Catholic militant," or as his own brother described him at his funeral, a "Catholic Nationalist."[98] Emilio Maza, another leader of the Montoneros killed soon after the Aramburu episode, was a former student leader at the Catholic University in Córdoba. Carlos Gustavo Ramos, co-founder of the movement with Abal Medina, was another student with a background in Tacuara. Finally, Mario Firmenich, the only leader of the Montoneros to survive the 1970s, was of Croatian origin and was educated at the Colegio Nacional de Buenos Aires, the most distinguished of the metropolitan high schools. As an adolescent, Firmenich served as the president of Acción Católica de la Juventud.[99]

The leading Montoneros were closely connected with groups of radical Catholic priests who appeared in the aftermath of the Second Vatican Council.[100] Among these priests was Juan Carlos García Elorrío who was a follower and disciple of Camilo Torres, the guerrilla priest killed a few years before in the jungles of Colombia. Until his own death in an automobile accident in 1970, García Elorrío edited the radical periodical *Cristianismo y Revolución*.[101] A second priest who influenced the Montoneros was Carlos Mugica, a man of upper-class background and the son of a prominent conservative politician who made his name as the champion of the poor in Buenos Aires. "Jesus," Mugica claimed, "was the most ambitious revolutionary throughout history, who wanted not only new structures ... but a new form of living unthinkable to mankind."[102] In Mugica's book, *Peronismo y cristianismo*, published in 1973, however, there were strong traces of the old clerical anticommunism. "To uphold the total equality of man," he wrote, "is to deny the reality of sin. ... Complete equality will only be achieved on the coming of the Lord. ... Marxism overemphasizes material man."[103]

García Elorrío, Mugica, and others became the links be-

tween the Montoneros and the Movement of the Third World
Priests. This leftist "postconciliar" movement considered the
church "out of step with the times" and identified "socialism
[as] the form of society most appropriate to our times and
to the spirit of the church."[104] In taking such stances, the
movement quickly came under attack from Nationalists. The
Third World priests, one Nationalist alleged, "want a church
that only promotes man, a church that is temporal, materialist
and democratic, and they imagine the people to be the subject
of all power."[105]

Yet within this clerical "New Left" that the Nationalists
deplored there were nevertheless numerous vestiges of the
Nationalist movement and the clerical Right. The Third
World priests, for example, depicted themselves like the Nationalists as "guiding elites," whose task was to link the
"masses" with the "revolution" and to create the "new
man."[106] In ways again reminiscent of the Nationalists, the
priests linked "capitalism" and "totalitarian atheism and collectivism" as the great enemies of humanity.[107] The Third
World priests echoed the old clerical objections to popular
democracy in the sense that they claimed the institutions of
representative government created only "an illusion of participation." Peronism, for example, declared a contributor to
Cristianismo y Revolución, was not a political party because
as such it would be no different from

the rest of the liberal parties that used democratic elections as the
last barrier against the revolution. . . . Reduced to a political party
within the system, Peronism would lose its chance to lead a real
revolution.[108]

In the early 1960s, Cooke, the Peronist intellectual and ac-
tivist, had expressed his contempt for the armed bands and a
willingness "to shoot the lot of them."[109] Yet alongside the
Third World priests, Cooke became the second great influence on the Montoneros. However, Cooke too had certain
ambiguous antecedents. The son of the prominent renegade
Radical Juan W. Cooke, who supported Perón in 1945, the
younger Cooke became a congressman in 1946. Cooke then
joined the small group of Peronists who followed the Nation-

alists and voted against the ratification of the treaty of Chapultepec. During this period, Cooke upheld links with the Rosas
Institute and was said to admire some of the texts of Nazi
political theorists such as Carl Schmitt.[110]

Cooke began moving leftward toward the end of Perón's
government, particularly under Aramburu when he became
the exiled Perón's "personal delegate" in Argentina. In this
role, he was constantly hatching plots for a guerrilla war led
by Peronists which would lead to a mass working-class revolt
and Perón's return to power.[111] In the early 1960s, Cooke
spent several years in Cuba, where he adopted Castro's doctrine that "imperialism is the true enemy."[112] Between his
return from Cuba in early 1964 and his death in 1968, Cooke
sought to refashion Peronism into a movement like Castro's
that would lead to a popular, leftist, and anti-imperialist revolution of "national liberation."[113]

While Cooke was alive, his ideas were either ignored or
strongly resisted by the now highly conservative Peronist
labor unions. Perón himself initially opposed the Cuban revolution because it destroyed the Batista regime he had long
supported. By 1968, however, as he observed the course of
events under Onganía and Krieger Vasena, Perón too was
moving sharply to the Left along the lines suggested by
Cooke. In *La hora de los pueblos* (Hour of the Peoples), published in 1968, Perón urged the replacement of "liberal democracy" by a "people's democracy" and pledged to lead his
movement into the struggle against "the oppressive yoke of
imperialism" now embodied in the Onganía regime. Henceforth, his aim was "liberation in the international sphere and
structural reform in the internal sphere."[114] By mid-1970, as
the guerrilla groups began to proliferate, Perón was ordering
his followers into "a total confrontation. . . . Violence already
reigns and only more violence can destroy it."[115]

As their name indicated, the Montoneros, who quickly ab-
sorbed the other Peronist guerrilla organizations, depicted
themselves as latter-day Federalist freedom fighters. In this
guise, they considered themselves a revolutionary elite
whose mission was to crystallize the revolutionary potential
of the masses. They intended to fight "gun in hand for the

seizure of power for Perón and his people."[116] *Si Evita vi-viera, sería Montonera* (If Evita were alive she would be a Montonero) became the best-known slogan of the Montoneros, which indicated they regarded the dubious career of Eva Perón as the inspiration for the violent struggle they were attempting to lead.

In sum, the Montoneros became yet another example of "that strange fusion or marriage between the Left and [Right]" that characterized so many of the political movements of the late 1960s and early 1970s.[117] Like Baxter's group, they were open to suspicion because of the "ease with which they crossed from the extreme right to the extreme left or vice versa."[118] Despite their alignment with the "national Left," the Montoneros adopted many of the general concepts that originated among the Nationalists. The slogan *La patria socialista, sin yanquis ni marxistas* (A Socialist nation with no "Yanks" or Marxists) evoked the Nationalist idea that Washington and Moscow were in league to subdue the country. The Montoneros often employed the old Nationalist metaphor "national being" (*ser nacional*), whose origins lay in the writings of Taine. The struggle the Montoneros pledged against the "imperialist infiltrator in the heart of the nation" echoed the old Nationalist conspiracy theories based on anti-Semitism and represented a kind of doctrine of national security in reverse, in which the term "imperialist" replaced "subversive."[119]

Borrowing yet another technique from the Nationalists, the Montoneros sought to exploit history for political purposes. Their own crude versions of historical revisionism contained a much stronger emphasis on the role of the "masses" than standard revisionism but still took as their starting point the cult of Rosas and other Federalist caudillos. The Peronists, declared the Montoneros, were "a historical continuation of our patriots who fought for independence and of the caudillos who followed Rosas."[120] Like the revisionists, the Montoneros placed "heroes and saints" at the center of their historical cosmography, although this time using such figures as the models for the so-called Socialist man.[121] Among the great historical heroes of the Montoneros was José Artigas, the leader of the independence struggle in Uruguay. In comic strip propaganda, Montonero publications depicted Artigas as the patriarchal landowner who was the "defender of the poor."[122]

On these grounds, the Montoneros could be depicted as the champions of "feudal socialism": they aspired to a political system in which they would become the lords and the "masses" their villeins. As the alienated children of the "old families of the landowning bourgeoisie" or of "senior military officers and public functionaries," in class terms, the leaders of the Montoneros bore some resemblance to the young Nationalists of *La Nueva República* forty years earlier. Unlike these forerunners, however, the Montoneros practiced cold-blooded violence. In September 1974, for example, Firmenich and his accomplices issued an almost nonchalant account of the way they had taken and killed Aramburu four years before.[123]

The highly authoritarian command structure used by the Montoneros created a situation in which in the battle between the guerrillas and the military, "two symmetrical military totalitarianisms" were confronting one another.[124] Others argued that the very idea of "national liberation" had its roots in Mussolini's concept of the "proletarian nation." This was an idea Mussolini had developed during World War I as he underwent his mutation from socialism into fascism. In Mussolini's view, nations possessed a relationship similar to that depicted by Socialists between the social classes, and he shifted the doctrine of class war into the struggle between "proletarian" and "plutocratic" nations.[125] Of his own fate if the Montoneros had ever won control, Timerman said, "I would have been placed against a wall and shot. The charge: counterrevolutionary Zionism. In this respect, as in so many others, Fascists of the Left and Right complement each other."[126]

These were some of the grounds that led one later observer to conclude that the Montoneros bore "a striking resemblance to a seldom recognized precursor: the radical wing of the European fascist movements." Among the resemblances were hostility to foreigners per se; an extraordinarily chauvinistic affirmation of the nation; exaltation of the leader in the person of Perón; the worship of violence [and] militant hostility to both Marxism and Liberalism. [The Montoneros upheld] profoundly militarist, authoritarian and elitist conceptions . . . of politics and their own organizations.[127]

But as Catholics, as well as militarists, authoritarians, and elitists, the Montoneros evoked the indigenous Nationalists more strongly than the foreign Fascists. There was no evidence that the Montoneros had any knowledge of Fascist doctrine. They claimed Perón, Eva Perón, Cooke, and Mugica as their intellectual mentors, along with other Peronists of very diverse background: ideologues like Hernández Arregui, revisionist historians like Rosa, renegade Communists such as Puiggrós, and relics of the FORJA like Jauretche. The Montoneros were neo-Peronists, but as "national socialists," they were also neo-Nationalists, another of the descendants of the primitive Nationalist movement.[128]

Following the first forays of the guerrilla groups in 1970, Argentina lurched from one government to another and in 1975, into the chasm of the "dirty war." In 1973, the Peronists replaced the military government, but the "restoration" survived for only three years until the military coup of March 1976. Up to around 1971, the Nationalists, like Sánchez Sorondo who had joined the swelling tide of opposition to Onganía's regime, attempted to create their own mass movement under a military leader. One of the results of this campaign was the abortive military rebellion of May 1971 led by General Eduardo Labanca against the recently established government of General Alejandro Lanusse. In his revolutionary proclamation, Labanca announced the inception of a new "national and popular movement," which would be "basically Christian." His aim, Labanca declared, was

to correct a state of injustice, and to establish a truly Christian society. This is not an exclusively military movement, and still less does it aim for an iron dictatorship of the totalitarian or fascist type. . . . It is a movement that is neither right- nor left-wing, but firmly Catholic, popular and nationalist.

Echoing the major conflicts of the Krieger Vasena era but drawing on the Nationalist antipathy to "liberals," Labanca attacked the "financial Right, the agent of British imperialism that has put Argentina in a state of dependency . . . making it into a great ranch made up of fat cows and thin workers."[129]

The Labanca episode revealed once more that on their own the Nationalists could command only little support among the military and were destined for failure. When the Labanca rebellion collapsed, many of the Nationalists finally put aside their memories of 1955 and enlisted with the Peronists. By early 1973, Sánchez Sorondo, for example, gained the nomination of the Peronist coalition known as FREJULI ("Justicialist" Liberation Front) as candidate for senator in Buenos Aires. Illustrating the way "Right" and "Left" were now completely entangled, during the election campaign, Sánchez Sorondo, the erstwhile militant right-winger, received the endorsement of both the left-wing Juventud Peronista (Peronist Youth) and the Montoneros. However, the Radicals, who unceasingly reminded the voters of Sánchez Sorondo's "Fascist" antecedents, defeated him in the election.[130]

In 1973, when the Peronists took over the government from the military, several other leading Nationalists carved a niche for themselves in the Peronist movement. Among them were historian José María Rosa and Basilio Serrano, one of the scions of the Ateneo de la República. Both these men were nominated for ambassadorships after the elections of March 1973.[131] In 1973, Jacovella, another prominent Nationalist and an expert in native arts and folklore, became the director of the Colón Theater in Buenos Aires. Under his control, national dance for a time took precedence in the Colón over the usual repertoire of classical opera.[132] In 1973, the Peronists even gained the support of persons closely identified with the 1955 revolution. General Lonardi's daughter, Marta Lonardi de Deheza, for example, declared herself willing to embrace the "movement for liberation," at least until the Peronists began to insult the memory of her father.[133]

The collusion between the Nationalist Right and Left became particularly visible in what was now the "National and Popular" University of Buenos Aires. In 1973, Puiggrós, the

former Communist, became rector of the university and issued a flood of rhetoric reminiscent of Martínez Zuviría thirty
years before. "All universities," Puiggrós declared, "whether
state or private, should reflect the national doctrine in their
teachings, and prevent the infiltration of liberalism, positivism, historicism and utilitarianism."[134] In 1973, while Montonero front organizations took over the student associations,
Puiggrós and his followers again purged the university faculties. Warnings that these measures amounted to "McCarthyism" and "witch hunts" and applied "conspiracy theories"
passed unheeded.[135] A prominent mathematician vainly
pleaded that the attempt by "xenophobic currents" to impose
the "national doctrine" on his own discipline implied "the
destruction of universal values that exist beyond any doubt."
"Whatever we call national should also include what is universal," he implored before an unyielding audience.[136]

During the next year or two, there were many other echoes
of the past campaigns waged by the Nationalists. When Perón
himself returned as president in October 1973, he immediately began rebuilding the corporatist institutions he had
used in the period 1946–1955. He restored the grip of the CGT
over the labor unions and attempted to consolidate its control
by allowing union congresses only once every four years.
Plans were soon afoot for another Peronist constitution, which
like its predecessor of 1949 would "banish forever the politicians, sectarianism and demagogy." A Peronist minister remarked in 1975 that political parties "only divide the citi-
zenry, favor their supporters in a demagogic way, and
undermine the soul of the nation."[137]

The Process of National
Reorganization

By 1975, with Perón himself now dead and the government in
the feeble grasp of Isabel Perón, the Peronist regime was
hurtling into self-destruction. Open war had erupted between
the Montoneros and the Peronist Right, which controlled the
sinister group of assassins known as the "Triple A," Alianza
Anticomunista Argentina (Argentine Anti-Communist Alli-

ance). The violent struggle between the factions went back to mid-1971 when death squads started to abduct and murder leftists.[138] In June 1973, as hundreds of thousands gathered at Ezeiza airport outside Buenos Aires to greet Perón on his return from exile in Spain, heavily armed right-wingers shot scores of leftists. In the ensuing turmoil, the Triple A emerged as a clandestine army financed and controlled by José López Rega, Perón's minister of social welfare. By late May 1975, the press reported more than five hundred assassinations over the past year, the vast majority of them leftists.[139] At stake was whether, as the Montoneros wished, the country would become a "socialist fatherland" in their grip or, as the followers of López Rega insisted, a "Peronist fatherland" controlled by the right-wing gangs and the reactionary labor unions.

As the violence and chaos mounted, the military, which had become the main target of the guerrilla groups, bided its time and waited for an opportunity to deal the death blow against "subversion." Throughout the early 1970s, military officers condemned the "mental confusion, the doctrinary chaos . . . among the masses, . . . the feeble liberal slogans, . . . the illiteracy, vice, corruption, and declining moral standards," conditions they blamed on the "farce of democracy." "Subversion" was taking hold of the country through "the penetration of the institutions of the state by secret teams and cells."[140]

In 1970, Genta, a leading critic of what he and others who were formerly linked with the hard-line colorado faction in the military called the "soft" Onganía regime (*la dictablanda*), urged the military to execute a counterrevolution.[141] The following year Genta issued another tract entitled *La guerra contrarrevolucionaria* (Counterrevolutionary War). Genta's grim agenda ran as follows:

Create a military state and a war policy to combat internal subversion; indoctrinate the military with a clear idea of its mission and with enthusiasm for this mission; mobilize the entire population for the counterrevolutionary war; free the nation from the power of international money; base everything in Christ, which means restore the natural hierarchies.[142]

"Today," Genta proclaimed, "the only option is military dictatorship."[143] The new dictatorship, he continued, would rest on the "ideological unity" of the armed services, the forging of a "single mind." "Unity," he wrote, "can only be achieved through a return to the Catholic, Roman and Hispanic principles on which the nation was founded, and which are those of the Christian west."[144]

In October 1974, the ERP gunned down Genta, but soon after, the influence of his doctrines reached its zenith. In early 1975, the government of Isabel Perón authorized the army to adopt any measures it wished to wipe out the guerrillas led by the Marxist ERP in the province of Tucumán and in September 1975 extended this authority to the rest of the country.[145] In September too a new defense law instituted a chain of military courts to try "subversives." In October, the Internal Security and National Defense councils placed the police under military command and gave the army the power to enter universities and factories.[146] Toward late 1975, the generals swore a formal pledge to the doctrine of national security and agreed on the tactic of "disappearances" to strike terror in the population and to prevent the guerrillas from gaining popular support. The reasoning ran that once isolated, the guerrillas could be annihilated.[147]

The military junta that followed the bankrupt government of Isabel Perón in March 1976 bore the ponderous but obscurely menacing title of the Process of National Reorganization, and it took power with a clear sense of purpose and "an entire philosophy of repression."[148] Henceforth, "the values of Christian morality would prevail"; the regime would uphold "national security, while eliminating subversion and the conditions that promote its existence"; soon Argentina would occupy "its due place within the western Christian world."[149]

The army commander General Jorge R. Videla, who became president of the junta, declared his "profound Christian belief in the preeminent dignity of man as a fundamental value," but his method of restoring such "dignity" was naked force.[150] The government would employ all the power it could muster, Videla warned, to shift the country in a new direction and transform its cultural and ideological foundations. Henceforth, the doctrine of national security would be applied to the letter and the country ruled as if it were "the operational theater for the global confrontation" against communism. This term "global" indicated that the junta had returned to the ideas the French put forward twenty years before. "The French version" of the doctrine was "more correct" than the American, one of the generals declared, because "the former pointed to a global approach, but the latter was exclusively, or almost exclusively, military."[151] In the war on subversion, it would no longer be possible to apply "judicial norms and standards."

In this type of struggle the secrecy with which our special operations must be conducted means that we cannot divulge whom we have captured and whom we want to capture; everything has to be enveloped in a cloud of silence.[152]

In June 1976, as its campaigns of kidnapping, torture, and mass murder were rapidly escalating, the regime issued a decree lifting the ban imposed under Isabel Perón on *Cabildo*, a Nationalist monthly magazine founded in 1974. *Cabildo* now became the forum for some of the original surviving Nationalists led by Julio Irazusta and Federico Ibarguren and at the same time for other Nationalists who were now dead.[153] Among the second group was Meinvielle, killed three years earlier by an automobile in the streets.[154] *Cabildo* advertised one of Meinvielle's last books, *The Jew and the Mystery of History*, and eulogized the assassinated Genta. Genta's *Counterrevolutionary War*, declared *Cabildo*, had been "originally written as a textbook for the school of military aviation, but [was] now a Nationalist classic, an irreplaceable tool for an understanding of the True Doctrine."[155]

Cabildo lashed out against "leftism," "agnosticism," and "romantic egalitarianism." Thanks to the recent coup, it exulted, "democracy has been buried forever." Irazusta indulged in attacks on the "ideologies that gnaw at the national spirit," while Ibarguren, now head of the department of history at the Catholic University of El Salvador, resumed his tirades against the intellectual heritage of Rousseau. Patricio Randle, a much younger contributor, thought it "unpardonable" to combat the guerrillas alone and to fail to act against the "underlying causes" of their actions, which he called the "ideological virus."[156]

Cabildo constantly deplored the coverage of current events in Argentina by the *New York Times* and by *Le Monde*, which it called "the daily bible of our intellectual Bolsheviks in Paris."[157] In early 1977, *Cabildo* attacked Jacobo Timerman, the owner of *La Opinión*, for having established a newspaper in Argentina broadly modeled on *Le Monde*.[158] Soon afterward, Timerman fell captive to the security forces, which then held him hidden away for two years before eventually allowing him to flee abroad.[159] Some months earlier, in September 1976, *Cabildo* named other persons and institutions it considered "crypto-Communists" or "agents of ideological contamination," accusations that also produced a spate of disappearances.[160]

In September 1976, *Cabildo* listed certain words and modish popular expressions it considered typical of "ideological subversion." Among them was "consensus," a term *Cabildo* rejected because it "deifies public opinion." "Methodology," it declared, was a pretentious left-wing embellishment of "method," empty of any other meaning. The word "couple" (*pareja*) bore the connotation of extramarital relationships between the sexes and could no longer be tolerated.[161] Reacting to criticisms in the United States of the grave violations of human rights now occurring in Argentina, in October 1976, *Cabildo* published a cartoon under the caption "Uncle Sam and the Guerrillas. Allies against the Nation." Some abuse of authority, *Cabildo* admitted, was occurring in Argentina, but it was "an unfortunate and inevitable" result of the war against the guerrillas. Anyone who failed to acknowledge this fact belonged to the "vast, unsubtle action of the international Left."[162]

Cabildo backed apartheid in South Africa and the reactionary breakaway Catholic movement led by Cardinal Marcel Lefèbvre in France and identified "the system established in Europe in 1945" as the source of the "ruin and chaos" in the contemporary world. By accepting the idea that six million Jews were slain by the Nazis during World War II, this "system" was guilty of "a gigantic falsification of history." In defining the type of "subversion" that should be "wiped out," *Cabildo* listed the teachings of Jews, Marxists, Freudians, Jehovah's Witnesses, Seventh-Day Adventists, and Mormons.[163] The aim of current policy, *Cabildo* insisted, was not only to destroy the guerrillas themselves but to eliminate the root causes that produced them: the habits of mind and the secular or "relativist" values on which the guerrillas allegedly fed.

The military regime of 1976 appointed Nationalists to the supreme court and to positions in the ministries of education and justice, the Central Bank, and numerous faculties in the universities.[164] Meanwhile, the church provided another avenue for the Nationalists to influence and support the regime. During this period, it was later alleged, priests sympathetic to the regime, some of them Spaniards, scoured the texts of Saint Thomas Aquinas and his successors for justifications for the use of torture by the state.[165] Throughout these years, priests who served as military chaplains attended torture sessions.[166] Ecclesiastical dignitaries described the regime's policies as a "defense of humanity [and] of God." "I pray for divine protection over this 'dirty war,'" one of them reportedly declared.[167]

In the late 1970s, the statements of senior military officers rang constantly with the language and figurative constructions of the Nationalists. Thus, the regime's enemies, declared Videla, were not only armed terrorists but all those who "spread ideas contrary to western civilization."[168] Political parties were unsuited to Argentina's needs because of "their vices and deformations."[169] Jews "transferred their secret practices and symbols into Freemasonry, which is now attempting to destroy the Christian idea."[170] The "subversive," declared General Ramón Camps, "has forfeited the right to call himself an Argentine."[171] The generals drew on the Nationalist eschatology to portray themselves as Christian commanders leading a struggle to extirpate the heretics and convert the unbelievers. "Since Marxism is the modern heresy," wrote Camps, "we are currently witnessing a war between Good and Evil."[172] The archaic organicist metaphors used by the Nationalists reappeared constantly in the terminology of military leaders. Thus, the navy, declared one officer, was a "healthy institution, uncontaminated by the ulcer of extremism, or by a Third World adulteration which does not recognize the true Christ, or by the tortuous and demagogic attitudes of hypocritical politicians."[173] The military commander of Bahía Blanca, General Edgardo Acdel Vilas, dubbed eighteenth-century "idealism, rationalism and empiricism" a "diabolical trilogy."[174]

The doctrine of national security remained the other major component of the discourse of the military. "Subversion in Argentina," asserted Camps, "belongs within the context of the subversive or terrorist action that has developed throughout the world since the end of World War II, when Russia recognized the need to find a new way to advance its imperialism."[175] "Local subversion," declared the ministry of culture and education, "is an appendix of something unitary and worldwide. It operates under the centralized direction of the leading Marxist-Leninist states that have made ideology the principal means of domination."[176]

The ideas that produced the guerrillas, the military claimed, stemmed from the mass media and from certain professions, above all, psychoanalysis. After 1976, the junta attacked and purged the media on a scale that dwarfed similar operations in the past. "We had to 'take out' [*aniquilar*] quite a few [journalists]," Camps blandly confessed, "because they were taking positions that threatened the prevailing institutions."[177] Argentina's production of books, which stood at 31.5 million in 1976, plummeted to only 8.7 million in 1979.[178] The regime would allow only those films to be screened "that portray man in his daily and perennial struggle against materialism and selfishness, . . . the men struggling for honor, religion, and values."[179]

Of the psychoanalysts, it was said that "no sector of the population suffered more," because their role, the military claimed, was "to bolster the spirits of the guerrillas."[180] The psychoanalysts became such a prominent target because they were now playing a role in society, particularly among the urban upper middle classes, that formerly belonged to the

priests and the church. The intellectual mentors of the psychoanalysts, such as Freud, claimed *Cabildo*, were attempting "to destroy the Christian concept of the family."[181] Scores,
if not hundreds, of psychoanalysts now perished in the secret
prisons maintained by the security forces.

Architects comprised another highly suspect group, principally because of their past ties with the Peronists. In the early
1970s, many young architects flocked into the Peronist movement convinced that in an era of profound social reform they
would play a leading role in the nation's physical reconstruction. The architects would redesign the universities to allow
students to display their power in mass demonstrations and
lay out vast new squares to hold "enormous groups of people,
the people in its entirety."[182] In the eyes of the military, while
the psychoanalysts molded the "mentality" of "subversion,"
the architects established its physical environment.

Another campaign focused on the schools. "Up until now,"
declared General Vilas in September 1976,

the struggle against subversion . . . has been directed at the movement's visible head, the subversive delinquent, but not against the
ideologues who generate and influence them. . . . We should eliminate the sources on which the subversive delinquent feeds . . . and
this source is in the universities and the secondary schools.[183]

Cabildo took a similar position. "In education," it insisted,
"you must act firmly to destroy the roots of subversion, and
show your students the falsehood of doctrines forced upon us
[from abroad] for so many years."[184] In the effort to create the
"virtuous subject," natural law once more occupied a dominant position in the curricula of the universities, while the
works of Marx, Freud, Einstein, and eventually hundreds of
other authors were banned. Einstein, it was said, for example,
had "destroyed the Christian concepts of time and space."[185]
In 1978, the ministry of education consulted the National
Academy of Exact and Natural Sciences as to whether "modern mathematics could be considered potentially subversive."[186] In the University of Buenos Aires, the government-
appointed intervenor, Alberto Ottalagano, commissioned a
priest to exorcise the institution of the "diabolical" influence

of student radicals. Ottalagano then dismissed 1,350 professors, telling them "to go teach Freud in Paris, and Marx in
Moscow."[187]

School textbooks now proclaimed that

for psychological and physical reasons, the male should be acknowledged as the authority. . . . By her nature the woman represents
kindness and love. Unless things are so, anarchy and dissatisfaction
become a fact. . . . To deny the father's authority is to tear the family
to pieces. The woman's obedience to authority has a great educational influence on the family.

The textbooks listed divorce alongside free love, abortion,
and pornography as an example of "the most recent Marxist
strategy to conquer the west." Among five school textbooks,
the word "democracy" appeared but once and then as a concept "independent of the form of government," relevant only
to "culture" rather than politics.[188]

A historical work by Federico Ibarguren which was published in 1978 provided another example of the kind of intellectual climate that prevailed during this period. Here Ibarguren repeated unchanged the ideas he had picked up from
his clerical instructors almost fifty years before. By specifying
where we have come from, his book explained, history explains
what we are and where we are bound; religion is the driving
force of civilization; nations were not created by Rousseau's
voluntary contract but by the pact between those destined to be
governors and those to be governed described by Saint Thomas
Aquinas and his successors; the "cross and the sword" had col-
onized and civilized Spanish America; the colonial cabildos
were prototypes of "true democracy"; the Reformation, followed by Descartes and his intellectual progeny, led the world
into damnation. "What then," Ibarguren finally asked himself
some five hundred pages later, "is the recipe for a future government?"

As always there will be a choice between a fit, select aristocracy to
lead the people toward the common good, or the sick opportunism
of corrupt adventurers who demagogically sell their tyrannized peoples. . . . There will be no nation unless it can train its ruling
class.[189]

In this way, the period that launched the doctrine of national security concluded in rampant military tyranny. One of the most striking features of the 1960–1980 period was the extent to which Nationalist influences were suddenly all-pervasive, soaked up by groups that were mortal enemies ostensibly occupying the opposite ends of the political spectrum. The newfound power of the Nationalists epitomized a society bordering on collapse and lurching into self-destruction.

The Nationalist Legacy

During the 1980s, Argentine politics underwent another major shift when the "Process" finally crumbled in the aftermath of the war of the Malvinas Islands during April–June 1982. The elected government of Raúl Alfonsín succeeded the juntas in December 1983, and the period 1984–1987, in particular, marked a determined effort to exact retribution from the military leaders for their actions during the previous decade while imposing the authority of the constitutional government over the armed forces. But as resistance to such policies stiffened, these years were again filled with examples of the values, attitudes, and mentalities that characterized the Nationalists and the national security doctrinaires.

"Myths and conspiracy theories," as the *New York Times* described them, continued to dominate the Argentine military.[190] In 1980, General Roberto Viola expatiated on the "indirect strategy" of the Communists during the nuclear age which would make the Third World their prime theater of operations.[191] "World War I," declared General Leopoldo Galtieri at around the same time, "was a struggle between armies, and World War II one between nations; World War III will be a conflict between ideologies."[192] In mangled resonances of the *Protocols of the Elders of Zion*, General Cristino Nicolaides urged the world to recognize "the Marxist-Communist international . . . that has been active since 500 B.C., and [since then] has thrown itself against the western world." According to Nicolaides, the struggle against subversion marked the prelude to World War III, although its origins lay in the "loss of values that began with modern liberalism."[193]

Veterans of the Malvinas war roaming the streets of Buenos Aires at the end of the conflict in mid-1982 echoed the Nationalist propaganda of the 1930s as they chanted, *"los bolches y los ingleses, los mismos intereses,"* which meant that the British were in league with Communists to destroy the country. When queried about his personal political loyalties in 1983, General Camps acknowledged that "on several points" he shared the views of Hitler, in particular, his determination, as he put it, "to save mankind and to struggle against the permanent Communist campaign that was so full of lies." Yet Camps denied he was a "Nazi" and called himself "a man of the right, a conservative, but an extreme humanist."[194]

In the 1980s, many of Argentina's generals remained convinced that during the "dirty war" they had saved society from destruction. In 1983, General Luciano B. Menéndez, who ruled the Córdoba region under the juntas, argued that the nation should be grateful to the military rather than vilifying it because "we acted in defense of society, meeting our obligations as soldiers."[195] Soon, he added, the nation would call on its soldiers once more when the need arose for another "total action" against subversion.[196]

The alliance between the military authoritarians and the clerical Nationalists continued intact during the 1980s. A military chaplain who accompanied the army during the invasion of the Malvinas Islands in 1982 described the expedition as symbolizing the unity of the "cross and the sword." The restoration of Argentina's sovereignty over the islands, he declared, would bring a sense of fulfillment to a people that was "Catholic, Hispanic and Roman . . . [who were fighting] for our nation and for Jesus Christ."[197] During the brief period that Argentine forces controlled the islands in April–June 1982, the governor of the Malvinas, General Mario Benjamín Menéndez, conducted an elaborate ceremony to invest the Virgin of Rosario as their patroness.[198] In January 1983, the air force commander, Basilio Lami Dozo, denied charges that his force was riddled with "Fascists" and that Genta's writings continued to be used to indoctrinate his officers. The truth was, he revealed, that the force was "Nationalist," wedded to "the social doctrine of the church."[199] Brigadier Augusto

Hughes, who became Lami Dozo's successor as air force commander in 1983, was widely known for his devotion to the
texts of Genta.[200]

Under Alfonsín, the Nationalist priests helped the military
to resist the new government. A group known as the FAMUS,
Familiares y Amigos de los Muertos por la Subversión (Relatives and Friends of the Victims of Subversion), which consisted of the leading supporters of the juntas, held monthly
masses to commemorate the victims of the guerrillas, rituals
that became an opportunity to glorify the juntas and to pour
scorn on the new democracy. Democratic leaders like Alfonsín, declared FAMUS in late 1983, represented "leftist eth-
ics, modernist culture, Anglo-Saxon Atlanticism, . . . international Jewry, Masonry."[201]

In 1985, the Alfonsín government placed the leaders of the
fallen military juntas on trial on charges of kidnap, torture,
and murder. The supreme council of the armed forces now
added to its loud defense of the military's actions in the 1970s
with the argument that "in war anything goes. There are no
limits to the use of force."[202] When the trials began, shady
gangs—relatives, it was said, of accused military leaders,
members of the intelligence services, or remnants of the Triple A—embarked on attempts at intimidation and political
destabilization by planting bombs and issuing assassination
lists.

The Nationalists made "national identity into a simple-
minded absolute value," concluded Alfonsín in 1985, reduc-
ing "the conflicts that were inevitable in a highly complex
society into an artificial, straitlaced [*autoritaria*] uniformity."
The Nationalists exemplified the "crusading spirit, the mystical slogans and the calls for direct action," he added, "which
had enjoyed their last great moment of frenetic splendor in
the hell of the 1970s." Under his own government, the Nationalists continued to resist democracy "with the same fanaticism they had shown fifty years before." Yet as the president
was forced to admit, "It should be recognized that Nationalist
ideas had become firmly rooted in national politics."[203]

In the 1980s, active support for the Nationalist movement
was still confined to a small fraction of the population. Yet its

influence pervaded the military, the church, sections of the Peronist party, and some of the trade unions. Public opinion polls in the 1980s found that still around one-third of the Argentine electorate showed inclinations toward "corporatism."[204] There were traces of Nationalist ideas even in the ruling Radical party which appeared when some of its factions urged Alfonsín to reconstitute his following as "the third historical movement" in succession to Yrigoyen and Perón.[205]

In the military schools, history classes continued to depict the "shining victories of dictators from the most remote times to the present."[206] Some of the labor unions remained willing to negotiate with Nationalists in the military to establish a new *pacto militar-sindical* (military-union pact), and union leaders insulted members of the government with anti-Semitic slurs.[207]

In the late 1980s, the Argentine church remained a focus of "preconciliar" conservatism.[208] Daniel María Rossi, a priest who attended one of the meetings of FAMUS in 1986, labeled all democrats as "pseudo-heroes" who embodied the nefarious legacy of the French Revolution.[209] In an echo of the Catholic concept of the "just war," military officers now referred to their actions during the 1970s as "good violence."[210] In March 1987, the members of FAMUS, among whom were numerous "elegantly dressed women," championed the repression as a "holy war for a just cause."[211]

Argentina's bishops claimed that the democratic government professed "materialist ideologies contrary to our Argentine way of life."[212] The clerical ideologues continued to demand a democracy based on "natural groups" that were "real expressions" of the people."[213] Antonio Plaza, a protegé of Mario Amadeo who served as bishop of La Plata between 1955 and 1986, criticized the Alfonsín government because of the "many Jews" within it.[214] At one of the masses held by FAMUS in 1987, the celebrants declared their determination to "have done with the Radical synagogue."[215]

Writing in the *Revista Militar* in 1987, General Villegas, the head of CONASE under Onganía, once more proclaimed the unceasing "integral war, the permanent war, the war amidst the peace" that aimed to capture the "psyche of men." According to Villegas, "subversion" meant "slow, silent infiltration." In Latin America, he continued, populist regimes would be followed by democratic, "then Socialist and finally Marxist" governments, while Marxism would lead to the destruction of the nation's "Greco-Roman culture enriched by Christianity."[216]

In secret meetings at the resort city of Mar del Plata in late 1987, senior military officers agreed that the "enemy within" remained active, and that the country was once more moving toward collapse "because of the infiltration at every level by Marxism."[217] General Camps attacked Alfonsín's efforts to engender a new democratic political culture as a "continuation of subversion by other means."[218] The Centro de Oficiales Retirados, an association of retired military and police officers, denounced the human rights groups, which led the campaigns against the military, as "subproducts of Marxism"; during Alfonsín's government, the center declared, "Marxism" had again taken over the mass media.[219]

In 1987–88, Alfonsín faced a succession of revolts led by the so-called carapintadas, dissident troops who opposed the trials and cuts in military spending and who launched their revolts in full combat dress, their faces daubed in camouflage paint. Two of these actions in April and December 1987 were led by Lieutenant-Colonel Aldo Rico, a decorated veteran of the Malvinas war and one of the first Argentine officers trained in the United States in the 1960s. However, Rico was also known as "a sympathizer of the extreme right" and as a supporter of a "strong state" serving "the common good."[220]

In April 1988, the police unearthed a Nationalist terrorist group, Alerta Nacional (National Alert), that was equipped with bombs, weapons, volumes of printed propaganda, and even helicopters. Alerta Nacional possessed links with Rico, the revisionist historian Rosa, some of the Peronists, the right-wing unions led by the metal workers, the police, and the intelligence services.[221] During this period, the supporters of Rico and Alerta Nacional paraded through the streets of Buenos Aires in green and black uniforms, delivered the Roman salute, and carried flags bearing emblems reminiscent of the swastika. They marched along to cries of "Down with Democracy! Long live Rico! Long live the church!"[222]

In December 1988, Colonel Mohamed Ali Seineldín led a third revolt of the carapintadas. Seineldín was a man from Entre Ríos, one of the old Nationalist strongholds and the birthplace of Gálvez, the Irazustas, and Carulla. Despite his Muslim origins, Seineldín was known as "a sworn foe of the United States and a fanatical Catholic who would like to see the cross replace the sun in the centre of Argentina's flag."[223] The Malvinas war, Seineldín reportedly declared, "should have led to a new Argentina [able] to fulfill the designs of the Virgin."[224] Seineldín belonged, according to his own army commander, to a "parallel army" that professed "fundamentalism, . . . an extreme sense of religion."[225]

In early December 1990, the carapintadas rebelled for a fourth time in three years. In a written statement, which ended with the slogan *"Dios, Patria . . . o Muerte,"* Seineldín acknowledged his "total responsibility" for this action in which around a score of persons died.[226] Seineldín, wrote a commentator, considered himself "a lord of the manor."

No one can give him orders . . . but his subordinates receive from him a feudal-like protection, a blood bond. The carapintadas are soldiers bonded together not only by common values but by a fundamentalist ideology [and] nationalism and faith in tradition and religion. [Their aim is to restore] the lost honor of the army, . . . to regenerate the army, and through the army the country as a whole which has lost its sense of direction precisely because, they believe, it has lost its most fundamental institution.[227]

In sixty years, the Nationalist movement had barely changed. It continued to "amalgamate the ethos of the premodern world with the reactionary ritualism of the military corporation." The movement betrayed the same "astonishing mixture of the most archaic dogmas of counter-revolutionary Catholic theology with the counter-insurgency content of the Doctrine of National Security." Its discourse still belonged to the sphere of religion rather than politics: "faithful," "soldiers," "orthodox," "heretics," "apostles."[228]

In 1990, under the new government of Carlos Menem, the

quest among Nationalists to restore "the principles of Christian civilization" continued. Yet another Nationalist periodical, *Patria Argentina*, edited by the aged but still active Federico Ibarguren, denounced Menem's officials as "Zionist agents." The Colombian drug cartel, it alleged, was using bases in the Argentine north helped by "international Zionism." "Since World War II," declared Walter Beveraggi Allende, another contributor to *Patria Argentina*, Argentina had been undermined by a "perverse plan to destroy its economy and impoverish its people." Letters to *Patria Argentina* from Paris, Helsinki, Valladolid, and Miami advertised for contacts in Argentina on behalf of numerous extreme right-wing organizations across the Western world. Ibarguren's diatribes, now directed against Antonio Gramsci and Mikhail Gorbachev as the two latest cult figures of the Left, also saluted the memory of Lugones: "Great Leopoldo! Burning prophet, the lover of heroism as well as your verses!"[229]

Chapter Eight

Conclusion

Throughout its history, from the clerical outbursts of the 1880s to the carapintadas in the 1980s, the keynote of the Nationalist movement was reactiveness and defensiveness. The indigenous roots of the movement lay in nineteenth-century federalism and clericalism and in the effort to subvert positivism around 1900. Most of the movement's specific ideas, by contrast, were of derivative, European provenance. The most powerful or influential Nationalists were men of provincial, rural, and native Argentine background, and three provinces in particular—Entre Ríos, Córdoba, and Salta—possessed the strongest links with the movement. With the striking exception of Lugones, the Nationalists of Córdoba and Salta identified closely with the church. In Entre Ríos, an area in which small immigrant, often Jewish colonies were set among marginal cattle ranches, the secular strains of the movement were more pronounced, although here too clerical influences were never absent. The leading Nationalists often belonged to prominent but declining native Argentine ranching families. In more recent times, persons of immigrant background like Genta or Seineldín achieved prominence in the movement, a shift that illustrated not only the country's changing ethnic structure but the way political issues affecting the older elites eventually embraced a range of other groups.

Many of the leading Nationalists belonged to the upper or upper middle classes but very few to the great landed elite of the province of Buenos Aires. As children and adolescents, the future Nationalists often received educations in leading high schools and universities; later, they trained for the professions, law, the priesthood, the military, or occasionally, like Carulla, medicine. At school, the older generation of Nationalists became steeped in Catholic thought and classics and were reared on a curriculum that began with Plato, Aristotle, and the medieval scholastics and ended in de Maistre and Maurras.[1] Organizations like Catholic Action and the Instituto Juan Manuel de Rosas, which preached historical revisionism, played a similarly important part in indoctrinating the Nationalist youth.

No women ever commanded influential positions in the Nationalist movement, although as the career of Eva Perón showed, Nationalist ideas could be attractive to female as well as to male politicians. A few of the leading Nationalists, notably, Federico Ibarguren and Marcelo Sánchez Sorondo, joined the movement under the influence of their fathers, but a majority started their careers as members of the established political parties. These men converted to the Nationalist movement as they became disillusioned with party politics, failed to achieve sufficient prominence within their parties, or for one reason or another came to regard the established system as a threat to their personal interests.

Thus, Carlos Ibarguren began his career as a conservative and turned to the Nationalist movement soon after the Radicals displaced the conservatives in the election of 1916. The Irazustas began as Radicals but became Nationalists when Yrigoyen centralized the political system, destroying the independence of the Radicals of Entre Ríos by federal interventions. Carulla abandoned his Socialist allegiances and began moving into the Nationalist camp during World War I when the European Socialists aligned themselves with the militarists. The Nationalists of succeeding generations were sometimes former Peronists.

The decision to enlist with the Nationalists often occurred in the midst of political traumas like the Semana Trágica or Perón's war on the church. Walter Beveraggi Allende, for example, became a Nationalist under Frondizi around 1960. The precipitating factor in his shift to the Nationalist movement was Frondizi's unexpected reversal of his long-proclaimed commitment to a nationalist oil policy.

The Nationalist movement filled the void created by the absence of a strong conservative party commanding popular support. As Carlos Ibarguren argued, by the end of World War I, it became essential to seek "a compensatory force and the means to put a brake on the excesses of democracy. Every extremist campaign will fail if the conservative classes, which are so discordant, put together a united defense."[2] The "united defense" Ibarguren aspired for, however, continually failed to materialize and led the more extreme conservatives to become sponsors of the military coup and dictatorship.

The emergence of the Nationalist movement illustrated the incapacity of the weaker segments of the upper classes to defend themselves against an avalanche of social and political change. The threat of uncontrollable change first appeared in the wake of immigration and the rise of yrigoyenismo; the threat then intensified after World War II as the country lurched toward the cataclysm of the 1970s. "How and why does dictatorship arise?" Carlos Ibarguren asked during the 1930s. "Dictatorship is always the result of anarchy. If anarchy is superficial, dictatorship is short-lived; if anarchy is profound, dictatorship becomes ruthless."[3]

Once closely identified with the movement, most Nationalists stayed there for life, and Carulla represented one of the few documented examples of an apostate Nationalist. But long commitment or loyalty to the movement did not prevent the Nationalists from entering into tactical alliances with the liberals or, like Sánchez Sorondo in the early 1970s, from enlisting for a period with the Peronists. The military governments led by Onganía in 1966–1970 and Videla in 1976–1981 represented a coalition of Nationalists and liberals, and both established a broad division of labor in which the Nationalists controlled the political and educational systems while the liberals directed the economy. In the late 1930s and particularly in 1968–1973, the Nationalists formed alliances with the "national Left" which played a major part in the formation of mass-based populist movements.

The Nationalist movement consistently failed to achieve

unity and homogeneity and throughout remained factionalized and hybrid. Even so, all the Nationalists subscribed to
the basic propositions that liberal democracy had failed, that
its eventual outcome lay in communism, and that authoritarian rule should replace democracy. While democracy en-
dured, demagogic upstarts and the mob would rule and the
"natural aristocracy" the Nationalists considered themselves
to represent would be destroyed. Equally, so long as the liberal order prevailed, the country would fall into the hands of
its foreign enemies: the international monopolies, the Masons, or the Jews. To the Nationalists, "liberalism"—a perennially amorphous term—embodied "materialism" and national degeneration.

The church was the source of many of the conceptual alternatives the Nationalists offered to the liberal order. Ultramon-
tanism became the most influential clerical doctrine in Argentina and provided the vital connection between the
Nationalist movement and the European counterrevolution.
On these foundations the Nationalists proclaimed such dogmas as the absolute validity of natural law, the rights of the
provinces and other "lesser cells" against those of the central
government, the idea that hierarchy and rank were "natural,"
the legitimacy of authoritarian government, the rights of the
church in education, and the necessity of "social justice."

The writings of ultraconservatives in France, Spain, and, to
a lesser extent, Italy continually reinforced and reinvigorated
these ideas. Among the European writers, Maurras possessed
the greatest influence in Argentina. "To demilitarize France,"
Maurras had declared during the Dreyfus affair of the 1890s,
"was to dechristianize France."[4] This idea reappeared in Argentina as recently as the 1980s as the military fought back
against Alfonsín's efforts to curb its powers. The tie with
Maurras placed the Nationalists within an international family of ideologues and political movements professing the
same basic ideas. In 1933, for example, T. S. Eliot addressed
the University of Virginia in terms virtually identical to those
of the *La Nueva República* group in Buenos Aires. Eliot defined "the struggle of our time" as the struggle "to concentrate
not to dissipate; to renew our traditional wisdom; to reestab-

lish the vital connection between the individual and the race;
the struggle, in a word, against Liberalism." During this period, Eliot too traversed the path of anti-Semitism, and in 1945,
he failed to speak out against the Holocaust.[5] The Nationalists, whose concepts and principles appear so dated and discredited today, thus possessed a close link with some of the
leading figures of the Western intellectual tradition.

The chief inspiration of historical revisionism lay in the
writings of Spanish conservatives, led by Menéndez Pelayo,
although he belonged to a broader tradition established by
Taine, whose roots lay in the German Enlightenment. Particularly in the late 1930s, Mussolini, himself a part-Maurrasian,
commanded considerable influence in Argentina, although he
affected Perón more strongly than the Nationalists. On this
issue, Carlos Waisman's judgment remains broadly valid: the
Nationalists "differed from the Fascist model in that their rejection of political modernity was total. . . . Their organicism
was purely authoritarian and anti-mobilizational."[6] As the
struggle against Perón in 1954–55 demonstrated, the Nationalists, who were constantly endorsing dictatorship, inveterately
opposed the totalitarian, atheist state. Similarly, in Argentina,
contrary to the claims of wartime American propagandists, the
influence of "the religion of Valhalla," as Franceschi dubbed
the ideology of Nazism, was never more than slight. Nazi-like
elements surfaced in the writings of Lugones, Carulla, and
Martínez Zuviría (and among some of the military leaders
in the 1970s), but the Maurrasian and hispanophile strains
continually predominated. Making these distinctions high-
lighted the reluctance or inability of the Nationalists to insti-
tutionalize a mass movement. The Nationalists could lead a
military coup, but they stayed in power only for as long as they
could rule by force. As authoritarians rather than Fascists, the
Nationalists could take power but rarely keep it.

Led by Alejandro E. Bunge in the period 1937–1944, some
of the Nationalists followed the military and began to support
economic self-sufficiency through industrial development.
Yet because the Nationalists continually looked backward
rather than forward, economic nationalism, as opposed to economic xenophobia, emerged grudgingly and remained

halfhearted and superficial. The chief concerns of the Nationalists lay in education and society rather than in the economy. They wanted to minimize the cultural influence of foreigners, mold a deferential and jingoistic mass mentality, and erect a society of gremios or corporations infused with the values they imagined had prevailed on the great cattle *estancias* under Rosas.

The difficulties the Nationalists encountered in winning mass support for these ideas continually forced them into the role of propagandists tied chiefly to the military. Strong Nationalist influences in the military command appeared at the end of World War I as the military began to develop its enduringly ambivalent identity as a "part of the Europeanized, modernized elite . . . but a bulwark of historical tradition and order."[7] Henceforth, the Nationalists were continually infiltrating the higher spheres of the military as "advisers" or "teachers." In the late 1920s, Carulla and his friends unflaggingly cultivated Uriburu; in the early 1940s, Genta and Sánchez Sorondo lectured to audiences of senior military officers; in the 1960s, associations like the Ateneo de la República and the Cursillos de Cristiandad effected the link; in the 1980s, FAMUS afforded the nexus. Throughout the Nationalists issued messages that a substantial proportion of the military wanted to hear: the military institution, they argued, was a natural ruling class whose status and power was ordained by divine law. The perennial receptiveness of the military to Nationalist teachings reflected broad similarities between them in social status. Nationalist sympathizers in the military tended to form part of a marginal or junior elite: like Uriburu or Seineldín, they belonged to provincial families; like the members of the GOU or Rico, they were usually colonels rather than generals.

For decades, the Nationalists infiltrated themselves in military academies, in seminaries, and in niches in the universities, especially the law schools and history faculties. The entrenched position the Nationalists commanded in the education system at large became visible in the strong authoritarian threads among the political parties and the broader political culture of Argentina, in the continuing mystical appeal of the organic national community, and in the ubiquitous popularity of conspiracy theories orchestrated by foreigners. Thus, although the Nationalists failed to gain a mass following, Amadeo could quite correctly claim that "there were some enduring elements in the movement which were eventually adopted by the people as a whole and became part of the public domain."[8]

The Nationalists became most powerful in periods of extreme political strain or breakdown, particularly during the eleven military coups in Argentina between 1930 and 1982. These episodes illustrated the way abrupt political change brought to the fore those who offered the simplest and most direct methods to reconstitute state power and authority. Conversely, the Nationalists exercised least influence in periods of relatively strong government, such as under Alvear in the mid-1920s, Justo in the mid-1930s, or Perón in 1945–1948. The renaissance of the Nationalist movement after 1950 reflected the political deadlock and the chronic economic slump that followed the decline and fall of Perón. In the 1970s, the Nationalists supplied the ideological weaponry for the military's violent confrontation with "subversion" and in the 1980s with the militant authoritarian assumptions on which the carapintadas sought to resist the restored democracy.

Some of the early-twentieth-century writings of the Nationalists contained an unexceptionable, at times even charming nostalgic ruralism. We may share the distaste of the Nationalists for "relativism," urban squalor, and exploitation, ponder their vision of a society composed of "cooperative man," or acknowledge the strong corporate, as opposed to individualistic, character of modern society. But we should not forget that the Nationalists exploited bigotry in the defense of privilege, defended dictatorship and repression in the name of justice, and practiced war and persecution in pursuit of a chimera of national unity.

Notes

Preface

1. *El Bimestre Político y Económico*, January 28, 1983. (Quoting General Ramón J. Camps, chief of police in Buenos Aires during the late 1970s.)

2. National Commission on the Disappeared, *Nunca Más*. With an introduction by Ronald Dworkin. New York: Farrar, Straus, Giroux, 1986, 7.

3. National Commission on the Disappeared, *Nunca Más*, 8.

4. National Commission on the Disappeared, *Nunca Más*, 4.

5. Ernst Nolte, *Three Faces of Fascism: Action Française, Italian Fascism, National Socialism*. Translated by Leila Verrewitz. New York: Holt, Rinehart and Winston, 1966, x.

6. Isidoro Cheresky, "Argentina: Régimen político de soberanía compartida," *Punto de Vista*, n.d., 19.

7. I have taken the expression "the dark underside of Argentine history" from Tulio Halperín Donghi and the phrase "second tradition" from Natalio Botana.

8. Enrique Zuleta Alvarez, *El nacionalismo argentino*. Vol. 2. Buenos Aires: La Bastilla, 1975, 722.

9. Quoted in F. L. Carstens, *The Rise of Fascism*. 2d ed. Berkeley and Los Angeles: University of California Press, 1980, 198.

10. National Commission on the Disappeared, *Nunca Más*, xiii.

11. For an assessment of Lugones, see below, pp. 95–96.

12. Cristián Buchrucker, *Nacionalismo y peronismo: La Argentina en la crisis ideológica mundial (1927–1955)*. Buenos Aires: Sudamericana, 1987, 200. Buchrucker comes closest among recent writers in treating the Nationalist movement as Fascist, arguing that Hitler's invasion of the Soviet Union in 1941 united the ultra-right-

wing clerical groups (like the Argentine Nationalists) behind the Nazis. I have seen little evidence that such unification occurred. My own text attempts to trace some of these issues in more detail in chapters 5 and 6 in reviewing the genesis and growth of Peronism. Even Buchrucker, it should be noted, prefers the term *filofascista*, which means an admirer of fascism.

13. Hugh Trevor-Roper, "The Phenomenon of Fascism." In *European Fascism*. Edited by S. J. Woolf. London: Weidenfeld and Nicholson, 1968, 28.

14. Eugen Weber, *Varieties of Fascism*. Princeton: D. Van Nostrand Co., 1964, 481.

15. Weber, *Varieties*, 134.

16. Weber, *Varieties*, 515.

17. Nolte, *Faces*, 461. Nolte, however, explicitly removes Peronism from this category.

18. Trevor-Roper, "Fascism," 28.

19. For discussion, see Stanley G. Payne, "Spanish Fascism in Comparative Perspective." In *New Appraisals of Fascism*. Edited by Henry A. Turner, Jr. New York: New Viewpoints, 1975, 144.

20. Marysa Navarro Gerassi, *Los nacionalistas*. Buenos Aires: Jorge Alvarez, 1969, 97.

21. *The European Right: A Historical Profile*. Edited by Hans Rogger and Eugen Weber. Berkeley and Los Angeles: University of California Press, 1966.

22. Federico Ibarguren, *Nuestra tradición histórica*. Buenos Aires: Dictio, 1978, 15, 30.

23. Walter Beveraggi Allende, *El dogma nacionalista*. Buenos Aires: Manuel Belgrano, 1969, 5.

24. Quoted in Carlos H. Waisman, "The Ideology of Right-wing Nationalism in Argentina: Capitalism, Socialism, and the Jews," *Proceedings of the Ninth World Congress of Jewish Studies*, Jerusalem, 1986, 338.

25. Osiris J. Villegas, "La estrategia integral de la lucha subversiva," *Revista Militar*, January–April 1987, 11–19.

26. Villegas, "Estrategia integral," 15.

27. Quoted in *El Bimestre Político y Económico*, November 5, 1983.

Chapter 1. The Incubus of Doctrine

1. See the discussion of Portuguese *integralismo* in H. Martins, "Portugal." In Woolf, *European Fascism*, 302–336.

2. Angelo Del Bocca and Mario Giovana, *Fascism Today: A World Survey*. New York: Pantheon Books, 1969, 53.

3. Quoted in *Criterio*, July 13, 1933.

4. Ronald C. Newton, "On 'Functional Groups,' 'Fragmentation' and 'Pluralism' in Spanish American Political Society." In *Politics and Social Change in Latin America: The Distinct Tradition*. Edited by Howard J. Wiarda. Amherst: University of Massachusetts Press, 1974, 79.

5. Howard J. Wiarda, "Toward a Framework for Analysis." In Wiarda, *Politics*, 203.

6. Zeev Sternhell, *La droite révolutionnaire, 1885–1914: Les origines françaises du fascisme*. Paris: Editions de Seuil, 1978, 27.

7. Martins, "Portugal."

8. Salvatore Saladino, "Italy." In Rogger and Weber, *European Right*, 239.

9. Among the other general parallels between Romania and Latin American nations, including Argentina, were the use of the state as an instrument of modernization, the development of the state bureaucracy as a social class, the role of foreign minorities, upper classes linked to foreign banks which aped Western European fashions, and conspiracy theories of politics. Cf. Eugen Weber, "Romania." In Rogger and Weber, *European Right*, 568.

10. Sinarquismo, however, possessed a larger popular (often peasant) base. Its adherents were "les mécontents, les pauvres, les jeunes de la classe moyenne urbaine, les petits proprietaires, les paysans sans terre." Cf. Jean Meyer, *La sinarquisme: Un fascisme mexicain? 1937–1947*. Paris: Hachette, 1977, 32.

11. Jesús Guisa Azevedo, *Doctrina política de la reacción*. Mexico, 1941, 6.

12. Augusto Garcia Rocha Dorea, *O pensamento revolucionária de Plínio Salgado*. São Paulo: Voz de Oeste, 1975, ix–xi, 10.

13. Sinclair Lewis, *Babbit*. New York: Signet, 1980, 151–155.

14. I obtained the catalog in 1985 from the Librería Huemul in Buenos Aires. The books listed were published by the Editorial Nuevo Orden.

15. This judgment on Maurras appears in Arturo Jauretche, *FORJA y la década infame*. Buenos Aires: A. Peña Lillo, 1984, 21.

16. *La Nueva República*, January 1, 1928.

17. Federico Ibarguren, *Los orígenes del nacionalismo argentino*. Buenos Aires: Calcius, 1969, 213–214.

18. Glen Dealy, "The Tradition of Monistic Democracy in Latin America." In Wiarda, *Politics*, 79.

19. Ibarguren, *Orígenes*, 365.
20. Jordán B. Genta, *Acerca de la libertad de enseñar y de la enseñanza de la libertad.* Buenos Aires: Dictio, 1976, 12.
21. Salvador Ferla, *Doctrina del nacionalismo.* Buenos Aires, 1947, 49.
22. Bernice Hamilton, *Political Thought in Sixteenth-Century Spain: A Study of the Political Ideas of Vitoria, De Soto, Suárez, and Molina.* Oxford: Clarendon Press, 1963, 33. (Quoting Francisco Suárez.)
23. Ibarguren, *Orígenes*, 54.
24. Quoted in Fredrick B. Pike, *Hispanism, 1898–1936: Spanish Conservatives and Liberals and Their Relations with Latin America.* Notre Dame: University of Notre Dame Press, 1971, 265.
25. John L. Phelan, *The People and the King: The Comunero Revolution in Colombia, 1781.* Madison: University of Wisconsin Press, 1978, 81–86.
26. Juan Villagra, quoted in Buchrucker, *Nacionalism y peronismo*, 115.
27. Hugo Wast, "El Kahal." In Hugo Wast, *Obras completas de Hugo Wast.* Madrid, 1956, 1726.
28. *La Nueva República*, June 2, 1928.
29. J. L. Talmon, *The Myth of the Nation and the Vision of Revolution.* Berkeley, Los Angeles, and London: University of California Press, 1981, 540.
30. Michael Sutton, *Nationalism, Positivism and Catholicism: The Politics of Charles Maurras and French Catholics, 1890–1914.* Cambridge: Cambridge University Press, 1982, 18–37.
31. *Criterio*, March 10, 1932.
32. Ibarguren, *Orígenes*, 80.
33. Zuleta Alvarez, *Nacionalismo*, 2:722. Castellani also mentioned several Italian writers: Libertoni, Taparelli, and D'Azeglio.
34. On de Maistre, see *La Nueva República*, April and May 1929; and Ibarguren, *Orígenes*, 384. On Bonald, see Comisión de Estudios de la Sociedad Argentina de la Defensa de la Tradición, Familia y Propiedad, *El nacionalismo: Una incógnita en constante evolución.* Buenos Aires: Comisión de Estudios, 1970, 19. On Donoso Cortés, see Ibarguren, *Orígenes*, 362. On Balmes, see Pike, *Hispanism*, 24. Menéndez Pelayo arrived in Argentina mostly, it seemed, by way of Ramiro de Maeztu, Spanish ambassador to Argentina in 1927–1929 who was shot by the Republicans on the outbreak of the Spanish civil war in 1936. Cf. Zuleta Alvarez, *Nacionalismo*, 1: 40, 217. Julio Irazusta acknowledged the influence of Burke, de Maistre, Bonald,

Maeztu, Balmes, Donoso Cortés, Menéndez Pelayo, Maurras, and Benedetto Croce. See *Homenaje a Julio Irazusta*. Edited by Enrique Zuleta Alvarez, Mario Guillermo Saraví, and Enrique Díaz Araujo. Mendoza, 1984, 13.

35. Joseph de Maistre, *Une politique expérimentale*. Introduction and selected texts by Bernard de Vaulx. Paris: Librairie Arthème Fayard, 1940.

36. De Maistre, *Politique*, 36.

37. De Maistre, *Politique*, 218.

38. De Maistre, *Politique*, 155.

39. *Criterio*, January 7, 1930.

40. Ibarguren, *Orígenes*, 384.

41. Gustave de Bonald, *Considérations sur la Révolution Française*. Preface by Louis de Montesquiou. Paris: Nouvelle Librairie National, n.d., vi.

42. Bonald, *Considérations*, vii.

43. Bonald, *Considérations*, 53.

44. Bonald, *Considérations*, 52–53.

45. John Weiss, *Conservativism in Europe, 1770–1945*. London: Thames and Hudson, 1977, 48.

46. Gustavo Franceschi in *Criterio*, April 30, 1931.

47. Ibarguren, *Orígenes*, 362.

48. Quoted in *La Nueva República*, May 26, 1928.

49. Pike, *Hispanism*, 21.

50. Rogger and Weber, *European Right*, 176.

51. Pike, *Hispanism*, 24.

52. Raymond Carr, *Spain, 1808–1975*. 2d ed. Oxford: Oxford University Press, 1982, 355. Also Javier Herrero, *Los orígenes del pensamiento reaccionario español*. Madrid: Cuadernos para el Diálogo, 1971. Menéndez Pelayo is often rendered Menéndez y Pelayo.

53. Marcelino Menéndez Pelayo, *Historia de los ortodoxos españoles*. Madrid: Editorial Católico, 1956, 1192.

54. Menéndez Pelayo, *Historia*, 1193.

55. Menéndez Pelayo, *Historia*, 1194.

56. Menéndez Pelayo, *Historia*, 367.

57. Menéndez Pelayo, *Historia*, 368.

58. Pike, *Hispanism*, 75.

59. John A. Armstrong, *Nations before Nationalism*. Chapel Hill: University of North Carolina Press, 1982, 72–74.

60. Pike, *Hispanism*, 78, 97.

61. Comisión de Estudios, *Nacionalismo*, 55.

62. Genta, *Libertad*, 459.

63. Ibarguren, *Orígenes*, 371.

64. Comisión de Estudios, *Nacionalismo*, 55.

65. Ibarguren, *Orígenes*, 232.

66. Ibarguren, *Orígenes*, 13.

67. Comisión de Estudios, *Nacionalismo*, 55.

68. Ibarguren, *Orígenes*, 189.

69. José M. Rosa, "Defensa y pérdida de nuestra independencia económica," *Revista de Economía Argentina* XLI, no. 287 (May 1942): 131.

70. José Enrique Rodó, *Ariel*. Edited by Gordon Brotherston. Cambridge: Cambridge University Press, 1967, 84.

71. H. Ramsden, *Angel Ganivet's Idearium Español: A Critical Study*. Manchester: Manchester University Press, 1967, 156.

72. Ramsden, *Ganivet*, 35, 75.

73. Ramsden, *Ganivet*, 99.

74. Ramsden, *Ganivet*, 115.

75. For Kant in this context, see Elie Kedourie, *Nationalism*. New York: Frederick A. Praeger, 1960, 23.

76. Kedourie, *Nationalism*, 39.

77. For comments on Fustel de Coulanges's *Histoire des institutions politiques de la France*, see *Criterio*, December 4, 1930.

78. Menéndez Pelayo, *Historia*, 1193.

79. Sternhell, *La droite*, 18.

80. For Taine's influence on Barrès, see William Curt Buthman, *The Rise of Integral Nationalism in France*. New York: Octagon Books, 1970, 55–70.

81. Buthman, *Nationalism*, 109.

82. Manuel Gálvez, *El solar de la raza*. 5th ed. Madrid: Saturnino Callejas, n.d.

83. Sternhell, *La droite*, 15.

84. Sternhell, *La droite*, 148.

85. Rogger and Weber, *European Right*, 22–23. For an acknowledgment of Sorel's influence, see Juan E. Carulla, *Al filo de medio siglo*. Paraná, 1951, 145.

86. Jane Burbank, *Intelligentsia and Revolutionary Russian Views of Bolshevism, 1917–1922*. New York: Oxford University Press, 1986, 200–205.

87. For acknowledgments of Maurras's influence, see Comisión de Estudios, *Nacionalismo*, 25; Ibarguren, *Orígenes*, 12; Zuleta Alvarez et al., *Julio Irazusta*, 13. Also see Rodolfo Irazusta, *Testimonios*. Buenos Aires: Huencul, 1980, 20.

88. Marcelo Sánchez Sorondo, *La revolución que anunciamos*. Buenos Aires: Nueva Política, 1945, 246.

89. Carulla, *Medio siglo*, 147.

90. Irazusta and Falcionelli, in *Dinámica Social*, no. 28 (Dec. 1952).

91. Zuleta Alvarez, *Nacionalismo*, 1, 27.

92. Charles Maurras, *L'Avenir de l'Intelligence*. Paris: Ernest Flammarion, 1927, vi, 15.

93. Maurras, *L'Avenir*, 15.

94. Sternhell, *La droite*, 384–395.

95. Sternhell, *La droite*, 379.

96. Buthman, *Nationalism*, 277.

97. Sutton, *Maurras*, 41.

98. Maurras, *L'Avenir*, 16.

99. Sternhell, *La droite*, 214.

100. Oscar A. Troncoso, *Los nacionalistas argentinos: Antecedentes y trayectoria*. Buenos Aires: S.A.G.A., 1957, 29.

101. *Criterio*, January 30, 1930.

102. *La Nueva República*, December 15, 1929.

103. Enrique P. Osés, *Medios y fines del nacionalismo*. Buenos Aires, 1941, 28.

104. Osés, *Medios*, 64.

105. Ibarguren, *Orígenes*, 231.

106. *Criterio*, October 7, 1930.

107. Ibarguren, *Orígenes*, 189.

108. Carlos Ibarguren, Jr., *Roberto de Laferrére: Periodismo-Política-Historia*. Buenos Aires: Editorial de la Universidad de Buenos Aires, 1970, 36.

109. Ferla, *Nacionalismo*, 49.

110. Ibarguren, *Orígenes*, 393.

111. Quoted in Ibarguren, *Orígenes*, 363.

112. Ibarguren, *Orígenes*, 181–187.

113. Talmon, *Myth*, 499.

114. Pike, *Hispanism*, 294.

115. Genta, *Libertad*, 179.

116. *Criterio*, April 24, 1930.

117. Genta, *Libertad*, 315.

118. Quoted in Talmon, *Myth*, 402.

119. Ibarguren, *Orígenes*, 244.

120. Leopoldo Lugones, *La grande Argentina*. Buenos Aires: Babel, 1930, 157. (This publication is a collection of articles published during the 1920s.)

121. Ibarguren, *Orígenes*, 398.

122. Ibarguren, *Orígenes*, 389.

123. Talmon, *Myth*, 367.
124. Talmon, *Myth*, 222–223.
125. *Criterio*, January 29, 1931.
126. Norman Cohn, *Warrant for Genocide*. New York: Harper and Row, 1967, 54.
127. Cohn, *Genocide*, 61.
128. Quoted in Joseph Katz, *Freemasons and Jews in Europe*. Cambridge: Harvard University Press, 1970, 150.
129. Menéndez Pelayo, *Historia*, 446.
130. Genta, *Libertad*, 182.
131. *Crisol*, February 14, 1933.
132. *Crisol*, November 25, 1935.
133. *La Maroma*, January 1940.
134. Raúl Scalabrini Ortiz, "Bases para la reconstrucción nacional." In *La década infame*. Edited by Alberto Ciria. Buenos Aires: Carlos Pérez, 1968, 198. On the relations between Scalabrini Ortiz (normally seen as a leftist) and the Nationalists, see below, pp. 123–124.
135. Osés, *Medios*, 45.
136. Ibarguren, *Orígenes*, 398.

Chapter 2. The Threads of Tradition

1. Ernest Gellner, *Nations and Nationalism*. Oxford: Basil Blackwell, 1983, 94.
2. Manuel Gálvez, *El diario de Gabriel Quiroga: Opiniones sobre la vida argentina*. Buenos Aires: Arnoldo Möen, 1910, 56.
3. Gustavo Franceschi, in *Criterio*, July 6, 1933.
4. E. J. M. Clemens, *The La Plata Countries of South America*. Philadelphia: J. B. Lippincott Co., 1886, 303.
5. Américo A. Tonda, *La iglesia argentina incomunicada con Roma (1810–1858): Problemas, conflictos, soluciones*. Santa Fe: Castelví, 1965.
6. Mercedes Gandolfo, *La iglesia, factor de poder en la Argentina*. Montevideo, 1968, 71.
7. Quoted in Samuel Trífolo, *La Argentina vista por viajeros ingleses, 1810–1860*. Buenos Aires: Gure, 1959, 79. (My retranslation.)
8. Guillermo Furlong, S. J., "El catolicismo argentino entre 1860 y 1930." In *Historia argentina contemporánea, 1862–1930*, 2:251. Edited by Academia Nacional de la Historia. Buenos Aires: El Ateneo, 1964.
9. John Lynch, "The Catholic Church in Latin America,

1830–1930." In *Cambridge History of Latin America*, 4:534. Edited by Leslie Bethell. Cambridge: Cambridge University Press, 1986.

10. Raúl H. Castagnino, *Rosas y los jesuitas*. Buenos Aires: Pleamar, 1970.

11. Furlong, "Catolicismo argentino," 252. Disputes with Rome concerned not only the patronato. Another contentious issue was the *exaquatur*, the claim of the local authorities to review messages and communications from Rome before they were released or published. Rome refused contact until the region's independence was recognized by Spain.

12. Austen A. Ivereigh, "Nationalist Catholic Thought in Argentina, 1930–1946: Monseñor Gustavo Franceschi and *Criterio* in the Search for a Post-liberal Order." M. A. thesis. Oxford University, 1990, 2.

13. John J. Kennedy, *Catholicism, Nationalism and Democracy in Argentina*. Notre Dame: University of Notre Dame Press, 1958, 50.

14. Domingo F. Sarmiento, *Life in the Argentine Republic in the Days of the Tyrants. With a Biographical Sketch of the Author by Mrs. Horace Mann*. New York: Collier Books, 1961, 98.

15. Manuel E. Macchi, *Urquiza y el catolicismo*. Santa Fe: Castelví, 1969.

16. Manuel Juan Sanguinetti, *La representación diplomática del Vaticano en los países del Plata*. Buenos Aires: Talleres Gráficos Abecé, 1954, 82.

17. Lynch, "Catholic Church," 534.

18. E. E. Y. Hales, *Pio Nono: A Study in European Politics and Religion in the Nineteenth Century*. London: Eyre and Spottiswood, 1954, 240–258.

19. A. C. Jemolo, *Church and State in Italy, 1850–1950*. Translated by David Moore. Oxford: Basil Blackwell, 1960, 13.

20. Ricaurte Soler, *El positivismo argentino*. Mexico: Universidad Autónoma de México, 1979, 51.

21. Néstor Tomás Auza, *Católicos y liberales en la generación del ochenta*. 2d ed. Buenos Aires: Ediciones Culturales Argentinas, 1981, 14.

22. Quoted in Héctor Recalde, *La iglesia y la cuestión social, 1871–1910*. Buenos Aires: Centro Editor de América Latina, 1985, 35.

23. Recalde, *Iglesia*, 35.

24. Recalde, *Iglesia*, 44.

25. The episode is recounted in Sanguinetti, *Representación diplomática*, 80.

26. Recalde, *Iglesia*, 228.

27. Sanguinetti, *Representación diplomática*, 94.

28. Clemens, *La Plata*, 304.

29. Cámara de Diputados, *Diario de Sesiones*, I: 529. 1883 (July 11, 1883).

30. Furlong, "Catolicismo argentino," 265.

31. Auza, *Católicos*, 14.

32. José Manuel Estrada, *Discursos*. Prologue by Tomás Casares. Buenos Aires: Estrada, 1943, 1:84.

33. Auza, *Católicos*, 430.

34. Auza, *Católicos*, 274.

35. Auza, *Católicos*, 230.

36. Estrada, *Discursos*, 99.

37. Estrada, *Discursos*, 235; Kennedy, *Catholics*, 98–105.

38. Auza, *Católicos*, 42.

39. Estrada, *Discursos*, 333.

40. Estrada, October 18, 1888. Quoted in Alicia S. García and Ricardo Rodríguez Molas, *El autoritismo y los argentinos: La hora de la espada (1924–1946)*. Buenos Aires: Centro Editor de América Latina, 1988, 15.

41. Quoted in *Criterio*, September 18, 1930.

42. For an extensive discussion of these social and political changes after 1890, see David Rock, *Politics in Argentina, 1890–1930: The Rise and Fall of Radicalism*. Cambridge: Cambridge University Press, 1975, chaps. 1–4.

43. *Rerum Novarum*, May 15, 1891. In *Seven Great Encyclicals*. 2d ed. Edited by William J. Gibbons, S. J. Glen Rock, N.J.: Paulist Press, 1963, 2.

44. Gibbons, *Rerum Novarum*, 2.

45. Gibbons, *Rerum Novarum*, 3.

46. Gibbons, *Rerum Novarum*, 8.

47. Gibbons, *Rerum Novarum*, 2.

48. Gibbons, *Rerum Novarum*, 18.

49. José Elías Níklison, "Acción social católica," *Boletín del Departamento Nacional del Trabajo*, no. 46 (March 1920):19.

50. For a lengthy description of these projects, see Alejandro E. Bunge, "La acción social obrera," *Revista de Economía Argentina* XL, no. 274 (April 1941): 124–131. (First published in 1913.) Catholic activities among women are examined in Sandra McGee Deutsch, "The Catholic Church, Work, and Womanhood in Argentina, 1890–1930." Mimeo.

51. For an account of Grote's activities, see Michael A. Burdick,

"For God and Fatherland: Religion and Politics in Argentina." Ph.D. diss. University of California, Santa Barbara, 1991, 35.

52. Níklison, "Acción," 120.

53. Níklison, "Acción," 197.

54. Níklison, "Acción," 255.

55. Quoted in Hobart E. Spalding, *La clase trabajadora argentina (Documentos para su historia, 1890–1912)*. Buenos Aires: Galerna, 1970, 544.

56. Soler, *Positivismo*, 49.

57. Soler, *Positivismo*, 13.

58. Carlos Ibarguren, *La historia que he vivido*. Buenos Aires: Peuser, 1955, 114.

59. Rodó, *Ariel*, 9.

60. Rodó, *Ariel*, 68.

61. Rodó, *Ariel*, 18.

62. Manuel Gálvez, *Amigos y maestros de mi juventud*. Buenos Aires: Hachette, 1961, 43.

63. Eduardo José Cárdenas and Carlos Manuel Payá, *El primer nacionalismo argentino en Manuel Gálvez y Ricardo Rojas*. Buenos Aires: A. Peña Lillo, 1978, 119.

64. Gálvez, *Amigos*, 147.

65. Manuel Gálvez, *Solar*, 15–16.

66. Quoted in Mónica Quijada, *Manuel Gálvez: 60 años de pensamiento nacionalista*. Buenos Aires: Centro Editor de América Latina, 1985, 31.

67. Belisario J. Montero, "De mi diario," *Ideas*, no. 13 (1904): 8–10.

68. Gálvez, *Amigos*, 43.

69. Oscar Cornblit, "Inmigrantes y empresarios en la política argentina." In *Los fragmentos del poder*. Edited by Torcuato S. Di Tella and Tulio Halperín Donghi. Buenos Aires: Jorge Alvarez, 1969, 389–438.

70. For a more extensive discussion, see Carl Solberg, *Immigration and Nationalism in Argentina and Chile, 1890–1914*. Austin: University of Texas Press, 1970.

71. Arturo Reynal O'Connor, "Los poetas argentinos," *Ideas*, no. 15 (1905):259.

72. José Hernández, *The gaucho Martín Fierro*. Adapted from the Spanish and Rendered into English Verse by Walter Owen with Drawings by Alberto Guiraldes. New York: Farrar and Rinehart, 1936, 40.

73. Quoted in Paul Everett Brown, "Ideological Origins of Mod-

ern Argentine Nationalism." Ph.D. diss. Claremont Graduate School, 1975, 229.

74. These issues are discussed in Tulio Halperín Donghi, "¿Para qué la inmigración? Ideología y política inmigratoria y aceleración del proceso modernizador: El caso argentino (1810–1914)," *Jahrbuch für Geschichte von Staat, Wirtschaft und Gesellschaft Lateinamerikas* 13 (1976):458–472.

75. Carlos H. Waisman, "The Question of Revolution and the Reversal of Development in Argentina." Mimeo, 64.

76. Halperín, "Inmigración," 472. Drumont himself plagiarized an earlier anti–Semite, Gougenot de Mousseaux. Cf. Cohn, *Genocide*, 50.

77. María Inés Barbero and Fernando Devoto, *Los nacionalistas*. Buenos Aires: Centro Editor de América Latina, 1983, 18.

78. Article in *La Nación*, June 20, 1906.

79. Gálvez, *Amigos*, 39.

80. Gálvez claimed to be the eighth-generation descendant of Juan de Garay, the founder of the cities of Santa Fe and Buenos Aires. Cf. Ignacio B. Anzoateguí, *Manuel Gálvez*. Buenos Aires: Ediciones Culturales Argentinas, 1961; Cárdenas and Payá, *Primer nacionalismo*, 54.

81. Esther Hadasah Scott Turner, "Hispanism in the Life and Works of Manuel Gálvez." Ph.D. diss. University of Washington, 1958, 174–177.

82. Gálvez, *Quiroga*, 129.

83. For a recent study of this issue, see Donna J. Guy, *Sex and Danger in Buenos Aires: Prostitution, Family, and Nation in Argentina*. Lincoln: University of Nebraska Press, 1991.

84. Manuel Gálvez, *Nacha Regules*. Buenos Aires: Tor, n.d., 26.

85. Ricardo Oliver, "Sinceridades," *Ideas*, no. 1 (1903):3.

86. Gálvez, *Quiroga*, 13.

87. Gálvez, *Amigos*, 238.

88. Gálvez, *Quiroga*, 34.

89. Gálvez, *Quiroga*, 51–53.

90. Gálvez, *Quiroga*, 100–103.

91. Gálvez, *Quiroga*, 219–223.

92. Gálvez, *Quiroga*, 230–232.

93. Gálvez, *Quiroga*, 67.

94. Gálvez, *Quiroga*, 124–125.

95. Ricardo Rojas, *La restauración nacionalista*. 2d ed. Buenos Aires, 1922, 25, 120. (The first edition appeared in 1909.) Educational issues during this period are discussed in Solberg, *Immigration*, 146–148.

96. Quoted in Barbero and Devoto, *Nacionalistas*, 19.

97. Rojas, *Restauración*, 120.

98. Rojas, *Restauración*, 121.

99. Rojas, *Restauración*, 125.

100. Ricardo Rojas, *Eurindia*. In Ricardo Rojas, *Obras de Ricardo Rojas*, 5:42. Buenos Aires: La Facultad, 1924.

101. Ibarguren, *Historia*, 17.

102. Ibarguren, *Historia*, 11.

103. Sandra McGee Deutsch, *Counterrevolution in Argentina, 1900–1932: The Argentine Patriotic League*. Lincoln: University of Nebraska Press, 1986, 61.

104. *Montonera* was the term applied to the nineteenth-century Federalist guerrillas in the Argentine interior.

105. Ibarguren, *Historia*, 13.

106. Ibarguren, *Historia*, 237.

107. Ibarguren, *Historia*, 241. Saenz Peña and Gómez were the chief architects of the suffrage law of 1911–12, which Ibarguren as a Nationalist later condemned. Ibarguren himself served as a minister in the Saenz Peña government.

108. Ibarguren, *Historia*, 263.

109. Rojas, *Restauración*, 116.

110. Gálvez, *Amigos*, 84.

111. Manuel Gálvez, *El espiritualismo español*. Buenos Aires: Bayardo, 1921, 10.

112. Quoted in Quijada, *Gálvez*, 27.

113. Gálvez, *Amigos*, 43.

114. Gálvez, *Solar*, 15–16.

115. Cárdenas and Payá, *Primer nacionalismo*, 123.

116. Ramsden, *Ganivet*, 59.

117. Pike, *Hispanismo*, 134.

118. Cárdenas and Payá, *Primer nacionalismo*, 72.

119. Arturo Caturelli, *El itinerario espiritual de Leopoldo Lugones*. Buenos Aires: Mikael, 1981, 6.

120. Leopoldo Lugones, Jr., *Mi padre: Biografía de Leopoldo Lugones*. Buenos Aires: Centurión, 1949, 27.

121. Julio Irazusta, *Genio y figura de Leopoldo Lugones*. Buenos Aires: Editorial de la Universidad de Buenos Aires, 1968, 23–24.

122. Quoted in Irazusta, *Lugones*, 23. The verse commemorates the services of Lugones's ancestor to the Spanish Crown for which he received *encomiendas* in Salta and Santiago del Estero.

123. Irazusta, *Lugones*, 23.

124. Cárdenas and Payá, *Primer nacionalismo*, 25.

125. Lugones, "Prometeo." In Leopoldo Lugones, Jr., ed., *Obras en prosa.* Mexico: Aguilar, 1962, 1005.

126. Lugones, "Prometeo," 1031.

127. Cf. Lugones, Jr., *Mi padre,* 113.

128. Caturelli, *Lugones,* 23.

129. Lugones, "Prometeo," 1050.

130. Lugones, Jr., *Mi padre,* 232.

131. Leopoldo Lugones, "El payador." In Leopoldo Lugones, Jr., ed., *Obras en prosa.* Mexico: Aguilar, 1962, 1079–1082.

132. Lugones, "El payador," 1085.

133. Quoted in Caturelli, *Lugones,* 32.

134. Gálvez, *Solar,* 14.

135. Lugones, "Prometeo," 778.

136. Lugones, "Prometeo," 1005.

137. Juan E. Carulla, *Al filo de medio siglo.* Paraná, 10–11.

138. Cárdenas and Payá, *Primer nacionalismo,* 52.

139. Irazusta, *Lugones,* 7.

140. Similar "declining classes" have been identified as supporters of early-twentieth-century nationalism in Poland. Cf. Talmon, *Myth,* 126.

141. Gálvez, *Amigos,* 125.

142. Cf. Cárdenas and Payá, *Primer nacionalismo,* 130.

143. Gálvez, *Amigos,* 39.

144. Rodó, *Ariel,* 6.

145. Gálvez, *Nacha Regules,* 9.

146. Lugones, "Prometeo," 1074.

147. Gálvez, *Amigos,* 12.

148. Níklison, "Acción," 200.

149. *Criterio,* July 6, 1933.

150. Quoted in Buchrucker, *Nacionalismo,* 51.

Chapter 3. Rule by the Capable

1. Quoted in Irazusta, *Lugones,* 111.

2. Turner, "Gálvez," 207.

3. Barbero and Devoto, *Nacionalistas,* 20–28.

4. Ibarguren, *Historia,* 234.

5. Ibarguren, *Historia,* 305. Ibarguren recalled the 1915 program in his memoirs published in 1955. The measures listed in 1915—state control of international trade, the development of a merchant marine, the use of exchange controls—were almost identical

to those instituted by Perón at the time Ibarguren was writing. Thus, Ibarguren was claiming intellectual authorship of Perón's measures.

6. Quoted in Waisman, "Revolution," 17.

7. Irazusta, *Lugones*, 28.

8. Lugones, "Prometeo," 1074–1075.

9. Irazusta, *Lugones*, 24.

10. Irazusta, *Lugones*, 32.

11. Quoted in Victoria Itzcovich, "La ideología golpista antes de 1930. (Los escritos políticos de Leopoldo Lugones),"*El Bimestre Político y Económico*, no. 30 (1986): 2.

12. Lugones, "El payador," 1293.

13. Irazusta, *Lugones*, 32.

14. Cárdenas and Payá, *Primer nacionalismo*, 92.

15. McGee Deutsch, *Counterrevolution*, 61.

16. *La Prensa*, May 9, 1919.

17. Iaacov Oveid, "El trasfondo histórico de la ley 4144, de residencia," *Desarrollo Económico* 16, no. 61 (April–June 1976): 123–150.

18. Rock, *Politics*, 67–94.

19. Solberg, *Nationalism*, 148–150.

20. Turner, "Gálvez," 187.

21. McGee Deutsch, *Counterrevolution*, 35–36. The events of 1909 and 1910 are also described in Solberg, *Nationalism*, 112–114.

22. *Diario de Sesiones*, Cámara de Diputados, vol. 1 (1910): 295, 325.

23. Gálvez, *Quiroga*, 232–234.

24. Gálvez, *Quiroga*, 77.

25. Gálvez, *Quiroga*, 232.

26. "Krausism" derived from Karl Christian Krause, a disciple of Kant. See Juan Lopez-Morillas, *The Krausist Movement and Ideological Change in Spain, 1854–1874*. Translated by Frances M. Lopez Morillas. Cambridge: Cambridge University Press, 1981. The movement's growth and influence in Argentina is discussed by Arturo Andrés Roig, *Los krausistas argentinos*. Puebla, Mexico: José N. Cajica, 1969.

27. Roig, *Krausistas*, 148, 217, 304, 492.

28. Hipólito Yrigoyen, *Pueblo y gobierno*. Edited by Roberto Etchepareborda. I. *La reparación fundamental*. Buenos Aires: Raigal, 1955, 86. Yrigoyen's writings are notoriously florid and obscure; my translations are very free.

29. Quoted in Gabriel del Mazo, *El radicalismo: Ensayo sobre su historia y doctrina*. I:55. Buenos Aires: Gure, 1957.

30. Yrigoyen, *Reparación*, 126.

31. Yrigoyen, *Reparación*, 126.

32. Yrigoyen, *Reparación*, 125.

33. Gardenia Vidal, "Los partidos políticos y la estabilidad del sistema democrático: El Partido Radical en Córdoba, 1916–1925." *Primeras Jornadas Inter-Escuelas Departamentos de Historia* (October 1988):5. Universidad Nacional de la Plata.

34. Rock, *Politics*, 59.

35. Roberto Etchepareborda, *Yrigoyen y el congreso*. Buenos Aires: Raigal, 1956.

36. Rock, *Politics*, 62.

37. Mitchell-Innes to Foreign Office, April 8, 1919. Despatch no. 94, April 9, 1919. FO 371–3504. (Public Record Office, London.)

38. Barbero and Devoto, *Nacionalismo*, 37.

39. *La Época*, December 27, 1918.

40. For a fuller discussion, see Rock, *Politics*, 125–156.

41. Ignacio D. Irigoyen, in *Diario de Sesiones*, Senadores, vol. 2 (1918–19):83.

42. Luis Agote, in *Diario de Sesiones*, Cámara de Diputados, vol. 15 (1918–19):70–72.

43. Rock, *Politics*, 169.

44. Ibarguren, *Historia*, 324.

45. García and Rodríguez Molas, *Autoritarismo*, 18. (Quoting Gen. José F. Uriburu in 1914.)

46. *La Prensa*, January 20, 1919. Military issues are examined in detail in Frederick M. Nunn, *European Military Professionalization in South America, 1890–1940*. Lincoln: University of Nebraska Press, 1983.

47. Pedro A. Echagüe in *Diario de Sesiones*, Senadores, vol. 2 (1918–19): 40.

48. Sandra F. McGee, "The Visible and Invisible Liga Patriótica Argentina, 1919–28: Gender Roles and the Right Wing," *Hispanic American Historical Review* 64, no. 2 (May 1984):233–258.

49. Manuel Carlés, speech to the Sociedad de Beneficencia, May 29, 1919. Quoted in Barbero and Devoto, *Nacionalistas*, 49.

50. McGee Deutsch, *Counterrevolution*, 137. The mazorqueros belonged to Rosas's police force, the *mazorca*.

51. Barbero and Devoto, *Nacionalistas*, 49. During the same era, Sinclair Lewis's character Babbit expressed the same ideas in more homespun language. He also attempted to create a movement like the Argentine Patriotic League in his hometown of Zenith known as the Good Citizen League. Cf. Lewis, *Babbit*, 152, 176, 311.

52. Ibarguren, *Historia*, 114.

53. Carlos Ibarguren, *La literatura y la gran guerra*. Buenos Aires: La Cooperativa Editorial "Buenos Aires," 1920, 7.

54. Ibarguren, *Historia*, 279.

55. Ibarguren, *Literatura*, 62.

56. Gálvez, *Espiritualismo*, 2–3.

57. Alejandro E. Bunge, *La economía argentina*. Vol. 1. Buenos Aires: Agencia General de Librerías y Publicaciones, 1928, 9. Bunge explained that Lugones had persuaded him to write the book.

58. Many of Bunge's ideas during the war and immediate post-war periods are reprinted in Alejandro E. Bunge, *Una nueva Argentina*. Buenos Aires: Kraft, 1940. See also A. E. Bunge, *La nueva política económica argentina: Introduccion al estudio de la industria nacional*. Buenos Aires: Unión Industrial Argentina, 1921.

59. Lugones, Jr., *Mi padre*, 281.

60. Lugones, Jr., *Mi padre*, 274.

61. Lugones, Jr., *Mi padre*, 293.

62. Speech in the Coliseo Theater, July 1923. Reprinted in Barbero and Devoto, *Nacionalistas*, 52.

63. Quoted in Barbero and Devoto, *Nacionalistas*, 52–55.

64. Itzcovich, "Lugones," 2.

65. Barbero and Devoto, *Nacionalistas*, 55.

66. Leopoldo Lugones, "El discurso de Ayacucho." In Leopoldo Lugones, *La patria fuerte*. Buenos Aires: Círculo Militar, 1930, 19.

67. Lugones, "Ayacucho," 19.

68. Irazusta, *Lugones*, 114.

69. Quoted in Itzcovich, "Lugones," 9.

70. Lugones, Jr., *Mi padre*, 326, 335.

71. *La Nación*, March 4, 1926.

72. *La Nación*, May 1, 1927.

73. *La Nueva República*, December 1, 1928.

74. Lugones, *La patria fuerte*, 52.

75. Lugones, *La patria fuerte*, 157.

76. Lugones, *La patria fuerte*, 49.

77. Lugones, *La patria fuerte*, 70.

78. Lugones, *La patria fuerte*, 9.

79. Caturelli, *Lugones*, 133.

80. *La Nueva República*, July 21, 1928.

81. Lugones, *La patria fuerte*, 167.

82. Ibarguren, *Historia*, 318.

83. *La Fronda*, May 20, 1928.

84. Barbero and Devoto, *Nacionalistas*, 37.

85. Manuel Carlés, *Conferencia pronunciada en el Centro de Almaceneros*. Buenos Aires: Centro de Almaceneros, 1926, 33–34.

86. Benjamín Villafañe, *Degenerados: Tiempos en que la mentira y el robo engendran apóstoles*. Buenos Aires, 1928, 10.

87. *La Fronda*, June 22, 1927.

88. Carulla, *Medio siglo*, 48, 80.

89. Carulla, *Medio siglo*, 150.

90. Carulla, *Medio siglo*, 16.

91. Carulla, *Medio siglo*, 159.

92. Zuleta Alvarez, *Nacionalismo*, 1, 205.

93. Carulla, *Medio siglo*, 175.

94. Zuleta Alvarez et al., *Julio Irazusta*, 13.

95. Carulla, *Medio siglo*, 167.

96. *La Nueva República*, December 1, 1927.

97. *La Nueva República*, June 14, 1930.

98. *La Nueva República*, December 1, 1927.

99. *La Nueva República*, December 12, 1928.

100. *La Nueva República*, July 7, 1928.

101. *La Nueva República*, December 1, 1928.

102. *La Nueva República*, March 1, 1928.

103. *La Nueva República*, January 31, 1928.

104. *La Nueva República*, October 20, November 3, December 1, 1928.

105. *La Nueva República*, April 22, 1928.

106. *La Nueva República*, July 7, 1928.

107. *La Nueva República*, April 1, 1928.

108. Uriburu attended the group's first anniversary banquet. Cf. *La Nueva República*, December 12, 1928.

109. *La Nueva República*, June 26, 1928.

110. *La Nueva República*, December 1, 1927.

111. Zuleta Alvarez et al., *Julio Irazusta*, 12, 73.

112. *La Nueva República*, December 1, 1927.

113. *La Nueva República*, April 23, 1928.

114. Zuleta Alvarez, *Nacionalismo*, I: 208; Irazusta, *Testimonios*, 20.

115. *La Nueva República*, December 1, 1928.

116. Irazusta, *Testimonios*, 21.

117. An example appears in one of Carulla's articles in *La Nueva República*, October 12, 1928.

118. Carulla, *Medio siglo*, 145. Another source shows that the alliance between Maurras and Sorel was created in 1911. Cf. Sternhell, *La droite*, 384.

119. Carulla, *Medio siglo*, 128, 147.
120. Carulla, *Medio siglo*, 145–147.
121. Carulla, *Medio siglo*, 166.
122. For a broader discussion of the Catholic revival, see Ivereigh, "Catholic Thought."
123. *La Nueva República*, January 15, 1928.
124. *La Nueva República*, January 4, 1928.
125. *La Nueva República*, April 23, 1928.
126. *La Nueva República*, June 26, 1928.
127. *La Nueva República*, March 1, 1928.
128. *La Nueva República*, May 26, 1928.
129. Carulla, *Medio siglo*, 175.
130. Quoted in Troncoso, *Nacionalistas*, 47.
131. *La Nueva República*, June 26, 1928.
132. *La Nueva República*, May 5, 1928.
133. *La Nueva República*, July 21, 1928.
134. Carulla, *Medio siglo*, 20.
135. *La Nueva República*, September 5, 1930.

Chapter 4. The Nationalist Crusade

1. Quoted in Ibarguren, *Orígenes*, 405.
2. Ibarguren, *Historia*, 305.
3. Matías Sánchez Sorondo, "6 de septiembre de 1930." In Ciria, *Década infame*, 54.
4. Rock, *Politics*, 212.
5. Carulla, *Medio siglo*, 180.
6. Carulla, *Medio siglo*, 182.
7. Roberto de Laferrère claimed to have created the Liga Republicana, but as Carulla claimed: "Without boasting I can say that my own efforts were important in stimulating the new organization" (Carulla, *Medio siglo*, 183).
8. Quoted in *La Vanguardia*, October 15, 1929.
9. *La Nueva República*, July 20, 1930.
10. *La Nueva República*, September 29, 1930.
11. *Criterio*, September 11, 1930.
12. Felix J. Weil, *Argentina Riddle*. New York: John Day, 1944, 39.
13. The revolutionary proclamation of September 6, 1930, quoted in García and Rodríguez Molas, *Autoritarismo*, 66.
14. García and Rodríguez Molas, *Autoritarismo*, 68, 105.
15. Manuel Lezica, *Recuerdos de un nacionalista*. Buenos Aires: Astral, 1968, 41.

16. Quoted in Lezica, *Recuerdos*, 33.

17. Ibarguren, *Historia*, 419.

18. Troncoso, *Nacionalistas*, 20.

19. Comisión de Estudios, *Nacionalismo*, 29.

20. *La Nueva República*, December 13, 1930.

21. Lezica, *Recuerdos*, 54–56.

22. García and Rodríguez Molas, *Autoritarismo*, 122.

23. Lezica, *Recuerdos*, 58.

24. Alain Rouquié, *Poder militar y sociedad política en la Argentina*. Vol. 1. Hasta 1943. Buenos Aires: Emecé, 1983, 249; also McGee Deutsch, *Counterrevolution*, 209–212.

25. Carulla, *Medio siglo*, 210.

26. Carulla, *Medio siglo*, 209.

27. García and Rodríguez Molas, *Autoritarismo*, 129.

28. *Crisol*, February 14, 1932.

29. Ibarguren, *Orígenes*, 303.

30. For comments on the social composition of the Nationalist bands in the 1930s, see Leonardo Castellani, in *Primera Plana*, May 16, 1967.

31. Navarro, *Nacionalistas*, 93.

32. *Crisol*, May 1, 1934.

33. *Criterio*, October 20, 1932.

34. García and Rodríguez Molas, *Autoritarismo*, 20.

35. García and Rodríguez Molas, *Autoritarismo*, 50.

36. *Crisol*, January 19, 1934.

37. Ibarguren, *Orígenes*, 325.

38. On Lugones's return to the church, see Irazusta, *Lugones*, 116.

39. Gálvez, *Amigos y maestros*, 208.

40. Jauretche, *FORJA*, 21–22.

41. Weil, *Riddle*, 20.

42. Norberto Galasso, *Raúl Scalabrini Ortiz y la penetración inglesa*. Buenos Aires: Centro Editor de América Latina, 1984, 37.

43. Carulla, *Medio siglo*, 223.

44. *La Vanguardia*, January 2, 1935.

45. Cf. *La Nueva República*, December 13, 1930.

46. Ibarguren, *Orígenes*, 228.

47. Cf. Ibarguren, *Orígenes*, 306.

48. Ronald H. Dolkart, "Manuel Fresco, Governor of the Province of Buenos Aires, 1936–1940: A Study of the Argentine Right and Its Response to Economic and Social Change." Ph.D. diss. University of California, Los Angeles, 1969, 80.

49. Carulla, *Medio siglo*, 221.

50. *La Voz Nacionalista, El nacionalismo argentino*. Buenos Aires, 1935, 14.

51. Marcelo Sánchez Sorondo, quoted in García and Rodríguez Molas, *Autoritarismo*, 150–151.

52. Ibarguren, *Orígenes*, 357.

53. Nunn, *Military*, 261–262. (Quoting Col. Enrique Rottjer.)

54. *La Vanguardia*, April 9, 1935.

55. Robert A. Potash, *The Army and Politics in Argentina, 1928–1965: Yrigoyen to Perón*. Stanford: Stanford University Press, 1969, 144–148, 163, 218.

56. Wast, *Obras*, xii.

57. C. Ibarguren, Jr., *Laferrère*, 7.

58. Ibarguren, *Orígenes*, 405.

59. Osés, *Medios*, 43.

60. Comisión de Estudios, *Nacionalismo*, 54.

61. Ibarguren, *Orígenes*, 227. In the following section, I have quoted extensively from this work, which is a collection of National-ist writings, programs, and treatises.

62. Ibarguren, *Orígenes*, 392.

63. Ibarguren, *Orígenes*, 393.

64. Ibarguren, *Orígenes*, 392.

65. Ivereigh, "Catholic Thought," 17, 20.

66. Hugo Wast, *Oro*. In Wast, *Obras completas*, 1767.

67. Ibarguren, *Orígenes*, 214.

68. Segments of the *Politeia* appear in Ibarguren, *Orígenes*, 385–386.

69. Comisión de Estudios, *Nacionalismo*, 54.

70. Ibarguren, *Orígenes*, 264. (Quoting Matías Sánchez Sorondo.)

71. Ibarguren, *Orígenes*, 303.

72. Ibarguren, *Orígenes*, 359.

73. C. Ibarguren, Jr., *Laferrère*, 69–70.

74. Lugones, *Grande Argentina*, 110.

75. *Crisol*, August 19, 1934.

76. Lugones, *Grande Argentina*, 172.

77. Ibarguren, *Orígenes*, 398.

78. Ibarguren, *Orígenes*, 26.

79. C. Ibarguren, Jr., *Laferrère*, 69.

80. C. Ibarguren, Jr., *Laferrère*, 69.

81. Lugones, *Grande Argentina*, 120.

82. Alejandro E. Bunge, "Esplendor y decadencia de la raza blanca," *Revista de Economía Argentina* XXXIX, no. 259 (Jan. 1940):9–23.

83. Ibarguren, *Orígenes*, 352.

84. Ibarguren, *Orígenes*, 281.

85. *Criterio*, February 23, 1933.

86. *Criterio*, January 12, 1933.

87. *Criterio*, June 11, 1931.

88. *Criterio*, January 12, 1933.

89. *Criterio*, September 29, 1932.

90. *Crisol*, January 24, 1935; Ibarguren, *Orígenes*, 367.

91. *Criterio*, June 23, 1932.

92. *Criterio*, April 9 and June 4, 1931. Anti-Semitism was strongest in *Criterio* during the editorship of Enrique Osés and declined when Franceschi took over in 1932. Franceschi himself expressed doubts over the authenticity of the *Protocols* in *Criterio*, July 28, 1932.

93. Wast, *Oro*, 1659.

94. Wast, *Oro*, 1665.

95. Wast, *Oro*, 1681.

96. Wast, *Oro*, 1702.

97. Wast, *Oro*, 1726.

98. Wast, *Oro*, 1766.

99. Wast, *Oro*, 1650. The distinction between "cultural" and "biological" anti-Semitism appears in Anthony D. S. Smith, *Nationalism in the Twentieth Century*. New York: New York University Press, 1979, 58.

100. *La Vanguardia*, June 5, 1935.

101. *Criterio*, April 16, 1931.

102. Harold Eugene Davis, *Latin American Political Thought: A Historical Introduction*. New York: Free Press, 1974, 177.

103. Quoted in Turner, "Gálvez," 180.

104. Quijada, *Gálvez*, 74, 77.

105. Osés, *Medios*, 43.

106. Osés, *Medios*, 220.

107. Ibarguren, *Orígenes*, 277.

108. *Criterio*, April 20, 1933.

109. Ibarguren, *Historia*, 469.

110. *Primera Plana*, May 16, 1967.

111. Sánchez Sorondo, *Revolución*, 180.

112. Comisión de Estudios, *Nacionalismo*, 110–111.

113. Troncoso, *Nacionalistas*, 58.

114. Ibarguren, *Orígenes*, 375.

115. Ibarguren, *Orígenes*, 277.

116. Navarro, *Nacionalistas*, 97–99.

117. *Criterio*, November 6, 1930.

118. *Criterio*, July 13, 1933.

119. *Criterio*, May 21, 1931.

120. Ibarguren, *Orígenes*, 405.

121. José María Estrada, *El legado de nacionalismo*. Buenos Aires: Gure, 1956, 50.

122. *Criterio*, March 8, 1933.

123. Ibarguren, *Orígenes*, 14.

124. *Criterio*, October 20, 1932.

125. *Criterio*, April 4, 1930.

126. *La Voz Nacionalista, Nacionalismo*, 20.

127. *Crisol*, June 12, 1936.

128. Mario Amadeo, *Hoy, Ayer, Mañana*. Buenos Aires: Gure, 1956, 113–114.

129. *La Nueva República*, September 20, 1930.

130. Ibarguren, *Orígenes*, 375.

131. *Criterio*, July 28, 1932.

132. *Criterio*, October 20, 1932.

133. Carulla, *Medio siglo*, 229.

134. Carulla, *Medio siglo*, 230.

135. Quoted in Stewart Edward Sutin, "The Impact of Nazism on the Germans of Argentina." Ph.D. diss. University of Texas, 1975, 68.

136. Sutin, "Nazism," 56. An estimated 180,000 persons in Argentina, most of them in Buenos Aires or the province of Misiones, spoke German as a first language during the late 1930s.

137. *Diario de Sesiones*, Cámara de Diputados, vol. 1, 1939, 639.

138. *Criterio*, June 18, 1931.

139. Ibarguren, *Orígenes*, 364.

140. Ivereigh, "Catholic Thought," 88.

141. Quijada, *Gálvez*, 88.

142. Navarro, *Nacionalistas*, 127, quoting Mario Amadeo.

143. *Criterio*, July 17, 1937.

144. Ibarguren, *Historia*, 470.

145. Cf. Mark Falcoff, "Argentina." In *The Spanish Civil War*. Edited by Mark Falcoff and Fredrick B. Pike. Lincoln: University of Nebraska Press, 1982, 321.

146. Ibarguren, *Orígenes*, 352.

147. Ibarguren, *Orígenes*, 392.

148. *Criterio*, April 20, 1933.

149. *Quadragesimo Anno*, in Gibbons, *Encyclicals*, 128–130.

150. Gibbons, *Encyclicals*, 139.

151. Gibbons, *Encyclicals*, 141.
152. Gibbons, *Encyclicals*, 144.
153. Gibbons, *Encyclicals*, 145.
154. Gibbons, *Encyclicals*, 147.
155. Gibbons, *Encyclicals*, 151, 154.
156. *Quadragesimo Anno* criticized Socialists much less than did *Rerum Novarum* and now found them at fault mainly because they were atheists, materialists, or "world oriented." The Nationalists drew on this approach and attacked socialism as a "philosophy of consumption," which would provoke such heavy demands on the state as to lead to its collapse. For the Nationalist position on socialism, see Julio Irazusta, in *Criterio*, July 13, 1933.
157. *Criterio*, June 23, 1932.
158. *Crisol*, March 22, 1932.
159. Ibarguren, *Orígenes*, 347–350.
160. *La Voz Nacionalista, Nacionalismo*, 5.
161. Quoted in Comisión de Estudios, *Nacionalismo*, 50.
162. Cf. Gustavo Sosa-Pujato, "Popular Culture." In *Prologue to Perón: Argentina in Depression and War, 1930–1943*. Edited by Mark Falcoff and Ronald H. Dolkart. Berkeley, Los Angeles, and London: University of California Press, 1975, 155.
163. Dolkart, "Fresco," 142.
164. Dolkart, "Fresco," 278.
165. Brown, "Nationalism," 186–197.
166. Rodolfo Irazusta and Julio Irazusta, *La Argentina y el imperio británico: Los eslabones de una cadena, 1806–1933*. Buenos Aires: Tor, 1934.
167. *Crisol*, July 11, 1936.
168. Sánchez Sorondo, *Revolución*, 35.
169. C. Ibarguren, Jr., *Laferrère*, 89.
170. *La Maroma*, January 1940.
171. *Crisol*, February 7, 1934.
172. Navarro, *Nacionalistas*, 148.
173. *Crisol*, May 13 and July 28, 1935.
174. *Crisol*, December 15, 1935.
175. Ernesto Palacio, *Catilina contra la oligarquía*. Buenos Aires: Rosso, 1935, 12, 25–26.
176. C. Ibarguren, Jr., *Laferrère*, 10.
177. Quoted in Zuleta Alvarez, *Nacionalismo*, 350.
178. Ibarguren, *Orígenes*, 371.
179. C. Ibarguren, Jr., *Laferrère*, 90.
180. C. Ibarguren, Jr., *Laferrère*, 90.

181. *La Vanguardia*, July 4, 1934.

182. *La Vanguardia*, July 28, 1934.

183. *Crisol*, July 31, 1934.

184. Halperín, *Revisionismo*, 14.

185. For an account of the ceremony, see Ibarguren, *Orígenes*, 399.

186. Quoted in Hebe Clementi, *Rosas en la historia nacional*. Buenos Aires: La Pleyade, 1970, 179.

187. Ibarguren, *Orígenes*, 383.

188. Rosa, "Defensa," 131.

189. Lugones, *Grande Argentina*, 16, 82–83, 96, 137.

190. García and Rodríguez Molas, *Autoritarismo*, II: 51.

191. Lugones, *Grande Argentina*, 22, 85.

192. Cf. Miguel Murmis and Juan Carlos Portantiero, *Estudios sobre los orígenes del peronismo*. Buenos Aires: Siglo XXI, 1970, 24.

193. *Criterio*, May 14, 1933.

194. Ibarguren, *Orígenes*, 74.

195. Ibarguren, *Orígenes*, 188.

196. Ibarguren, *Orígenes*, 190.

197. *Crisol*, September 20, 1933.

198. Potash, *Army and Politics*, 152.

199. Mark Falcoff, "Argentine Nationalism on the Eve of Perón: Force of Radical Orientation of Young Argentina and Its Rivals." Ph.D. diss. Princeton University, 1970. Arthur P. Whitaker and David C. Jordan, *Nationalism in Contemporary Latin America*. New York: Free Press, 1966, 63–66.

200. Arturo Jauretche, in Ciria, *Década infame*, 191.

201. J. J. Hernández Arregui, *La formación de la conciencia nacional*. 2d ed. Buenos Aires: Plus Ultra, 1973, 306–313.

202. Osés, *Medios*, 79.

203. This version of Yrigoyen's career began to develop following the publication of a biography by Gálvez. See Manuel Gálvez, *Vida de Hipólito Yrigoyen*. Buenos Aires: Tor, 1933.

204. Raúl Scalabrini Ortiz, *Historia de los ferrocarriles argentinos*. 4th ed. Buenos Aires: Reconquista, 1940.

205. Falcoff, "Argentine Nationalism," 97.

206. Quoted in Hernández Arreguí, *Formación*, 330.

207. Falcoff, "Argentine Nationalism," 97.

208. Raúl Scalabrini Ortiz, "Bases para la reconstrucción nacional," in Ciria, *Década infame*, 198.

209. Troncoso, *Nacionalistas*, 61. Scalabrini Ortiz's career is examined more sympathetically in Galasso, *Raúl Scalabrini Ortiz*.

See also Mark Falcoff, "Raúl Scalabrini Ortiz: The Making of the Argentine Nationalist," *Hispanic American Historical Review* 52, no. 1 (Feb. 1972):74–101.

Chapter 5. The Nationalist Revolution

1. The most recent survey of foreign policy issues during the war is *Argentina Between the Great Powers, 1939–46*. Edited by Guido Di Tella and D. Cameron Watt. Pittsburgh: University of Pittsburgh Press, 1989.

2. Irazusta, *Testimonios*, 60.

3. Nicholas John Spykman, *America's Strategy in World Politics: The United States and the Balance of Power*. New York: Harcourt, Brace and Co., 1942, 328.

4. Sumner Welles, *Where Are We Heading?* New York: Harper and Brothers, 1946, 191.

5. "El plan de reactivación económica ante el Honorable Senado," *Desarrollo Económico* 19, no. 75 (1979): 404.

6. "El plan," 426.

7. Rodolfo Puiggrós, *El peronismo: Sus causas*. Buenos Aires: Carlos Pérez, 1971, 41–51, 134.

8. Trevor-Roper, "Fascism," 23.

9. Ibarguren, *Orígenes*, 395.

10. Ivereigh, "Catholic Thought," 111.

11. Osés, *Medios*, 18.

12. C. Ibarguren, Jr., *Laferrère*, 76, recounts a duel between Laferrère and Rodolfo Irazusta.

13. *La Maroma*, October 1939.

14. *La Maroma*, October 1939.

15. On German influences, see Ronald C. Newton, "Disorderly Succession: Great Britain, the United States and the 'Nazi Menace' in Argentina, 1939–1946," in Di Tella and Watt, *Argentina Between the Great Powers*, 111–134. According to Newton, 114, "No evidence has appeared to substantiate the nightmarish vision of grandiose Germanic strategic designs that fuelled the imagination of exile and Argentine anti-fascists and of much of official Washington in the late 1930s and early 1940s." This issue is now exhaustively, if not definitively, examined in Ronald C. Newton, *The "Nazi Menace" in Argentina, 1931–1947*. Stanford: Stanford University Press, 1992.

16. Carulla, *Medio siglo*, 241.

17. Nunn, *Military*, 264.

18. For comments on *El Pampero*, see Ysabel Rennie, *The Argentine Republic*. New York: Macmillan, 1945, 273.

19. *El Fortín*, January 1941.

20. C. Ibarguren, Jr., *Laferrère*, 94.

21. *El Fortín*, February 1941.

22. For an example of enlistment with the "Blue Brigade," see below, p. 188. I have found little evidence to support Buchrucker's view that the Nationalists pledged themselves to the Nazi cause following the invasion of the Soviet Union. (Cf. Buchrucker, *Nacionalismo*, 200.)

23. Rennie, *Argentine Republic*, 287.

24. *El Fortín*, May 1941.

25. *El Fortín*, August 28, 1941.

26. *El Fortín*, September 15, 1941.

27. Quoted in García and Rodríguez Molas, *Autoritarismo*, 150.

28. Genta, *Libertad*, 36. (Speech of September 5, 1941.)

29. Estatutos del Consejo Superior del Nacionalismo. Buenos Aires, 1941.

30. See *Revista Militar*, April 1941 and August 1943, and *Revista de Economía Argentina*, May 1941 and November 1942.

31. *El Fortín*, January 1941.

32. *El Fortín*, February 6, 1942.

33. *El Ríoplatense*, December 24, 1942.

34. Sánchez Sorondo, *Revolución*, 246.

35. Ray Josephs, *Argentine Diary: The Inside Story of the Coming of Fascism*. New York: Random House, 1944, 267.

36. In mid-1943, the title of this group was changed to Alianza Libertadora Nacionalista.

37. Josephs, *Diary*, xi.

38. Leonardo Castellani, in Sánchez Sorondo, *Revolución*, 267.

39. Irazusta, *Testimonios*, 156.

40. *Perón y el GOU: Los documentos de una logia secreta*. Compiled by Robert A. Potash. Buenos Aires: Sudamericana, 1984, 199.

41. Potash, *GOU*, 101–102.

42. Potash, *GOU*, 103.

43. Potash, *GOU*, 200.

44. Potash, *GOU*, 235.

45. Quoted in García and Rodríguez Molas, *Autoritarismo*, 201.

46. García and Rodríguez Molas, *Autoritarismo*, 228, quoting President Ramírez on June 7, 1943.

47. García and Rodríguez Molas, *Autoritarismo*, 225.

48. García and Rodríguez Molas, *Autoritarismo*, 221.

49. Potash, *GOU*, 220.

50. Potash, *GOU*, 134.

51. Josephs, *Diary*, 47.

52. Josephs, *Diary*, 234.

53. Genta, *Libertad*, 80, 90.

54. For a fuller account of relations with the United States under the military junta, see Rennie, *Argentine Republic*, 353–356.

55. Josephs, *Diary*, 142.

56. These measures are listed in Rennie, *Argentine Republic*, 373–378.

57. *Cabildo*, January 1, 1944.

58. *Cabildo*, November 15, 1943.

59. Weil, *Riddle*, 52.

60. *Cabildo*, November 2, 1943.

61. José Peter, *Crónicas proletarias*. Buenos Aires: Esfera, 1968, 214.

62. C.T.A.L. (Confederación de Trabajadores de América Latina), *White and Blue Book: In Defense of the Argentine People and against the Fascist Regime Oppressing It*. Mexico City, February 20, 1946, 24.

63. *Cabildo*, October 28, 1943.

64. Josephs, *Diary*, 217.

65. Josephs, *Diary*, 141–142.

66. Josephs, *Diary*, 271.

67. Paul W. Lewis, *The Crisis of Argentine Capitalism*. Chapel Hill: University of North Carolina Press, 1990, 134.

68. Nunn, *Military*, 260–262.

69. Colonel Juan Perón, "Comandos de montaña," *Revista Militar*, April 1943, 705.

70. Potash, *GOU*, 25.

71. *Cabildo*, September 29, 1943. (Quoting Alberto Baldrich.)

72. Sánchez Sorondo, *Revolución*, 246.

73. *La Razón*, June 8, 1943.

74. *La Razón*, June 9, 1943.

75. *Cabildo*, November 11, 1943.

76. *Cabildo*, November 11, 1943.

77. *La Razón*, November 30, 1943.

78. Josephs, *Diary*, 256.

79. *Cabildo*, November 30, 1943.

80. *La Razón*, December 10, 1943.

81. Hiroschi Matsushita, *Movimiento obrero argentino, 1930–1945: Sus proyecciones en la historia del peronismo*. Buenos Aires: Siglo Veinte, 1983, 268.

82. *Cabildo*, January 12, 1944.

83. Troncoso, *Nacionalistas*, 68.

84. Weil, *Riddle*, 54.

85. Farrell's speech on June 6, 1944, in *Revista Militar*, 1944, 1069–1070.

86. Baldrich, in *Revista Militar*, 1944, 1101.

87. *Cabildo*, June 24, 1944.

88. Weil, *Riddle*, 189; Rennie, *Argentine Republic*, 371.

89. *Cabildo*, July 29, 1944.

90. *Cabildo*, October 15, 1944.

91. Rennie, *Argentine Republic*, 381.

92. *Cabildo*, March 21, 1944.

93. *Cabildo*, June 28, 1944.

94. Coronel Juan Perón, *El pueblo quiere saber de qué se trata*. Buenos Aires, 1944, 71–82.

95. *La Prensa*, June 11, 1944.

96. *Noticias Gráficas*, August 26, 1944; September 7, 1944.

97. Quoted in Germán Arciniegas, *The State of Latin America*. Translated by Harriet de Onís. New York: Knopf, 1952, 50.

98. Congress of Industrial Organizations, Committee on Latin American Affairs, *The Argentine Regime: Facts and Recommendations to the United Nations*. New York, 1946, 128.

99. Congress of Industrial Relations, *Argentine Regime*, vii.

100. *New York Herald Tribune*, December 27, 1945.

101. Herbert Matthews, quoted in Arciniegas, *Latin America*, 63.

102. Américo Ghioldi, *De la tiranía a la democracia social*. Buenos Aires: Gure, 1956, 80. On Perón and fascism, see Paul H. Lewis, "Was Perón a Fascist? An Inquiry into the Nature of Fascism," *The Journal of Politics* 42 (1980): 242–256.

103. Quoted in Eduardo Crawley, *A House Divided: Argentina 1880–1980*. New York: St. Martin's Press, 1984, 65.

104. Puiggrós, *Peronismo*, 11. Also see Felix Luna, *El '45*. Buenos Aires: Sudamericana, 1971, 59.

105. Luna, *'45*, 58.

106. Puiggrós, *Peronismo*, 12.

107. Esteban Peicovich, *Hola Perón*. Buenos Aires: Jorge Alvarez, 1965, 40.

108. *El pueblo quiere saber de qué se trata* was a common Nationalist slogan of this period, adopted as a banner, for example, by *Cabildo* in 1942.

109. Perón, *Pueblo*, 9.

110. Perón, *Pueblo*, 17.

111. Perón, *Pueblo*, 166.

112. Perón, *Pueblo*, 24.

113. Perón, *Pueblo*, 98.

114. Perón, *Pueblo*, 29.

115. Perón, *Pueblo*, 31.

116. Perón, *Pueblo*, 160, 165.

117. Perón, *Pueblo*, 79.

118. Perón, *Pueblo*, 228. Despite his frequent references to the papal encyclicals, Perón did not seem to recognize the Catholic origins of the concept of social justice. The French Revolution, he confusingly claimed, did not achieve "the fulfillment of its ideas" in the sphere of social justice because "its legislation . . . was inspired by the absolute individualism" of Voltaire. The Nationalists seized on this issue as one of the features distinguishing themselves and Peronism.

119. Perón, *Pueblo*, 202.

120. Perón, *Pueblo*, 91.

121. Speech defining the functions of the Postwar Council. *Noticias Gráficas*, September 6, 1944.

122. Quoted in Silvia Sigal and Eliseo Verón, *Perón o muerte: Los fundamentos discursivos del fenómeno peronista*. Buenos Aires: Legasa, 1986, 41.

123. For a discussion of the relationship between fascism and national integration, see William Sheridan Allen, "The Appeal of Fascism and the Problem of National Disintegration," in *Reappraisals of Fascism*. Edited by Henry A. Turner, Jr. New York: New Viewpoints, 1975, 45–52. Perón, however, claimed that the intellectual source of the "nation in arms" was the late-nineteenth-century German military theorist Colmar Freiherr von der Goltz. See Juan Perón, "Significación de la defensa nacional desde el punto de vista militar," *Revista Militar*, 1944, 1115–1136.

124. *Noticias Gráficas*, July 8, 1944.

125. Perón, *Pueblo*, 198.

126. Perón, *Pueblo*, 21.

127. Perón, *Pueblo*, 199.

128. Congress of Industrial Relations, *Argentine Regime*, 94.

129. Perón, *Pueblo*, 99.

130. Perón, *Pueblo*, 151.

131. C.T.A.L., *White and Blue Book*, 24–25.

132. Congress of Industrial Relations, *Argentine Regime*, 110.

133. Luna, '45, 211. Luna's account of this incident appeared several years before the formation of the group known as the Madres de la Plaza de Mayo of the 1970s.

134. Perón, *Pueblo*, 202.

135. Perón, *Pueblo*, 225.

136. *Noticias Gráficas*, July 12, 1944.

137. *Noticias Gráficas*, August 2, 1944.

138. *Noticias Gráficas*, August 2, 1944.

139. *Noticias Gráficas*, August 13, 1944.

140. *Noticias Gráficas*, September 3, 1944.

141. Luna, '45, 118.

142. Perón, *Pueblo*, 9.

143. *Noticias Gráficas*, May 31, 1945.

144. Luna, '45, 134.

145. Luna, '45, 156.

146. Puiggrós, *Peronismo*, 156.

147. *Noticias Gráficas*, July 27, 1945.

148. *Noticias Gráficas*, July 30, 1945.

149. *Noticias Gráficas*, September 19, 1945.

150. Juan Perón, *Perón Expounds His Doctrine*. Buenos Aires, 1948, 55.

151. For a comprehensive study of the 1946 election, see Manuel Mora y Araujo and Ignacio Llorente, *El voto peronista: Ensayos de sociología electoral argentina*. Buenos Aires: Sudamericana, 1980.

152. United States, Department of State, *Memorandum of the United States Government among the American Republics with Respect to the Argentine Situation*. Washington, D.C.: February 1946, 66–67. The above citation should not be understood as an endorsement of the Blue Book, which in most respects proved wildly inaccurate. For a recent evaluation, see Callum A. McDonald, "The Braden Campaign and Anglo-Argentine Relations in Argentina 1945–6," in Di Tella and Watt, *Argentina Between the Great Powers*, 150.

153. *Criterio*, December 24, 1932.

154. Amadeo, *Hoy*, 18.

155. Amadeo, *Hoy*, 18.

156. Amadeo, *Hoy*, 114.

157. Amadeo, *Hoy*, 119.

158. Buchrucker, *Nacionalismo*, 290.

159. Daniel James, *Resistance and Integration: Peronism and the Argentine Working Class, 1946–1976*. Cambridge: Cambridge University Press, 1988, 22.

160. *Cabildo*, January 13, 1944.

161. Luna, '45, 173.

162. Luna, '45, 73.

163. Luna, '45, 400.

164. Juan José Hernández Arregui, *Nacionalismo y liberación: Metrópolis y colonias en la era del imperialismo.* Buenos Aires: Hachea, 1969, 16.

165. Puiggrós, *Peronismo*, 130; Buchrucker, *Nacionalismo*, 289.

Chapter 6.　Perón and After

1. Juan Perón, *Doctrina peronista.* Buenos Aires, 1948, xxxi.

2. María Eva Duarte de Perón, *La mujer puede y debe votar.* Buenos Aires, n.d., 1. Legislation enfranchising women was passed in September 1947. See *Primera Plana*, January 3, 1967, "Historia del peronismo," no. 27.

3. T. C. McCormick, *Problems of the Post-War World.* New York: McGraw Hill, 1945, 3.

4. McCormick, *Problems*, 4.

5. Stanley Hoffman and Charles Maier, *The Marshall Plan: A Retrospective.* Boulder: Westview Press, 1984, 29.

6. Juan Perón, *Doctrinary Principles of the Social Policy of His Excellency, the President of the Argentine Republic, General Juan Perón.* Buenos Aires, 1947, 8–9.

7. Perón, *Doctrina*, 32. (Speech of February 24, 1947.)

8. Perón, *Doctrina*, 383. (Speech of August 2, 1947.)

9. Alberto Ciria, *Política y cultura popular: La Argentine peronista, 1946–1955.* Buenos Aires: Ediciones de la Flor, 1983, 216.

10. Juan José Hernández Arregui, in *Azul y Blanco*, October 8, 1957.

11. *Primera Plana*, October 4, 1966, "Historia del peronismo," no. 19.

12. Juan Carlos Torre, "Argentina since 1956." Mimeo.

13. Arciniegas, *Latin America*, 63.

14. Juan Perón, *La fuerza es el derecho de las bestias.* Buenos Aires, 1958, 17.

15. Quoted in Sigal and Verón, *Perón o muerte*, 69.

16. Sigal and Verón, *Perón o muerte*, 68.

17. *Primera Plana*, April 11, 1967, "Historia del peronismo," no. 39. María Flores, *The Woman with a Whip: Eva Perón.* New York: Doubleday and Co., 1952, 218.

18. Flores, *Eva Perón*, 238.

19. Ciria, *Política*, 295.

20. Eva Perón, *Clases y escritos completos 1946–1952.* 3: 21. Buenos Aires: Megafón, 1987.

21. Flores, *Eva Perón*, 276.

22. Quoted in Ciria, *Política*, 181.

23. Duarte de Perón, *La mujer*, 13.
24. Duarte de Perón, *La mujer*, 10.
25. Duarte de Perón, *La mujer*, 20.
26. *Primera Plana*, January 3, 1967, "Historia del peronismo," no. 27.
27. Juan Perón, *The General Confederation of Labor Listens to Perón*. Buenos Aires, 1950, 5.
28. Juan Perón, *La comunidad organizada*. Buenos Aires: El Túnel, 1974, 12.
29. Quoted in Tomás Eloy Martinez, *The Perón Novel*. Translated by Asa Latz. New York: Pantheon Books, 1988, 164.
30. Perón, *Comunidad organizada*, 79–80.
31. Perón, *General Confederation*, 27.
32. *Dinámica Social*, November 1951.
33. Brown, "Nationalism," 175.
34. Brown, "Nationalism," 176–183.
35. *Dinámica Social*, November 1951.
36. Brown, "Nationalism," 268, quoting a 1953 article by Rodolfo de Tecera del Franco published by the *Boletín del Instituto de Sociología*.
37. *Dinámica Social*, November 1951.
38. *Primera Plana*, June 7, 1966, "Historia del peronismo," no. 5. Luna, '45, 485, shows the Nationalist vote at 75,000 nationally or a fraction under 1 percent.
39. *Primera Plana*, May 10, 1966, "Historia del peronismo," no. 1.
40. *Primera Plana*, June 7, 1966, "Historia del peronismo," no. 5.
41. *Primera Plana*, January 3, 1967, "Historia del peronismo," no. 27.
42. Julio Meinvielle, *Política argentina 1949–1956*. Buenos Aires: Trafac, 1956, 36.
43. Meinvielle, *Política*, 160.
44. Osés retreated into complete obscurity in late 1944 and died in late 1954.
45. Julio Irazusta, *Perón y la crisis argentina*. 3d ed. Buenos Aires: Independencia, 1983, 9. *Azul y Blanco*, February 1, 1967.
46. Facultad de Derecho y Ciencias Sociales, *Encuesta sobre la revisión constitucional*. Buenos Aires: Facultad de Derecho y Ciencias Sociales de la Universidad de Buenos Aires, 1948, 181.
47. Ernesto Goldar, "La literatura peronista." In *El peronismo*. Edited by Gonzalo Cárdenas et al. Buenos Aires: Carlos Pérez, 1969, 144–145.

278 *Notes to pages 166–172*

48. *Dinámica Social*, August 1951.
49. *Dinámica Social*, December 1952.
50. Amadeo, *Hoy*, 33.
51. *Dinámica Social*, October 1950.
52. *Dinámica Social*, March 1951.
53. *Dinámica Social*, August 1951.
54. *Dinámica Social*, November 1950.
55. *Dinámica Social*, November 1951.
56. Troncoso, *Nacionalistas*, 77.
57. Bruno C. Jacovella, *Fiestas tradicionales argentinas*. Buenos Aires: Lejouane, 1953, 5.
58. Ferla, *Doctrina*, introduction.
59. Ferla, *Doctrina*, 45.
60. Ferla, *Doctrina*, 68.
61. Ferla, *Doctrina*, 49–50.
62. Ferla, *Doctrina*, 20.
63. *Dinámica Social*, July 1951.
64. Quoted in Clementi, *Rosas*, 179.
65. Ludovico García de Loydi, *La iglesia frente al peronismo: Bosquejo histórico*. Buenos Aires: C.I.C., 1956, 18.
66. Estrada, *Nacionalismo*, 43.
67. Estrada, *Nacionalismo*, 44.
68. Estrada, *Nacionalismo*, 47.
69. Estrada, *Nacionalismo*, 50.
70. Estrada, *Nacionalismo*, 87.
71. Meinvielle, *Política*, 179–180.
72. Silvestre Pérez, *Filosofía del federalismo en el Río de la Plata*. Montevideo: Tipografía Atlántida, 1948, 15.
73. Pérez, *Federalismo*, 25.
74. *Dinámica Social*, December 1954.
75. *Dinámica Social*, February 1955.
76. *Criterio*, January 17 and January 24, 1946.
77. *Criterio*, January 31 and July 18, 1946.
78. *Criterio*, October 24, 1946.
79. *Criterio*, November 14, 1946.
80. *Primera Plana*, May 16, 1967, "Historia del peronismo," no. 44.
81. *Azul y Blanco*, September 4, 1967.
82. *Primera Plana*, October 18, 1966, "Historia del peronismo," no. 22.
83. Virgilio Filippo, *El plan quinquenal de Perón y los comunistas*. Buenos Aires: Lista Blanca, 1948, 9.

84. Filippo, *Plan quinquenal*, 41.
85. Filippo, *Plan quinquenal*, 9.
86. For background on Kelly, see *El Bimestre Económico y Social*, July 1, 1983.
87. *Primera Plana*, April 2, 1964.
88. *Azul y Blanco*, May 29, 1967.
89. Amadeo, *Hoy*, 21.
90. Irazusta, *Perón*, 239.
91. Meinvielle, *Política*, 25.
92. Meinvielle, *Política*, 176.
93. Meinvielle, *Política*, 115.
94. *Criterio*, February 21, 1946.
95. *Dinámica Social*, December 1954.
96. Meinvielle, *Política*, 233.
97. Meinvielle, *Política*, 7.
98. Meinvielle, *Política*, 8.
99. Meinvielle, *Política*, 17.
100. Meinvielle, *Política*, 233.
101. Troncoso, *Nacionalistas*, 70.
102. Hugo Gambini, *Perón y la iglesia*. Buenos Aires: Centro Editor de América Latina, 1971, 41.
103. *Primera Plana*, May 16, 1967.
104. Irazusta, *Perón*, 242.
105. *Primera Plana*, May 16, 1967.
106. Amadeo, *Hoy*, 8.
107. Amadeo, *Hoy*, 115.
108. *Criterio*, September 30, 1948.
109. *Criterio*, October 13, 1955.
110. *Primera Plana*, October 18, 1966, "Historia del peronismo," no. 21; Ivereigh, "Catholic Thought," 148.
111. *Primera Plana*, November 1, 1966, "Historia del peronismo," no. 22; Gambini, *Perón*, 29.
112. Robert J. Alexander, *The Perón Era*. New York: Columbia University Press, 1951, 132.
113. Juan Perón, *Justicialismo y la doctrina social cristiana*. Buenos Aires, 1951, 9.
114. Perón, *Doctrina social*, 22.
115. Burdick, "Religion and Politics," 89.
116. *Criterio*, October 13, 1955.
117. *Primera Plana*, July 18 and July 25, 1967, "Historia del peronismo," nos. 52 and 53.
118. Robert A. Potash, *The Army and Politics in Argentina, 1945–1962*. Stanford: Stanford University Press, 1980, 132.

119. C. Ibarguren, Jr., *Laferrère*, 110–111.

120. *Primera Plana*, October 1 and October 8, 1968, "La segunda presidencia," nos. 19 and 20.

121. García de Loydi, *Iglesia*, 103.

122. *Criterio*, June 12, 1952.

123. *Criterio*, August 8, 1952.

124. The activities of Hicks were openly condemned by bishops. *Primera Plana*, December 24, 1968, "La segunda presidencia," no. 30.

125. *Criterio*, January 28, 1954. For other criticisms of the worker-priests, see *Dinámica Social*, April 1954.

126. *Criterio*, February 25, 1954.

127. *Criterio*, April 8, 1954.

128. Julio Godio, *La caída de Perón: De junio a septiembre de 1955*. Buenos Aires: Gránica, 1973, 19.

129. *Criterio*, August 12, 1954.

130. *Criterio*, April 7, 1955.

131. *Criterio*, April 28, 1955.

132. *Criterio*, July 28, 1955.

133. *Primera Plana*, January 7, 1969, "La segunda presidencia," no. 32.

134. *Criterio*, July 14, 1955.

135. Pedro Santos Martínez Constanzo, *La nueva argentina: 1946–1955*. Vol. I. Buenos Aires: La Bastilla, 1976, 277.

136. Ernesto López, *Seguridad nacional y sedición militar*. Buenos Aires: Legasa, 1987, 105.

137. Irazusta, *Perón*, 9; Meinvielle, *Política*, 290. For details of the last weeks of Perón's regime, see *Primera Plana*, May 6–August 5, 1969.

138. C. Ibarguren, Jr., *Laferrère*, 109. Written correctly, the Italian would read, *"Cosa è parlare de morte e altro morire."*

139. *Criterio*, October 10, 1955.

140. *Criterio*, October 27, 1955.

141. Marcelo Sánchez Sorondo, *Libertades prestadas*. Buenos Aires: A. Peña Lillo, 1970, 92.

142. García de Loydi, *Iglesia*, 83.

143. García de Loydi, *Iglesia*, 28.

144. García de Loydi, *Iglesia*, 8, 15.

145. García de Loydi, *Iglesia*, 94.

146. Amadeo, *Hoy*, 92.

147. *Azul y Blanco*, May 29, 1967.

148. Felix Lafiandra, Jr., *Los panfletos: Su aporte a la revolución libertadora*. 2d ed. Buenos Aires: Itinerarium, 1955, 158.

149. Lafiandra, *Panfletos*, 162.

150. Lafiandra, *Panfletos*, 163.

151. *Criterio*, November 24, 1955.

152. Lonardi took this "Nationalist" position on relations with the Peronists, although his own exact sympathies remained unclear. Palacio, for example, commented that "Lonardi was neither a Nationalist nor a Social Christian, but a gentleman of liberal background." See *Primera Plana*, May 16, 1967.

153. Quoted in "La caída de Lonardi," *Primera Plana*, November 10, 1970.

154. *Criterio*, November 24, 1955.

155. *Primera Plana*, May 16, 1967.

156. *Primera Plana*, May 16, 1967.

157. Sánchez Sorondo, *Libertades*, 57.

158. *Azul y Blanco*, May 7, 1957.

159. Troncoso, *Nacionalistas*, 71.

160. *Azul y Blanco*, February 27 and April 24, 1957.

161. *Azul y Blanco*, May 25 and August 15, 1956.

162. Troncoso, *Nacionalistas*, 80.

163. Quoted in Troncoso, *Nacionalistas*, 71.

164. Troncoso, *Nacionalistas*, 78.

165. Troncoso, *Nacionalistas*, preface.

166. *Azul y Blanco*, March 11, 1958.

167. *Azul y Blanco*, July 7 and 21, 1966.

168. *Azul y Blanco*, August 4, 1966.

169. *Primera Plana*, May 16, 1967. Sánchez Sorondo turned down the offer.

170. *Azul y Blanco*, December 15, 1966; *Primera Plana*, April 8, 1969.

171. *Primera Plana*, November 13, 1962.

172. *Primera Plana*, July 18, 1963. The *Boletín del Instituto Juan Manuel de Rosas de Investigaciones Históricas* provides information on the institute's development and activities.

173. Clementi, *Rosas*, 60. (Quoting Julio Irazusta.)

174. *Azul y Blanco*, June 11, 1957.

175. Cf. *Azul y Blanco*, May 21, 1968.

176. Letter from a fifth-year law student in *Azul y Blanco*, May 29, 1967.

177. *Azul y Blanco*, October 6, 1966.

178. *Primera Plana*, December 12, 1963.

179. *Primera Plana*, December 4, 1962.

180. *Azul y Blanco*, August 25, 1966.

181. *Azul y Blanco*, June 18, 1968. Oliva belonged to the *colorado* faction of the military. See below, pp. 195–196.

182. *Primera Plana*, May 16, 1967. The youth groups are discussed below, pp. 205–209.

183. *Primera Plana*, December 4, 1962.

184. *Primera Plana*, December 4, 1962.

185. *Primera Plana*, June 28, 1968.

186. Interview in *Primera Plana*, February 27, 1968.

187. *Azul y Blanco*, July 10, 1967.

188. *Azul y Blanco*, June 19, 1967.

189. *Azul y Blanco*, July 8, 1969. The book reviewed was Marysa Navarro Gerassi's *Los nacionalistas*.

190. Genta, *Libertad*, 286.

191. *Primera Plana*, March 10, 1964.

192. *Azul y Blanco*, February 1, 1967.

193. Comisión de Estudios, *Nacionalismo*, 25.

194. Comisión de Estudios, *Nacionalismo*, 103.

195. Comisión de Estudios, *Nacionalismo*, 32.

196. Comisión de Estudios, *Nacionalismo*, 71.

197. Beveraggi Allende, *Dogma*, 62.

198. Interview in *Azul y Blanco*, October 16, 1967.

199. Beveraggi Allende, *Dogma*, 5.

200. Beveraggi Allende, *Dogma*, 10.

201. Beveraggi Allende, *Dogma*, 97.

202. Beveraggi Allende, *Dogma*, 71.

203. Beveraggi Allende, *Dogma*, 71.

Chapter 7. Authoritarians, Populists, and Revolutionaries

1. For details of these military conflicts, see *Primera Plana*, April 15 and July 9, 1963; May 10, 1966.

2. Daniel Frontalini and María Cristina Caiti, *El mito de la guerra sucia*. Buenos Aires: Centro de Estudios Legales y Sociales, 1984, 31.

3. López, *Seguridad nacional*, 138–147.

4. Quoted in José Teófilo Goyret, *Geopolítica y subversión*. Buenos Aires: De Palma, 1980, 132.

5. For details of the Plan CONINTES, see *Clarín*, March 12, 1960.

6. Villegas later acknowledged French influences on his own ideas. *Primera Plana*, July 27, 1969.

7. Osiris G. Villegas, *Guerra revolucionaria comunista*. Buenos Aires: Pleamar, 1963, 181–182.

8. Villegas, *Guerra comunista*, 9.

9. Villegas, *Guerra comunista*, 10.

10. Villegas, *Guerra comunista*, 11, 58.

11. Villegas, *Guerra comunista*, 177.

12. Villegas, *Guerra comunista*, 12.

13. Villegas, *Guerra comunista*, 87.

14. Villegas, *Guerra comunista*, 180.

15. Villegas, *Guerra comunista*, 186.

16. On Brazil, see Alain Rouquié, *The Military and the State in Latin America*. Translated by Paul E. Sigmund. Berkeley, Los Angeles, and London: University of California Press, 1987, 282. In 1952, a Brazilian officer wrote that "national security lies . . . in the battle for production [and] in the provision of stability and a reasonable standard of living." Quoted in Brian Loveman and Thomas M. Davies, Jr., *The Politics of Antipolitics: The Military in Latin America*. 2d ed. Lincoln: University of Nebraska Press, 1989, 8.

17. López, *Seguridad nacional*, 61–63.

18. *Primera Plana*, February 25, 1964.

19. The full text of Onganía's speech is reproduced in *Primera Plana*, May 10, 1966.

20. *Primera Plana*, May 5, 1964.

21. *Primera Plana*, June 7, 1966.

22. *Acta de la Revolución Argentina*. Quoted in Osiris Guillermo Villegas, *Políticas y estrategias para el desarrollo y la seguridad nacional*. Buenos Aires: Pleamar, 1969, 253. See also William C. Smith, *Authoritarianism and the Crisis of the Argentine Political Economy*. Stanford: Stanford University Press, 1989, 50.

23. *Mensaje de la Junta Revolucionaria al Pueblo Argentino*. Quoted in Villegas, *Políticas*, 257–260. See also Smith, *Authoritarianism*, 49–50, who surprisingly calls this "new language."

24. Villegas, *Políticas*, 257–260. For further discussion, see José Comblin, *The Church and the National Security State*. Maryknoll, N.Y.: Orbis Books, 1979, 73–90.

25. *Primera Plana*, July 26, 1966. Opus Dei was founded in 1939 and the Cursillos in 1950. Cf. Gustavo Roca, *Las dictaduras militares del cono sur*. Córdoba: El Cid, 1984, 217–218.

26. *Primera Plana*, December 4, 1962; November 11, 1966.

27. Quoted in Guillermo O'Donnell, *Bureaucratic Authoritarianism: Argentina, 1966–1973, in Comparative Perspective*. Translated by James McGuire in collaboration with Rae Flory. Berkeley, Los Angeles, and London: University of California Press, 1988, 59.

28. Villegas, *Políticas*, for a lengthy discussion of how these two bodies were meant to function and interract.

29. General Benjamín Rattenbach, in prologue to Villegas, *Políticas*.

30. Villegas, *Políticas*, 35.

31. O'Donnell, *Bureaucratic Authoritarianism*, 55.

32. *Primera Plana*, July 12, 1966.

33. *Azul y Blanco*, August 4, 1966.

34. *Azul y Blanco*, August 4, 1966.

35. Ernesto Garzón Valdés, "La emigración argentina—acerca de sus causas ético-políticas." In *El poder militar en la Argentina*. Edited by Peter Waldmann and Ernesto Garzón Valdés. Frankfurt: Verlag Klaus Dieter Vervuert, 1982, 181.

36. *Primera Plana*, May 12, 1967.

37. *Primera Plana*, January 3, 1968.

38. *Primera Plana*, November 22, 1966.

39. *Primera Plana*, January 3, 1968.

40. *Primera Plana*, January 3, 1968.

41. Smith, *Authoritarianism*, 61.

42. *Primera Plana*, October 10, 1967.

43. *Primera Plana*, July 9, 1968; April 1, 1969.

44. *Primera Plana*, October 17, 1967.

45. Smith, *Authoritarianism*, 132, 183.

46. *Primera Plana*, December 4, 1962.

47. *Primera Plana*, April 18, 1963.

48. *Primera Plana*, March 10, 1964.

49. *Primera Plana*, March 31, 1964.

50. Juan José Sebreli, *Los deseos imaginarios del peronismo*. Buenos Aires: Legasa, 1983, 169.

51. *Primera Plana*, March 31, 1964.

52. Quoted in Del Bocca and Giovana, *Fascism*, 377.

53. For details, see *Primera Plana*, May 16, 1967.

54. *Primera Plana*, November 26, 1963.

55. In 1973, Baxter was killed in a plane crash at Orly airport outside Paris. See *La Opinión*, July 4, 1973.

56. *Primera Plana*, March 10, 1963.

57. *Primera Plana*, March 17, 1964.

58. *Primera Plana*, March 10, 1964.

59. *Primera Plana*, May 16, 1967.

60. John W. Cooke, *Perón-Cooke Correspondencia*. Buenos Aires, 1973, 2:202.

61. *Primera Plana*, March 31, 1964.

62. *Primera Plana*, March 31, 1964.

63. *Primera Plana*, March 17, 1964.

64. *Primera Plana*, July 19, 1966.

65. *Primera Plana*, September 20, 1966.

66. Donald C. Hodges, *Argentina, 1943–1987: The National Revolution and Resistance.* 2d ed. Albuquerque: University of New Mexico Press, 1987, 52.

67. John William Cooke, *Peronismo y revolución. El país y el golpe del estado. Informe a las bases.* Buenos Aires: Papiro, 1971, 233. This document was written in 1966.

68. For discussion of this issue, see *Primera Plana*, November 13, 1962.

69. *Primera Plana*, May 16, 1967.

70. *Azul y Blanco*, November 27, 1966. Timerman, better known as the owner of *La Opinión*, was also the owner-founder of *Primera Plana*.

71. *Azul y Blanco*, July 19, 1967.

72. *Primera Plana*, February 6, 1968.

73. *Azul y Blanco*, May 14, 1968.

74. *Azul y Blanco*, October 8, 1968.

75. *Azul y Blanco*, October 9, 1967. Another extensive report followed on July 9, 1968.

76. *Azul y Blanco*, June 19, 1967.

77. *Azul y Blanco*, July 19, 1967.

78. *Azul y Blanco*, October 23, 1967.

79. *Azul y Blanco*, April 10, 1967.

80. *Primera Plana*, November 21, 1967.

81. Meinvielle, in *Azul y Blanco*, July 19, 1967.

82. *Azul y Blanco*, May 21, 1968.

83. *Azul y Blanco*, June 25, 1968.

84. *Azul y Blanco*, August 20, 1968.

85. *Azul y Blanco*, September 10, 1968. (Advertisements by Editorial Sudestada.)

86. *Azul y Blanco*, September 24, 1968.

87. *Azul y Blanco*, October 1, 1968.

88. *Azul y Blanco*, October 22, 1968.

89. *Azul y Blanco*, October 1, 1968.

90. *Azul y Blanco*, September 3, 1968.

91. *Azul y Blanco*, July 1, 1969.

92. *Primera Plana*, September 20, 1966; October 7, 1968.

93. *Primera Plana*, October 31, 1967.

94. *Primera Plana*, April 29, 1969.

95. *Primera Plana*, July 8, 1969.

96. *La Opinión*, June 2, July 27, and July 30, 1971.

97. Lewis, *Argentine Capitalism*, 367.

98. Claudia Hilb and Daniel Lutzky, *La nueva izquierda argentina: 1960–1980. Política y violencia.* Buenos Aires: Centro Editor de América Latina, 1984, 63–64; *Primera Plana*, September 15, 1970.

99. Hodges, *Argentina*, 65.

100. Hilb and Lutzky, *Nueva izquierda*, 90.

101. Cf. Burdick, "Religion and Politics," 204.

102. Quoted in *La Opinión*, June 24, 1971.

103. Padre Carlos Mugica, *Peronismo y cristianismo.* Buenos Aires: Merlín, 1973, 31.

104. *La Opinión*, July 28, 1973.

105. Quoted in Burdick, "Religion and Politics," 224.

106. *La Opinión*, July 14, 1971.

107. *La Opinión*, July 14, 1971.

108. *Cristianismo y Revolución*, September 1971. Quoted in Hilb and Lutzky, *Nueva izquierda*, 55. For a full account of the Movement of Third World Priests in Argentina, see Burdick, "Religion and Politics," 180–320.

109. See above, p. 208.

110. *Azul y Blanco*, January 10, 1968; Sebreli, *Deseos*, 65.

111. Hodges, *Argentina*, 45.

112. Cooke, *Perón-Cooke*, 2:167.

113. John William Cooke, *La lucha por la liberación nacional.* Buenos Aires, 1971, 7.

114. Juan Perón, *La hora de los pueblos.* Buenos Aires: El Norte, 1968, 5,12.

115. Quoted in Lester A. Sobel, *Argentina and Perón.* New York: Facts on File, 1975, 13.

116. Richard Gillespie, *Los soldados de Perón: Los Montoneros.* Buenos Aires: Grijalbo, 1987, 9.

117. Hilb and Lutzky, *Nueva izquierda*, 105.

118. Sebreli, *Deseos*, 167.

119. Hilb and Lutzky, *Nueva izquierda*, 46.

120. Quoted in Hilb and Lutzky, *Nueva izquierda*, 51.

121. Sebreli, *Deseos*, 177.

122. *El Descamisado*, September 29, 1973.

123. *La Causa Peronista*, September 6, 1974.

124. Hilb and Lutzky, *Nueva izquierda*, 100–106.

125. Sebreli, *Deseos*, 140; Talmon, *Myth*, 494; Saladino, "Italy," 242.

126. Jacobo Timerman, *Prisoner without a Name, Cell without a Number*. Translated by Toby Talbot. New York: Knopf, 1989, 79.

127. O'Donnell, *Bureaucratic Authoritarianism*, 307.

128. My own view on this issue is much the same as follows: "If the influence of the Mussolinean model on Perón had been indeed significant, it had been more marginal on mainstream Peronism; on a movement such as the Montoneros . . . it was all but negligible." Tulio Halperín Donghi, "Argentina's Unmastered Past." Mimeo.

129. *La Opinión*, May 29, 1971.

130. *La Opinión*, January 21, March 30, April 13, and April 17, 1973.

131. *La Opinión*, April 17, 1973.

132. *La Opinión*, July 27, 1973.

133. *La Opinión*, July 27, 1973.

134. Garzón Valdés, "Emigración," 182.

135. *La Opinión*, May 12, 1973.

136. *La Opinión*, July 17, 1973.

137. Rouquié, *The Military*, 348.

138. *La Opinión*, July 20, 1971.

139. *Buenos Aires Herald*, May 29, 1975.

140. Alberto Daniel Faleroni, *La guerra de la cuarta dimensión*. Buenos Aires: Luis Lassere, 1970, 105, 126.

141. Jordán B. Genta, *Seguridad y desarrollo: Reflexiones sobre el terror en la Argentina*. Buenos Aires: Cultura Argentina, 1970.

142. Genta, *Libertad*, 333.

143. Genta, *Libertad*, 348.

144. Genta, *Libertad*, 454.

145. Cf. Frontalini and Caiti, *Guerra sucia*, 74.

146. Hodges, *Argentina*, 188.

147. Frontalini and Caiti, *Guerra sucia*, 32–33.

148. Timerman, *Prisoner*, 154.

149. Arnold Spitta, "El 'Proceso de Reorganización Nacional' de 1976–1981: Los objetivos básicos y su realización práctica. Ensayo sobre elementos de la realidad política cotidiana bajo un régimen militar." In Waldmann and Garzón Valdés, eds., *El poder militar en la Argentina*, 79.

150. Press reports, March 27, 1976.

151. Frontalini and Caiti, *Guerra sucia*, 32. (Quoting General Ramón J. Camps.)

152. National Commission on the Disappeared, *Nunca Más*, 397.

153. Irazusta died in May 1982 during the brief period Argentina held control over the Malvinas Islands.

154. *La Opinión*, August 3, 1973.

155. *Cabildo*, September 16, 1976.

156. *Cabildo*, August 1976.

157. *Cabildo*, August 1976.

158. *Cabildo*, February 1977.

159. Timerman, *Prisoner.*

160. *Cabildo*, September 1976.

161. *Cabildo*, September 1976.

162. *Cabildo*, October 1976.

163. *Cabildo*, October 1976.

164. Emilio F. Mignone, *Iglesia y dictadura: El papel de la iglesia a la luz de sus relaciones con el régimen militar.* 3d ed. Buenos Aires: Ediciones del Pensamiento Nacional, 1986, 222.

165. Mignone, *Iglesia*, 20, 38.

166. Mignone, *Iglesia*, 32; National Commission on the Disappeared, *Nunca Más*, 53.

167. Mignone, *Iglesia*, 24.

168. Quoted in *Gente*, November 22, 1976. The following section, quoting members of the military in 1976–1983, benefited from an early draft of Frank Graziano, *Divine Violence. Spectacle, Psychosexuality, and Radical Christianity in the Argentine "Dirty War."* Boulder: Westview Press, 1992.

169. Frontalini and Caiti, *Guerra sucia*, 30. (Quoting General Albano Harguindegay.)

170. Mignone, *Iglesia*, 193. (Quoting General Justo Jácobo Rojas Alcorta.)

171. Donald C. Hodges, "The Process of National Destruction in Argentina." Mimeo, 277.

172. Ramón J. Camps, *Caso Timerman: Punto final.* Buenos Aires: Tribuna Abierta, 1982, 21.

173. National Commission on the Disappeared, *Nunca Más*, 445.

174. Quoted in Waisman, "Ideology," 19.

175. Frontalini and Caiti, *Guerra sucia*, 13.

176. República Argentina, *Conozcamos nuestro enemigo: Subversión en el ámbito educativo.* Buenos Aires: Ministerio de Cultura y Educación, 1978, 13.

177. Quoted in *El Bimestre Político y Económico*, November 5, 1983.

178. Garzón Valdés, "Emigración," 184.

179. Patricio J. Crichigno, "Political Regimes and Legitimacy in Argentina: An Alternative Framework for the Study of Political Instability and the Dynamics of Social Change." Ph.D. diss. University of California, Santa Barbara, 1989, chap. 6, 27.

180. Timerman, *Prisoner*, 95.

181. Timerman, *Prisoner*, 130.

182. *La Opinión*, May 16, 1973.

183. *Cabildo*, September 16, 1976.

184. Jimmy Burns, *The Land that Lost Its Heroes*. London: Bloomsbury Press, 1987, 152.

185. Timerman, *Prisoner*, 130.

186. Garzón Valdés, "Emigración," 184.

187. Garzón Valdés, "Emigración," 183.

188. Spitta, "Proceso," 91.

189. Federico Ibarguren, *Nuestra tradición*, 487.

190. Quoted in *La Prensa*, June 20, 1982.

191. Roberto Viola, blurb in José Teófilo Goyret, *Geopolítica y subversión*. Buenos Aires: De Palma, 1980.

192. Quoted in National Commission on the Disappeared, *Nunca Más*, 443.

193. Frontalini and Caiti, *Guerra sucia*, 78. (Quoting *Clarín*, April 24, 1981.)

194. Interview in *La Semana*, December 29, 1983.

195. *El Bimestre Político y Económico*, May 3, 1983.

196. *El Bimestre Político y Económico*, November 27, 1983.

197. Quoted in Burns, *Land*, 69.

198. Burdick, "Religion and Politics," 353.

199. *El Bimestre Político y Económico*, January 29, 1983.

200. Burns, *Land*, 108.

201. *El Bimestre Político y Económico*, December 10, 1983.

202. *El Bimestre Político y Económico*, March 3, 1987.

203. Raúl Alfonsín, quoted in Oscar Landi, *Reconstrucciones: Las nuevas formas de la cultura política*. Buenos Aires: Puntosur, 1988, 101.

204. Manuel Mora y Araujo, "The Nature of the Alfonsín Coalition. In *Elections and Democratization in Latin America*. Edited by Paul W. Drake and Eduardo Silva. La Jolla: University of California, San Diego, 1986, 186.

205. David Rock, "Political Movements in Argentina." In *From Military Rule to Liberal Democracy in Argentina*. Edited by Monica Peralta Ramos and Carlos H. Waisman. Boulder: Westview Press, 1987, 3–19.

206. Daniel Poneman, *Argentina: Democracy on Trial*. New York: Paragon House, 1987, 80.

207. Saúl Ubaldini, head of the General Confederation of Labor, referred to Radical leader César Jaroslavsky as *"un judío compadre."* Cf. *El Bimestre Político y Económico*, March 26, 1986.

208. Mignone, *Iglesia*, 211.

209. Mignone, *Iglesia*, 192.

210. Mignone, *Iglesia*, 193.

211. *El Bimestre Político y Económico*, March 20, 1987.

212. *El Bimestre Político y Económico*, August 8, 1987.

213. Burdick, "Religion and Politics," 385.

214. From a report in *El Bimestre Político y Económico*, March 4, 1987.

215. *El Bimestre Político y Económico*, April 22, 1987.

216. Osiris G. Villegas, "Estrategia integral," 12.

217. *Latin America: Weekly Report*, April 15, 1988.

218. *El Bimestre Político y Económico*, August 6, 1987.

219. *El Bimestre Político y Económico*, July 5, 1987.

220. *El Bimestre Político y Económico*, March 18, 1988.

221. *El Bimestre Político y Económico*, April 5 and April 12, 1988.

222. *El Bimestre Político y Económico*, April 12, 1988.

223. *Times* (London), November 5, 1989.

224. *Latin America: Weekly Report*, December 15, 1988.

225. *El Bimestre Político y Económico*, June 19, 1989.

226. *La Nación*, December 5, 1990.

227. *Noticias de la Semana*, December 6, 1990. During preliminary court hearings held in May 1991, Seineldín's attorney condemned "the systematic campaign against the military since 1983" while thanking "the government of 1976–1983 on account of which Argentina is not Cuba." (See *La Prensa*, May 16, 1991.) On the same day, the press reported the arrest of a person caught desecrating a Jewish cemetery. "Yes I'm a Nazi," he declared. "Long live Rico! Long live Argentina!" (*La Opinión*, Los Angeles, May 16, 1991.) This incident followed others like it in France and elsewhere in 1990 and 1991. (My thanks to Fernando Rocchi for providing me with this information.)

228. Atilio Borón, "Authoritarian Ideological Traditions and Transitions towards Democracy in Argentina," *Papers on Latin America*, Institute of Latin American and Iberian Studies, Columbia University, no. 8 (1989):10, 31, 36.

229. *Patria Argentina*, nos. 34–35, June 1990.

Chapter 8. Conclusion

1. Interview with Máximo Etchecopar, Buenos Aires, June 1990.

2. Ibarguren, *Historia*, 249.

3. Quoted in Clementi, *Rosas*, 57.

4. Quoted in Nunn, *Military*, 79.

5. David Daiches, in *Times Literary Supplement* 20–26, 1989.

6. Waisman, *Reversal of Development*, 275.

7. Nunn, *Military*, 22.

8. Amadeo, *Hoy*, 114.

Select Bibliography

Materials for this book were assembled from the libraries of the University of California, Santa Barbara and Los Angeles, and from the Biblioteca Nacional in Buenos Aires. I drew on the resources of numerous libraries in the United States thanks to the facilities of interlibrary loan. I wish to acknowledge the great help and support of the staff at the University of California, Santa Barbara, in obtaining books, newspapers, and other documentation from outside sources.

The following bibliographical list represents a substantial proportion of the materials available on the Argentine Nationalists, but it is by no means comprehensive and presents only the material used in this book.

Alexander, Robert J. *The Perón Era*. New York: Columbia University Press, 1951.

Allen, William Sheridan. "The Appeal of Fascism and the Problem of National Disintegration." In *Reappraisals of Fascism*, edited by Henry A. Turner, Jr., 45–52. New York: New Viewpoints, 1975.

Amadeo, Mario. *Hoy, Ayer, Mañana*. Buenos Aires: Gure, 1956.

Anzoategui, Ignacio B. *Manuel Gálvez*. Buenos Aires: Ediciones Culturales Argentinas, 1961.

Arciniegas, Germán. *The State of Latin America*. Translated by Harriet de Onís. New York: Knopf, 1952.

Armstrong, John A. *Nations before Nationalism*. Chapel Hill: University of North Carolina Press, 1982.

Auza, Néstor Tomás. *Católicos y liberales en la generación del ochenta*. 2d ed. Buenos Aires: Ediciones Culturales Argentinas, 1981.

Azul y Blanco. Buenos Aires, 1956–1958 and 1966–1969.

Barbero, María Inés, and Fernando Devoto. *Los nacionalistas*. Buenos Aires: Centro Editor de América Latina, 1983.

Beveraggi Allende, Walter. *El dogma nacionalista*. Buenos Aires: Manuel Belgrano, 1969.

El Bimestre Político y Económico. Buenos Aires, 1982–1988.

Bonald, Gustave de. *Considérations sur la Révolution Française*. Preface by Louis de Montesquiou. Paris: Nouvelle Librairie National, n.d.

Borón, Atilio. "Authoritarian Ideological Traditions and Transitions towards Democracy in Argentina." *Papers on Latin America*, Institute of Latin American and Iberian Studies, Columbia University, no. 8 (1989).

Brown, Paul Everett. "Ideological Origins of Modern Argentine Nationalism." Ph.D. diss. Claremont Graduate School, 1975.

Buchrucker, Cristián. *Nacionalism y peronismo: La Argentina en la crisis ideológica mundial (1927–1955)*. Buenos Aires: Sudamericana, 1987.

Bunge, Alejandro E. "La acción social obrera." *Revista de Economía Argentina* XL, no. 274 (April 1941): 124–131.

———. *La economía argentina*. Vol. 1. Buenos Aires: Agencia General de Librerías y Publicaciones, 1928.

———. "Esplendor y decadencia de la raza blanca." *Revista de Economía Argentina* XXXIX, no. 259 (Jan. 1940):9–23.

———. *La nueva política económica argentina: Introducción al estudio de la industria nacional*. Buenos Aires: Unión Industrial Argentina, 1921.

———. *Una nueva Argentina*. Buenos Aires: Kraft, 1940.

Burbank, Jane. *Intelligentsia and Revolutionary Russian Views of Bolshevism, 1917–1922*. New York: Oxford University Press, 1986.

Burdick, Michael A. "For God and Fatherland: Religion and Politics in Argentina." Ph.D. diss. University of California, Santa Barbara, 1991.

Burns, Jimmy. *The Land that Lost Its Heroes*. London: Bloomsbury Press, 1987.

Buthman, William Curt. *The Rise of Integral Nationalism in France*. New York: Octagon Books, 1970.

Cabildo. Buenos Aires, 1943–1944 and 1976–1977.

Camps, Ramón J. *Caso Timerman: Punto final*. Buenos Aires: Tribuna Abierta, 1982.

Cárdenas, Eduardo José, and Carlos Manuel Payá. *El primer nacionalismo argentino en Manuel Gálvez y Ricardo Rojas*. Buenos Aires: A. Peña Lillo, 1978.

Carlés, Manuel. *Conferencia pronunciada en el Centro de Almaceneros*. Buenos Aires: Centro de Almaceneros, 1926.

Carr, Raymond. *Spain, 1808–1975*. 2d ed. Oxford: Oxford University Press, 1982.

Carstens, F. L. *The Rise of Fascism*. 2d ed. Berkeley and Los Angeles: University of California Press, 1980.

Carulla, Juan E. *Al filo de medio siglo*. Paraná, 1951.

Castagnino, Raúl H. *Rosas y los jesuitas*. Buenos Aires: Pleamar, 1970.

Caturelli, Arturo. *El itinerario espiritual de Leopoldo Lugones*. Buenos Aires: Mikael, 1981.

La Causa Peronista. Buenos Aires, 1974.

Cheresky, Isidoro. "Argentina: Régimen político de soberanía compartida." *Punto de Vista*, n.d.

Ciria, Alberto. *Política y cultura popular: La Argentina peronista, 1946–1955*. Buenos Aires: Ediciones de la Flor, 1983.

Clarín. Buenos Aires, March 1960.

Clemens, E. J. M. *The La Plata Countries of South America*. Philadelphia: J. B. Lippincott Co., 1886.

Clementi, Hebe. *Rosas en la historia nacional*. Buenos Aires: La Pleyade, 1970.

Cohn, Norman. *Warrant for Genocide*. New York: Harper and Row, 1981.

Comblin, José. *The Church and the National Security State*. Maryknoll, N.Y.: Orbis Books, 1979.

Comisión de Estudios de la Sociedad Argentina de la Defensa de la Tradición, Familia y Propiedad. *El nacionalismo: Una incógnita en constante evolución*. Buenos Aires: Comisión de Estudios de la Sociedad Argentina de la Defensa de la Tradición, 1970.

Congress of Industrial Organizations, Committee on Latin American Affairs. *The Argentine Regime: Facts and Recommendations to the United Nations*. New York, 1946.

Cooke, John W. *La lucha por la liberación nacional*. Buenos Aires, 1971.

———. *Perón-Cooke Correspondencia*. 2 vols. Buenos Aires, 1973.

———. *Peronismo y revolución. El país y el golpe del estado. Informe a las bases*. Buenos Aires: Papiro, 1971.

Cornblit, Oscar. "Inmigrantes y empresarios en la política argentina." In *Los fragmentos del poder*, edited by Torcuato S. Di Tella and Tulio Halperín Donghi, 389–438. Buenos Aires: Jorge Alvarez, 1969.

Crawley, Eduardo. *A House Divided: Argentina 1880–1980*. New York: St. Martin's Press, 1984.

Crichigno, Patricio J. "Political Regimes and Legitimacy in Argentina: An Alternative Framework for the Study of Political Instability and the Dynamics of Social Change." Ph.D. diss. University of California, Santa Barbara, 1989.

Crisol. Buenos Aires, 1933–1937.

Criterio. Buenos Aires, 1929–1935 and 1946–1955.

C.T.A.L. (Confederación de Trabajadores de América Latina). *White and Blue Book: In Defense of the Argentine People and against the Fascist Regime Oppressing It.* Mexico City, February 20, 1946.

D'Atri, Norberto. "El revisionismo histórico: Su historiografía." In *Política nacionalista y revisionismo histórico*, edited by Arturo Jauretche, 111–167. Buenos Aires: A. Peña Lillo, 1982.

Davis, Harold Eugene. *Latin American Political Thought: A Historical Introduction.* New York: Free Press, 1974.

Dealy, Glen. "The Tradition of Monistic Discovery in Latin America." In *Politics and Change in Latin America: The Distinct Tradition*, by Howard J. Wiarda, 71–104. Amherst: University of Massachusetts Press, 1974.

Del Bocca, Angelo, and Mario Giovana. *Fascism Today: A World Survey.* New York: Pantheon Books, 1969.

Del Mazo, Gabriel. *El radicalismo: Ensayo sobre su historia y doctrina.* Vol. I. Buenos Aires: Gure, 1957.

De Maistre, Joseph. *Une politique expérimentale.* Introduction and selected texts by Bernard de Vaulx. Paris: Librairie Arthème Fayard, 1940.

El Descamisado. Buenos Aires, 1973.

Diario de Sesiones, Cámara de Diputados, vol. 1 (1910), vol. 15 (1918–19), vol. 1 (1939).

Diario de Sesiones, Senadores, vol. 2 (1918–19).

Dinámica Social. Buenos Aires, 1951–1955.

Di Tella, Guido, and D. Cameron Watt. *Argentina Between the Great Powers, 1939–46.* Pittsburgh: University of Pittsburgh Press, 1989.

Di Tella, Torcuato S., and Tulio Halperín Donghi. *Los Fragmentos del Poder.* Buenos Aires: Jorge Alvarez, 1969.

Dolkart, Ronald H. "Manuel Fresco, Governor of the Province of Buenos Aires, 1936–1940: A Study of the Argentine Right and Its Response to Economic and Social Change." Ph.D. diss. University of California, Los Angeles, 1969.

Drake, Paul W., and Eduardo Silva, eds. *Elections and Democratization in Latin America.* La Jolla: University of California, San Diego, 1986.

Duarte de Perón, María Eva. *La mujer puede y debe votar.* Buenos Aires, n.d.

Estatutos del Consejo Superior del Nacionalismo. Buenos Aires, 1941.

Estrada, José Manuel. *Discursos.* Prologue by Tomás Casares. Buenos Aires: Estrada, 1943.

Estrada, José María de. *El legado de nacionalismo.* Buenos Aires: Gure, 1956.

Etchepareborda, Roberto. *Yrigoyen y el congreso.* Buenos Aires: Raigal, 1956.

Facultad de Derecho y Ciencias Sociales. *Encuesta sobre la revisión constitucional.* Buenos Aires: Facultad de Derecho y Ciencias Sociales de la Universidad de Buenos Aires, 1948.

Falcoff, Mark. "Argentina." In *The Spanish Civil War*, edited by Mark Falcoff and Fredrick B. Pike. Lincoln: University of Nebraska Press, 1982.

———. "Argentine Nationalism on the Eve of Perón: Force of Radical Orientation of Young Argentina and Its Rivals." Ph.D. diss. Princeton University, 1970.

———. "Raul Scalabrini Ortiz: The Making of an Argentine Nationalist." *Hispanic American Historical Review* 52, no. 1 (Feb. 1972):74–101.

Faleroni, Alberto Daniel. *La guerra de la cuarta dimensión.* Buenos Aires: Luis Lassere, 1970.

Ferla, Salvador. *Doctrina del nacionalismo.* Buenos Aires, 1947.

Filippo, Virgilio. *El plan quinquenal de Perón y los comunistas.* Buenos Aires: Lista Blanca, 1948.

Flores, María. *The Woman with a Whip: Eva Perón.* New York: Doubleday and Co., 1952.

El Fortín. Buenos Aires, 1941–42.

La Fronda. Buenos Aires, 1927, 1928.

Frontalini, Daniel, and María Cristina Caiti. *El mito de la guerra sucia.* Buenos Aires: Centro de Estudios Legales y Sociales, 1984.

Furlong, Guillermo, S.J. "El catolicismo argentino entre 1860 y 1930." In *Historia argentina contemporánea, 1862–1930*, edited by Academia Nacional de la Historia, 2:251. Buenos Aires: El Ateneo, 1964.

Galasso, Norberto. *Raúl Scalabrini Ortiz y la penetración inglesa.* Buenos Aires: Centro Editor de América Latina, 1984.

Gálvez, Manuel. *Amigos y maestros de mi juventud.* Buenos Aires: Hachette, 1961.

———. *El diario de Gabriel Quiroga: Opiniones sobre la vida argentina.* Buenos Aires: Arnoldo Möen, 1910.

———. *El espiritualismo español*. Buenos Aires: Bayardo, 1921.

———. *El solar de la raza*. 5th ed. Madrid: Saturnino Callejas, n.d.

———. *Nacha Regules*. Buenos Aires: Tor, n.d.

———. *Vida de Hipólito Yrigoyen*. Buenos Aires: Tor, 1933.

Gambini, Hugo. *Perón y la iglesia*. Buenos Aires: Centro Editor de América Latina, 1971.

Gandolfo, Mercedes. *La iglesia, factor de poder en la Argentina*. Montevideo, 1968.

García, Alicia S., and Ricardo Rodríguez Molas. *El autoritismo y los argentinos: La hora de la espada (1924–1946)*. Buenos Aires: Centro Editor de América Latina, 1988.

García de Loydi, Ludovico. *La iglesia frente al peronismo: Bosquejo histórico*. Buenos Aires: C.I.C., 1956.

Garcia Rocha Dorea, Augusto. *O pensamento revolucionária de Plínio Salgado*. São Paulo: Voz de Oeste, 1975.

Garzón Valdés, Ernesto. "La emigración argentina—acerca de sus causas ético-políticas." In *El poder militar en la Argentina*, edited by Peter Waldmann and Ernesto Garzón Valdés. Frankfurt: Verlag Klaus Dieter Vervuert, 1982.

Gellner, Ernest. *Nations and Nationalism*. Oxford: Basil Blackwell, 1983.

Genta, Jordán B. *Acerca de la libertad de enseñar y de la enseñanza de la libertad*. Buenos Aires: Dictio, 1976.

———. *Seguridad y desarrollo: Reflexiones sobre el terror en la Argentina*. Buenos Aires: Cultura Argentina, 1970.

Ghioldi, Américo. *De la tiranía a la democracia social*. Buenos Aires: Gure, 1956.

Gillespie, Richard. *Los soldados de Perón: Los Montoneros*. Buenos Aires: Grijalbo, 1987.

Godio, Julio. *La caída de Perón: De junio a septiembre de 1955*. Buenos Aires: Gránica, 1973.

Goldar, Ernesto. "La literatura peronista." In *El peronismo*, edited by Gonzalo Cárdenas et al., 139–186. Buenos Aires: Carlos Pérez, 1969.

Goyret, José Teófilo. *Geopolítica y subversión*. Buenos Aires: De Palma, 1980.

Graziano, Frank. *Divine Violence. Spectacle, Psychosexuality, and Radical Christianity in the Argentine "Dirty War."* Boulder: Westview Press, 1992.

Guisa Azevedo, Jesús. *Doctrina política de la reacción*. Mexico, 1941.

Guy, Donna J. *Sex and Danger in Buenos Aires: Prostitution, Fam-*

ily, and Nation in Argentina. Lincoln: University of Nebraska Press, 1991.

Hales, E. E. Y. *Pio Nono: A Study in European Politics and Religion in the Nineteenth Century.* London: Eyre and Spottiswood, 1954.

Halperín Donghi, Tulio. "Argentina's Unmastered Past." Mimeo.

———. "¿Para qué la inmigración? Ideología y política inmigratoria y aceleración del proceso modernizador: El caso argentino (1810–1914)." *Jahrbuch für Geschichte von Staat, Wirtschaft und Gesellschaft Lateinamerikas* 13 (1976):458–472.

———. *El revisionismo histórico argentino.* Buenos Aires: Siglo XXI, 1971.

Hamilton, Bernice. *Political Thought in Sixteenth-Century Spain: A Study of the Political Ideas of Vitoria, De Soto, Suárez, and Molina.* Oxford: Clarendon Press, 1963.

Hernández, José. *The gaucho Martín Fierro.* Adapted from the Spanish and Rendered into English Verse by Walter Owen with Drawings by Alberto Guiraldes. New York: Farrar and Rinehart, 1936.

Hernández Arregui, Juan José. *La formación de la conciencia nacional.* 2d ed. Buenos Aires: Plus Ultra, 1973.

———. *Nacionalismo y liberación: Metrópolis y colonias en la era del imperialismo.* Buenos Aires: Hachea, 1969.

Herrero, Javier. *Los orígenes del pensamiento reaccionario español.* Madrid: Cuadernos para el Diálogo, 1971.

Hilb, Claudia, and Daniel Lutzky. *La nueva izquierda argentina: 1960–1980. Política y violencia.* Buenos Aires: Centro Editor de América Latina, 1984.

Hodges, Donald C. *Argentina, 1943–1987: The National Revolution and Resistance.* 2d ed. Albuquerque: University of New Mexico Press, 1987.

———. "The Process of National Destruction in Argentina." Mimeo.

Hoffman, Stanley, and Charles Maier. *The Marshall Plan: A Retrospective.* Boulder: Westview Press, 1984.

Ibarguren, Carlos. *La historia que he vivido.* Buenos Aires: Peuser, 1955.

———. *La literatura y la gran guerra.* Buenos Aires: La Cooperativa Editorial "Buenos Aires," 1920.

Ibarguren, Carlos, Jr. *Roberto de Laferrère: Periodismo-Política-Historia.* Buenos Aires: Editorial de la Universidad de Buenos Aires, 1970.

Ibarguren, Federico. *Los orígenes del nacionalismo argentino.* Buenos Aires: Calcius, 1969.

————. *Nuestra tradición histórica.* Buenos Aires: Dictio, 1978.

Irazusta, Julio. *Genio y figura de Leopoldo Lugones.* Buenos Aires: Editorial de la Universidad de Buenos Aires, 1968.

————. *Perón y la crisis argentina.* 3d ed. Buenos Aires: Independencia, 1983.

Irazusta, Rodolfo. *Testimonios.* Buenos Aires: Huencul, 1980.

Irazusta, Rodolfo, and Julio Irazusta. *La Argentina y el imperio británico: Los eslabones de una cadena, 1806–1933.* Buenos Aires: Tor, 1934.

Itzcovich, Victoria. "La ideología golpista antes de 1930. (Los escritos políticos de Leopoldo Lugones.)" *El Bimestre Político y Económico,* no. 30 (1986):5–14.

Ivereigh, Austen A. "Nationalist Catholic Thought in Argentina, 1930–1946: Monseñor Gustavo Franceschi and *Criterio* in the Search for a Post-liberal Order." M.A. thesis. Oxford University, 1990.

Jacovella, Bruno C. *Fiestas tradicionales argentinas.* Buenos Aires: Lejouane, 1953.

James, Daniel. *Resistance and Integration: Peronism and the Argentine Working Class, 1946–1976.* Cambridge: Cambridge University Press, 1988.

Jauretche, Arturo. *FORJA y la década infame.* Buenos Aires: A. Peña Lillo, 1984.

Jemolo, A. C. *Church and State in Italy, 1850–1950.* Translated by David Moore. Oxford: Basil Blackwell, 1960.

Josephs, Ray. *Argentine Diary: The Inside Story of the Coming of Fascism.* New York: Random House, 1944.

Katz, Joseph. *Freemasons and Jews in Europe.* Cambridge: Harvard University Press, 1970.

Kedourie, Elie. *Nationalism.* New York: Frederick A. Praeger, 1960.

Kennedy, John J. *Catholicism, Nationalism and Democracy in Argentina.* Notre Dame: University of Notre Dame Press, 1958.

Lafiandra, Felix, Jr. *Los panfletos: Su aporte a la revolución libertadora.* 2d ed. Buenos Aires: Itinerarium, 1955.

Landi, Oscar. *Reconstrucciones: Las nuevas formas de la cultura política.* Buenos Aires: Puntosur, 1988.

Lewis, Paul W. *The Crisis of Argentine Capitalism.* Chapel Hill: University of North Carolina Press, 1990.

————. "Was Perón a Fascist? An Inquiry into the Nature of Fascism." *The Journal of Politics* 42 (1980):242–256.

Lewis, Sinclair. *Babbit.* New York: Signet, 1980.

Lezica, Manuel. *Recuerdos de un nacionalista*. Buenos Aires: Astral, 1968.

López, Ernesto. *Seguridad nacional y sedición militar*. Buenos Aires: Legasa, 1987.

Lopez-Morillas, Juan. *The Krausist Movement and Ideological Change in Spain, 1854–1874*. Translated by Frances M. Lopez Morillas. Cambridge: Cambridge University Press, 1981.

Loveman, Brian, and Thomas M. Davies, Jr. *The Politics of Antipolitics: The Military in Latin America*. 2d ed. Lincoln: University of Nebraska Press, 1989.

Lugones, Leopoldo. *La grande Argentina*. Buenos Aires: Babel, 1930.

———. *La patria fuerte*. Buenos Aires: Círculo Militar, 1930.

———. "El payador." In *Obras en prosa*, edited by Leopoldo Lugones, Jr., 1079–1341. Mexico: Aguilar, 1962.

———. "Prometeo." In *Obras en prosa*, edited by Leopoldo Lugones, Jr. Mexico: Aguilar, 1962.

Lugones, Leopoldo, Jr. *Mi padre: Biografía de Leopoldo Lugones*. Buenos Aires: Centurión, 1949.

———. *Obras en prosa*. Mexico: Aguilar, 1962.

Luna, Felix. *El '45*. Buenos Aires: Sudamericana, 1971.

Lynch, John. "The Catholic Church in Latin America, 1830–1930." In *Cambridge History of Latin America*, edited by Leslie Bethell, 4:527–595. Cambridge: Cambridge University Press, 1986.

Macchi, Manuel E. *Urquiza y el catolicismo*. Santa Fe: Castelvi, 1969.

McCormick, T. C. *Problems of the Post-War World*. New York: McGraw Hill, 1945.

McDonald, Callum A. "The Braden Campaign and Anglo-Argentine Relations in Argentina, 1945–6. In *Argentina Between the Great Powers, 1939–46*, edited by Guido Di Tella and D. Cameron Watt, 137–157. Pittsburgh: Pittsburgh University Press, 1989.

McGee, Sandra F. "The Visible and Invisible Liga Patriótica Argentina, 1919–29: Gender Roles and the Right Wing." *Hispanic American Historical Review* 64, no. 2 (May 1984):233–258.

McGee Deutsch, Sandra. "The Catholic Church, Work, and Womanhood in Argentina, 1890–1930." Mimeo.

———. *Counterrevolution in Argentina, 1900–1932: The Argentine Patriotic League*. Lincoln: University of Nebraska Press, 1986.

Martínez, Tomás Eloy. *The Perón Novel*. Translated by Asa Latz. New York: Pantheon Books, 1988.

Martínez Constanzo, Pedro Santos. *La nueva argentina: 1946–1955.* Vol. I. Buenos Aires: La Bastilla, 1976.

Martins, H. "Portugal." In *European Fascism*, edited by S. J. Woolf, 302–336. London: Weidenfeld and Nicholson, 1968.

La Maroma. Buenos Aires, 1939–40.

Matsushita, Hiroschi. *Movimiento obrero argentino, 1930–1945: Sus proyecciones en la historia del peronismo.* Buenos Aires: Siglo Veinte, 1983.

Maurras, Charles. *L'Avenir de l'Intelligence.* Paris: Ernest Flammarion, 1927.

Meinvielle, Julio. *Política argentina 1949–1956.* Buenos Aires: Trafac, 1956.

Menéndez Pelayo, Marcelino. *Historia de los ortodoxos españoles.* Madrid: Editorial Católico, 1956.

Meyer, Jean. *La sinarquisme: Un fascisme mexicain?* 1937–1947. Paris: Hachette, 1977.

Mignone, Emilio F. *Iglesia y dictadura: El papel de la iglesia a la luz de sus relaciones con el régimen militar.* 3d ed. Buenos Aires: Ediciones del Pensamiento Nacional, 1986.

Montero, Belisario J. "De mi diario." *Ideas*, no. 13 (1904):8–10.

Mora y Araujo, Manuel. "The Nature of the Alfonsín Coalition." In *Elections and Democratization in Latin America*, edited by Paul W. Drake and Eduardo Silva, 175–188. La Jolla: University of California, San Diego, 1986.

Mora y Araujo, Manuel, and Ignacio Llorente. *El voto peronista: Ensayos de sociología electoral argentina.* Buenos Aires: Sudamericana, 1980.

Mugica, Padre Carlos. *Peronismo y cristianismo.* Buenos Aires: Merlín, 1973.

Murmis, Miguel, and Juan Carlos Portantiero. *Estudios sobre los orígenes del peronismo.* Buenos Aires: Siglo XXI, 1970.

La Nación. Buenos Aires, 1904, 1926–1928.

Navarro Gerassi, Marysa. *Los nacionalistas.* Buenos Aires: Jorge Alvarez, 1969.

National Commission on the Disappeared. *Nunca Más.* With an Introduction by Ronald Dworkin. New York: Farrar, Straus, Giroux, 1986.

Newton, Ronald C. "Disorderly Succession: Great Britain, the United States and the 'Nazi Menace' in Argentina, 1939–1946." In *Argentina Between the Great Powers*, edited by Guido Di Tella and D. Cameron Watt, 111–134. Pittsburgh: University of Pittsburgh Press, 1989.

————. "On 'Functional Groups,' 'Fragmentation' and 'Pluralism' in Spanish American Political Society." In *Politics and Social Change in Latin America: The Distinct Tradition*, edited by Howard J. Wiarda, 129–156. Amherst: University of Massachusetts Press, 1974.

————. *The "Nazi Menace" in Argentina, 1931–1947*. Stanford: Stanford University Press, 1992.

New York Herald Tribune. New York, December 27, 1945.

Níklison, José Elías. "Acción social católica." *Boletín del Departamento Nacional del Trabajo*, no. 46 (March 1920).

Nolte, Ernst. *Three Faces of Fascism: Action Française, Italian Fascism, National Socialism*. Translated by Leila Verrewitz. New York: Holt, Rinehart, and Winston, 1966.

Noticias Gráficas. Buenos Aires, 1944–45.

Noticias de la Semana. Buenos Aires, December 6, 1990.

La Nueva República. Buenos Aires, 1927–1931.

Nunn, Frederick M. *European Military Professionalization in South America, 1890–1940*. Lincoln: University of Nebraska Press, 1983.

O'Donnell, Guillermo. *Bureaucratic Authoritarianism: Argentina, 1966–1973, in Comparative Perspective*. Translated by James McGuire in collaboration with Rae Flory. Berkeley, Los Angeles, and London: University of California Press, 1988.

Oliver, Ricardo. "Sinceridades." *Ideas*, no. 1 (1903):3–8.

La Opinión. Buenos Aires, 1971–1973.

Osés, Enrique P. *Medios y fines del nacionalismo*. Buenos Aires, 1941.

Oveid, Iaacov. "El trasfondo histórico de la ley 4144, de residencia." *Desarrollo Económico* 16, no. 61 (April–June 1976):123–150.

Palacio, Ernesto. *Catilina contra la oligarquía*. Buenos Aires: Rosso, 1935.

Patria Argentina. Buenos Aires, June 1990.

Payne, Stanley G. "Spanish Fascism in Comparative Perspective." In *New Appraisals of Fascism*, edited by Henry A. Turner, Jr., 144–171. New York: New Viewpoints, 1975.

Peicovich, Esteban. *Hola Perón*. Buenos Aires: Jorge Alvarez, 1965.

Pérez, Silvestre. *Filosofía del federalismo en el Río de la Plata*. Montevideo: Tipografía Atlántida, 1948.

Perón, Eva. *Clases y escritos completos 1946–1952*. Vol. 3. Buenos Aires: Megafón, 1987.

Perón, Coronel Juan. "Comandos de montaña." *Revista Militar*, April 1943, 705.

———. *El pueblo quiere saber de qué se trata.* Buenos Aires, 1944.

Perón, Juan. *La comunidad organizada.* Buenos Aires: El Túnel, 1974.

———. *Doctrina peronista.* Buenos Aires, 1948.

———. *Doctrinary Principles of the Social Policy of His Excellency, the President of the Argentine Republic, General Juan Perón.* Buenos Aires, 1947.

———. *La fuerza es el derecho de las bestias.* Buenos Aires, 1958.

———. *The General Confederation of Labor Listens to Perón.* Buenos Aires, 1950.

———. *La hora de los pueblos.* Buenos Aires: El Norte, 1968.

———. *Justicialismo y la doctrina social cristiana.* Buenos Aires, 1951.

———. *Perón Expounds His Doctrine.* Buenos Aires, 1948.

———. "Significación de la defensa nacional desde el punto de vista militar." *Revista Militar,* 1944, 1115–1136.

Peter, José. *Crónicas proletarias.* Buenos Aires: Esfera, 1968.

Phelan, John L. *The People and the King: The Comunero Revolution in Colombia, 1781.* Madison: University of Wisconsin Press, 1978.

Pike, Fredrick B. *Hispanism, 1898–1936: Spanish Conservatives and Liberals and Their Relations with Latin America.* Notre Dame: University of Notre Dame Press, 1971.

"El plan de reactivación económica ante el Honorable Senado." *Desarrollo Ecónomico* 19, no. 75 (1979):403–426.

Poneman, Daniel. *Argentina: Democracy on Trial.* New York: Paragon House, 1987.

Potash, Robert A. *The Army and Politics in Argentina, 1928–1945: Yrigoyen to Perón.* Stanford: Stanford University Press, 1969.

———. *The Army and Politics in Argentina, 1945–1962.* Stanford: Stanford University Press, 1980.

———. *Perón y el GOU: Los documentos de una logia secreta.* Buenos Aires: Sudamericana, 1984.

La Prensa. Buenos Aires, 1918, 1919, 1944.

Primera Plana. Buenos Aires, 1962–1969.

Puiggrós, Rodolfo. *El peronismo: Sus causas.* Buenos Aires: Carlos Pérez, 1971.

Quadragesimo Anno. In *Seven Great Encyclicals,* edited by William J. Gibbons, S. J., 125–166. 2d ed. Glen Rock, N.J.: Paulist Press, 1963.

Quijada, Mónica. *Manuel Gálvez: 60 años de pensamiento nacionalista.* Buenos Aires: Centro Editor de América Latina, 1985.

Ramsden, H. *Angel Ganivet's Idearium Español: A Critical Study.* Manchester: Manchester University Press, 1967.

La Razón. Buenos Aires, 1943.

Recalde, Héctor. *La iglesia y la cuestión social, 1871–1910.* Buenos Aires: Centro Editor de América Latina, 1985.

Rennie, Ysabel. *The Argentine Republic.* New York: Macmillan, 1945.

República Argentina. *Conozcamos nuestro enemigo: Subversión en el ámbito educativo.* Buenos Aires: Ministerio de Cultura y Educación, 1978.

Rerum Novarum. In *Seven Great Encyclicals*, edited by William J. Gibbons, S.J., 1–24. 2d ed. Glen Rock, N.J.: Paulist Press, 1963.

Revista de Economía Argentina. Buenos Aires, May 1941 and November 1942.

Revista Militar. Buenos Aires, 1941–1944, 1987.

Reynal O'Connor, Arturo. "Los poetas argentinos." *Ideas*, no. 15 (1905):246–268.

El Ríoplatense. Buenos Aires, December 24, 1942.

Roca, Gustavo. *Las dictadures militares del cono sur.* Córdoba: El Cid, 1984.

Rock, David. "Political Movements in Argentina." In *From Military Rule to Liberal Democracy in Argentina*, edited by Monica Peralta Ramos and Carlos H. Waisman, 3–20. Boulder: Westview Press, 1987.

———. *Politics in Argentina, 1890–1930: The Rise and Fall of Radicalism.* Cambridge: Cambridge University Press, 1975.

Rodó, José Enrique. *Ariel*, edited by Gordon Brotherston. Cambridge: Cambridge University Press, 1967.

Rogger, Hans, and Eugen Weber. *The European Right: A Historical Profile.* Berkeley and Los Angeles: University of California Press, 1966.

Roig, Arturo Andrés. *Los krausistas argentinos.* Puebla, Mexico: José N. Cajica, 1969.

Rojas, Ricardo. *Eurindia.* In *Obras de Ricardo Rojas*, by Ricardo Rojas. Vol. 5. Buenos Aires: La Facultad, 1924.

———. *La restauración nacionalista.* 2d ed. Buenos Aires, 1922.

Rosa, José M. "Defensa y pérdida de nuestra independencia económica." *Revista de Economía Argentina* XLI, no. 287 (May 1942):131–138.

Rouquié, Alain. *The Military and the State in Latin America.* Translated by Paul E. Sigmund. Berkeley and Los Angeles: University of California Press, 1987.

———. *Poder militar y sociedad política en la Argentina.* Vol. 1. Hasta 1943. Buenos Aires: Emecé, 1983.

Saladino, Salvatore. "Italy." In *The European Right: A Historical Profile,* edited by Hans Rogger and Eugen Weber, 210–260. Berkeley and Los Angeles: University of California Press, 1966.

Sánchez Sorondo, Marcelo. *Libertades prestadas.* Buenos Aires: A. Peña Lillo, 1970.

———. *La revolución que anunciamos.* Buenos Aires: Nueva Política, 1945.

Sánchez Sorondo, Matías. "6 de septiembre de 1930." In *La década infame,* edited by Alberto Ciria, 51–64. Buenos Aires: Carlos Pérez, 1968.

Sanguinetti, Manuel Juan. *La representación diplomática del Vaticano en los países del Plata.* Buenos Aires: Talleres Gráficos Abecé, 1954.

Sarmiento, Domingo F. *Life in the Argentine Republic in the Days of the Tyrants. With a Biographical Sketch of the Author by Mrs. Horace Mann.* New York: Collier Books, 1961.

Scalabrini Ortiz, Raúl. "Bases para la reconstrucción nacional." In *La década infame,* edited by Alberto Ciria, 213–220. Buenos Aires: Carlos Pérez, 1968.

———. *Historia de los ferrocarriles argentinos.* 4th ed. Buenos Aires: Reconquista, 1940.

Scott Turner, Esther Hadasah. "Hispanism in the Life and Works of Manuel Gálvez." Ph.D. diss. University of Washington, 1958.

Sebreli, Juan José. *Los deseos imaginarios del peronismo.* Buenos Aires: Legasa, 1983.

Sigal, Silvia, and Eliseo Verón. *Perón o muerte: Los fundamentos discursivos del fenómeno peronista.* Buenos Aires: Legasa, 1986.

Smith, Anthony D. S. *Nationalism in the Twentieth Century.* New York: New York University Press, 1979.

Smith, William C. *Authoritarianism and the Crisis of the Argentine Political Economy.* Stanford: Stanford University Press, 1989.

Sobel, Lester A. *Argentina and Perón.* New York: Facts on File, 1975.

Solberg, Carl. *Immigration and Nationalism in Argentina and Chile, 1890–1914.* Austin: University of Texas Press, 1970.

Soler, Ricaurte. *El positivismo argentino.* Mexico: Universidad Autónoma de México, 1979.

Sosa-Pujato, Gustavo. "Popular Culture." In *Prologue to Perón: Argentina in Depression and War, 1930–1943,* edited by Mark Falcoff and Ronald H. Dolkart, 136–163. Berkeley and Los Angeles: University of California Press, 1975.

Spalding, Hobart E. *La clase trabajadora argentina (Documentos para su historia, 1890–1912)*. Buenos Aires: Galerna, 1970.

Spitta, Arnold. "El 'Proceso de Reorganización Nacional' de 1976–1981: Los objetivos básicos y su realización práctica. Ensayo sobre elementos de la realidad política cotidiana bajo un régimen militar." In *El poder militar en la Argentina*, edited by Peter Waldmann and Ernesto Garzón Valdés, 77–100. Frankfurt: Verlag Klaus Dieter Vervuert, 1982.

Spykman, Nicholas John. *America's Strategy in World Politics: The United States and the Balance of Power*. New York: Harcourt, Brace and Co., 1942.

Sternhell, Zeev. *La droite révolutionnaire, 1885–1914: Les origines françaises du fascisme*. Paris: Editions de Seuil, 1978.

Sutin, Stewart Edward. "The Impact of Nazism on the Germans of Argentina." Ph.D. diss. University of Texas, 1975.

Sutton, Michael. *Nationalism, Positivism and Catholicism: The Politics of Charles Maurras and French Catholics, 1890–1914*. Cambridge: Cambridge University Press, 1982.

Talmon, J. L. *The Myth of the Nation and the Vision of Revolution*. Berkeley and Los Angeles: University of California Press, 1981.

Timerman, Jacobo. *Prisoner without a Name, Cell without a Number*. Translated by Toby Talbot. New York: Knopf, 1989.

Tonda, Américo A. *La iglesia argentina incomunicada con Roma (1810–1858): Problemas, conflictos, soluciones*. Santa Fe: Castelví, 1965.

Torre, Juan Carlos. "Argentina since 1956." Mimeo.

Trevor-Roper, Hugh. "The Phenomenon of Fascism." In *European Fascism*, edited by S. J. Woolf, 18–38. London: Weidenfeld and Nicholson, 1968.

Trífolo, Samuel. *La Argentina vista por viajeros ingleses, 1810–1860*. Buenos Aires: Gure, 1959.

Troncoso, Oscar A. *Los nacionalistas argentinos: Antecedentes y trayectoria*. Buenos Aires: S.A.G.A., 1957.

United States, Department of State. *Memorandum of the United States Government among the American Republics with Respect to the Argentine Situation*. Washington, D.C.: February 1946.

La Vanguardia. Buenos Aires, 1934–1937.

Vidal, Gardenia. "Los partidos políticos y la estabilidad del sistema democrático: El Partido Radical en Córdoba, 1916–1925." *Primeras Jornadas Inter-Escuelas Departamentos de Historia*, Universidad Nacional de la Plata (October 1988).

Villafañe, Benjamín. *Degenerados: Tiempos en que la mentira y el robo engendran apóstoles*. Buenos Aires, 1928.

Villegas, Osiris G. "La estrategia integral de la lucha subversiva." *Revista Militar*, January–April 1987, 11–19.

———. *Guerra revolucionaria comunista*. Buenos Aires: Pleamar, 1963.

———. *Políticas y estrategias para el desarrollo y la seguridad nacional*. Buenos Aires: Pleamar, 1969.

La Voz Nacionalista. El nacionalismo argentino. Buenos Aires, 1935.

Waisman, Carlos H. "The Ideology of Right-Wing Nationalism in Argentina: Capitalism, Socialism, and the Jews." *Proceedings of the Ninth World Congress of Jewish Studies*. Jerusalem, 1986.

———. "The Question of Revolution and the Reversal of Development in Argentina." Mimeo.

———. *Reversal of Development in Argentina: Postwar Counterrevolutionary Politics and Their Structural Consequences*. Princeton: Princeton University Press, 1987.

Wast, Hugo. "El Kahal." In *Obras completas de Hugo Wast*, by Hugo Wast. Madrid, 1956.

———. "Oro." In *Obras completas de Hugo Wast*, by Hugo Wast. Madrid, 1956.

Weber, Eugen. "Romania." In *The European Right: A Historical Profile*, edited by Hans Rogger and Eugen Weber, 500–574. Berkeley and Los Angeles: University of California Press, 1966.

———. *Varieties of Fascism*. Princeton: D. Van Nostrand and Co., 1964.

Weil, Felix J. *Argentina Riddle*. New York: John Day, 1944.

Weiss, John. *Conservativism in Europe, 1770–1945*. London: Thames and Hudson, 1977.

Welles, Sumner. *Where Are We Heading?* New York: Harper and Brothers, 1946.

Whitaker, Arthur P., and David C. Jordan. *Nationalism in Contemporary Latin America*. New York: Free Press, 1966.

Wiarda, Howard J. *Politics and Social Change in Latin America: The Distinct Tradition*. Amherst: University of Massachusetts Press, 1974.

———. "Law and Political Development in Latin America: Toward a Framework for Analysis." In *Politics and Social Change in Latin America: The Distinct Tradition*, edited by Howard J. Wiarda, 199–230. Amherst: University of Massachusetts Press, 1974.

Woolf, S. J. *European Fascism*. London: Weidenfeld and Nicholson, 1968.

Yrigoyen, Hipólito. *Pueblo y gobierno*, edited by Roberto Etchepareborda. Vol. I. *La reparación fundamental*. Buenos Aires: Raigal, 1955.

Zuleta Alvarez, Enrique. *El nacionalismo argentino*. 2 vols. Buenos Aires: La Bastilla, 1975.

Zuleta Alvarez, Enrique, Mario Guillermo Saraví, and Enrique Díaz Araujo, editors, *Homenaje a Julio Irazusta*. Mendoza, 1984.

Index

309